THE AMERICAN TWENTIES

THE AMERICAN TWENTIES

A Literary Panorama

Edited by

JOHN K. HUTCHENS

J. B. LIPPINCOTT COMPANY

PHILADELPHIA AND NEW YORK

CONTENTS

Editor's Note: Throughout this book, ellipses indicated by dots are the author's own; those indicated by asterisks are the editor's.

THE AMERICAN TWENTIES

JOHN K. HUTCHENS

A Note on the
Nineteen Twenties

FOR survivors of the Nineteen Twenties in the United States this volume will be, perhaps, a kind of memory-book. For younger generations it is designed to say, in effect, "This is how it was"— or something of how it was—with certain American writers and writing in the era that began with Armistice, 1918, and ended with the Big Crash in October, 1929.

There are sundry dangers, of course, in dwelling upon the Twenties. One of them is sentimentality. Over that decade, so innocent of terrors yet to come, hovers now a deceptively romantic haze akin to that which the Twenties thought to see over the Nineties. Yet it seems incontestable that 1918-1929 really was a good time for the American writer, the best he had known since New England's Golden Day. If his post-World War I disillusion was bitter, it was so to speak a creative disillusion, as witness the uses to which it was put by Ernest Hemingway, Ring Lardner, F. Scott Fitzgerald, E. E. Cummings, T. S. Eliot. If the civilization of this country was intensely materialistic ("The business of the government is business," said Calvin Coolidge), it was an ugly fact against which writers could and did react with brilliant intensity in satire and realism— one must believe that the older ones reacted with a special energy

II

after the failure of that era of "automatic progress" in which they had matured and which they saw betrayed. The revolution in manners, morals and thinking for which "The Jazz Age" is so foolishly inadequate a label was, in short, profound and challenging. It inspired and liberated some artists, it destroyed others. Historically, the important fact about it was that it was personal and individualistic, and therefore it made for good writing. The literary "climate" (as the term did not then go) was excellent.

All through the Twenties, then, ran an excitement and concern about writing for its own sake that have not since existed here. A good deal of nonsense found its way into this—coterie snobbishness, insignificant little magazines that died in a month—but, even so, the excitement had a compelling value of its own. Literature and the people who made it were actually news in daily papers, apart from the reviewing columns. The New Yorker opening the morning *World* to F.P.A.'s "Conning Tower," the *Post* to Christopher Morley's "Bowling Green," the *Sun* to Don Marquis' "Sun Dial," shared vicariously in this literary life, as did Chicagoans reading Bert Leston Taylor and Keith Preston. In turn, these personal columns of comment and criticism and lively contributions stirred curiosity, built reputations, shaped taste. There are no such columns today, and the lack is significant. (It must be that newspaper publishers have simply decided that not many readers would be interested or have the time.) In the theatre the awareness of artistic renascence was even more startling, if ultimately less important, than in the novel, the short story and poetry. Never had there been an American playwright with a gift that could remotely be described as greatness. Almost overnight Eugene O'Neill arrived, and one knew that America had at last a dramatist in the major tradition. Art, as well as Bayard Veiller's *The Thirteenth Chair,* could be box-office.

If there is the danger of sentimentalizing about the Twenties, there is even more danger in over-simplifying. It is too easy to think of the era's writing as happening suddenly, whereas, of course, the preparation for much that was characteristic in it had been in the making for twenty years. Ellen Glasgow, H. L. Mencken, Theodore Dreiser, Robert Frost, Vachel Lindsay, Van Wyck Brooks, had made their names and created substantial bodies of work before America entered World War I. The war on the genteel tradition reached a climax in the Twenties, but early steps had been taken by forerunners as distant as William Dean Howells in mid-career, and the fight had been carried on with critical brilliance by James Gibbons Huneker, Francis Hackett, Randolph Bourne. Margaret Anderson's *Little Review,* inclined to be inhospitable to native talent, nevertheless was a pioneer esthetic influence. From 1914 on, the Mencken-Nathan *Smart Set* (they had been its literary and drama critics, respectively, since 1908) published authors who had no haven elsewhere, as *The New Yorker* was to do a few years later. The spadework had been distinguished.

Nor is it safe to generalize about the "tone" of the Twenties, as if a prevailing mood dominated them. With the failure of Wilsonian idealism, intellectuals despaired. Reform was dead. Reaction brought the ugly pressures of conformity. Harding had been sent to the White House by the electorate's fond dream that pre-1917 might be restored, and people who got in the way—"radicals"—were apt to find themselves in trouble. If foreign-born, they might be deported. If native, they might be set upon by such sturdy defenders of the weal as the California organization that censured Sinclair Lewis' *Main Street* for creating "a distaste for the conventional good life of the American." All this is true—and yet, as the Twenties dawned, the young knew a kind of delight as they realized that an unprecedented freedom was at hand. For better or worse, the literary reputation of the Twenties hinges on the use they made of it.

While the older intellectuals despaired, the young seized on the romance of disillusion and had a fine, fevered time with it. They were a generation "lost," Gertrude Stein told Ernest Hemingway; whether they were really lost or not, they enjoyed enormously the drama of thinking so. If the decade had a theme song, it was the gorgeous melancholy of Gershwin's *Rhapsody in Blue.* If it had a journal it was *The New Yorker,* which, starting in 1925, watched the parade with an amused and searching gaze, did not mistake accuracy for solemnity, and developed new techniques of comment and reporting with its Talk of the Town, Profile and Reporter-at-Large departments. "America was going on the greatest, gaudiest spree in history and there was going to be plenty to tell about it," Fitzgerald said. There was indeed, and no one told an aspect of it so well as he did. In Greenwich Village's bohemia, Malcolm Cowley was to recall from the vantage point of *Exile's Return* (1934), the doctrine of ideas specifically included "the idea of self-expression—each man's, each woman's, purpose in life is to express himself; the idea of paganism—the body is a temple in which there is nothing unclean, a shrine to be adorned for the ritual of love; the idea of living for the moment—it is stupid to pile up treasures that we can enjoy only in old age; the idea of psychological adjustment—we are unhappy because we are maladjusted, and maladjusted because we are repressed; the idea of changing place—'they do things better in Europe' —by expatriating himself, by living in Paris, Capri or the South of France, the artist can break the puritan shackles, drink, live freely and be wholly creative." The doctrine, as Cowley notes, traveled quickly across the land to a thousand would-be Greenwich Villages. Old standards went out the window; so did a good deal of hypocrisy and inhibiting convention. Indeed, the older generation—after exercising its historic right to denounce the loose ways of the younger —crashed the party. And, since most good writing draws on experience, this abrupt change in American mores was at once reflected in American literature. The pre-World War I American woman who valued her reputation did not visit saloons. The post-war trend toward social equality of the sexes found her using the speakeasy as casually as a club and without, necessarily, picking up a scarlet letter. None of this would be very significant today as literary history if the writers of the Twenties had not been scrupulous craftsmen. The best of them were. Even those burned out by dissipation worked hard and honestly, if irregularly. They thought and talked about their art. One wonders if ever, before or since, American writers have in general so concentrated on form and method. It is something to think about when you hear the Twenties discussed as a sort of musical comedy peopled by John Held, Jr. characters playing Mah Jong while resting up between sex-and-gin bouts. The bouts took place, all right. It was a feverish time, this sudden liberation in a country still in nervous high-gear from a war in which it had not been physically exhausted. But among people who worked in the arts, it was also a hard-working time.

If the result of their work had been art-colony sterility, those who sit in judgment on the Twenties would be nearer right when they say, severely, that the decade's major writers failed because they had little interest in social and political reform. (This is the utilitarian view that demands of a work of art that it perform a palpable social function; we were to see in the following decade what happened when novelists became reformers and pamphleteers.) It is true that few of the creative writers of the Twenties had specific suggestions about ridding the country of its materialism. They even prided themselves on their political indifference, and inevitably they must disappoint the critic who now imposes politico-sociological standards upon them. But to say that Fitzgerald's *The Great Gatsby* was not a searching critical comment on the society of his time, or that *Babbitt* failed because countless American Babbitts did not go out of business after the book was published, is to read with no sensibility. Method and form, on which the writers of the Twenties concentrated so intensely, had a value of their own and a vitality whose effect is still fortunately with us. Few American prose writers of today would be what they are if Hemingway, Anderson, Fitzgerald, one or another of them, had not gone before; few poets have not felt the influence of Eliot or Frost, Cummings or Stevens. There is a certain irony in the fact that these rebels, sometimes called "nihilists," have endured in their fashion longer than the dreams of eternal prosperity widely held in right-thinking circles prior to 1929. Not for the first time, the artist was the truly sound builder in the society in which he lived.

Not all the writers in this book, it will be instantly apparent, were artists. Most assuredly some of them were and are: Hemingway and Anderson, Glasgow and Lardner, O'Neill, Fitzgerald, and most of the poets. Others are here for the flavor they recall of that mordant, light-hearted, serious-minded, complex and seminal time. All of them belong in some fashion to the pattern of the Twenties, though one survivor would be the first to admit that the pattern is incompletely represented in this selective (as distinguished from comprehensive) book, and that "pattern" is a dangerously rigid word anyhow for so fluid a time. At least one major figure is conspicuously absent: Willa Cather's will excludes the reprinting in anthology form of work she did in the period covered by this book. Some others are missing for reasons that doubtless are debatable. William Faulkner, Katherine Anne Porter, Thornton Wilder, John Dos Passos were of course writing in the Twenties, but seem to belong essentially to a later time, though there will be found here a preview (from *Manhattan Transfer*) of the camera-eye device Dos Passos was to use so brilliantly in the Thirties in *U.S.A.;* the preview took the form of chapter-headings which, in sum, make a poem about New York. Dreiser's major work of this period was *An American Tragedy,* so difficult to excerpt within reasonable length that this book represents him with a selection in less familiar vein—that warm and tender personality sketch of his brother which manages also to be a vivid period study of an earlier Broadway. Other selections represent an editor's notion that writing which is good of its kind has a claim to the attention, such as Damon Runyon's story of the opening of the Snyder-Gray trial for the *New York American:* a gaudy event, of a kind the Twenties specialized in, captured in the cynical style of a Broadwayite who was a highly accomplished reporter. A happily inclusive word, "flavor" explains also the glimpse here of James Branch Cabell's *Jurgen.* Some judges of excellent taste deemed *Jurgen* quite wonderful for its wit, its oblique wisdom, and whatnot. Others, even at the time, thought it not quite readable. Almost anyone would admit it as an exhibit, the subject of a news event when John Sumner staged one of his celebrated forays into the market place on behalf of the New York Society for the Suppression of Vice. The row was prodigious. Mr. Sumner, and the virtue on which he held a sort of patent, retired in defeat.

While cultivating the attitude of indifference, the Twenties grew excited easily. It was one of their more endearing, if occasionally exasperating, charms, depending, as usual in such cases, on one's interest in what was causing the excitement. It is hard not to smile now at the furore Ernest Boyd set up with his "Aesthete: Model

1924" in the first issue of the Mencken-Nathan *American Mercury*, a composite portrait whose aftermath you will see reported by Burton Rascoe in his vivid "Bookman's Daybook" column from the *New York Tribune* (Malcolm Cowley described it some years later in *Exile's Return*). The row was silly, but in fact it says something about the period that so trivial a piece of literary business was a matter of public interest. Writers, as has been noted, were news, as Rascoe was demonstrating regularly with such sharp portraits as those republished here of Miss Cather and Dreiser. The teapot had a similar tempest when Joseph Conrad arrived for the first time in New York, and Christopher Morley's account of the event in his "Bowling Green" column—containing a valuable word-picture of Conrad—was challenged by Rascoe and others. The mild uproar mattered no more than did the *Mercury* fracas; but it too is a footnote to the time and the "climate."

The principal weapon of attack on these and similar occasions was the wisecrack. Departing suddenly from the old homespun American tradition, the Twenties' humor was usually insulting or at least supercilious and almost always consciously urbane, with a few outstanding exceptions like that of Robert Benchley, whose wonderful sense of the ridiculous fell into no pattern, and Kin Hubbard of Indiana, whose shrewd Abe Martin was the wit Will Rogers tried to be. Almost alone, *The New Yorker* changed the American idea of what constituted a joke. For the most part the period's effective humor was in that magazine and in the polished light verse of Dorothy Parker and Samuel Hoffenstein (why, F.P.A. wondered, did no one ever mention *heavy* verse?), in the curiously savage-sentimental theatre reviews of Alexander Woollcott, in the amused, Broadway suavity of Percy Hammond surveying the world of the first nighters, in the disdain of George Jean Nathan as expressed in "Code of a Critic," in the thundering invective of the H. L. Mencken who rejected the farmer's claim to be regarded as a member of the human race. Samples of each are here. But again, let there be no hasty generalizing, because the samples are less than final. For here also are Mrs. Parker's somber, compassionate short story "Big Blonde," one of the finest of the Twenties, and Mencken's "The Hills of Zion," a classic example of a great reporter at work. It is further to be remembered how Mencken, as pioneering critic, fought for the recognition of Dreiser, how Nathan was the first major critic to champion O'Neill. Any reader of the *New York World* in the Twenties recalls with gratitude and delight some hundreds of columns of Heywood Broun's that touched warmly and amusingly on almost everything in the news. They are apt to remember even more vividly his passionate scorn when he saw justice all too blind. Here is one of the columns on the Sacco-Vanzetti case that led to his departure from the *World,* which was then four years from its grave and less courageous than it had once been. The "Jazz Age," you see, could go crusading with the same intensity with which it went partying, whether it crusaded for justice or art. Does Gilbert Seldes' essay on Chaplin seem a little strained now? Perhaps it did then. But his *The Seven Lively Arts,* from which it comes, was a healthy, pathfinding book that led down from the ivory tower. In general, the not-so-delirious Twenties took their artistic discoveries seriously. In the name of art some colossal frauds were perpetrated, though none so obvious, I think, as the "proletarian novel" that captivated the Thirties. One of the few entirely safe generalizations about the Twenties is that they had an aversion to dullness. Generally speaking, dullness in a writer was a crime. The effort to avoid it could be ludicrous, as in the purplish novels of Carl Van Vechten. But the motive was not contemptible.

Of all the Twenties' literary perfectionists the most consistent were, as one might expect, the poets. At the same time they were the most unpredictable artists of an unpredictable decade, adding to the discipline inherent in the writing of poetry a sustained richness of invention. There can be only a suggestion in this volume of their extraordinary range and variety, but it may suffice to indicate the later stages of that American "poetic renaissance" that began approximately with Harriet Monroe's founding of *Poetry* magazine in 1912. By 1920 most of the thirteen represented here had won the battle for recognition and acceptance, though Eliot and Frost had first to win it abroad, and at home the storm over free verse was still roaring in the mid-Twenties. One of them, Robert Frost, would become the best loved and most popular American poet of his time. Another, Edna St. Vincent Millay, would be the lyric voice of the newly liberated and uninhibited young. Eliot was to be the most complexly controversial literary figure of his generation, in part for reasons bearing as much on his politics and religion as on his art. Almost without exception these and about thirty others would find their place increasingly certain as time passed, and they went on to more mature work, and their audience matured with them.

The old battle cries of Imagism and free verse are dim now, but the work that provoked them is not. Amy Lowell (whose services to poetry included promotion and financing) and "H.D." (Hilda Doolittle) learned well from Ezra Pound on their way to being early Imagists. Their poems are still fresh and alive, and to be read with pleasure. So are Sandburg's, some thirty years after Harriet Monroe first published him. In his free-swinging, melodic reporting he was the Midwest minstrel taking his legends and stories and verbal cartoons around the countryside, putting on a poetic show, now and then kidding the customers a little, often leaving them with a line that would haunt them indefinitely. It was the direct, immediately understandable approach of the showman, poetry for the man in the gallery as well as the orchestra seat. That quick intelligibility was a major aspect also of Frost, who established his personal idiom within conventional forms and gave his subtleties the deceptive plainness of a pastoral. How much of music and wisdom lay behind that seeming simplicity is one of the fine achievements of American literature considered as popular art, as—on a broader plane—is Stephen Vincent Benét's *John Brown's Body,* with its vivid lyricism and movielike scenic appeal. That is to say, it is all but impossible that having once read "Stopping by Woods on a Snowy Evening," one could ever quite forget it; or "Mending Wall" or "Road Not Taken" or a dozen other poems in which Frost transformed the ordinary particular into the universal. Thus, too, the vision of America with which Benét concluded his narrative. It declaims, it all but waves the flag, it joins the company of all those others—poems, speeches, stories—that have made instant and lasting contact, struck a common chord. On this plane of memorability is poem after poem by Edna St. Vincent

Millay, whose lyric gift is now strangely in shadow. She wrote beyond the power to sustain that gift, a fault common enough among good writers, and not really important beside the fact that "Renascence" is a fine poem and that, as in "Euclid—," she gave a new life to the sonnet in her time. So, it may be supposed, has Conrad Aiken written too much, and with too great facility—novels, stories, poems, essays—but again one is inclined to say, "What of it?" Why not, at this point, simply be concerned with his best?; with a novel like *Blue Voyage,* stories like "Mr. Arcularis" and "The Dark City," a lyric like "When Trout Swim Down Great Ormond Street." His music—his "subaqueous music," Louis Untermeyer has called it—ripples, his wit is keen. One is grateful for Aiken, as one is grateful and perpetually surprised by E. E. Cummings. The author of the remarkable *The Enormous Room,* a World War I chronicle like no other, has also a vaudevillish wit that makes syntactical and typographical jokes. Further, he is a poet of lyric love, and of traditional measures, as in "All in Green Went My Love Riding." The sentiment hides behind a cloak of skepticism, but of course that was characteristic of the Twenties, which were inclined to be chary of the heart on the sleeve. Elinor Wylie polished a line until it dazzled with its controlled precision. Marianne Moore and Wallace Stevens describe image and scene with a scrupulousness that led into a kind of high, grave comedy. What is it about? It isn't always easy to be certain, the point being made sometimes by association of sound. But the humor is worth waiting for, the imagery is rich and rewarding in itself, just as in Hart Crane's "At Melville's Tomb" the images march by with a somber eloquence and authority of their own.

All of them, whether or not they were directly influenced by Eliot, were of course, intensely aware of him. Who could not be, after *The Waste Land* was published in *The Dial* in November, 1922, and at once became a turning point in the history of poetry written in English? A statement of despair, it reflected exactly the tone of post-war disillusion. As an intellectual program—renunciation of the present and anarchy, return to the past and authority—it worried younger poets who saw in Eliot the supreme technician of his time. It did not worry them to the point where they refrained

from learning what they could of dramatic phrasing, irony and de-
tachment, of music, structure and precise diction; after which they
would go their own ways, richer for the experience even while they
denounced their master for his announcement that he was an Anglo-
Catholic in religion, a royalist in politics, a classicist in literature. The
influence remained, and still does, and "Gerontion"—written on the
way to *The Waste Land*—will partly explain why.

Even categories which had flourished in a tradition of what might
be called permissible dullness had sparkle. The late Twenties brought
Vernon L. Parrington's enormous *Main Currents in American Thought*,
and if time reveals increasingly its faults of esthetic judgment, its
own great literary virtues remain. Among them are the style, at once
lucid and vigorous; the brilliant character-portraits; the extraordinary
sense of immediacy he conveyed in evoking the past. They are all
in his pages here on the Gilded Age—a post-war era with which,
incidentally, the Twenties knew a certain affinity. Indeed, for an era
that allegedly lived only for the moment, the Twenties had a marked
regard for the past, providing the past was restored with spirit.
Thomas Beer recaptured the Nineties in a book, *The Mauve Decade*,
that shimmered like an impressionist painting—and was packed with
learning and insights not to be hidden beneath its langorous expression. It was a book utterly characteristic of its time: sophisticated,
witty, addressed to the knowing, a little impatient with the unknow-
ing, put together with the most artful craftsmanship. Beer wrote of
the rich, but knew too much about them to be (like Fitzgerald) deceived. He understood Mark Hanna. He also understood Stephen
Crane. He wrote some remarkable short stories around an Ohio
farm wife he called Mrs. Egg. He was one of the decade's "conscious stylists," an ambiguous term somehow suggesting decadence,
as if writers as a rule were unconscious of style. Beer was successful,
and so, at his best, was Joseph Hergesheimer, whose flair for interior decoration has moved critics unfairly to overlook the narrative
gift, the skill with which he restored the glitter and taste of the
American romantic past, in *The Three Black Pennys* and *Java Head*.
They continue to be effective novels, and his *San Cristóbal de la
Habana* is a winning and excellent travel book. It proves nothing

very much, I suppose, except that Hergesheimer had an interesting
time in Cuba and came back with the materials for a lively costume
romance he would call *The Bright Shawl!*

The Twenties did not deem Hergesheimer a great writer or even
a very important one, but they had a place for him, and for a large
number of others who wrote well and honorably on their own
terms: Zona Gale, Glenway Wescott, Thomas Boyd, Louis Bromfield, Anne Parrish. It was both a more hospitable and a more toler-
ant literary time than the present, and, despite the fevered legend,
a relatively relaxed one, when writers had the benefit of an audience
or many audiences that had not yet been lured away in large numbers by competing attractions. The new book clubs that arrived shortly
after the mid-Twenties were ridiculed at the time as one more
standardizing influence in American life, but actually they had a
function. They delivered books in far corners of the country where
books were not ordinarily available, and along with the mediocrity
they enhanced was the intelligent reading they encouraged. (In the
three years beginning in 1926, the Book-of-the-Month Club dis-
tributed, among other selections, Remarque's *All Quiet on the Western Front,* Walter Lippmann's *A Preface to Morals,* Francis Hackett's *Henry the Eighth,* Shaw's *The Intelligent Woman's Guide to
Socialism,* Carl Sandburg's *The Prairie Years,* Ellen Glasgow's *The
Romantic Comedians,* Rölvaag's *Giants of the Earth,* Stephen Vincent
Benét's *John Brown's Body.*) Between 1919 and 1929 E. Halde-
mann-Julius sold 100 million of his Little Blue Books (five cents
each), classics and junk together. The point is, America was reading avidly. And while the economics of publishing were as always
grim, the newcomer then had less difficulty getting into print than
he now has, and that too bore directly on the day-to-day culture.
Experimentation was taken for granted, was in the air. Little magazines flourished by the hundred, and somewhere among them—from
The Dial to *Blast*—was a starting place for almost anyone. The first
novel's first printing was apt to be small, but somehow there *was*
usually a first printing; probably the publisher expected to lose
money, but he was investing in the author's future, a speculative
gesture he cannot so often afford today. A good many writers and

their readers came of age together, starting in the early post-war period. Even some of the established performers—Lardner, Anderson, Frost—had in fact not been writing very long; and for such veterans as Dreiser, Ellen Glasgow and Willa Cather, the most fruitful days were ahead as 1920 arrived.

Ford cars and chain-owned newspapers may have been standardizing the United States, but the writers were extraordinary in their variety. More than ever, as one goes back over the roster of works and authors, one wonders how the writing of the Twenties has come to be regarded as a quite homogeneous unit, as if the expatriates had produced most of it, or as if it were entirely a literature of protest or despair. A good deal of it was, but then we come back to the persistently curious paradox of the Twenties: while saying in effect that life was scarcely worth living, writers who said it were living it strenuously; and most of their readers were living it prosperously and agreeably. The Depression Thirties, the Wartorn Forties, were far off. The revolts—the revolt from the village, the revolt from idealism, the revolt from America—were conducted with enormous gusto. The affirmation of negation was distinctly affirmative, as was apparent when Harold Stearns, assembling a symposium called *Civilization in the United States,* was told with splendid vigor by thirty contributors that American civilization was virtually dead.

The revolt from the village, as Carl Van Doren called it, had been bitterly forecast in 1915 by Edgar Lee Masters' *Spoon River Anthology.* Sherwood Anderson, in *Winesburg,* Ohio (1919) dissected the small town with Masters' realism and his own deep sympathy. ("A naturalist with a skirl of music," was Francis Hackett's fine phrase for him.) Next to Hemingway, no prose writer influenced other writers of the Twenties as did Anderson—and even Hemingway seems to have felt obliged to exorcise the fear of that influence by a savage parody, *The Torrents of Spring.* Hemingway was of course to become one of the exact users of the language. Sentence for sentence Anderson remains, especially in his novels, a bumbler—and in great flashes a profoundly moving storyteller, almost, it sometimes seemed, in spite of himself, writing as the storytellers talked in the Ohio town in which he grew up: one hears the drawl, the start-and-stop, the searching for a word. Above all there is the sense of a man trying to tell the inner, mystically apprehended truth about places, people, and himself. The struggle for simplicity was often anything but simple. It was tortuous and, as Hemingway demonstrated, unfortunate. But when he achieved it, there were stories like "I'm a Fool," "I Want to Know Why," and "The Return," stories with a countryman's feeling for weather and animals, with a sensitive small-town man's awareness of the melancholy lying just under the surface of ordinary lives around him. His poet's eye saw the loneliness in others, a loneliness often related to sexual unhappiness, and with his intuitive understanding he was quick to build stories around them. He himself had walked away from a dull business life into the personal freedom of the artist, and thereafter his religion was to be freedom. He moved into the great world, but in the meaning of art he never left the small towns and the county fairs and the slow-talking village people among whom he had grown up. He was a troubadour who sang the same song, with only slight variations, but sang it superbly in the prime of his career, and however widely he traveled he always came home once more. Anderson could not really revolt from the village when the essence of his art, the chief reason for his being an artist at all, was there.

No more could Sinclair Lewis, as he led his fierce-looking charges on Gopher Prairie in *Main Street* and on Zenith in *Babbitt*. He seemed, when those books burst on the country in 1920 and 1922, to be the most slashing of satirists, and there is every reason to think he intended to be. The sometime janitor of Upton Sinclair's Helicon Hall utopia was surely one to scorn the business life of Zenith, in the State of Winnemac, and to do its social life to precisely the deadly turn you will find in the chapters on the select dinner party given by the Babbitts for the beauty and chivalry of Floral Heights. One must believe too that Lewis, the young radical who had matured in the Wilsonian New Freedom, felt a further anger as he looked at a thousand Zeniths and Gopher Prairies and saw what had happened to Progress. What a fine time he had, what a fine time he gave everyone else, with those murderous pictures of the service club luncheons and their hearty jocularity, the mildly shady business practices of George F. Babbitt, the felonious activities of the Reverend Elmer Gantry! To all but those for whom it came somewhat too close to home, the satire was one of the great entertainments of the decade. It rang with the passion of a man who meant what he was saying. It crackled with vitality. But then time brought a subtle change. The satire dimmed to a kind of friendly, though still exact, photography, and it seemed perfectly clear, if it had not been so before, that Lewis and George F. Babbitt were friends, that Babbitt's little gesture toward freedom was more tragic than anything else, that Lewis really loved Zenith and was comfortably at home there, reserving only the right to be pretty frank with his pals at the Kiwanis Club. The sting of the satire is gone, then, and some of the impact of the themes; and one sees now that the dialogue which at first hearing seemed an exact transcription was not exact at all but a language on which Lewis had imposed his own accent and rhythms. In the best of his big books there remain the characters he created so completely. Re-reading *Babbitt, Arrowsmith, Dodsworth,* one realizes that—so far as it is possible to guess at such a thing at this point—these people have come to stay, that at least one of them is part of the language, a figure so perfectly caught that he is now a symbol, as surely as Micawber or Becky Sharp. After those big books Lewis could not hold the pace; his later work was so tired that it seemed a feeble imitation or an unkind parody. But in *Babbitt,* among the towers that "were neither citadels nor churches but frankly and beautifully office buildings," Lewis was a novelist at the height of his career.

So, in the Twenties, was Ellen Glasgow, whose revolt was against a tradition. The tradition was that body of Southern myth designed to mitigate the result of the War Between the States. Born into the legend, she left it behind only occasionally; chiefly she stayed and satirized it, though no one of her novels is exclusively satiric, and some of them not at all. Her delicate irony was always close to tragedy—the plight of the elderly Judge Bland, in *The Romantic Comedians,* married to a girl whose appeal lay in her dissimilarity to his late, respected and unloved wife; the long, unforgettable, central section of *The Sheltered Life;* the situation in which, in the chapter reprinted in this book from *They Stooped to Conquer,* Virginius Littlepage wrestles between desire for an appetizing temptress and the code governing his conduct toward his wife. Miss Glasgow was so completely of the world of which she wrote that no one, I imagine, ever thought of calling her a "regionalist," a word then coming into fashion for writers adept in presenting "local color." Her knowledge of that world was as pervasive, and as unobtrusive, as the skill with which she obtained any effect she sought. She was one of the absolutely sure-footed artists among all American writers, in purity of craftsmanship the equal of such of her contemporaries as Hemingway, Fitzgerald, Edith Wharton, Lardner, Willa Cather. How widely read is she now, one wonders, and is she merely taken for granted? Do readers pass by *The Sheltered Life, Barren Ground,* and the others, thinking that for all their fame they must have a parochial basis? In the first half of 1952 only one of her novels, *Vein of Iron,* was in print in the United States.

On the other hand, the place of the American Twenties' most ferocious satirist, and one of the most skillful and sensitive realists, grows constantly more secure. Of Ring Lardner Maxwell Perkins once wrote to Hemingway, "If he had written much more he would have been a great writer perhaps." Perhaps, too, it is remarkable that in his forty-eight years he left so much that endures so well, when one thinks of the time and energy that went into syndicate pot-boiling. He was savage and funny, often at the same time. His loathing for Broadway heels, small-town sadists, prize-fight hangers-on, was finely distilled venom, the deadlier for the objectivity with which he destroyed them, or, rather, seemed to stage-manage their self-destruction. These portraits are definitive—the practical joker in "Haircut," the movie producer and his wife in "The Love Nest," the prizefighter in "Champion," the Broadway producer in "A Day with Conrad Green." With the dumb ballplayer in "You Know Me, Al" he was somewhat more patient. The busher with the swelled head and the fast ball is only pathetic and ridiculous. One thinks of Lardner as an utterly dispassionate clinician with a very dark view of the world and most of the people in it, and of all the things they sweat for and pride themselves on. But he was no more to be categorized than Miss Glasgow. His humor was usually ironic, but not always, and he could be suddenly and unexpectedly tender, as in "The Golden Honeymoon," a story less characteristic of him than a dozen others, and presented here because one reader finds it impossible to omit it. Less characteristic, to be sure, and yet it exemplifies two of Lardner's great gifts—his unerring control over whatever material he used, and the faultless ear he brought to American speech, its representation in phonetic spelling that had certain humorous values but was even more important in making the reader *hear* as well as see. As surely as Fitzgerald himself, the Lardner of the few and fine short stories fitted the Twenties' reputed mold: the work was virtually perfect of its kind, it was without illusions, it stopped too soon.

They understood each other very well, one is certain on reading Fitzgerald's appreciation of Lardner after the latter's death in 1933: a little essay that says much about Fitzgerald as well. His regret that Lardner had not written as much as he might have, reflects Fitzgerald's own preoccupation with time. The first of the Twenties' writers of enduring importance fully to "arrive" after the decade began, he seemed forever conscious of the speed with which time flowed past him. And now, sooner or later, any consideration of the Twenties must come back to him and linger there. Their pace and despairs, their successes and self-induced tragedies, filled in almost too perfect measure the life of one whose first novel was a new generation's declaration of independence. *This Side of Paradise* (1920) was not in most respects a good novel; either was its successor, *The Beautiful and Damned;* either was subject to the kind of virulence in which Frances Newman indulged in a newspaper review of the former—a review which, together with Fitzgerald's rejoinder and Miss Newman's reply, makes a curious episode revealing some interesting facets of the principals and a sideline observer, Mr. Cabell. Yet even Fitzgerald's early, uncertain work had a distinction, a combination of candor, intelligence and extreme sensitiveness to environment; and the best, it seems certain now, belongs with the absolutely first-rate American writing of his lifetime. When he died at forty-four in Hollywood in 1940, the press obituaries said nothing much of him except to remember that he was "the historian of the Jazz Age," which was true but absurdly far from being the whole truth. The neglect in which he had worked since 1934 (when *Tender Is the Night* failed with the public and most critics) continued until the re-evaluation began with understanding post-mortems by people who had read him with care. In 1945 Edmund Wilson edited *The Crack-up*, a miscellany of autobiographical essays, notebooks, letters; 1951 brought a brilliant full-length biography, Arthur Mizener's *The Far Side of Paradise,* and a collection of stories finely edited and introduced by Malcolm Cowley. The revival was on, and if it seems preposterous that there should be any question of having to "revive" the author of *The Great Gatsby*— well, we are a restless people who tend to neglect established artists suddenly while we go in pursuit of fresh discoveries. Like most such revivals, this one has already brought a reaction, including denials of a greatness that is not claimed for Fitzgerald even by his most ardent supporters. The revival does make it unlikely, from now on, that his reputation will be allowed again to fall into the shadow it knew in the Thirties, which had no particular place for a novelist as intent as Fitzgerald was on grace, romantic love, the psychotic problems of the rich, and whose subject matter in some of his finest work was a projection of himself. Before *The Great Gatsby* was over Gatsby, as Fitzgerald said, had become Fitzgerald; so, in *Tender Is the Night,* had Richard Diver; and one can guess at how much of personal remorse he wrote into that haunting return to the Twenties, the short story called "Babylon Revisited." It is true that Fitzgerald was to pay a penalty for his dependence as a writer on aspects of his own life. He came at last to the "emotional bankruptcy" he had always dreaded: while there was to be a final flash of his old power in the unfinished *Last Tycoon,* the vein of the earlier books and stories was worked thin. How rich was that vein at its full strength is not a matter of mere nostalgia, or of enthusiasm cherished out of loyalty to writing that was an event in readers' lives. One has only to go back to *The Great Gatsby* (1925) or "The Rich Boy," the long short story published the following year. They are right where they were, with their first freshness of tone, the vitality of their romantic realism, their dramatic overtones of disaster—and that central fact of wealth that was pivotal in Fitzgerald's life and work. With something like envy though never, I think, with mere snobbery, there ran through all his early work the fascination money held for him, or what he thought money brought of grace and charm. At the same time there stood by, like an observant guard, his wary moral sense, what he called "the spoiled priest" in him. The dramatic tension this conflict produced was a major factor in his writing, a tension the more vibrant because of Fitzgerald's implicit honesty. For one feels that while he was deceived, notably by the role of wealth, he never consciously deceived himself. Above all there remains "the wise and tragic sense of life" of which, toward the end of his life, he wrote to his daughter. Of his writing in the Twenties it especially enriched *The Great Gatsby* and is to be seen, if necessarily on a smaller scale, in the story of Anson Hunter, the Rich Boy whose character, shaped by wealth, forced him to dominate at the cost of love.

Writing the truth as he saw it, Fitzgerald employed recognizable and generally romantic models until he achieved a technique, a tone, of his own. Ernest Hemingway, also writing the truth, wrote it as no writer had quite seen it before him. Hemingway too had his teachers, less formal than Fitzgerald's. Sherwood Anderson taught him something about simplicity. Gertrude Stein talked to him about sentences. Ezra Pound cut adjectives out of the manuscripts Hemingway sent to him—the pre-Fascist, pre-psychiatric ward Pound, who ultimately would be more important as critic and editor than as poet, who liked nothing better than to take what he called the "cold fat," the "emotional slither," the "upholstered" words out of writing. Since 1923 no one's writing has been more free of cold fat, slither and upholstery than that of Miss Stein's and Pound's pupil, who came into their world after a Midwestern boyhood, ambulance driving and a serious wound on the Italian front in World War I, and European correspondence for the Toronto *Star*. Here was the very archetype of the young post-war American, utterly disillusioned by what he had experienced. Fitzgerald had, at least, his glamour and his gold-specked dreams. Hemingway, haunted then as later by the fact of death, seemed to put his faith only in writing. No cant, no big words like "sacrifice" and "glory," the esthetic reality of physical sensation and especially of violence, the necessity to endure through personal courage an existence containing very little that compensated for all the agony: these were articles of faith. For the artists there was art; for them and for others there was liquor and sex; somehow one would survive. A somewhat narrow world, a rather negative vision, as Hemingway's critics have not tired of pointing out from that day to this. What more, one sometimes wonders, do they really ask of him? A more sharply defined social interest, mainly. But Hemingway's "whole work is a criticism of society," as Edmund Wilson has noted, and most effectively so when it is least direct. His most pronounced failures have occurred in works in which the attack was frontal, as in *To Have and Have Not,* where indignation came first and characters became caricatures, or in *The Fifth Column,* where his political thinking had a kind of shortsightedness of which the Communists made grateful use. Critics not of the left could certainly wish that Hemingway's characters were less stylized to fit a personal philosophy and therefore were more memorable as individuals, in particular the women, who almost without exception are submissive shadows. A good many other changes could probably be asked; which demands, if satisfied, would make of him a very different author. It is hard to know what the purpose of this critical daydreaming is, when the important thing is to recognize what he has meant since 1925, when *In Our Time* introduced him to his own country with the cleansing shock of cold water. Here was hard, clear writing, dazzling in its concentration, saying exactly what it was intended to say, without waste, and with great emotion. It is not easy to recapture that arrival because, between that time and now, imitators by the thousand have obscured the view, wandering in and out of his novels and stories, making off with a mannerism or device here, a character or even a story idea there. His actual technique has been harder to borrow because it involves the methods by which he functions as a creator, and these in turn relate to his motives and his personality, as indicated in a now celebrated passage in his *Death in the Afternoon:*

"I was trying to write then and I found the greatest difficulty, aside from knowing truly what you felt, rather than what you were supposed to feel, and had been taught to feel, was to put down what really happened in action; what the actual things were which produced the emotion that you experienced. In writing for a newspaper you told what happened and, with one trick and another, you communicated the emotion aided by the element of timeliness which gives a certain emotion to any account of something that has happened on that day; but the real thing, the sequence of motion and fact which made the emotion and which would be valid in a year or in ten years or, with luck and if you stated it purely enough, always, was beyond me and I was working very hard to try to get it * * * I was trying to learn to write, commencing with the simplest things, and one of the simplest things of all and the most fundamental is violent death."

Not so simple, though the imitators keep trying because on the surface it does look very simple indeed: the straight declarative sentences, bare of adjectives and adverbs; the curt dialogue; the flexible, swinging cadences of the linked sentences. "This too remember," he wrote elsewhere in the same book, which the imitators have not read with sufficient care. "If a man writes clearly enough any one can see if he fakes. If he mystifies to avoid a straight statement, which is very different from breaking so-called rules of syntax or grammar to make an effect which can be obtained in no other way, the writer takes a longer time to be known as a fake and other writers who are afflicted by the same necessity will praise him in their own defense."

Having rejected the technique which achieves emotion by describing it, Hemingway could scarcely have faked or mystified if he had wanted to. He was committed to exactness, and if his material was limited the method by which it was treated was absolutely right. It portrayed the world of nature with incomparable brilliance and the precision of the poet. It "froze" action until action could be fully seen and felt and the emotional impact of a moment or a story got under way. It had the laconic, unemphatic air of the Hemingway heroes who specialize in "grace under pressure," like Lieutenant

Henry in *A Farewell to Arms,* or pure pride of craft, like the aging
bullfighter in "The Undefeated," a symbol of that personal gallantry
which is at the very center of Hemingway's moral scheme, as duty
was in Conrad's. As Hemingway progressed from his early, intensely
cultivated simplicity into the use of more complex symbols, his writing in general shared that greater complexity. The fatalism faded a
little that he had brought from a war which saw the end of idealism
for a generation. There remained the superb gift of direct communication, the "cold fat" all cleared away, the certainty (and how truly
rare it is) that behind this story or that book was a writer who, at
the time he wrote it, could think of no way of making it better. In
that insistence lies at least one aspect of the romanticism Hemingway's critics are always finding in him, with a slight air of accusation. Very well, then, it is romanticism. It belongs with the articles
of faith. It may have been the most important single thing that happened to American writing in the Twenties.

"It was an age of miracles, it was an age of art, it was an age of
excess, and it was an age of satire," Fitzgerald was to say of it, and
suddenly it was gone. In retrospect, at least, the ending seems sudden,
though in fact it was less explosion than fadeout. In the autumn of
the decade's very last year *A Farewll to Arms* was published, full of
that melancholy disenchantment the Twenties bore so happily, like
a flag. *Tender Is the Night,* which among other things was a definitive portrait of the American expatriate lost between a world he had
renounced and a world he could never really join, was still five years
away. Miss Glasgow's finest novel, *The Sheltered Life,* would not
appear until 1932. Nevertheless, an era had ended with Black Friday, and one had to be aware of it even at the time. The "climate"
changed perceptibly. The casual acceptance that had marked so much
of American life for ten years disappeared in a flash. The easy money
vanished, and with it the air of unconcern. The party was over, the
hangover was beginning. The literature of social protest would be
in full bloom soon, notably with the opening of Dos Passos' *U.S.A.,*
but first there was to be a dramatic entrance, just before the final curtain. Out of the South, and published in that fateful October, came
Thomas Wolfe's *Look Homeward, Angel* to conclude the Twenties

with a touch of curious irony—namely, that after a decade of experimentation and new forms, the Twenties should end with a novel
that owed much to Whitman and Melville and nothing to Anderson
or Hemingway. It was the first installment of what would be in effect
a multi-volume novel about Thomas Wolfe and America, and if it
had any particular characteristic of the Twenties it was that the
author was the hero and in revolt against his environment. Critics
and readers hailed, justly, its vitality and use of sensuous detail,
as in the evocative passage of the dawning consciousness of little
Eugene Gant. About its rhetoric they weren't always so comfortable:
it ran from true eloquence down to an extravagance that had the
air of a compulsion to write so many words a day. The critics and
the readers had, after all, just lived through a decade in which "form"
and "discipline" were important, and this was a writer who had no
use for either, whose major objective appeared to be a catalog of
everything he could remember. It was tumultuously personal, lyrical,
ecstatic, verbose, grotesquely comic, utterly without the sophistication of the decade just then passing, and perhaps the welcome it
received was the warmer because of that. Looked back upon from
the late fall of 1929, a good deal that was still vivid in memory
did appear to be sinister or silly—Teapot Dome scandals, acceptance
of corruption, flagpole sitters, Scopes Trial, Dr. Coué and his formula for self-improvement ("day by day in every way I am getting
better and better"), the great confidence game known as the Florida
Boom, intellectual forums on the new national institution called the
petting party, de-bunking of traditional heroes, bobbed hair, dance
marathons. If those things seemed, as 1930 arrived, to belong almost to another country, perhaps it was because there was a certain
subconscious embarrassment, along with a cynical amusement, that
they had ever happened or been allowed to seem important. Something new was in order, not necessarily better, but new. But the
good writing of the Twenties, like its painting and its music, would
not remain behind. Because the disillusion was positive, the values
held up. That concentration on art which so dismays the social
scientists gave the novels and the poems and the stories an enduring
base. It was a good time, we see now, for a writer to learn his craft,

as we are reminded when a writer of that era carries on into this one: the most eagerly awaited novel of 1952 would be Ernest Hemingway's. Above all, though we did not entirely realize it then, the Twenties brought to a decisive end America's status as a literary colony. That was the use that writers made of their new freedom, and it was a fine, rewarding use, a triumph worth all the work, heartbreak and failures that went into it.

JOHN K. HUTCHENS

SHORT STORIES

RING LARDNER

The Golden Honeymoon

MOTHER says that when I start talking I never know when to stop. But I tell her the only time I get a chance is when she ain't around, so I have to make the most of it. I guess the fact is neither one of us would be welcome in a Quaker meeting, but as I tell Mother, what did God give us tongues for if He didn't want we should use them? Only she says He didn't give them to us to say the same thing over and over again, like I do, and repeat myself. But I say:

"Well, Mother," I say, "when people is like you and I and been married fifty years, do you expect everything I say will be something you ain't heard me say before? But it may be new to others, as they ain't nobody else lived with me as long as you have."

So she says:

"You can bet they ain't, as they couldn't nobody else stand you that long."

"Well," I tell her, "you look pretty healthy."

"Maybe I do," she will say, "but I looked even healthier before I married you."

You can't get ahead of Mother.

Yes, sir, we was married just fifty years ago the seventeenth day of last December and my daughter and son-in-law was over from Trenton to help us celebrate the Golden Wedding. My son-in-law is John H. Kramer, the real estate man. He made $12,000 one year and is pretty well thought of around Trenton; a good, steady, hard worker. The Rotarians was after him a long time to join, but he kept telling them his home was his club. But Edie finally made him join. That's my daughter.

Well, anyway, they come over to help us celebrate the Golden Wedding and it was pretty crimpy weather and the furnace don't seem to heat up no more like it used to and Mother made the remark that she hoped this winter wouldn't be as cold as the last, referring to the winter previous. So Edie said if she was us, and nothing to keep us home, she certainly wouldn't spend no more winters up here and why didn't we just shut off the water and close up the house and go down to Tampa, Florida? You know we was there four winters ago and staid five weeks, but it cost us over three hundred and fifty dollars for hotel bill alone. So Mother said we wasn't going no place to be robbed. So my son-in-law spoke up and said that Tampa wasn't the only place in the South, and besides we didn't have to stop at no high price hotel but could rent us a couple of rooms and board out somewheres, and he had heard that St. Petersburg, Florida, was *the* spot and if we said the word he would write down there and make inquiries.

Well, to make a long story short, we decided to do it and Edie said it would be our Golden Honeymoon and for a present my son-in-law paid the difference between a section and a compartment so as we could have a compartment and have more privatecy. In a compartment you have an upper and lower berth just like the regular sleeper, but it is a shut in room by itself and got a wash bowl. The car we went in was all compartments and no regular berths at all. It was all compartments.

We went to Trenton the night before and staid at my daughter and son-in-law and we left Trenton the next afternoon at 3.23 P.M.

This was the twelfth day of January. Mother set facing the front of the train, as it makes her giddy to ride backwards. I set facing her, which does not affect me. We reached North Philadelphia at

4.03 P.M. and we reached West Philadelphia at 4.14, but did not go into Broad Street. We reached Baltimore at 6.30 and Washington, D. C., at 7.25. Our train laid over in Washington two hours till another train come along to pick us up and I got out and strolled up the platform and into the Union Station. When I come back, our car had been switched on to another track, but I remembered the name of it, the La Belle, as I had once visited my aunt out in Oconomowoc, Wisconsin, where there was a lake of that name, so I had no difficulty in getting located. But Mother had nearly fretted herself sick for fear I would be left.

"Well," I said, "I would of followed you on the next train."

"You couldn't of," said Mother, and she pointed out that she had the money.

"Well," I said, "we are in Washington and I could of borrowed from the United States Treasury. I would of pretended I was an Englishman."

Mother caught the point and laughed heartily.

Our train pulled out of Washington at 9.40 P.M. and Mother and I turned in early, I taking the upper. During the night we passed through the green fields of old Virginia, though it was too dark to tell if they was green or what color. When we got up in the morning, we was at Fayetteville, North Carolina. We had breakfast in the dining car and after breakfast I got in conversation with the man in the next compartment to ours. He was from Lebanon, New Hampshire, and a man about eighty years of age. His wife was with him, and two unmarried daughters and I made the remark that I should think the four of them would be crowded in one compartment, but he said they had made the trip every winter for fifteen years and knowed how to keep out of each other's way. He said they was bound for Tarpon Springs.

We reached Charleston, South Carolina, at 12.50 P.M. and arrived at Savannah, Georgia, at 4.20. We reached Jacksonville, Florida, at 8.45 P.M. and had an hour and a quarter to lay over there, but Mother made a fuss about me getting off the train, so we had the darky make up our berths and retired before we left Jacksonville. I didn't sleep good as the train done a lot of hemming and hawing, and Mother never sleeps good on a train as she says she is always worrying that I will fall out. She says she would rather have the upper herself, as then she would not have to worry about me, but I tell her I can't take the risk of having it get out that I allowed my wife to sleep in an upper berth. It would make talk.

We was up in the morning in time to see our friends from New Hampshire get off at Tarpon Springs, which we reached at 6.53 A.M.

Several of our fellow passengers got off at Clearwater and some at Belleair, where the train backs right up to the door of the mammoth hotel. Belleair is the winter headquarters for the golf dudes and everybody that got off there had their bag of sticks, as many as ten and twelve in a bag. Women and all. When I was a young man we called it shinny and only needed one club to play with and about one game of it would of been a-plenty for some of these dudes, the way we played it.

The train pulled into St. Petersburg at 8.20 and when we got off the train you would think it was a riot, what with all the darkies barking for the different hotels.

I said to Mother, I said:

"It is a good thing we have got a place picked out to go to and don't have to choose a hotel, as it would be hard to choose amongst them if every one of them is the best."

She laughed.

We found a jitney and I give him the address of the room my son-in-law got for us and soon we was there and introduced ourselves to the lady that owns the house, a young widow about forty-eight years of age. She showed us our room, which was light and airy with a comfortable bed and bureau and washstand. It was twelve dollars a week, but the location was good, only three blocks from Williams Park.

St. Pete is what folks calls the town, though they also call it the Sunshine City, as they claim they's no other place in the country where they's fewer days when Old Sol don't smile down on Mother Earth, and one of the newspapers gives away all their copies free every day when the sun don't shine. They claim to of only give them away some sixty-odd times in the last eleven years. Another nickname they have got for the town is "the Poor Man's Palm Beach," but I guess they's men that comes there that could borrow as much from the bank as some of the Willie boys over to the other Palm Beach.

During our stay we paid a visit to the Lewis Tent City, which is the headquarters for the Tin Can Tourists. But maybe you ain't heard about them. Well, they are an organization that takes their vacation trips by auto and carries everything with them. That is, they bring along their tents to sleep in and cook in and they don't patronize no hotels or cafeterias, but they have got to be bona fide auto campers or they can't belong to the organization.

They tell me they's over 200,000 members to it and they call themselves the Tin Canners on account of most of their food being put up in tin cans. One couple we seen in the Tent City was a couple from Brady, Texas, named Mr. and Mrs. Pence, which the old man is over eighty years of age and they had come in their auto all the way from home, a distance of 1,641 miles. They took five weeks for the trip, Mr. Pence driving the entire distance.

The Tin Canners hails from every State in the Union and in the summer time they visit places like New England and the Great Lakes region, but in the winter the most of them comes to Florida and scatters all over the State. While we was down there, they was a national convention of them at Gainesville, Florida, and they elected a Fredonia, New York, man as their president. His title is Royal Tin Can Opener of the World. They have got a song wrote up which everybody has got to learn it before they are a member:

> "The tin can forever! Hurrah, boys! Hurrah!
> Up with the tin can! Down with the foe!
> We will rally round the campfire, we'll rally once again,
> Shouting, 'We auto camp forever!'"

That is something like it. And the members has also got to have a tin can fastened on to the front of their machine.

I asked Mother how she would like to travel around that way and she said:

"Fine, but not with an old rattle brain like you driving."

"Well," I said, "I am eight years younger than this Mr. Pence who drove here from Texas."

"Yes," she said, "but he is old enough to not be skittish."

You can't get ahead of Mother.

Well, one of the first things we done in St. Petersburg was to go to the Chamber of Commerce and register our names and where we was from as they's great rivalry amongst the different States in regards to the number of their citizens visiting in town and of course our little State don't stand much of a show, but still every little bit helps, as the fella says. All and all, the man told us, they was eleven thousand names registered, Ohio leading with some fifteen hundred-odd and New York State next with twelve hundred. Then come Michigan, Pennsylvania and so on down, with one man each from Cuba and Nevada.

The first night we was there, they was a meeting of the New York-New Jersey Society at the Congregational Church and a man from Ogdensburg, New York State, made the talk. His subject was Rainbow Chasing. He is a Rotarian and a very convicting speaker, though I forget his name.

Our first business, of course, was to find a place to eat and after trying several places we run on to a cafeteria on Central Avenue that suited us up and down. We eat pretty near all our meals there and it averaged about two dollars per day for the two of us, but the food was well cooked and everything nice and clean. A man don't mind paying the price if things is clean and well cooked.

On the third day of February, which is Mother's birthday, we spread ourselves and eat supper at the Poinsettia Hotel and they charged us seventy-five cents for a sirloin steak that wasn't hardly big enough for one.

I said to Mother: "Well," I said, "I guess it's a good thing every day ain't your birthday or we would be in the poorhouse."

"No," says Mother, "because if every day was my birthday, I would be old enough by this time to of been in my grave long ago."

You can't get ahead of Mother.

In the hotel they had a card-room where they was several men and ladies playing five hundred and this new fangled whist bridge.

We also seen a place where they was dancing, so I asked Mother would she like to trip the light fantastic toe and she said no, she was too old to squirm like you have got to do now days. We watched some of the young folks at it awhile till Mother got disgusted and said we would have to see a good movie to take the taste out of our mouth. Mother is a great movie heroyne and we go twice a week here at home.

But I want to tell you about the Park. The second day we was there we visited the Park, which is a good deal like the one in Tampa, only bigger, and they's more fun goes on here every day than you could shake a stick at. In the middle they's a big bandstand and chairs for the folks to set and listen to the concerts, which they give you music for all tastes, from Dixie up to classical pieces like Hearts and Flowers.

Then all around they's places marked off for different sports and games—chess and checkers and dominoes for folks that enjoys those kind of games, and roque and horse-shoes for the nimbler ones. I used to pitch a pretty fair shoe myself, but ain't done much of it in the last twenty years.

Well, anyway, we bought a membership ticket in the club which costs one dollar for the season, and they tell me that up to a couple years ago it was fifty cents, but they had to raise it to keep out the riffraff.

Well, Mother and I put in a great day watching the pitchers and she wanted I should get in the game, but I told her I was all out of practice and would make a fool of myself, though I seen several men pitching who I guess I could take their measure without no practice. However, they was some good pitchers, too, and one boy from Akron, Ohio, who could certainly throw a pretty shoe. They told me it looked like he would win the championship of the United States in the February tournament. We come away a few days before they held that and I never did hear if he win. I forget his name, but he was a clean cut young fella and he has got a brother in Cleveland that's a Rotarian.

Well, we just stood around and watched the different games for two or three days and finally I set down in a checker game with a man named Weaver from Danville, Illinois. He was a pretty fair checker player, but he wasn't no match for me, and I hope that don't sound like bragging. But I always could hold my own on a checkerboard and the folks around here will tell you the same thing. I played with this Weaver pretty near all morning for two or three mornings and he beat me one game and the only other time it looked like he had a chance, the noon whistle blowed and we had to quit and go to dinner.

While I was playing checkers, Mother would set and listen to the band, as she loves music, classical or no matter what kind, but anyway she was setting there one day and between selections the woman next to her opened up a conversation. She was a woman about Mother's own age, seventy or seventy-one, and finally she asked Mother's name and Mother told her her name and where she was from and Mother asked her the same question, and who do you think the woman was?

Well, sir, it was the wife of Frank M. Hartsell, the man who was engaged to Mother till I stepped in and cut him out, fifty-two years ago!

Yes, sir!

You can imagine Mother's surprise! And Mrs. Hartsell was surprised, too, when Mother told her she had once been friends with her husband, though Mother didn't say how close friends they had been, or that Mother and I was the cause of Hartsell going out West. But that's what we was. Hartsell left his town a month after the engagement was broke off and ain't never been back since. He had went out to Michigan and become a veterinary, and that is where he had settled down, in Hillsdale, Michigan, and finally married his wife.

Well, Mother screwed up her courage to ask if Frank was still living and Mrs. Hartsell took her over to where they was pitching horse-shoes and there was old Frank, waiting his turn. And he knowed Mother as soon as he seen her, though it was over fifty years. He said he knowed her by her eyes.

"Why, it's Lucy Frost!" he says, and he throwed down his shoes and quit the game.

Then they come over and hunted me up and I will confess I wouldn't of knowed him. Him and I is the same age to the month, but he seems to show it more, some way. He is balder for one thing. And his beard is all white, where mine has still got a streak of brown in it. The very first thing I said to him, I said:

"Well, Frank, that beard of yours makes me feel like I was back north. It looks like a regular blizzard."

"Well," he said, "I guess yourn would be just as white if you had it dry cleaned."

But Mother wouldn't stand that.

"Is that so!" she said to Frank. "Well, Charley ain't had no tobacco in his mouth for over ten years!"

And I ain't!

Well, I excused myself from the checker game and it was pretty close to noon, so we decided to all have dinner together and they was nothing for it only we must try their cafeteria on Third Avenue. It was a little more expensive than ours and not near as good, I thought. I and Mother had about the same dinner we had been having every day and our bill was $1.10. Frank's check was $1.20 for he and his wife. The same meal wouldn't of cost them more than a dollar at our place.

After dinner we made them come up to our house and we all set in the parlor, which the young woman had give us the use of to entertain company. We begun talking over old times and Mother said she was a-scared Mrs. Hartsell would find it tiresome listening to we three talk over old times, but as it turned out they wasn't much chance for nobody else to talk with Mrs. Hartsell in the company. I have heard lots of women that could go it, but Hartsell's wife takes the cake of all the women I ever seen. She told us the family history of everybody in the State of Michigan and bragged for a half hour about her son, who she said is in the drug business in Grand Rapids, and a Rotarian.

When I and Hartsell could get a word in edgeways we joked one another back and forth and I chafed him about being a horse doctor.

"Well, Frank," I said, "you look pretty prosperous, so I suppose they's been plenty of glanders around Hillsdale."

"Well," he said, "I've managed to make more than a fair living. But I've worked pretty hard."

"Yes," I said, "and I suppose you get called out all hours of the night to attend births and so on."

Mother made me shut up.

Well, I thought they wouldn't never go home and I and Mother was in misery trying to keep awake, as the both of us generally always takes a nap after dinner. Finally they went, after we had made an engagement to meet them in the Park the next morning, and Mrs. Hartsell also invited us to come to their place the next night and play five hundred. But she had forgot that they was a meeting of the Michigan Society that evening, so it was not till two evenings later that we had our first card game.

Hartsell and his wife lived in a house on Third Avenue North and had a private setting room besides their bedroom. Mrs. Hartsell couldn't quit talking about their private setting room like it was something wonderful. We played cards with them, with Mother and Hartsell partners against his wife and I. Mrs. Hartsell is a miserable card player and we certainly got the worst of it.

After the game she brought out a dish of oranges and we had to pretend it was just what we wanted, though oranges down there is like a young man's whiskers; you enjoy them at first, but they get to be a pesky nuisance.

We played cards again the next night at our place with the same partners and I and Mrs. Hartsell was beat again. Mother and Hartsell was full of compliments for each other on what a good team they made, but the both of them knowed well enough where the secret of their success laid. I guess all and all we must of played ten different evenings and they was only one night when Mrs. Hartsell and I come out ahead. And that one night wasn't no fault of hern.

When we had been down there about two weeks, we spent one evening as their guest in the Congregational Church, at a social give by the Michigan Society. A talk was made by a man named Bitting of Detroit, Michigan, on How I was Cured of Story Telling. He is a big man in the Rotarians and give a witty talk.

A woman named Mrs. Oxford rendered some selections which Mrs. Hartsell said was grand opera music, but whatever they was my daughter Edie could of give her cards and spades and not made such a hullaballoo about it neither.

Then they was a ventriloquist from Grand Rapids and a young woman about forty-five years of age that mimicked different kinds of birds. I whispered to Mother that they all sounded like a chicken, but she nudged me to shut up.

After the show we stopped in a drug store and I set up the refreshments and it was pretty close to ten o'clock before we finally turned in. Mother and I would of preferred tending the movies, but Mother said we mustn't offend Mrs. Hartsell, though I asked her had we came to Florida to enjoy ourselves or to just not offend an old chatter-box from Michigan.

I felt sorry for Hartsell one morning. The women folks both had an engagement down to the chiropodist's and I run across Hartsell in the Park and he foolishly offered to play me checkers.

It was him that suggested it, not me, and I guess he repented himself before we had played one game. But he was too stubborn to give up and set there while I beat him game after game and the worst part of it was that a crowd of folks had got in the habit of watching me play and there they all was, looking on, and finally they seen what a fool Frank was making of himself, and they began to chafe him and pass remarks. Like one of them said:

"Who ever told you you was a checker player!"

And:

"You might maybe be good for tiddle-de-winks, but not checkers!"

I almost felt like letting him beat me a couple games. But the crowd would of knowed it was a put up job.

Well, the women folks joined us in the Park and I wasn't going to mention our little game, but Hartsell told about it himself and admitted he wasn't no match for me.

"Well," said Mrs. Hartsell, "checkers ain't much of a game anyway, is it?" She said: "It's more of a children's game, ain't it? At least, I know my boy's children used to play it a good deal."

"Yes, ma'am," I said. "It's a children's game the way your husband plays it, too."

Mother wanted to smooth things over, so she said:

"Maybe they's other games where Frank can beat you."

"Yes," said Mrs. Hartsell, "and I bet he could beat you pitching horse-shoes."

"Well," I said, "I would give him a chance to try, only I ain't pitched a shoe in over sixteen years."

"Well," said Hartsell, "I ain't played checkers in twenty years."

"You ain't never played it," I said.

"Anyway," says Frank, "Lucy and I is your master at five hundred."

Well, I could of told him why that was, but had decency enough to hold my tongue.

It had got so now that he wanted to play cards every night and when I or Mother wanted to go to a movie, any one of us would have to pretend we had a headache and then trust to goodness that they wouldn't see us sneak into the theater. I don't mind playing cards when my partner keeps their mind on the game, but you take a woman like Hartsell's wife and how can they play cards when they have got to stop every couple seconds and brag about their son in Grand Rapids?

Well, the New York-New Jersey Society announced that they was goin to give a social evening too and I said to Mother, I said:

"Well, that is one evening when we will have an excuse not to play five hundred."

"Yes," she said, "but we will have to ask Frank and his wife to go to the social with us as they asked us to go to the Michigan social."

"Well," I said, "I had rather stay home than drag that chatter-box everywheres we go."

So Mother said:

"You are getting too cranky. Maybe she does talk a little too much but she is good hearted. And Frank is always good company."

So I said:

"I suppose if he is such good company you wished you had of married him."

Mother laughed and said I sounded like I was jealous. Jealous of a cow doctor!

Anyway we had to drag them along to the social and I will say that we give them a much better entertainment than they had given us.

Judge Lane of Paterson made a fine talk on business conditions and a Mrs. Newell of Westfield imitated birds, only you could really tell what they was the way she done it. Two young women from Red Bank sung a choral selection and we clapped them back and they gave us Home to Our Mountains and Mother and Mrs. Hartsell both had tears in their eyes. And Hartsell, too.

Well, some way or another the chairman got wind that I was there and asked me to make a talk and I wasn't even going to get up, but Mother made me, so I got up and said:

"Ladies and gentlemen," I said. "I didn't expect to be called on for a speech on an occasion like this or no other occasion as I do not set myself up as a speech maker, so will have to do the best I can, which I often say is the best anybody can do."

Then I told them the story about Pat and the motorcycle, using the brogue, and it seemed to tickle them and I told them one or two other stories, but altogether I wasn't on my feet more than twenty or twenty-five minutes and you ought to of heard the clapping and hollering when I set down. Even Mrs. Hartsell admitted that I am quite a speechifier and said if I ever went to Grand Rapids, Michigan, her son would make me talk to the Rotarians.

When it was over, Hartsell wanted we should go to their house and play cards, but his wife reminded him that it was after 9.30 P.M., rather a late hour to start a card game, but he had went crazy on the subject of cards, probably because he didn't have to play partners with his wife. Anyway, we got rid of them and went home to bed.

It was the next morning, when he met over to the Park, that Mrs. Hartsell made the remark that she wasn't getting no exercise so I suggested that why didn't she take part in the roque game.

She said she had not played a game of roque in twenty years, but if Mother would play she would play. Well, at first Mother wouldn't hear of it, but finally consented, more to please Mrs. Hartsell than anything else.

Well, they had a game with a Mrs. Ryan from Eagle, Nebraska, and a young Mrs. Morse from Rutland, Vermont, who Mother had met down to the chiropodist's. Well, Mother couldn't hit a flea and they all laughed at her and I couldn't help from laughing at her myself and finally she quit and said her back was too lame to stoop over. So they got another lady and kept on playing and soon Mrs. Hartsell was the one everybody was laughing at, as she had a long shot to hit the black ball, and as she made the effort her teeth fell out on to the court. I never seen a woman so flustered in my life. And I never heard so much laughing, only Mrs. Hartsell didn't join in and she was madder than a hornet and wouldn't play no more, so the game broke up.

Mrs. Hartsell went home without speaking to nobody, but Hartsell stayed around and finally he said to me, he said:

"Well, I played you checkers the other day and you beat me bad and now what do you say if you and me play a game of horse-shoes?"

I told him I hadn't pitched a shoe in sixteen years, but Mother said:

"Go ahead and play. You used to be good at it and maybe it will come back to you."

Well, to make a long story short, I give in. I oughtn't to of never tried it, as I hadn't pitched a shoe in sixteen years, and I only done it to humor Hartsell.

Before we started, Mother patted me on the back and told me to do my best, so we started in and I seen right off that I was in for it, as I hadn't pitched a shoe in sixteen years and didn't have my distance. And besides, the plating had wore off the shoes so that they was points right where they stuck into my thumb and I hadn't throwed more than two or three times when my thumb was raw and it pretty near killed me to hang on to the shoe, let alone pitch it.

Well, Hartsell throws the awkwardest shoe I ever seen pitched and to see him pitch you wouldn't think he would ever come no-wheres near, but he is also the luckiest pitcher I ever seen and he made some pitches where the shoe lit five and six feet short and then schoonered up and was a ringer. They's no use trying to beat that kind of luck.

They was a pretty fair size crowd watching us and four or five other ladies besides Mother, and it seems like, when Hartsell pitches, he has got to chew and it kept the ladies on the anxious seat as he don't seem to care which way he is facing when he leaves go.

You would think a man as old as him would of learnt more manners.

Well, to make a long story short, I was just beginning to get my distance when I had to give up on account of my thumb, which I showed it to Hartsell and he seen I couldn't go on, as it was raw and bleeding. Even if I could of stood it to go on myself, Mother wouldn't of allowed it after she seen my thumb. So anyway I quit and Hartsell said the score was nineteen to six, but I don't know what it was. Or don't care, neither.

Well, Mother and I went home and I said I hoped we was through with the Hartsells as I was sick and tired of them, but it seemed like she had promised we would go over to their house that evening for another game of their everlasting cards.

Well, my thumb was giving me considerable pain and I felt kind of out of sorts and I guess maybe I forgot myself, but anyway, when we was about through playing Hartsell made the remark that he wouldn't never lose a game of cards if he could always have Mother for a partner:

So I said:

"Well, you had a chance fifty years ago to always have her for a partner, but you wasn't man enough to keep her."

I was sorry the minute I had said it and Hartsell didn't know what to say and for once his wife couldn't say nothing. Mother tried to smooth things over by making the remark that I must of had something stronger than tea or I wouldn't talk so silly. But Mrs. Hartsell had froze up like an iceberg and hardly said good night to us and I bet her and Frank put in a pleasant hour after we was gone.

As we was leaving, Mother said to him: "Never mind Charley's nonsense, Frank. He is just mad because you beat him all hollow pitching horseshoes and playing cards."

She said that to make up for my slip, but at the same time she certainly riled me. I tried to keep ahold of myself, but as soon as we was out of the house she had to open up the subject and begun to scold me for the break I had made.

Well, I wasn't in no mood to be scolded. So I said:

"I guess he is such a wonderful pitcher and card player that you wished you had married him."

"Well," she said, "at least he ain't a baby to give up pitching because his thumb has got a few scratches."

"And how about you," I said, "making a fool of yourself on the roque court and then pretending your back is lame and you can't play no more!"

"Yes," she said, "but when you hurt your thumb I didn't laugh at you, and why did you laugh at me when I sprained my back?"

"Who could help from laughing!" I said.

"Well," she said, "Frank Hartsell didn't laugh."

"Well," I said, "why didn't you marry him?"

"Well," said Mother, "I almost wished I had!"

"And I wished so, too!" I said.

"I'll remember that!" said Mother, and that's the last word she said to me for two days.

We seen the Hartsells the next day in the Park and I was willing to apologize, but they just nodded to us. And a couple days later we heard they had left for Orlando, where they have got relatives.

I wished they had went there in the first place.

Mother and I made it up setting on a bench.

"Listen, Charley," she said. "This is our Golden Honeymoon and we don't want the whole thing spoilt with a silly old quarrel."

"Well," I said, "did you mean that about wishing you had married Hartsell?"

"Of course not," she said, "that is, if you didn't mean that you wished I had, too."

So I said:

"I was just tired and all wrought up. I thank God you chose me instead of him as they's no other woman in the world who I could of lived with all these years."

"How about Mrs. Hartsell?" says Mother.

"Good gracious!" I said. "Imagine being married to a woman that plays five hundred like she does and drops her teeth on the roque court!"

"Well," said Mother, "it wouldn't be no worse than being married to a man that expectorates towards ladies and is such a fool in a checker game."

So I put my arm around her shoulder and she stroked my hand and I guess we got kind of spoony.

They was two days left of our stay in St. Petersburg and the next to the last day Mother introduced me to a Mrs. Kendall from Kingston, Rhode Island, who she had met at the chiropodist's.

Mrs. Kendall made us acquainted with her husband, who is in the grocery business. They have got two sons and five grandchildren and one great-grandchild. One of their sons lives in Providence and is way up in the Elks as well as a Rotarian.

We found them very congenial people and we played cards with them the last two nights we was there. They was both experts and I only wished we had met them sooner instead of running into the Hartsells. But the Kendalls will be there again next winter and we will see more of them, that is, if we decide to make the trip again.

We left the Sunshine City on the eleventh day of February, at 11 A.M. This give us a day trip through Florida and we seen all the country we had passed through at night on the way down.

We reached Jacksonville at 7 P.M. and pulled out of there at 8.10 P.M. We reached Fayetteville, North Carolina, at nine o'clock the following morning, and reached Washington, D. C., at 6.30 P.M., laying over there half an hour.

We reached Trenton at 11.01 P.M. and had wired ahead to my daughter and son-in-law and they met us at the train and we went to their house and they put us up for the night. John would of made us stay up all night, telling about our trip, but Edie said we must be tired and made us go to bed. That's my daughter.

The next day we took our train for home and arrived safe and sound, having been gone just one month and a day.

Here comes Mother, so I guess I better shut up.

SHERWOOD ANDERSON

The Return

EIGHTEEN years. Well, he was driving a good car, an expensive roadster, he was well clad, a rather solid fine-looking man, not too heavy. When he had left the Middle-Western town to go live in New York City he was twenty-two, and now, on his way back there, he was forty. He drove toward the town from the east, stopping for lunch at another town ten miles away.

When he went away from Caxton, after his mother died, he used to write letters to friends at home, but after several months the replies began to come with less and less frequency. On the day when he sat eating his lunch at a small hotel in the town ten miles east of Caxton he suddenly thought of the reason, and was ashamed. "Am I going back there on this visit for the same reason I wrote the letters?" he asked himself. For a moment he thought he might not go on. There was still time to turn back.

Outside, in the principal business street of the town, people were walking about. The sun shone warmly. Although he had lived for so many years in New York, he had always kept, buried away in him somewhere, a hankering for his own country. All the day before he had been driving through the eastern Ohio country, crossing many small streams, running down through small valleys, seeing the white farm-houses set back from the road, and the big red barns.

The elders were still in bloom along the fences, boys were swimming in a creek, the wheat had been cut, and now the corn was shoulder-high. Everywhere the drone of bees; in patches of woodland along the road a heavy, mysterious silence.

Now, however, he began thinking of something else. Shame crept over him. "When I first left Caxton, I wrote letters back to my boyhood friends there, but I wrote always of myself. When I had written a letter telling what I was doing in the city, what friends I was making, what my prospects were, I put, at the very end of the letter perhaps, a little inquiry. 'I hope you are well. How are things going with you?' Something of that sort."

The returning native—his name was John Holden—had grown very uneasy. After eighteen years it seemed to him he could see, lying before him, one of the letters written eighteen years before when he had first come into the strange Eastern city. His mother's brother, a successful architect in the city, had given him such and such an opportunity: he had been at the theater to see Mansfield as *Brutus,* he had taken the night boat up-river to Albany with his aunt; there were two very handsome girls on the boat.

Everything then must have been in the same tone. His uncle had given him a rare opportunity, and he had taken advantage of it. In time he had also become a successful architect. In New York City there were certain great buildings, two or three skyscrapers, several huge industrial plants, any number of handsome and expensive residences, that were the products of his brain.

When it came down to the scratch, John Holden had to admit that his uncle had not been excessively fond of him. It had just happened that his aunt and uncle had no children of their own. He did his work in the office well and carefully, had developed a certain rather striking knack for design. The aunt had liked him better. She had always tried to think of him as her own son, had treated him as a son. Sometimes she called him son. Once or twice, after his uncle died, he had a notion. His aunt was a good woman, but sometimes he thought she would rather have enjoyed having him,

John Holden, go in a bit more for wickedness, go a little on the loose, now and then. He never did anything she had to forgive him for. Perhaps she hungered for the opportunity to forgive.

Odd thoughts, eh? Well, what was a fellow to do? One had but the one life to live. One had to think of oneself.

Botheration! John Holden had rather counted on the trip back to Caxton, had really counted on it more than he realized. It was a bright summer day. He had been driving for days over the mountains of Pennsylvania, through New York State, through eastern Ohio. Gertrude, his wife, had died during the summer before, and his one son, a lad of twelve, had gone away for the summer to a boys' camp in Vermont.

The idea had just come to him. "I'll drive the car along slowly through the country, drinking it in. I need a rest, time to think. What I really need is to renew old acquaintances. I'll go back to Caxton and stay several days. I'll see Herman and Frank and Joe. Then I'll go call on Lillian and Kate. What a lot of fun, really!" It might just be that when he got to Caxton, the Caxton ball team would be playing a game, say with a team from Yerington. Lillian might go to the game with him. It was in his mind faintly that Lillian had never married. How did he know that? He had heard nothing from Caxton for many years. The ball game would be in Heffler's field, and he and Lillian would go out there, walking under the maple-trees along Turner Street, past the old stave factory, then in the dust of the road, past where the sawmill used to stand, and on into the field itself. He would be carrying a sunshade over Lillian's head, and Bob French would be standing at the gate where you went into the field and charging the people twenty-five cents to see the game.

Well, it would not be Bob; his son perhaps. There would be something very nice in the notion of Lillian's going off to a ball game that way with an old sweetheart. A crowd of boys, women and men, going through a cattle-gate into Heffler's field, tramping through the dust, young men with their sweethearts, a few gray-haired women, mothers of boys who belonged to the team, Lillian and he sitting in the rickety grand-stand in the hot sun.

Once it had been—how they had felt, he and Lillian, sitting there together! It had been rather hard to keep the attention centered on the players in the field. One couldn't ask a neighbor, "Who's ahead now, Caxton or Yerington?" Lillian's hands lay in her lap. What white, delicate, expressive hands they were! Once—that was just before he went away to live in the city with his uncle and but a month after his mother died—he and Lillian went to the ball-field together at night. His father had died when he was a young lad, and he had no relatives left in the town. Going off to the ball-field at night was maybe a risky thing for Lillian to do,—risky for her reputation if any one found it out,—but she had seemed willing enough. You know how small-town girls of that age are?

Her father owned a retail shoestore in Caxton and was a good, respectable man; but the Holdens—John's father had been a lawyer.

After they got back from the ball-field that night—it must have been after midnight—they went to sit on the front porch before her father's house. He must have known. A daughter cavorting about half the night with a young man that way! They had clung to each other with a sort of queer, desperate feeling neither understood. She did not go into the house until after three o'clock, and went then only because he insisted. He hadn't wanted to ruin her reputation. Why, he might have— She was like a little frightened child at the thought of his going away. He was twenty-two then, and she must have been about eighteen.

Eighteen and twenty-two are forty. John Holden was forty on the day when he sat at lunch at the hotel in the town ten miles from Caxton.

Now, he thought, he might be able to walk through the streets of Caxton to the ball-park with Lillian with a certain effect. You know how it is. One has to accept the fact that youth is gone. If there should turn out to be such a ball game and Lillian would go with him, he would leave the car in the garage and ask her to walk. One saw pictures of that sort of thing in the movies—a man coming back to his native village after twenty years; a new beauty taking the place of the beauty of youth—something like that. In the spring the leaves on maple-trees are lovely, but they are even more lovely in the fall—a flame of color; manhood and womanhood.

After he had finished his lunch John did not feel very comfortable. The road to Caxton—it used to take nearly three hours to travel the distance with a horse and buggy, but now, and without any effort, the distance could be made in twenty minutes.

He lit a cigar and went for a walk not in the streets of Caxton, but in the streets of the town ten miles away. If he got to Caxton in the evening, just at dusk, say, now—

With an inward pang John realized that he wanted darkness, the kindliness of soft evening lights. Lillian, Joe, Herman, and the rest. It had been eighteen years for the others as well as for himself. Now he had succeeded, a little, in twisting his fear of Caxton into fear for the others, and it made him feel somewhat better; but at once he realized what he was doing and again felt uncomfortable. One had to look out for changes, new people, new buildings, middle-aged people grown old, youth grown middle-aged. At any rate, he was thinking of the other now; he wasn't, as when he wrote letters home eighteen years before, thinking only of himself. "Am I?" It was a question.

An absurd situation, really. He had sailed along so gaily through upper New York State, through western Pennsylvania, through eastern Ohio. Men were at work in the fields and in the towns, farmers drove into towns in their cars, clouds of dust arose on some distant road, seen across a valley. Once he had stopped his car near a bridge and had gone for a walk along the banks of a creek where it wound through a wood.

He was liking people. Well, he had never before given much time to people, to thinking of them and their affairs. "I hadn't time," he told himself. He had always realized that, while he was a good enough architect, things move fast in America. New men were coming on. He couldn't take chances of going on forever on his uncle's reputation. A man had to be always on the alert. Fortunately, his marriage had been a help. It had made valuable connections for him.

Twice he had picked up people on the road. There was a lad of sixteen from some town of eastern Pennsylvania, working his way westward toward the Pacific coast by picking up rides in cars—a summer's adventure. John had carried him all of one day and had listened to his talk with keen pleasure. And so this was the younger generation. The boy had nice eyes and an eager, friendly manner. He smoked cigarettes, and once, when they had a puncture, he was very quick and eager about changing the tire. "Now, don't you soil your hands, Mister; I can do it like a flash," he said, and he did. The boy said he intended working his way overland to the Pacific coast, where he would try to get a job of some kind on an ocean freighter, and that, if he did, he would go on around the world. "But do you speak any foreign languages?" The boy did not. Across John Holden's mind flashed pictures of hot Eastern deserts, crowded Asiatic towns, wild half-savage mountain countries. As a young architect, and before his uncle died, he had spent two years in foreign travel, studying building in many countries; but he said nothing of this thought to the boy. Vast plans entered into with eager boyish abandon, a world tour undertaken as he, when a young man, might have undertaken to find his way from his uncle's house in East Eighty-first Street downtown to the Battery. "How do I know—perhaps he will do it," John thought. The day in company with the boy had been very pleasant, and he had been on the alert to pick him up again the next morning; but the boy had gone on his way, had caught a ride with some earlier riser. Why hadn't John invited him to his hotel for the night? The notion hadn't come to him until too late.

Youth, rather wild and undisciplined, running wild, eh? I wonder why I never did it, never wanted to do it.

If he had been a bit wilder, more reckless—that night, that time when he and Lillian— "It's all right being reckless with yourself, but when some one else is involved, a young girl in a small town, you yourself lighting out"— He remembered sharply that on the night, long before, as he sat with Lillian on the porch before her father's house his hand— It had seemed as though Lillian, on that evening, might not have objected to anything he wanted to do. He had thought—well, he had thought of the consequences. Women must be protected by men, all that sort of thing. Lillian had seemed rather stunned when he walked away, even though it was three o'clock in the morning. She had been rather like a person waiting at a railroad station for the coming of a train. There is a blackboard, and a strange man comes out and writes on it, "Train Number 287 has been discontinued"—something like that.

Well, it had been all right, everything had been all right.

Later, four years later, he had married a New York woman of good family. Even in a city like New York, where there are so many people, her family had been well known. They had connections.

After marriage, sometimes, it is true, he had wondered. Gertrude used to look at him sometimes with an odd light in her eyes. That boy he picked up in the road—once during the day when he said something to the boy, the same queer look came into his eyes. It would be rather upsetting if one knew that the boy had purposely avoided him next morning. There had been Gertrude's cousin. Once, after his marriage, John heard a rumor that Gertrude had wanted to marry that cousin, but of course he had said nothing to her. Why should he have? She was his wife. There had been, he had heard, a good deal of family objection to the cousin. He was reputed to be wild, a gambler and drinker.

Once the cousin came to the Holden apartment at two in the morning, drunk and demanding that he be allowed to see Gertrude, and she slipped on a dressing-gown and went down to him. That was in the hallway of the apartment, down-stairs, where almost any one might have come in and seen her. As a matter of fact, the elevator boy and the janitor did see her. She had stood in the hallway below talking for nearly an hour. What about? He had never asked Gertrude directly, and she had never told him anything. When she came up-stairs again and had got into her bed, he lay in his own bed trembling, but remained silent. He had been afraid that if he spoke he might say something rude; better keep still. The cousin had disappeared. John had a suspicion that Gertrude later supplied him with money. He went out West somewhere.

Now Gertrude was dead. She had always seemed very well, but suddenly she was attacked by a baffling kind of slow fever that lasted nearly a year. Sometimes she seemed about to get better, and then suddenly the fever grew worse. It might be that she did not want to live. What a notion! John had been at the bedside with the doctor when she died. It was at night, and as the boy was asleep, he was not called. There was something of the same feeling he had that night of his youth when he went with Lillian to the ball-field, an odd sense of futility, of inadequacy. There was no doubt that in some subtle way both women had accused him.

Of what? There had always been, in some vague, indefinable way, a kind of accusation in the attitude toward him of his uncle, the architect, and of his aunt. They had left him their money, but— It was as though the uncle had said, as though Lillian during that night long ago had said—

Had they all said the same thing, and was Gertrude his wife saying it as she lay dying? A smile, "You have always taken such good care of yourself, haven't you, John dear? You have observed the rules. You have taken no chances for yourself or the others." She had actually said something of that sort to him once in a moment of anger.

2

In the small town ten miles from Caxton there wasn't any park to which a man could go to sit. If one stayed about the hotel, some one from Caxton might come in. "Hello, what are you doing here?" It would be inconvenient to explain: "I didn't want to go to Caxton in the daylight. I want the kindliness of evening light for myself and the people I may see there."

John Holden's boy—he was but twelve—one might say his character had not begun to form yet. One felt in him sometimes a sort of unconscious and casual selfishness, an unawareness of others, a rather unhealthy sharpness about getting the best of others. It was a thing that should be corrected in him and at once. John Holden had got himself into a small panic. "I must write him a letter at once. Such a habit gets fixed in a boy and then in the man, and it cannot later be shaken off. There are such a lot of people living in the world! Every man and woman has his own point of view. To be civilized, really, is to be aware of the others, their hopes, their gladnesses, their disillusionments in life."

John Holden was now walking along a residence street of a small Ohio town composing in fancy a letter to his son in the boys' camp up in Vermont. He was a man who wrote to his son every day. "I think a man should," he told himself. "One should remember that now the boy has no mother."

He had come to an outlying railroad station. It was neat, with grass and flowers growing in a round bed in the very center of a lawn. Some man, the station agent and telegraph operator perhaps, passed him and went inside the station. John followed him in. On the wall of the waiting-room there was a framed copy of the time-table, and he stood studying it. A train went to Caxton at five. Another train came from Caxton and passed through the town he was now in at seven-forty-three, the seven-nineteen out of Caxton. The man in the small business section of the station opened a sliding-panel and looked at him. The two men just stared at each other without speaking, and then the panel was slid shut again.

John looked at his watch. Two-twenty-eight. At about six he could drive over to Caxton and dine at the hotel there. After he had dined, it would be evening, and people would be coming into the main street.

The seven-nineteen would come in. When John was a lad, sometimes, he, Joe, Herman, and often several other lads climbed on the front of the baggage- or mail-car and stole a ride to the very town he was now in. What a thrill, crouched down in the gathering darkness on the platform as the train ran the ten miles, the car rocking from side to side! When it got a little dark, in the fall or spring, the fields beside the track were lighted up when the fireman opened his fire-box to throw in coal. Once John saw a rabbit running along in the glare of light beside the track. He could have reached down and caught it with his hand. In the neighboring town the boys went into saloons and played pool and drank beer. They could depend upon catching a ride back home on the local freight that got to Caxton at about ten-thirty. On one of the adventures John and Herman got drunk, and Joe had to help them into an empty coalcar and later get them out at Caxton. Herman got sick, and when they were getting off the freight at Caxton, he stumbled and came very near falling under the wheels of the moving train. John wasn't as drunk as Herman. When the others weren't looking, he had poured several of the glasses of beer into a spittoon. In Caxton he and Joe had to walk about with Herman for several hours, and when John finally got home, his mother was still awake and was worried. He had to lie to her. "I drove out into the country with Herman, and a wheel broke. We had to walk home." The reason Joe could carry his beer so well was because he was German. His father owned the town meat-market, and the family had beer on the table at home. No wonder it did not knock him out as it did Herman and John.

There was a bench at the side of the railroad station, in the shade, and John sat there for a long time—two hours, three hours. Why hadn't he brought a book? In fancy he composed a letter to his son and in it he spoke of the fields lying beside the road outside the town of Caxton, of his greeting old friends there, of things that had happened when he was a boy. He even spoke of his former sweetheart, of Lillian. If he now thought out just what he was going to say in the letter, he could write it in his room at the hotel over in Caxton in a few minutes without having to stop and think what he was going to say. You can't always be too fussy about what you say to a young boy. Really, sometimes, you should take him into your confidence, into your life, make him a part of your life.

It was six-twenty when John drove into Caxton and went to the hotel, where he registered, and was shown to a room. On the street as he drove into town he saw Billy Baker, who, when he was a young man, had a paralyzed leg that dragged along the sidewalk when he walked. Now he was getting old; his face seemed wrinkled and faded, like a dried lemon, and his clothes had spots down the front. People, even sick people, live a long time in small Ohio towns. It is surprising how they hang on.

John had put his car, of a rather expensive make, into a garage beside the hotel. Formerly, in his day, the building had been used as a livery-barn. There used to be pictures of famous trotting and pacing horses on the walls of the little office at the front. Old Dave

Grey, who owned race-horses of his own, ran the livery-barn then, and John occasionally hired a rig there. He hired a rig and took Lillian for a ride into the country, along moonlit roads. By a lonely farm-house a dog barked. Sometimes they drove along a little dirt road lined with elders and stopped the horse. How still everything was! What a queer feeling they had! They couldn't talk. Sometimes they sat in silence thus, very near each other, for a long, long time. Once they got out of the buggy, having tied the horse to the fence, and walked in a newly cut hayfield. The cut hay lay all about in little cocks. John wanted to lie on one of the hay-cocks with Lillian, but did not dare suggest it.

At the hotel John ate his dinner in silence. There wasn't even a traveling-salesman in the dining-room, and presently the proprietor's wife came and stood by his table to talk with him. They had a good many tourists, but this just happened to be a quiet day. Dull days came that way in the hotel business. The woman's husband was a traveling-man and had bought the hotel to give his wife something to keep her interested while he was on the road. He was away from home so much! They had come to Caxton from Pittsburgh.

After he had dined, John went up to his room, and presently the woman followed. The door leading into the hall had been left open, and she came and stood in the doorway. Really, she was rather handsome. She only wanted to be sure that everything was all right, that he had towels and soap and everything he needed.

For a time she lingered by the door talking of the town.

"It's a good little town. General Hurst is buried here. You should drive out to the cemetery and see the statue." He wondered who General Hurst was. In what war had he fought? Odd that he hadn't remembered about him. The town had a piano factory, and there was a watch company from Cincinnati talking of putting up a plant. "They figure there is less chance of labor trouble in a small town like this."

The woman went, going reluctantly. As she was going along the hallway she stopped once and looked back. There was something a little queer. They were both self-conscious. "I hope you'll be comfortable," she said. At forty a man did not come home to his own home town to start— A traveling-man's wife, eh? Well! well!

At seven-forty-five John went out for a walk on Main Street and almost at once he met Tom Ballard, who at once recognized him, a fact that pleased Tom. He bragged about it. "Once I see a face, I never forget. Well! well!" When John was twenty-two, Tom must have been about fifteen. His father was the leading doctor of the town. He took John in tow, walked back with him toward the hotel. He kept exclaiming: "I knew you at once. You haven't changed much, really."

Tom was in his turn a doctor, and there was about him some-thing— Right away John guessed what it was. They went up into John's room, and John, having in his bag a bottle of whisky, poured Tom a drink, which he took somewhat too eagerly, John thought. There was talk. After Tom had taken the drink he sat on the edge of the bed, still holding the bottle John had passed to him. Herman was running a dray now. He had married Kit Small and had five kids. Joe was working for the International Harvester Company. "I don't know whether he's in town or not. He's a trouble-shooter, a swell mechanic, a good fellow," Tom said. They drank again.

As for Lillian, mentioned with an air of being casual by John, he, John, knew of course that she had been married and divorced. There was some sort of trouble about another man. Her husband married again later, and now she lived with her mother, her father, the shoe merchant, having died. Tom spoke somewhat guardedly, as though protecting a friend.

"I guess she's all right now, going straight and all. Good thing she never had any kids. She's a little nervous and queer; has lost her looks a good deal."

The two men went down-stairs and, walking along Main Street, got into a car belonging to the doctor.

"I'll take you for a little ride," Tom said; but as he was about to pull away from the curb where the car had been parked, he turned and smiled at his passenger. "We ought to celebrate a little, account of your coming back here," he said. "What do you say to a quart?"

John handed him a ten-dollar bill, and he disappeared into a near-by drug-store. When he came back he laughed.

"I used your name all right. They didn't recognize it. In the prescription I wrote out I said you had a general breakdown, that you needed to be built up. I recommended that you take a teaspoonful three times a day. Lord! my prescription-book is getting almost empty." The drug-store belonged to a man named Will Bennett. "You remember him, maybe. He's Ed Bennett's son; married Carrie Wyatt." The names were but dim things in John's mind. "This man is going to get drunk. He is going to try to get me drunk, too," he thought.

When they had turned out of Main Street and into Walnut Street they stopped midway between two street lights and had another drink, John holding the bottle to his lips, but putting his tongue over the opening. He remembered the evenings with Joe and Herman when he had secretly poured his beer into a spittoon. He felt cold and lonely. Walnut Street was one along which he used to walk, coming home late at night from Lillian's house. He remembered people who then lived along the street, and a list of names began running through his head. Often the names remained, but did not call up images of people. They were just names. He hoped the doctor would not turn the car into the street in which the Holdens had lived. Lillian had lived over in another part of town, in what was called "the Red House District." Just why it had been called that John did not know.

3

They drove silently along, up a small hill, and came to the edge of town, going south. Stopping before a house that had evidently been built since John's time, Tom sounded his horn.

"Didn't the fair-ground used to stand about here?" John asked. The doctor turned and nodded his head.

"Yes, just here," he said. He kept on sounding his horn, and a man and woman came out of the house and stood in the road beside the car.

"Let's get Maud and Alf and all go over to Lylse's Point," Tom said. He had indeed taken John into tow. For a time John wondered if he was to be introduced. "We got some hooch. Meet John Holden; used to live here years ago." At the fair-ground, when John was a lad, Dave Grey, the livery man, used to work out his race-horses in the early morning. Herman, who was a horse enthusiast, who then dreamed of some day becoming a horseman, came often to John's house in the early morning, and the two boys went off to the fair-ground without breakfast. Herman had got some sandwiches made of slices of bread and cold meat out of his mother's pantry. They went 'cross-lots, climbing fences and eating the sandwiches. In a meadow they had to cross there was heavy dew on the grass, and meadow larks flew up before them. Herman had at least come somewhere near expressing in his life his youthful passion: he still lived about horses; he owned a dray. With a little inward qualm John wondered. Perhaps Herman ran a motor-truck.

The man and woman got into the car, the woman on the back seat with John, the husband in front with Tom, and they drove away to another house. John could not keep track of the streets they passed through. Occasionally he asked the woman, "What street are we in now?" They were joined by Maud and Alf, who also crowded into the back seat. Maud was a slender woman of twenty-eight or thirty, with yellow hair and blue eyes, and at once she seemed determined to make up to John. "I don't take more than an inch of room," she said, laughing and squeezing herself in between John and the first woman, whose name he could not later remember.

He rather liked Maud. When the car had been driven some eighteen miles along a gravel road, they came to Lylse's farm-house, which had been converted into a road-house, and got out. Maud had been silent most of the way, but she sat very close to John, and as he felt cold and lonely, he was grateful for the warmth of her slender body. Occasionally she spoke to him in a half-whisper. "Ain't the night swell! Gee! I like it out in the dark this way."

Lylse's Point was at a bend of the Samson River, a small stream to which John as a lad had occasionally gone on fishing excursions with his father. Later he went out there several times with crowds of young fellows and their girls. They drove out then in Grey's old bus, and the trip out and back took several hours. On the way home at night they had great fun singing at the top of their voices and waking the sleeping farmers along the road. Occasionally some of the party got out and walked for a ways. It was a chance for a fellow to kiss his girl when the others could not see. By hurrying a little, they could later easily enough catch up with the bus.

A rather heavy-faced Italian named Francisco owned Lylse's, and it had a dance-hall and dining-room. Drinks could be had if you knew the ropes, and it was evident the doctor and his friends were old acquaintances. At once they declared John should not buy anything, the declaration, in fact, being made before he had offered. "You're our guest now; don't you forget that. When we come sometime to your town, then it will be all right," Tom said. He laughed. "And that makes me think. I forgot your change," he said, handing John a five-dollar bill. The whisky got at the drug-store had been consumed on the way out, all except John and Maud drinking heartily. "I don't like the stuff. Do you, Mr. Holden?" Maud said and giggled. Twice during the trip out her fingers had crept over and touched lightly his fingers, and each time she had apologized. "Oh, do excuse me!" she said. John felt a little as he had felt earlier in the evening when the woman of the hotel had come to stand at the door of his room and had seemed reluctant about going away.

After they got out of the car at Lylse's, he felt uncomfortably old and queer. "What am I doing here with these people?" he kept asking himself. When they had got into the light, he stole a look at his watch. It was not yet nine o'clock. Several other cars, most of them, the doctor explained, from Yerington, stood before the door, and when they had taken several drinks of rather mild Italian red wine, all of the party except Maud and John went into the dance-hall to dance. The doctor took John aside and whispered to him. "Lay off Maud," he said. He explained hurriedly that Alf and Maud had been having a row and that for several days they had not spoken to each other, although they lived in the same house, ate at the same table, and slept in the same bed. "He thinks she gets too gay with the men," Tom explained. "You better look out a little."

The woman and man sat on a bench under a tree on the lawn

before the house, and when the others had danced, they came out, bringing more drinks. Tom had got some more whisky. "It's moon, but pretty good stuff," he declared. In the clear sky overhead stars were shining, and when the others were dancing, John turned his head and saw across the road and between the trees that lined its banks the stars reflected in the water of the Samson. A light from the house fell on Maud's face, a rather strikingly lovely face in that light, but when looked at closely, rather petulant. "A good deal of the spoiled child in her," John thought.

She began asking him about life in the city of New York.

"I was there once, but for only three days. It was when I went to school in the East. A girl I knew lived there. She married a lawyer named Trigan, or something like that. You didn't know him, I guess."

And now there was a hungry, dissatisfied look on her face.

"God! I'd like to live in a place like that, not in this hole! There hadn't no man better tempt me." When she said that she giggled again. Once during the evening they walked across the dusty road and stood for a time by the river's-edge, but got back to the bench before the others had finished their dance. Maud persistently refused to dance.

At ten-thirty, all of the others having got a little drunk, they drove back to town, Maud again sitting beside John. On the drive Alf went to sleep, Maud pressed her slender body against John's, and after two or three futile moves to which he made no special response, she boldly put her hand into his. The second woman and her husband talked with Tom of people they had seen at Lylse's. "Do you think there's anything up between Fanny and Joe? No; I think she's on the square."

They got to John's hotel at eleven-thirty, and bidding them all good night, he went up-stairs. Alf had awakened. When they were parting, he leaned out of the car and looked closely at John. "What did you say your name was?" he asked.

John went up a dark stairway and sat on the bed in his room. Lillian had lost her looks. She had married, and her husband had divorced her. Joe was a trouble-shooter. He worked for the International Harvester Company, a swell mechanic. Herman was a dray-man. He had five kids.

Three men in a room next to John's were playing poker. They laughed and talked, and their voices came clearly to John. "You think so, do you? Well, I'll prove you're wrong." A mild quarrel began. As it was summer, the windows of John's room were open, and he went to one to stand, looking out. A moon had come up, and he could see down into an alleyway. Two men came out of a street and stood in the alleyway, whispering. After they left, two cats crept along a roof and began a love-making scene. The game in the next room broke up. John could hear voices in the hallway.

"Now, forget it. I tell you, you're both wrong." John thought of his son at the camp up in Vermont. "I haven't written him a letter to-day." He felt guilty.

Opening his bag, he took out paper and sat down to write; but after two or three attempts gave it up and put the paper away again. How fine the night had been as he sat on the bench beside the woman at Lylse's! Now the woman was in bed with her husband. They were not speaking to each other.

"Could I do it?" John asked himself, and then, for the first time that evening, a smile came to his lips.

"Why not?" he asked himself.

With his bag in his hand he went down the dark hallway and into the hotel office and began pounding on a desk. A fat old man with thin red hair and sleep-heavy eyes appeared from somewhere. John explained.

"I can't sleep. I think I'll drive on. I want to get to Pittsburgh and as I can't sleep, I might as well be driving." He paid his bill.

Then he asked the clerk to go and arouse the man in the garage, and gave him an extra dollar. "If I need gas, is there any place open?" he asked, but evidently the man did not hear. Perhaps he thought the question absurd.

He stood in the moonlight on the sidewalk before the door of the hotel and heard the clerk pounding on a door. Presently voices were heard, and the head-lights of his car shone. The car appeared, driven by a boy. He seemed very alive and alert.

"I saw you out to Lylse's," he said, and, without being asked, went to look at the tank. "You're all right; you got 'most eight gallons," he assured John as he climbed into the driver's seat.

How friendly the car, how friendly the night! John was not one who enjoyed fast driving, but he went out of the town at very high speed. "You go down two blocks, turn to your right, and go three. There you hit the cement. Go right straight to the east. You can't miss it."

John was taking the turns at racing speed. At the edge of town some one shouted to him from the darkness, but he did not stop. He hungered to get into the road going east.

"I'll let her out," he thought. "Lord! it will be fun! I'll let her out."

ERNEST HEMINGWAY

The Undefeated

MANUEL GARCIA climbed the stairs to Don Miguel Retana's office. He set down his suitcase and knocked on the door. There was no answer. Manuel, standing in the hallway, felt there was some one in the room. He felt it through the door.

"Retana," he said, listening.

There was no answer.

He's there, all right, Manuel thought.

"Retana," he said and banged the door.

"Who's there?" said some one in the office.

"Me, Manolo," Manuel said.

"What do you want?" asked the voice.

"I want to work," Manuel said.

Something in the door clicked several times and it swung open. Manuel went in, carrying his suitcase.

A little man sat behind a desk at the far side of the room. Over his head was a bull's head, stuffed by a Madrid taxidermist; on the walls were framed photographs and bull-fight posters.

The little man sat looking at Manuel.

"I thought they'd killed you," he said.

Manuel knocked with his knuckles on the desk. The little man sat looking at him across the desk.

"How many corridas you had this year?" Retana asked.

"One," he answered.

"Just that one?" the little man asked.

"That's all."

"I read about it in the papers," Retana said. He leaned back in the chair and looked at Manuel.

Manuel looked up at the stuffed bull. He had seen it often before. He felt a certain family interest in it. It had killed his brother, the promising one, about nine years ago. Manuel remembered the day. There was a brass plate on the oak shield the bull's head was mounted on. Manuel could not read it, but he imagined it was in memory of his brother. Well, he had been a good kid.

The plate said: "The Bull 'Mariposa' of the Duke of Veragua, which accepted 9 varas for 7 caballos, and caused the death of Antonio Garcia, Novillero, April 27, 1909."

Retana saw him looking at the stuffed bull's head.

"The lot the Duke sent me for Sunday will make a scandal," he said. "They're all bad in the legs. What do they say about them at the Café?"

"I don't know," Manuel said. "I just got in."

"Yes," Retana said. "You still have your bag."

He looked at Manuel, leaning back behind the big desk.

"Sit down," he said. "Take off your cap."

Manuel sat down; his cap off, his face was changed. He looked pale, and his coleta pinned forward on his head, so that it would not show under the cap, gave him a strange look.

"You don't look well," Retana said.

"I just got out of the hospital," Manuel said.

"I heard they'd cut your leg off," Retana said.

"No," said Manuel. "It got all right."

Retana leaned forward across the desk and pushed a wooden box of cigarettes toward Manuel.

"Have a cigarette," he said.

"Thanks."

Manuel lit it.

"Smoke?" he said, offering the match to Retana.

"No," Retana waved his hand, "I never smoke."

Retana watched him smoking.

"Why don't you get a job and go to work?" he said.

"I don't want to work," Manuel said. "I am a bull-fighter."

"There aren't any bull-fighters any more," Retana said.

"I'm a bull-fighter," Manuel said.

"Yes, while you're in there," Retana said.

Manuel laughed.

Retana sat, saying nothing and looking at Manuel.

"I'll put you in a nocturnal if you want," Retana offered.

"When?" Manuel asked.

"To-morrow night."

"I don't like to substitute for anybody," Manuel said. "That was the way they all got killed. That was the way Salvador got killed." He tapped with his knuckles on the table.

"It's all I've got," Retana said.

"Why don't you put me on next week?" Manuel suggested.

"You wouldn't draw," Retana said. "All they want is Litri and Rubito and La Torre. Those kids are good."

"They'd come to see me get it," Manuel said, hopefully.

"No, they wouldn't. They don't know who you are any more."

"I've got a lot of stuff," Manuel said.

"I'm offering to put you on to-morrow night," Retana said. "You can work with young Hernandez and kill two novillos after the Charlots."

"Whose novillos?" Manuel asked.

"I don't know. Whatever stuff they've got in the corrals. What the veterinaries won't pass in the daytime."

"I don't like to substitute," Manuel said.

"You can take it or leave it," Retana said. He leaned forward over the papers. He was no longer interested. The appeal that Manuel had made to him for a moment when he thought of the old days was gone. He would like to get him to substitute for Larita because he could get him cheaply. He could get others cheaply too.

He would like to help him though. Still he had given him the chance. It was up to him.

"How much do I get?" Manuel asked. He was still playing with the idea of refusing. But he knew he could not refuse.

"Two hundred and fifty pesetas," Retana said. He had thought of five hundred, but when he opened his mouth it said two hundred and fifty.

"You pay Villalta seven thousand," Manuel said.

"You're not Villalta," Retana said.

"I know it," Manuel said.

"He draws it, Manolo," Retana said in explanation.

"Sure," said Manuel. He stood up. "Give me three hundred, Retana."

"All right," Retana agreed. He reached in the drawer for a paper.

"Can I have fifty now?" Manuel asked.

"Sure," said Retana. He took a fifty peseta note out of his pocketbook and laid it, spread out flat, on the table.

Manuel picked it up and put it in his pocket.

"What about a cuadrilla?" he asked.

"There's the boys that always work for me nights," Retana said. "They're all right."

"How about picadors?" Manuel asked.

"They're not much," Retana admitted.

"I've got to have one good pic," Manuel said.

"Get him then," Retana said. "Go and get him."

"Not out of this," Manuel said. "I'm not paying for any cuadrilla out of sixty duros."

Retana said nothing but looked at Manuel across the big desk.

"You know I've got to have one good pic," Manuel said.

Retana said nothing but looked at Manuel from a long way off.

"It isn't right," said Manuel.

Retana was still considering him, leaning back in his chair, considering him from a long way away.

"There're the regular pics," he offered.

"I know," Manuel said. "I know your regular pics."

Retana did not smile. Manuel knew it was over.

"All I want is an even break," Manuel said reasoningly. "When I go out there I want to be able to call my shots on the bull. It only takes one good picador."

He was talking to a man who was no longer listening.

"If you want something extra," Retana said, "go and get it. There will be a regular cuadrilla out there. Bring as many of your own pics as you want. The charlotada is over by 10.30."

"All right," Manuel said. "If that's the way you feel about it."

"That's the way," Retana said.

"I'll see you to-morrow night," Manuel said.

"I'll be out there," Retana said.

Manuel picked up his suitcase and went out.

"Shut the door," Retana called.

Manuel looked back. Retana was sitting forward looking at some papers. Manuel pulled the door tight until it clicked.

He went down the stairs and out of the door into the hot brightness of the street. It was very hot in the street and the light on the white buildings was sudden and hard on his eyes. He walked down the shady side of the steep street toward the Puerto del Sol. The shade felt solid and cool as running water. The heat came suddenly as he crossed the intersecting streets. Manuel saw no one he knew in all the people he passed.

Just before the Puerto del Sol he turned into a café.

It was quiet in the café. There were a few men sitting at tables against the wall. At one table four men played cards. Most of the men sat against the wall smoking, empty coffee-cups and liqueur-glasses before them on the tables. Manuel went through the long room to a small room in back. A man sat at a table in the corner asleep. Manuel sat down at one of the tables.

A waiter came in and stood beside Manuel's table.

"Have you seen Zurito?" Manuel asked him.

"He was in before lunch," the waiter answered. "He won't be back before five o'clock."

"Bring me some coffee and milk and a shot of the ordinary," Manuel said.

The waiter came back into the room carrying a tray with a big coffee-glass and a liqueur-glass on it. In his left hand he held a bottle of brandy. He swung these down to the table and a boy who had followed him poured coffee and milk into the glass from two shiny, spouted pots with long handles.

Manuel took off his cap and the waiter noticed his pigtail pinned forward on his head. He winked at the coffee-boy as he poured out the brandy into the little glass beside Manuel's coffee. The coffee-boy looked at Manuel's pale face curiously.

"You fighting here?" asked the waiter, corking up the bottle.

"Yes," Manuel said. "To-morrow."

The waiter stood there, holding the bottle on one hip.

"You in the Charlie Chaplins?" he asked.

The coffee-boy looked away, embarrassed.

"No. In the ordinary."

"I thought they were going to have Chaves and Hernandez," the waiter said.

"No. Me and another."

"Who? Chaves or Hernandez?"

"Hernandez, I think."

"What's the matter with Chaves?"

"He got hurt."

"Where did you hear that?"

"Retana."

"Hey, Looie," the waiter called to the next room, "Chaves got cogida."

Manuel had taken the wrapper off the lumps of sugar and dropped them into his coffee. He stirred it and drank it down, sweet, hot, and warming in his empty stomach. He drank off the brandy.

"Give me another shot of that," he said to the waiter.

The waiter uncorked the bottle and poured the glass full, slopping another drink into the saucer. Another waiter had come up in front of the table. The coffee-boy had gone.

"Is Chaves hurt bad?" the second waiter asked Manuel.

"I don't know," Manuel said, "Retana didn't say."

"A hell of a lot he cares," the tall waiter said. Manuel had not seen him before. He must have just come up.

"If you stand in with Retana in this town, you're a made man," the tall waiter said. "If you aren't in with him, you might just as well go out and shoot yourself."

"You said it," the other waiter who had come in said. "You said it then."

"You're right I said it," said the tall waiter. "I know what I'm talking about when I talk about that bird."

"Look what he's done for Villalta," the first waiter said.

"And that ain't all," the tall waiter said. "Look what he's done for Marcial Lalanda. Look what he's done for Nacional."

"You said it, kid," agreed the short waiter.

Manuel looked at them, standing talking in front of his table. He had drunk his second brandy. They had forgotten about him. They were not interested in him.

"Look at that bunch of camels," the tall waiter went on. "Did you ever see this Nacional II?"

"I seen him last Sunday didn't I?" the original waiter said.

"He's a giraffe," the short waiter said.

"What did I tell you?" the tall waiter said. "Those are Retana's boys."

"Say, give me another shot of that," Manuel said. He had poured the brandy the waiter had slopped over in the saucer into his glass and drank it while they were talking.

The original waiter poured his glass full mechanically, and the three of them went out of the room talking.

In the far corner the man was still asleep, snoring slightly on the intaking breath, his head back against the wall.

Manuel drank his brandy. He felt sleepy himself. It was too hot to go out into the town. Besides there was nothing to do. He wanted to see Zurito. He would go to sleep while he waited. He kicked his suitcase under the table to be sure it was there. Perhaps it would be better to put it back under the seat, against the wall. He leaned down and shoved it under. Then he leaned forward on the table and went to sleep.

When he woke there was some one sitting across the table from him. It was a big man with a heavy brown face like an Indian. He had been sitting there some time. He had waved the waiter away and sat reading the paper and occasionally looking down at Manuel, asleep, his head on the table. He read the paper laboriously, forming the words with his lips as he read. When it tired him he looked at Manuel. He sat heavily in the chair, his black Cordoba hat tipped forward.

Manuel sat up and looked at him.

"Hello, kid," the big man said.

"I've been asleep." Manuel rubbed his forehead with the back of his fist.

"I thought maybe you were."

"How's everything?"

"Good. How is everything with you?"

"Not so good."

They were both silent. Zurito, the picador, looked at Manuel's white face. Manuel looked down at the picador's enormous hands folding the paper to put away in his pocket.

"I got a favor to ask you, Manos," Manuel said.

Manosduros was Zurito's nickname. He never heard it without thinking of his huge hands. He put them forward on the table self-consciously.

"Let's have a drink," he said.

"Sure," said Manuel.

The waiter came and went and came again. He went out of the room looking back at the two men at the table.

"What's the matter, Manolo?" Zurito set down his glass.

"Would you pic two bulls for me to-morrow night?" Manuel asked, looking up at Zurito across the table.

"No," said Zurito. "I'm not pic-ing."

Manuel looked down at his glass. He had expected that answer; now he had it. Well, he had it.

"I'm sorry, Manolo, but I'm not pic-ing." Zurito looked at his hands.

"That's all right," Manuel said.

"I'm too old," Zurito said.

"I just asked you," Manuel said.

"Is it the nocturnal to-morrow?"

"That's it. I figured if I had just one good pic, I could get away with it."

"How much are you getting?"

"Three hundred pesetas."

"I get more than that for pic-ing."

"I know," said Manuel. "I didn't have any right to ask you."

"What do you keep on doing it for?" Zurito asked. "Why don't you cut off your coleta, Manolo?"

"I don't know," Manuel said.

"You're pretty near as old as I am," Zurito said.

"I don't know," Manuel said. "I got to do it. If I can fix it so that I get an even break, that's all I want. I got to stick with it, Manos."

"No, you don't."

"Yes, I do. I've tried keeping away from it."

"I know how you feel. But it isn't right. You ought to get out and stay out."

"I can't do it. Besides, I've been going good lately."

Zurito looked at his face.

"You've been in the hospital."

"But I was going great when I got hurt."

Zurito said nothing. He tipped the cognac out of his saucer into his glass.

"The papers said they never saw a better faena," Manuel said.

Zurito looked at him.

"You know when I get going I'm good," Manuel said.

"You're too old," the picador said.

"No," said Manuel. "You're ten years older than I am."

"With me it's different."

"I'm not too old," Manuel said.

They sat silent, Manuel watching the picador's face.

"I was going great till I got hurt," Manuel offered.

"You ought to have seen me, Manos," Manuel said, reproach-fully.

"I don't want to see you," Zurito said. "It makes me nervous."

"You haven't seen me lately."

"I've seen you plenty."

Zurito looked at Manuel, avoiding his eyes.

"You ought to quit it, Manolo."

"I can't," Manuel said. "I'm going good now, I tell you."

Zurito leaned forward, his hands on the table.

"Listen. I'll pic for you and if you don't go big to-morrow night, you'll quit. See? Will you do that?"

"Sure."

Zurito leaned back, relieved.

"You got to quit," he said. "No monkey business. You got to cut the coleta."

"I won't have to quit," Manuel said. "You watch me. I've got the stuff."

Zurito stood up. He felt tired from arguing.

"You got to quit," he said. "I'll cut your coleta myself."

"No, you won't," Manuel said. "You won't have a chance."

Zurito called the waiter.

"Come on," said Zurito. "Come on up to the house."

Manuel reached under the seat for his suitcase. He was happy. He knew Zurito would pic for him. He was the best picador living. It was all simple now.

"Come on up to the house and we'll eat," Zurito said.

Manuel stood in the patio de caballos waiting for the Charlie Chaplins to be over. Zurito stood beside him. Where they stood it was dark. The high door that led into the bull-ring was shut. Above them they heard a shout, then another shout of laughter. Then there was silence. Manuel liked the smell of the stables about the patio de caballos. It smelt good in the dark. There was another roar from the arena and then applause, prolonged applause, going on and on.

"You ever see these fellows?" Zurito asked, big and looming beside Manuel in the dark.

"No," Manuel said.

"They're pretty funny," Zurito said. He smiled to himself in the dark.

The high, double, tight-fitting door into the bull-ring swung open and Manuel saw the ring in the hard light of the arc-lights, the plaza, dark all the way around, rising high; around the edge of the ring were running and bowing two men dressed like tramps, followed by a third in the uniform of a hotel bell-boy who stooped and picked up the hats and canes thrown down onto the sand and tossed them back up into the darkness.

The electric light went on in the patio.

"I'll climb onto one of those ponies while you collect the kids," Zurito said.

Behind them came the jingle of the mules, coming out to go into the arena and be hitched onto the dead bull.

The members of the cuadrilla, who had been watching the burlesque from the runway between the barrera and the seats, came walking back and stood in a group talking, under the electric light in the patio. A good-looking lad in a silver-and-orange suit came up to Manuel and smiled.

"I'm Hernandez," he said and put out his hand.

Manuel shook it.

"They're regular elephants we've got to-night," the boy said cheerfully.

"They're big ones with horns," Manuel agreed.

"You drew the worst lot," the boy said.

"That's all right," Manuel said. "The bigger they are, the more meat for the poor."

"Where did you get that one?" Hernandez grinned.

"That's an old one," Manuel said. "You line up your cuadrilla, so I can see what I've got."

"You've got some good kids," Hernandez said. He was very cheerful. He had been on twice before in nocturnals and was beginning to get a following in Madrid. He was happy the fight would start in a few minutes.

"Where are the pics?" Manuel asked.

"They're back in the corrals fighting about who gets the beautiful horses," Hernandez grinned.

The mules came through the gate in a rush, the whips snapping, bells jangling and the young bull ploughing a furrow of sand.

They formed up for the paseo as soon as the bull had gone through.

Manuel and Hernandez stood in front. The youths of the cuadrillas were behind, their heavy capes furled over their arms. In back, the four picadors, mounted, holding their steel-tipped push-poles erect in the half-dark of the corral.

"It's a wonder Retana wouldn't give us enough light to see the horses by," one picador said.

"He knows we'll be happier if we don't get too good a look at these skins," another pic answered.

"This thing I'm on barely keeps me off the ground," the first picador said.

"Well, they're horses."

"Sure, they're horses."

They talked, sitting their gaunt horses in the dark.

Zurito said nothing. He had the only steady horse of the lot. He had tried him, wheeling him in the corrals and he responded to the bit and the spurs. He had taken the bandage off his right eye and cut the strings where they had tied his ears tight shut at the base. He was a good, solid horse, solid on his legs. That was all he needed. He intended to ride him all through the corrida. He had already, since he had mounted, sitting in the half-dark in the big, quilted saddle, waiting for the paseo, pic-ed through the whole corrida in his mind. The other picadors went on talking on both sides of him. He did not hear them.

The two matadors stood together in front of their three peones, their capes furled over their left arms in the same fashion. Manuel was thinking about the three lads in back of him. They were all three Madrilenos, like Hernandez, boys about nineteen. One of them, a gypsy, serious, aloof, and dark-faced, he liked the look of. He turned.

"What's your name, kid?" he asked the gypsy.

"Fuentes," the gypsy said.

"That's a good name," Manuel said.

The gypsy smiled, showing his teeth.

"You take the bull and give him a little run when he comes out," Manuel said.

"All right," the gypsy said. His face was serious. He began to think about just what he would do.

"Here she goes," Manuel said to Hernandez.

"All right. We'll go."

Heads up, swinging with the music, their right arms swinging free, they stepped out, crossing the sanded arena under the arc-lights, the cuadrillas opening out behind, the picadors riding after, behind came the bull-ring servants and the jingling mules. The crowd applauded Hernandez as they marched across the arena. Arrogant, swinging, they looked straight ahead as they marched.

They bowed before the president, and the procession broke up into its component parts. The bull-fighters went over to the barrera and changed their heavy mantles for the light fighting capes. The mules went out. The picadors galloped jerkily around the ring, and two rode out the gate they had come in by. The servants swept the sand smooth.

Manuel drank a glass of water poured for him by one of Retana's deputies, who was acting as his manager and sword-handler. Hernandez came over from speaking with his own manager.

"You got a good hand, kid," Manuel complimented him.

"They like me," Hernandez said happily.

"How did the paseo go?" Manuel asked Retana's man.

"Like a wedding," said the handler. "Fine. You came out like Joselito and Belmonte."

Zurito rode by, a bulky equestrian statue. He wheeled his horse and faced him toward the toril on the far side of the ring where the bull would come out. It was strange under the arc-light. He pic-ed in the hot afternoon sun for big money. He didn't like this arc-light business. He wished they would get started.

Manuel went up to him.

"Pic him, Manos," he said. "Cut him down to size for me."

"I'll pic him, kid," Zurito spat on the sand. "I'll make him jump out of the ring."

"Lean on him, Manos," Manuel said.

"I'll lean on him," Zurito said. "What's holding it up?"

"He's coming now," Manuel said.

Zurito sat there, his feet in the box-stirrups, his great legs in the buckskin-covered armor gripping the horse, the reins in his left hand, the long pic held in his right hand, his broad hat well down over his eyes to shade them from the lights, watching the distant door of the toril. His horse's ears quivered. Zurito patted him with his left hand.

The red door of the toril swung back and for a moment Zurito looked into the empty passageway far across the arena. Then the bull came out in a rush, skidding on his four legs as he came out under the lights, then charging in a gallop, moving softly in a fast gallop, silent except as he woofed through wide nostrils as he charged, glad to be free after the dark pen.

In the first row of seats, slightly bored, leaning forward to write on the cement wall in front of his knees, the substitute bull-fight critic of *El Heraldo* scribbled: "Campagnero, Negro, 42, came out at 90 miles an hour with plenty of gas——"

Manuel, leaning against the barrera, watching the bull, waved his hand and the gypsy ran out, trailing his cape. The bull, in full gallop, pivoted and charged the cape, his head down, his tail rising. The gypsy moved in a zigzag, and as he passed, the bull caught sight of him and abandoned the cape to charge the man. The gyp sprinted and vaulted the red fence of the barrera as the bull struck it with his horns. He tossed into it twice with his horns, banging into the wood blindly.

The critic of *El Heraldo* lit a cigarette and tossed the match at the bull, then wrote in his note-book, "large and with enough horns to satisfy the cash customers. Campagnero showed a tendency to cut into the terrane of the bullfighters."

Manuel stepped out on the hard sand as the bull banged into the fence. Out of the corner of his eye he saw Zurito sitting the white horse close to the barrera, about a quarter of the way around the ring to the left. Manuel held the cape close in front of him, a fold in each hand, and shouted at the bull. "Huh! Huh!" The bull turned,

seemed to brace against the fence as he charged in a scramble, driving into the cape as Manuel side-stepped, pivoted on his heels with
the charge of the bull, and swung the cape just ahead of the horns.
At the end of the swing he was facing the bull again and held the
cape in the same position close in front of his body, and pivoted
again as the bull recharged. Each time, as he swung, the crowd
shouted.

Four times he swung with the bull, lifting the cape so it billowed
full, and each time bringing the bull around to charge again. Then,
at the end of the fifth swing, he held the cape against his hip and
pivoted, so the cape swung out like a ballet dancer's skirt and
wound the bull around himself like a belt, to step clear, leaving
the bull facing Zurito on the white horse, come up and planted
firm, the horse facing the bull, its ears forward, its lips nervous,
Zurito, his hat over his eyes, leaning forward, the long pole sticking
out before and behind in a sharp angle under his right arm, held
halfway down, the triangular iron point facing the bull.

El Heraldo's second-string critic, drawing on his cigarette, his
eyes on the bull, wrote: "the veteran Manolo designed a series of
acceptable veronicas, ending in a very Belmontistic recorte that
earned applause from the regulars, and we entered the tercio of the
cavalry."

Zurito sat his horse, measuring the distance between the bull and
the end of the pic. As he looked, the bull gathered himself together
and charged, his eyes on the horse's chest. As he lowered his head
to hook, Zurito sunk the point of the pic in the swelling hump of
muscle above the bull's shoulder, leaned all his weight on the
shaft, and with his left hand pulled the white horse into the air,
front hoofs pawing, and swung him to the right as he pushed the
bull under and through so the horns passed safely under the horse's
belly and the horse came down, quivering, the bull's tail brushing
his chest as he charged the cape Hernandez offered him.

Hernandez ran sideways, taking the bull out and away with the
cape, toward the other picador. He fixed him with a swing of the
cape, squarely facing the horse and rider, and stepped back. As
the bull saw the horse he charged. The picador's lance slid along his

back, and as the shock of the charge lifted the horse, the picador was already half-way out of the saddle, lifting his right leg clear as he missed with the lance and falling to the left side to keep the horse between him and the bull. The horse, lifted and gored, crashed over with the bull driving into him, the picador gave a shove with his boots against the horse and lay clear, waiting to be lifted and hauled away and put on his feet.

Manuel let the bull drive into the fallen horse; he was in no hurry, the picador was safe; besides, it did a picador like that good to worry. He'd stay on longer next time. Lousy pics! He looked across the sand at Zurito a little way out from the barrera, his horse rigid, waiting.

"Huh!" he called to the bull, "Tomar!" holding the cape in both hands so it would catch his eye. The bull detached himself from the horse and charged the cape, and Manuel, running sideways and holding the cape spread wide, stopped, swung on his heels, and brought the bull sharply around facing Zurito.

"Campagnero accepted a pair of varas for the death of one rosinante, with Hernandez and Manolo at the quites," *El Heraldo's* critic wrote. "He pressed on the iron and clearly showed he was no horse-lover. The veteran Zurito resurrected some of his old stuff with the pike-pole, notably the suerte——"

"Olé! Olé!" the man sitting beside him shouted. The shout was lost in the roar of the crowd, and he slapped the critic on the back. The critic looked up to see Zurito, directly below him, leaning far out over his horse, the length of the pic rising in a sharp angle under his armpit, holding the pic almost by the point, bearing down with all his weight, holding the bull off, the bull pushing and driving to get at the horse, and Zurito, far out, on top of him, holding him, holding him, and slowly pivoting the horse against the pressure, so that at last he was clear. Zurito felt the moment when the horse was clear and the bull could come past, and relaxed the absolute steel lock of his resistance, and the triangular steel point of the pic ripped in the bull's hump of shoulder muscle as he tore loose to find Hernandez's cape before his muzzle. He charged blindly into the cape and the boy took him out into the open arena.

Zurito sat patting his horse and looking at the bull charging the cape that Hernandez swung for him under the bright light while the crowd shouted.

"You see that one?" he said to Manuel.

"It was a wonder," Manuel said.

"I got him that time," Zurito said. "Look at him now."

At the conclusion of a closely turned pass of the cape the bull slid to his knees. He was up at once, but far out across the sand Manuel and Zurito saw the shine of the pumping flow of blood, smooth against the black of the bull's shoulder.

"I got him that time," Zurito said.

"He's a good bull," Manuel said.

"If they gave me another shot at him, I'd kill him," Zurito said.

"They'll change the thirds on us," Manuel said.

"Look at him now," Zurito said.

"I got to go over there," Manuel said, and started on a run for the other side of the ring, where the monos were leading a horse out by the bridle toward the bull, whacking him on the legs with rods and all, in a procession, trying to get him toward the bull, who stood, dropping his head, pawing, unable to make up his mind to charge.

Zurito, sitting his horse, walking him toward the scene, not missing any detail, scowled.

Finally the bull charged, the horse leaders ran for the barrera, the picador hit too far back, and the bull got under the horse, lifted him, threw him onto his back.

Zurito watched. The monos, in their red shirts, running out to drag the picador clear. The picador, now on his feet, swearing and flopping his arms. Manuel and Hernandez standing ready with their capes. And the bull, the great, black bull, with a horse on his back, hooves dangling, the bridle caught in the horns. Black bull with a horse on his back, staggering short-legged, then arching his neck and lifting, thrusting, charging to slide the horse off, horse sliding down. Then the bull into a lunging charge at the cape Manuel spread for him.

The bull was slower now, Manuel felt. He was bleeding badly. There was a sheen of blood all down his flank.

Manuel offered him the cape again. There he came, eyes open, ugly, watching the cape. Manuel stepped to the side and raised his arms, tightening the cape ahead of the bull for the veronica.

Now he was facing the bull. Yes, his head was going down a little. He was carrying it lower. That was Zurito.

Manuel flopped the cape; there he comes; he side-stepped and swung in another veronica. He's shooting awfully accurately, he thought. He's had enough fight, so he's watching now. He's hunting now. Got his eye on me. But I always give him the cape.

He shook the cape at the bull; there he comes; he side-stepped. Awful close that time. I don't want to work that close to him.

The edge of the cape was wet with blood where it had swept along the bull's back as he went by.

All right, here's the last one.

Manuel, facing the bull, having turned with him each charge, offered the cape with his two hands. The bull looked at him. Eyes watching, horns straight forward, the bull looked at him, watching.

"Huh!" Manuel said, "Toro!" and leaning back, swung the cape forward. Here he comes. He side-stepped, swung the cape in back of him, and pivoted, so the bull followed a swirl of cape and then was left with nothing, fixed by the pass, dominated by the cape. Manuel swung the cape under his muzzle with one hand, to show the bull was fixed, and walked away.

There was no applause.

Manuel walked across the sand toward the barrera, while Zurito rode out of the ring. The trumpet had blown to change the act to the planting of the banderillos while Manuel had been working with the bull. He had not consciously noticed it. The monos were spreading canvas over the two dead horses and sprinkling sawdust around them.

Manuel came up to the barrera for a drink of water. Retana's man handed him the heavy porous jug.

Fuentes, the tall gypsy, was standing holding a pair of banderillos, holding them together, slim, red sticks, fish-hook points out. He looked at Manuel.

"Go on out there," Manuel said.

The gypsy trotted out. Manuel set down the jug and watched. He wiped his face with his handkerchief.

The critic of *El Heraldo* reached for the bottle of warm champagne that stood between his feet, took a drink, and finished his paragraph.

"—the aged Manolo rated no applause for a vulgar series of lances with the cape and we entered the third of the palings."

Alone in the centre of the ring the bull stood, still fixed. Fuentes, tall, flat-backed, walking toward him arrogantly, his arms spread out, the two slim, red sticks, one in each hand, held by the fingers, points straight forward. Fuentes walked forward. Back of him and to one side was a peon with a cape. The bull looked at him and was no longer fixed.

His eyes watched Fuentes, now standing still. Now he leaned back, calling to him. Fuentes twitched the two banderillos and the light on the steel points caught the bull's eye.

His tail went up and he charged.

He came straight, his eyes on the man. Fuentes stood still, leaning back, the banderillos pointing forward. As the bull lowered his head to hook, Fuentes leaned backward, his arms came together and rose, his two hands touching, the banderillos two descending red lines, and leaning forward drove the points into the bull's shoulder, leaning far in over the bull's horns and pivoting on the two upright sticks, his legs tight together, his body curving to one side to let the bull pass.

"Olé!" from the crowd.

The bull was hooking wildly, jumping like a trout, all four feet off the ground. The red shaft of the banderillos tossed as he jumped. Manuel standing at the barrera, noticed that he hooked always to the right.

"Tell him to drop the next pair on the right," he said to the kid who started to run out to Fuentes with the new banderillos.

A heavy hand fell on his shoulder. It was Zurito.

"How do you feel, kid?" he asked.

Manuel was watching the bull.

Zurito leaned forward on the barrera, leaning the weight of his body on his arms. Manuel turned to him.

"You're going good," Zurito said.

Manuel shook his head. He had nothing to do now until the next third. The gypsy was very good with the banderillos. The bull would come to him in the next third in good shape. He was a good bull. It had all been easy up to now. The final stuff with the sword was all he worried about. He did not really worry. He did not even think about it. But standing there he had a heavy sense of apprehension. He looked out at the bull, planning his faena, his work with the red cloth that was to reduce the bull, to make him manageable.

The gypsy was walking out toward the bull again, walking heel-and-toe, insultingly, like a ball-room dancer, the red shafts of the banderillos twitching with his walk. The bull watched him, not fixed now, hunting him, but waiting to get close enough so he could be sure of getting him, getting the horns into him.

As Fuentes walked forward the bull charged. Fuentes ran across the quarter of a circle as the bull charged and, as he passed running backward, stopped, swung forward, rose on his toes, arms straight out, and sunk the banderillos straight down into the tight of the big shoulder muscles as the bull missed him.

The crowd were wild about it.

"That kid won't stay in this night stuff long," Retana's man said to Zurito.

"He's good," Zurito said.

"Watch him now."

They watched.

Fuentes was standing with his back against the barrera. Two of the cuadrilla were back of him, with their capes ready to flop over the fence to distract the bull.

The bull, with his tongue out, his barrel heaving, was watching the gypsy. He thought he had him now. Back against the red planks. Only a short charge away. The bull watched him.

The gypsy bent back, drew back his arms, the banderillos pointing at the bull. He called to the bull, stamped one foot. The bull was suspicious. He wanted the man. No more barbs in the shoulder.

Fuentes walked a little closer to the bull. Bent back. Called again. Somebody in the crowd shouted a warning.

"He's too damn close," Zurito said.

"Watch him," Retana's man said.

Leaning back, inciting the bull with the banderillos, Fuentes jumped, both feet off the ground. As he jumped the bull's tail rose and he charged. Fuentes came down on his toes, arms straight out, whole body arching forward, and drove the shafts straight down as he swung his body clear of the right horn.

The bull crashed into the barrera where the flopping capes had attracted his eye as he lost the man.

The gypsy came running along the barrera toward Manuel, taking the applause of the crowd. His vest was ripped where he had not quite cleared the point of the horn. He was happy about it, showing it to the spectators. He made the tour of the ring. Zurito saw him go by, smiling, pointing at his vest. He smiled.

Somebody else was planting the last pair of banderillos. Nobody was paying any attention.

Retana's man tucked a baton inside the red cloth of a muleta, folded the cloth over it, and handed it over the barrera to Manuel. He reached in the leather sword-case, took out a sword, and holding it by its leather scabbard, reached it over the fence to Manuel. Manuel pulled the blade out by the red hilt and the scabbard fell limp.

He looked at Zurito. The big man saw he was sweating.

"Now you get him, kid," Zurito said.

Manuel nodded.

"He's in good shape," Zurito said.

"Just like you want him," Retana's man assured him.

Manuel nodded.

The trumpeter, up under the roof, blew for the final act, and Manuel walked across the arena toward where, up in the dark boxes, the president must be.

In the front row of seats the substitute bull-fight critic of *El Her-*

aldo took a long drink of the warm champagne. He had decided it was not worth while to write a running story and would write up the corrida back in the office. What the hell was it anyway? Only a nocturnal. If he missed anything he would get it out of the morning papers. He took another drink of the champagne. He had a date at Maxim's at twelve. Who were these bull-fighters anyway? Kids and bums. A bunch of bums. He put his pad of paper in his pocket and looked over toward Manuel, standing very much alone in the ring, gesturing with his hat in a salute toward a box he could not see high up in the dark plaza. Out in the ring the bull stood quiet, looking at nothing.

"I dedicate this bull to you, Mr. President, and to the public of Madrid, the most intelligent and generous of the world," was what Manuel was saying. It was a formula. He said it all. It was a little long for nocturnal use.

He bowed at the dark, straightened, tossed his hat over his shoulder, and, carrying the muleta in his left hand and the sword in his right, walked out toward the bull.

Manuel walked toward the bull. The bull looked at him; his eyes were quick. Manuel noticed the way the banderillos hung down on his left shoulder and the steady sheen of blood from Zurito's picing. He noticed the way the bull's feet were. As he walked forward, holding the muleta in his left hand and the sword in his right, he watched the bull's feet. The bull could not charge without gathering his feet together. Now he stood square on them, dully.

Manuel walked toward him, watching his feet. This was all right. He could do this. He must work to get the bull's head down, so he could go in past the horns and kill him. He did not think about the sword, not about killing the bull. He thought about one thing at a time. The coming things oppressed him, though. Walking forward, watching the bull's feet, he saw successively his eyes, his wet muzzle, and the wide, forward-pointing spread of his horns. The bull had light circles about his eyes. His eyes watched Manuel. He felt he was going to get this little one with the white face.

Standing still now and spreading the red cloth of the muleta with the sword, pricking the point into the cloth so that the sword, now held in his left hand, spread the red flannel like the jib of a boat, Manuel noticed the points of the bull's horns. One of them was splintered from banging against the barrera. The other was sharp as a porcupine quill. Manuel noticed while spreading the muleta that the white base of the horn was stained red. While he noticed these things he did not lose sight of the bull's feet. The bull watched Manuel steadily.

He's on the defensive now, Manuel thought. He's reserving himself. I've got to bring him out of that and get his head down. Always get his head down. Zurito had his head down once, but he's come back. He'll bleed when I start him going and that will bring it down.

Holding the muleta, with the sword in his left hand widening it in front of him, he called to the bull.

The bull looked at him.

He leaned back insultingly and shook the wide-spread flannel.

The bull saw the muleta. It was a bright scarlet under the arc-light. The bull's legs tightened.

Here he comes. Whoosh! Manuel turned as the bull came and raised the muleta so that it passed over the bull's horns and swept down his broad back from head to tail. The bull had gone clean up in the air with the charge. Manuel had not moved.

At the end of the pass the bull turned like a cat coming around a corner and faced Manuel.

He was on the offensive again. His heaviness was gone. Manuel noted the fresh blood shining down the black shoulder and dripping down the bull's leg. He drew the sword out of the muleta and held it in his right hand. The muleta held low down in his left hand, leaning toward the left, he called to the bull. The bull's legs tightened, his eyes on the muleta. Here he comes, Manuel thought. Yuh!

He swung with the charge, sweeping the muleta ahead of the bull, his feet firm, the sword following the curve, a point of light under the arcs.

The bull recharged as the pase natural finished and Manuel raised the muleta for a pase de pecho. Firmly planted, the bull came by his chest under the raised muleta. Manuel leaned his head back to avoid the clattering banderillo shafts. The hot, black bull body touched his chest as it passed.

Too damn close, Manuel thought. Zurito, leaning on the barrera, spoke rapidly to the gypsy, who trotted out toward Manuel with a cape. Zurito pulled his hat down low and looked out across the arena at Manuel.

Manuel was facing the bull again, the muleta held low and to the left. The bull's head was down as he watched the muleta.

"If it was Belmonte doing that stuff, they'd go crazy," Retana's man said.

Zurito said nothing. He was watching Manuel out in the centre of the arena.

"Where did the boss dig this fellow up?" Retana's man asked.

"Out of the hospital," Zurito said.

"That's where he's going damn quick," Retana's man said.

Zurito turned on him.

"Knock on that," he said, pointing to the barrera.

"I was just kidding, man," Retana's man said.

"Knock on the wood."

Retana's man leaned forward and knocked three times on the barrera.

"Watch the faena," Zurito said.

Out in the centre of the ring, under the lights, Manuel was kneeling, facing the bull, and as he raised the muleta in both hands the bull charged, tail up.

Manuel swung his body clear and, as the bull recharged, brought around the muleta in a half-circle that pulled the bull to his knees.

"Why, that one's a great bull-fighter," Retana's man said.

"No, he's not," said Zurito.

Manuel stood up and, the muleta in his left hand, the sword in his right, acknowledged the applause from the dark plaza.

The bull had humped himself up from his knees and stood waiting, his head hung low.

Zurito spoke to two of the other lads of the cuadrilla and they ran out to stand back of Manuel with their capes. There were four men back of him now. Hernandez had followed him since he first came out with the muleta. Fuentes stood watching, his cape held against his body, tall, in repose, watching, lazy-eyed. Now the two came up. Hernandez motioned them to stand one at each side. Manuel stood alone, facing the bull.

Manuel waved back the men with the capes. Stepping back cautiously, they saw his face was white and sweating.

Didn't they know enough to keep back? Did they want to catch the bull's eye with the capes after he was fixed and ready? He had enough to worry about without that kind of thing.

The bull was standing, his four feet square, looking at the muleta. Manuel furled the muleta in his left hand. The bull's eyes watched it. His body was heavy on his feet. He carried his head low, but not too low.

Manuel lifted the muleta at him. The bull did not move. Only his eyes watched.

He's all lead, Manuel thought. He's all square. He's framed right. He'll take it.

He thought in bull-fight terms. Sometimes he had a thought and the particular piece of slang would not come into his mind and he could not realize the thought. His instincts and his knowledge worked automatically, and his brain worked slowly and in words. He knew all about bulls. He did not have to think about them. He just did the right thing. His eyes noted things and his body performed the necessary measures without thought. If he thought about it, he would be gone.

Now, facing the bull, he was conscious of many things at the same time. There were the horns, the one splintered, the other smoothly sharp, the need to profile himself toward the left horn, lance himself short and straight, lower the muleta so the bull would follow it, and, going in over the horns, put the sword all the way into a little spot about as big as a five-peseta piece straight in back of the neck, between the sharp pitch of the bull's shoulders. He must do all this and must then come out from between the horns. He was conscious he must do all this, but his only thought was in words: "Corto y derecho."

"Corto y derecho," he thought, furling the muleta. Short and straight. Corto y derecho, he drew the sword out of the muleta, profiled on the splintered left horn, dropped the muleta across his body, so his right hand with the sword on the level with his eye made the sign of the cross, and, rising on his toes, sighted along the dipping blade of the sword at the spot high up between the bull's shoulders.

Corto y derecho he lanced himself on the bull.

There was a shock, and he felt himself go up in the air. He pushed on the sword as he went up and over, and it flew out of his hand. He hit the ground and the bull was on him. Manuel, lying on the ground, kicked at the bull's muzzle with his slippered feet. Kicking, kicking, the bull after him, missed him in his excitement, bumping him with his head, driving the horns into the sand. Kicking like a man keeping a ball in the air, Manuel kept the bull from getting a clean thrust at him.

Manuel felt the wind on his back from the capes flopping at the bull, and then the bull was gone, gone over him in a rush. Dark, as his belly went over. Not even stepped on.

Manuel stood up and picked up the muleta. Fuentes handed him the sword. It was bent where it had struck the shoulderblade. Manuel straightened it on his knee and ran toward the bull, standing now beside one of the dead horses. As he ran, his jacket flopped where it had been ripped under his armpit.

"Get him out of there," Manuel shouted to the gypsy. The bull had smelled the blood of the dead horse and ripped into the canvas-cover with his horns. He charged Fuente's cape, with the canvas hanging from his splintered horn, and the crowd laughed. Out in the ring, he tossed his head to rid himself of the canvas. Hernandez, running up from behind him, grabbed the end of the canvas and neatly lifted it off the horn.

The bull followed it in a half-charge and stopped still. He was on the defensive again. Manuel was walking toward him with the sword and muleta. Manuel swung the muleta before him. The bull would not charge.

Manuel profiled toward the bull, sighting along the dipping blade of the sword. The bull was motionless, seemingly dead on his feet, incapable of another charge.

Manuel rose to his toes, sighting along the steel, and charged.

Again there was the shock and he felt himself being borne back in a rush, to strike hard on the sand. There was no chance of kicking this time. The bull was on top of him. Manuel lay as though dead, his head on his arms, and the bull bumped him. Bumped his back, bumped his face in the sand. He felt the horn go into the sand between his folded arms. The bull hit him in the small of the back. His face drove into the sand. The horn drove through one of his sleeves and the bull ripped it off. Manuel was tossed clear and the bull followed the capes.

Manuel got up, found the sword and muleta, tried the point of the sword with his thumb, and then ran toward the barrera for a new sword.

Retana's man handed him the sword over the edge of the barrera. "Wipe off your face," he said.

Manuel, running again toward the bull, wiped his bloody face with his handkerchief. He had not seen Zurito. Where was Zurito?

The cuadrilla had stepped away from the bull and waited with their capes. The bull stood, heavy and dull again after the action.

Manuel walked toward him with the muleta. He stopped and shook it. The bull did not respond. He passed it right and left, left and right before the bull's muzzle. The bull's eyes watched it and turned with the swing, but he would not charge. He was waiting for Manuel.

Manuel was worried. There was nothing to do but go in. Corto y derecho. He profiled close to the bull, crossed the muleta in front of his body and charged. As he pushed in the sword, he jerked his body to the left to clear the horn. The bull passed him and the sword shot up in the air, twinkling under the arc-lights, to fall red-hilted on the sand.

Manuel ran over and picked it up. It was bent and he straightened it over his knee.

As he came running toward the bull, fixed again now, he passed Hernandez standing with his cape.

"He's all bone," the boy said encouragingly.

Manuel nodded, wiping his face. He put the bloody handkerchief in his pocket.

There was the bull. He was close to the barrera now. Damn him. Maybe he was all bone. Maybe there was not any place for the sword to go in. The hell there wasn't! He'd show them.

He tried a pass with the muleta and the bull did not move. Manuel chopped the muleta back and forth in front of the bull. Nothing doing.

He furled the muleta, drew the sword out, profiled and drove in on the bull. He felt the sword buckle as he shoved it in, leaning his weight on it, and then it shot high in the air, end-over-ending into the crowd. Manuel had jerked clear as the sword jumped.

The first cushions thrown down out of the dark missed him. Then one hit him in the face, his bloody face looking toward the crowd. They were coming down fast. Spotting the sand. Somebody threw an empty champagne-bottle from close range. It hit Manuel on the foot. He stood there watching the dark, where the things were coming from. Then something whished through the air and struck by him. Manuel leaned over and picked it up. It was his sword. He straightened it over his knee and gestured with it to the crowd.

"Thank you," he said. "Thank you."

Oh, the dirty bastards! Dirty bastards! Oh, the lousy, dirty bastards! He kicked into a cushion as he ran.

There was the bull. The same as ever. All right, you dirty, lousy bastard!

Manuel passed the muleta in front of the bull's black muzzle.

Nothing doing.

You won't! All right. He stepped close and jammed the sharp peak of the muleta into the bull's damp muzzle.

The bull was on him as he jumped back and as he tripped on a cushion he felt the horn go into him, into his side. He grabbed the horn with his two hands and rode backward, holding tight onto the place. The bull tossed him and he was clear. He lay still. It was all right. The bull was gone.

He got up coughing and feeling broken and gone. The dirty bastards!

"Give me the sword," he shouted. "Give me the stuff."

Fuentes came up with the muleta and the sword.

Hernandez put his arm around him.

"Go on to the infirmary, man," he said. "Don't be a damn fool."

"Get away from me," Manuel said. "Get to hell away from me."

He twisted free. Hernandez shrugged his shoulders. Manuel ran toward the bull.

There was the bull standing, heavy, firmly planted.

All right, you bastard! Manuel drew the sword out of the muleta, sighted with the same movement, and flung himself onto the bull. He felt the sword go in all the way. Right up to guard. Four fingers and his thumb into the bull. The blood was hot on his knuckles, and he was on top of the bull.

The bull lurched with him as he lay on, and seemed to sink; then he was standing clear. He looked at the bull going down slowly over on his side, then suddenly four feet in the air.

Then he gestured at the crowd, his hand warm from the bull blood.

All right, you bastards! He wanted to say something, but he started to cough. It was hot and choking. He looked down for the muleta. He must go over and salute the president. President hell! He was sitting down looking at something. It was the bull. His four feet up. Thick tongue out. Things crawling around on his belly and under his legs. Crawling where the hair was thin. Dead bull. To hell with the bull! To hell with them all! He started to get to his feet and commenced to cough. He sat down again, coughing. Somebody came and pushed him up.

They carried him across the ring to the infirmary, running with him across the sand, standing blocked at the gate as the mules came in, then around under the dark passageway, men grunting as they took him up the stairway, and then laid him down.

The doctor and two men in white were waiting for him. They laid him out on the table. They were cutting away his shirt. Manuel felt tired. His whole chest felt scalding inside. He started to cough and they held something to his mouth. Everybody was very busy.

There was an electric light in his eyes. He shut his eyes.

He heard some one coming very heavily up the stairs. Then he did not hear it. Then he heard a noise far off. That was the crowd.

Well, somebody would have to kill his other bull. They had cut away all his shirt. The doctor smiled at him. There was Retana.

"Hello, Retana!" Manuel said. He could not hear his voice.

Retana smiled at him and said something. Manuel could not hear it.

Zurito stood beside the table, bending over where the doctor was working. He was in his picador clothes, without his hat.

Zurito said something to him. Manuel could not hear it.

Zurito was speaking to Retana. One of the men in white smiled and handed Retana a pair of scissors. Retana gave them to Zurito. Zurito said something to Manuel. He could not hear it.

To hell with this operating-table! He'd been on plenty of operating-tables before. He was not going to die. There would be a priest if he was going to die.

Zurito was saying something to him. Holding up the scissors.

That was it. They were going to cut off his coleta. They were going to cut off his pigtail.

Manuel sat up on the operating-table. The doctor stepped back, angry. Some one grabbed him and held him.

"You couldn't do a thing like that, Manos," he said.

He heard suddenly, clearly, Zurito's voice.

"That's all right," Zurito said. "I won't do it. I was joking."

"I was going good," Manuel said. "I didn't have any luck. That was all."

Manuel lay back. They had put something over his face. It was all familiar. He inhaled deeply. He felt very tired. He was very, very tired. They took the thing away from his face.

"I was going good," Manuel said weakly. "I was going great."

Retana looked at Zurito and started for the door.

"I'll stay here with him," Zurito said.

Retana shrugged his shoulders.

Manuel opened his eyes and looked at Zurito.

"Wasn't I going good, Manos?" he asked, for confirmation.

"Sure," said Zurito. "You were going great."

The doctor's assistant put the cone over Manuel's face and he inhaled deeply. Zurito stood awkwardly, watching.

F. SCOTT FITZGERALD

The Rich Boy

BEGIN with an individual, and before you know it you find that you have created a type; begin with a type, and you find that you have created—nothing. That is because we are all queer fish, queerer behind our faces and voices than we want any one to know or than we know ourselves. When I hear a man proclaiming himself an "average, honest, open fellow," I feel pretty sure that he has some definite and perhaps terrible abnormality which he has agreed to conceal—and his protestation of being average and honest and open is his way of reminding himself of his misprision.

There are no types, no plurals. There is a rich boy, and this is his and not his brothers' story. All my life I have lived among his brothers but this one has been my friend. Besides, if I wrote about his brothers I should have to begin by attacking all the lies that the poor have told about the rich and the rich have told about themselves—such a wild structure they have erected that when we pick up a book about the rich, some instinct prepares us for unreality. Even the intelligent and impassioned reporters of life have made the country of the rich as unreal as fairy-land.

Let me tell you about the very rich. They are different from you and me. They possess and enjoy early, and it does something to them,

makes them soft where we are hard, and cynical where we are trust-
ful, in a way that, unless you were born rich, it is very difficult to
understand. They think, deep in their hearts, that they are better
than we are because we had to discover the compensations and re-
fuges of life for ourselves. Even when they enter deep into our
world or sink below us, they still think that they are better than we
are. They are different. The only way I can describe young Anson
Hunter is to approach him as if he were a foreigner and cling stubbornly to my point of view. If I accept his for a moment I am lost—I
have nothing to show but a preposterous movie.

II

Anson was the eldest of six children who would some day divide
a fortune of fifteen million dollars, and he reached the age of reason
—is it seven?—at the beginning of the century when daring young
women were already gliding along Fifth Avenue in electric "mo-
biles." In those days he and his brother had an English governess who
spoke the language very clearly and crisply and well, so that the two
boys grew to speak as she did—their words and sentences were all
crisp and clear and not run together as ours are. They didn't talk
exactly like English children but acquired an accent that is peculiar to
fashionable people in the city of New York.

In the summer the six children were moved from the house on
71st Street to a big estate in northern Connecticut. It was not a
fashionable locality—Anson's father wanted to delay as long as possible his children's knowledge of that side of life. He was a man
somewhat superior to his class, which composed New York society,
and to his period, which was the snobbish and formalized vulgarity
of the Gilded Age, and he wanted his sons to learn habits of concentration and have sound constitutions and grow up into right-living
and successful men. He and his wife kept an eye on them as well as
they were able until the two older boys went away to school, but in
huge establishments this is difficult—it was much simpler in the series
of small and medium-sized houses in which my own youth was
spent—I was never far out of the reach of my mother's voice, of the
sense of her presence, her approval or disapproval.

Anson's first sense of his superiority came to him when he realized the half-grudging American deference that was paid to him in the Connecticut village. The parents of the boys he played with always inquired after his father and mother, and were vaguely excited when their own children were asked to the Hunters' house. He accepted this as the natural state of things, and a sort of impatience with all groups of which he was not the centre—in money, in position, in authority—remained with him for the rest of his life. He disdained to struggle with other boys for precedence—he expected it to be given him freely, and when it wasn't he withdrew into his family. His family was sufficient, for in the East money is still a somewhat feudal thing, a clan-forming thing. In the snobbish West, money separates families to form "sets."

At eighteen, when he went to New Haven, Anson was tall and thick-set, with a clear complexion and a healthy color from the ordered life he had led in school. His hair was yellow and grew in a funny way on his head, his nose was beaked—these two things kept him from being handsome—but he had a confident charm and a certain brusque style, and the upper-class men who passed him on the street knew without being told that he was a rich boy and had gone to one of the best schools. Nevertheless, his very superiority kept him from being a success in college—the independence was mistaken for egotism, and the refusal to accept Yale standards with the proper awe seemed to belittle all those who had. So, long before he graduated, he began to shift the centre of his life to New York.

He was at home in New York—there was his own house with "the kind of servants you can't get any more"—and his own family, of which, because of his good humor and a certain ability to make things go, he was rapidly becoming the centre, and the débutante parties, and the correct manly world of the men's clubs, and the occasional wild spree with the gallant girls whom New Haven only knew from the fifth row. His aspirations were conventional enough—they included even the irreproachable shadow he would some day marry, but they differed from the aspirations of the majority of young men in that there was no mist over them, none of that quality which is variously known as "idealism" or "illusion." Anson accepted without reservation the world of high finance and high extravagance, of divorce and dissipation, of snobbery and of privilege. Most of our lives end as a compromise—it was as a compromise that his life began.

He and I first met in the late summer of 1917, when he was just out of Yale, and, like the rest of us, was swept up into the systematized hysteria of the war. In the blue-green uniform of the naval aviation he came down to Pensacola, where the hotel orchestras played "I'm sorry, dear," and we young officers danced with the girls. Every one liked him, and though he ran with the drinkers and wasn't an especially good pilot, even the instructors treated him with a certain respect. He was always having long talks with them in his confident, logical voice—talks which ended by his getting himself, or, more frequently, another officer, out of some impending trouble. He was convivial, bawdy, robustly avid for pleasure, and we were all surprised when he fell in love with a conservative and rather proper girl.

Her name was Paula Legendre, a dark, serious beauty from somewhere in California. Her family kept a winter residence just outside of town, and in spite of her primness she was enormously popular; there is a large class of men whose egotism can't endure humor in a woman. But Anson wasn't that sort, and I couldn't understand the attraction of her "sincerity"—that was the thing to say about her—for his keen and somewhat sardonic mind.

Nevertheless, they fell in love—and on her terms. He no longer joined the twilight gathering at the De Soto bar, and whenever they were seen together they were engaged in a long, serious dialogue, which must have gone on several weeks. Long afterward he told me that it was not about anything in particular but was composed on both sides of immature and even meaningless statements—the emotional content that gradually came to fill it grew up not out of the words but out of its enormous seriousness. It was a sort of hypnosis. Often it was interrupted, giving way to that emasculated humor we call fun; when they were alone it was resumed again, solemn, low-keyed, and pitched so as to give each other a sense of unity in feeling and thought. They came to resent any interruptions of it, to be unresponsive to facetiousness about life, even to the mild cynicism of their contemporaries. They were only happy when the dialogue was going on, and its seriousness bathed them like the amber glow of an open fire. Toward the end there came an interruption they did not resent—it began to be interrupted by passion.

Oddly enough, Anson was as engrossed in the dialogue as she was and as profoundly affected by it, yet at the same time aware that on his side much was insincere, and on hers much was merely simple. At first, too, he despised her emotional simplicity as well, but with his love her nature deepened and blossomed, and he could despise it no longer. He felt that if he could enter into Paula's warm safe life he would be happy. The long preparation of the dialogue removed any constraint—he taught her some of what he had learned from more adventurous women, and she responded with a rapt holy intensity. One evening after a dance they agreed to marry, and he wrote a long letter about her to his mother. The next day Paula told him that she was rich, that she had a personal fortune of nearly a million dollars.

III

It was exactly as if they could say "Neither of us has anything: we shall be poor together"—just as delightful that they should be rich instead. It gave them the same communion of adventure. Yet when Anson got leave in April, and Paula and her mother accompanied him North, she was impressed with the standing of his family in New York and with the scale on which they lived. Alone with Anson for the first time in the rooms where he had played as a boy, she was filled with a comfortable emotion, as though she were pre-eminently safe and taken care of. The pictures of Anson in a skull cap at his first school, of Anson on horseback with the sweetheart of a mysterious forgotten summer, of Anson in a gay group of ushers and bridesmaids at a wedding, made her jealous of his life apart from her in the past, and so completely did his authoritative person seem to sum up and typify these possessions of his that she was inspired with the idea of being married immediately and returning to Pensacola as his wife.

But an immediate marriage wasn't discussed—even the engagement was to be secret until after the war. When she realized that only two days of his leave remained, her dissatisfaction crystallized in the intention of making him as unwilling to wait as she was. They were driving to the country for dinner and she determined to force the issue that night.

Now a cousin of Paula's was staying with them at the Ritz, a severe, bitter girl who loved Paula but was somewhat jealous of her impressive engagement, and as Paula was late in dressing, the cousin, who wasn't going to the party, received Anson in the parlor of the suite.

Anson had met friends at five o'clock and drunk freely and indiscreetly with them for an hour. He left the Yale Club at a proper time, and his mother's chauffeur drove him to the Ritz, but his usual capacity was not in evidence, and the impact of the steam-heated sitting-room made him suddenly dizzy. He knew it, and he was both amused and sorry.

Paula's cousin was twenty-five, but she was exceptionally naïve, and at first failed to realize what was up. She had never met Anson before, and she was surprised when he mumbled strange information and nearly fell off his chair, but until Paula appeared it didn't occur to her that what she had taken for the odor of a dry-cleaned uniform was really whiskey. But Paula understood as soon as she appeared; her only thought was to get Anson away before her mother saw him, and at the look in her eyes the cousin understood too.

When Paula and Anson descended to the limousine they found two men inside, both asleep; they were the men with whom he had been drinking at the Yale Club, and they were also going to the party. He had entirely forgotten their presence in the car. On the way to Hempstead they awoke and sang. Some of the songs were rough, and though Paula tried to reconcile herself to the fact that Anson had few verbal inhibitions, her lips tightened with shame and distaste.

Back at the hotel the cousin, confused and agitated, considered the incident, and then walked into Mrs. Legendre's bedroom, saying: "Isn't he funny?"

"Who is funny?"

"Why—Mr. Hunter. He seemed so funny."

Mrs. Legendre looked at her sharply.

"How is he funny?"

"Why, he said he was French. I didn't know he was French."

"That's absurd. You must have misunderstood." She smiled: "It was a joke."

The cousin shook her head stubbornly.

"No. He said he was brought up in France. He said he couldn't speak any English, and that's why he couldn't talk to me. And he couldn't!"

Mrs. Legendre looked away with impatience just as the cousin added thoughtfully, "Perhaps it was because he was so drunk," and walked out of the room.

This curious report was true. Anson, finding his voice thick and uncontrollable, had taken the unusual refuge of announcing that he spoke no English. Years afterwards he used to tell that part of the story, and he invariably communicated the uproarious laughter which the memory aroused in him.

Five times in the next hour Mrs. Legendre tried to get Hempstead on the phone. When she succeeded, there was a ten-minute delay before she heard Paula's voice on the wire.

"Cousin Jo told me Anson was intoxicated."

"Oh, no. . . ."

"Oh, yes. Cousin Jo says he was intoxicated. He told her he was French, and fell off his chair and behaved as if he was very intoxicated. I don't want you to come home with him."

"Mother, he's all right! Please don't worry about——"

"But I do worry. I think it's dreadful. I want you to promise me not to come home with him."

"I'll take care of it, mother. . . ."

"I don't want you to come home with him."

"All right, mother. Good-by."

"Be sure now, Paula. Ask some one to bring you."

Deliberately Paula took the receiver from her ear and hung it up. Her face was flushed with helpless annoyance. Anson was stretched out asleep in a bedroom up-stairs, while the dinner-party below was proceeding lamely toward conclusion.

The hour's drive had sobered him somewhat—his arrival was merely hilarious—and Paula hoped that the evening was not spoiled, after all, but two imprudent cocktails before dinner completed the disaster. He talked boisterously and somewhat offensively to the party at large for fifteen minutes, and then slid silently under the table; like a man in an old print—but, unlike an old print, it was rather horrible without being at all quaint. None of the young girls present remarked upon the incident—it seemed to merit only silence. His uncle and two other men carried him up-stairs, and it was just after this that Paula was called to the phone.

An hour later Anson awoke in a fog of nervous agony, through which he perceived after a moment the figure of his uncle Robert standing by the door.

". . . I said are you better?"

"What?"

"Do you feel better, old man?"

"Terrible," said Anson.

"I'm going to try you on another bromo-seltzer. If you can hold it down, it'll do you good to sleep."

With an effort Anson slid his legs from the bed and stood up.

"I'm all right," he said dully.

"Take it easy."

"I thin' if you gave me a glassbrandy I could go down-stairs."

"Oh, no——"

"Yes, that's the only thin'. I'm all right now. . . . I suppose I'm in Dutch dow' there."

"They know you're a little under the weather," said his uncle deprecatingly. "But don't worry about it. Schuyler didn't even get here. He passed away in the locker-room over at the Links."

Indifferent to any opinion, except Paula's, Anson was nevertheless determined to save the débris of the evening, but when after a cold bath he made his appearance most of the party had already left. Paula got up immediately to go home.

In the limousine the old serious dialogue began. She had known that he drank, she admitted, but she had never expected anything like this—it seemed to her that perhaps they were not suited to each other, after all. Their ideas about life were too different, and so forth. When she finished speaking, Anson spoke in turn, very soberly. Then Paula said she'd have to think it over; she wouldn't decide to-night; she was not angry but she was terribly sorry. Nor would she let him come into the hotel with her, but just before she got out of the car she leaned and kissed him unhappily on the cheek.

The next afternoon Anson had a long talk with Mrs. Legendre while Paula sat listening in silence. It was agreed that Paula was to brood over the incident for a proper period and then, if mother and daughter thought it best, they would follow Anson to Pensacola. On his part he apologized with sincerity and dignity—that was all; with every card in her hand Mrs. Legendre was unable to establish any advantage over him. He made no promises, showed no humility, only delivered a few serious comments on life which brought him off with rather a moral superiority at the end. When they came South three weeks later, neither Anson in his satisfaction nor Paula in her relief at the reunion realized that the psychological moment had passed forever.

IV

He dominated and attracted her, and at the same time filled her with anxiety. Confused by his mixture of solidity and self-indulgence, of sentiment and cynicism—incongruities which her gentle mind was unable to resolve—Paula grew to think of him as two alternating personalities. When she saw him alone, or at a formal party, or with his casual inferiors, she felt a tremendous pride in his strong, attractive presence, the paternal, understanding stature of his mind. In other company she became uneasy when what had been a fine imperviousness to mere gentility showed its other face. The other face was gross, humorous, reckless of everything but pleasure. It startled her mind temporarily away from him, even led her into a short covert experiment with an old beau, but it was no use—after four months of Anson's enveloping vitality there was an anæmic pallor in all other men.

In July he was ordered abroad, and their tenderness and desire reached a crescendo. Paula considered a last-minute marriage—decided against it only because there were always cocktails on his breath now, but the parting itself made her physically ill with grief. After his departure she wrote him long letters of regret for the days of love they had missed by waiting. In August Anson's plane slipped down into the North Sea. He was pulled onto a destroyer after a night in the water and sent to hospital with pneumonia; the armistice was signed before he was finally sent home.

Then, with every opportunity given back to them, with no material obstacle to overcome, the secret weavings of their temperaments came between them, drying up their kisses and their tears, making their voices less loud to one another, muffling the intimate chatter of their hearts until the old communication was only possible by letters, from far away. One afternoon a society reporter waited for two hours in the Hunters' house for a confirmation of their engagement. Anson denied it; nevertheless an early issue carried the report as a leading paragraph—they were "constantly seen together at South-hampton, Hot Springs, and Tuxedo Park." But the serious dialogue had turned a corner into a long-sustained quarrel, and the affair was almost played out. Anson got drunk flagrantly and missed an engagement with her, whereupon Paula made certain behavioristic demands. His despair was helpless before his pride and his knowledge of himself: the engagement was definitely broken.

"Dearest," said their letters now, "Dearest, Dearest, when I wake up in the middle of the night and realize that after all it was not to be, I feel that I want to die. I can't go on living any more. Perhaps when we meet this summer we may talk things over and decide differently—we were so excited and sad that day, and I don't feel that I can live all my life without you. You speak of other people. Don't you know there are no other people for me, but only you. . . ."

But as Paula drifted here and there around the East she would sometimes mention her gaieties to make him wonder. Anson was too acute to wonder. When he saw a man's name in her letters he felt more sure of her and a little disdainful—he was always superior to such things. But he still hoped that they would some day marry.

Meanwhile he plunged vigorously into all the movement and glitter of post-bellum New York, entering a brokerage house, joining half a dozen clubs, dancing late, and moving in three worlds—his own world, the world of young Yale graduates, and that section of the half-world which rests one end on Broadway. But there was always a thorough and infrangible eight hours devoted to his work in Wall Street, where the combination of his influential family connection, his sharp intelligence, and his abundance of sheer physical energy brought him almost immediately forward. He had one of those invaluable minds with partitions in it; sometimes he appeared at his office refreshed by less than an hour's sleep, but such occurrences were rare. So early as 1920 his income in salary and commissions exceeded twelve thousand dollars.

As the Yale tradition slipped into the past he became more and more of a popular figure among his classmates in New York, more popular than he had ever been in college. He lived in a great house, and had the means of introducing young men into other great houses. Moreover, his life already seemed secure, while theirs, for the most part, had arrived again at precarious beginnings. They commenced to turn to him for amusement and escape, and Anson responded readily, taking pleasure in helping people and arranging their affairs.

There were no men in Paula's letters now, but a note of tenderness ran through them that had not been there before. From several sources he heard that she had "a heavy beau," Lowell Thayer, a Bostonian of wealth and position, and though he was sure she still loved him, it made him uneasy to think that he might lose her, after all. Save for one unsatisfactory day she had not been in New York for almost five months, and as the rumors multiplied he became increasingly anxious to see her. In February he took his vacation and went down to Florida.

Palm Beach sprawled plump and opulent between the sparkling sapphire of Lake Worth, flawed here and there by house-boats at anchor, and the great turquoise bar of the Atlantic Ocean. The huge bulks of the Breakers and the Royal Poinciana rose as twin paunches from the bright level of the sand, and around them clustered the Dancing Glade, Bradley's House of Chance, and a dozen modistes and milliners with goods at triple prices from New York. Upon the trellised veranda of the Breakers two hundred women stepped right, stepped left, wheeled, and slid in that then celebrated calisthenic known as the double-shuffle, while in half-time to the music two thousand bracelets clicked up and down on two hundred arms.

At the Everglades Club after dark Paula and Lowell Thayer and Anson and a casual fourth played bridge with hot cards. It seemed to Anson that her kind, serious face was wan and tired—she had been around now for four, five, years. He had known her for three.

"Two spades."

"Cigarette? . . . Oh, I beg your pardon. By me."

"By."

"I'll double three spades."

There were a dozen tables of bridge in the room, which was filling up with smoke. Anson's eyes met Paula's, held them persistently even when Thayer's glance fell between them. . . .

"What was bid?" he asked abstractedly.

"Rose of Washington Square"

sang the young people in the corners:

> *"I'm withering there*
> *In basement air——"*

The smoke banked like fog, and the opening of a door filled the room with blown swirls of ectoplasm. Little Bright Eyes streaked past the tables seeking Mr. Conan Doyle among the Englishmen who were posing as Englishmen about the lobby.

"You could cut it with a knife."

". . . cut it with a knife."

". . . a knife."

At the end of the rubber Paula suddenly got up and spoke to Anson in a tense, low voice. With scarcely a glance at Lowell Thayer, they walked out the door and descended a long flight of stone steps— in a moment they were walking hand in hand along the moonlit beach.

"Darling, darling. . . ." They embraced recklessly, passionately, in a shadow. . . . Then Paula drew back her face to let his lips say what she wanted to hear—she could feel the words forming as they kissed again. . . . Again she broke away, listening, but as he pulled her close once more she realized that he had said nothing—only *"Darling! Darling!"* in that deep, sad whisper that always made her cry. Humbly, obediently, her emotions yielded to him and the tears streamed down her face, but her heart kept on crying: "Ask me—oh, Anson, dearest, ask me!"

"Paula. . . . *Paula!"*

The words wrung her heart like hands, and Anson, feeling her tremble, knew that emotion was enough. He need say no more, commit their destinies to no practical enigma. Why should he, when he might hold her so, biding his own time, for another year—forever? He was considering them both, her more than himself. For a moment, when she said suddenly that she must go back to her hotel, he hesitated, thinking, first, "This is the moment, after all," and then: "No, let it wait—she is mine. . . ."

He had forgotten that Paula too was worn away inside with the strain of three years. Her mood passed forever in the night.

He went back to New York next morning filled with a certain restless dissatisfaction. Late in April, without warning, he received a telegram from Bar Harbor in which Paula told him that she was engaged to Lowell Thayer, and that they would be married immediately in Boston. What he never really believed could happen had happened at last.

Anson filled himself with whiskey that morning, and going to the office, carried on his work without a break—rather with a fear of what would happen if he stopped. In the evening he went out as usual, saying nothing of what had occurred; he was cordial, humorous, unabstracted. But one thing he could not help—for three days, in any place, in any company, he would suddenly bend his head into his hands and cry like a child.

V

In 1922 when Anson went abroad with the junior partner to investigate some London loans, the journey intimated that he was to be taken into the firm. He was twenty-seven now, a little heavy without being definitely stout, and with a manner older than his years. Old people and young people liked him and trusted him, and mothers felt safe when their daughters were in his charge, for he had a way, when he came into a room, of putting himself on a footing with the oldest and most conservative people there. "You and I," he seemed to say, "we're solid. We understand."

He had an instinctive and rather charitable knowledge of the weaknesses of men and women, and, like a priest, it made him the more concerned for the maintenance of outward forms. It was typical of him that every Sunday morning he taught in a fashionable Episcopal Sunday-school—even though a cold shower and a quick change into a cutaway coat were all that separated him from the wild night before.

After his father's death he was the practical head of his family, and, in effect, guided the destinies of the younger children. Through a complication his authority did not extend to his father's estate, which was administrated by his Uncle Robert, who was the horsey member of the family, a good-natured, hard-drinking member of that set which centres about Wheatley Hills.

Uncle Robert and his wife, Edna, had been great friends of Anson's youth, and the former was disappointed when his nephew's superiority failed to take a horsey form. He backed him for a city club which was the most difficult in America to enter—one could only join if one's family had "helped to build up New York" (or, in other words, were rich before 1880)—and when Anson, after his election, neglected it for the Yale Club, Uncle Robert gave him a little talk on the subject. But when on top of that Anson declined to enter Robert Hunter's own conservative and somewhat neglected brokerage house, his manner grew cooler. Like a primary teacher who has taught all he knew, he slipped out of Anson's life.

There were so many friends in Anson's life—scarcely one for whom he had not done some unusual kindness and scarcely one whom he did not occasionally embarrass by his bursts of rough conversation or his habit of getting drunk whenever and however he liked. It annoyed him when any one else blundered in that regard—

about his own lapses he was always humorous. Odd things happened to him and he told them with infectious laughter.

I was working in New York that spring, and I used to lunch with him at the Yale Club, which my university was sharing until the completion of our own. I had read of Paula's marriage, and one afternoon, when I asked him about her, something moved him to tell me the story. After that he frequently invited me to family dinners at his house and behaved as though there was a special relation between us, as though with his confidence a little of that consuming memory had passed into me.

I found that despite the trusting mothers, his attitude toward girls was not indiscriminately protective. It was up to the girl—if she showed an inclination toward looseness, she must take care of herself, even with him.

"Life," he would explain sometimes, "has made a cynic of me."

By life he meant Paula. Sometimes, especially when he was drinking, it became a little twisted in his mind, and he thought that she had callously thrown him over.

This "cynicism," or rather his realization that naturally fast girls were not worth sparing, led to his affair with Dolly Karger. It wasn't his only affair in those years, but it came nearest to touching him deeply, and it had a profound effect upon his attitude toward life.

Dolly was the daughter of a notorious "publicist" who had married into society. She herself grew up into the Junior League, came out at the Plaza, and went to the Assembly; and only a few old families like the Hunters could question whether or not she "belonged," for her picture was often in the papers, and she had more enviable attention than many girls who undoubtedly did. She was dark-haired, with carmine lips and a high, lovely color, which she concealed under pinkish-gray powder all through the first year out, because high color was unfashionable—Victorian-pale was the thing to be. She wore black, severe suits and stood with her hands in her pockets leaning a little forward, with a humorous restraint on her face. She danced exquisitely—better than anything she liked to dance—better than anything except making love. Since she was ten she had always been in love, and, usually, with some boy who didn't respond to her. Those who did—and there were many—bored her after a brief encounter, but for her failures she reserved the warmest spot in her heart. When she met them she would always try once more—sometimes she succeeded, more often she failed.

It never occurred to this gypsy of the unattainable that there was a certain resemblance in those who refused to love her—they shared a hard intuition that saw through to her weakness, not a weakness of emotion but a weakness of rudder. Anson perceived this when he first met her, less than a month after Paula's marriage. He was drinking rather heavily, and he pretended for a week that he was falling in love with her. Then he dropped her abruptly and forgot—immediately he took up the commanding position in her heart.

Like so many girls of that day Dolly was slackly and indiscreetly wild. The unconventionality of a slightly older generation had been simply one facet of a post-war movement to discredit obsolete manners—Dolly's was both older and shabbier, and she saw in Anson the two extremes which the emotionally shiftless woman seeks, an abandon to indulgence alternating with a protective strength. In his character she felt both the sybarite and the solid rock, and these two satisfied every need of her nature.

She felt that it was going to be difficult, but she mistook the reason —she thought that Anson and his family expected a more spectacular marriage, but she guessed immediately that her advantage lay in his tendency to drink.

They met at the large débutante dances, but as her infatuation increased they managed to be more and more together. Like most mothers, Mrs. Karger believed that Anson was exceptionally reliable, so she allowed Dolly to go with him him to distant country clubs and suburban houses without inquiring closely into their activities or questioning her explanations when they came in late. At first these explanations might have been accurate, but Dolly's worldly ideas of capturing Anson were soon engulfed in the rising sweep of her emotion. Kisses in the back of taxis and motor-cars were no longer enough; they did a curious thing:

They dropped out of their world for a while and made another world just beneath it where Anson's tippling and Dolly's irregular hours would be less noticed and commented on. It was composed, this world, of varying elements—several of Anson's Yale friends and their wives, two or three young brokers and bond salesmen and a handful of unattached men, fresh from college, with money and a propensity to dissipation. What this world lacked in spaciousness and scale it made up for by allowing them a liberty that it scarcely permitted itself. Moreover, it centred around them and permitted Dolly the pleasure of a faint condescension—a pleasure which Anson, whose whole life was a condescension from the certitudes of his childhood, was unable to share.

He was not in love with her, and in the long feverish winter of their affair he frequently told her so. In the spring he was weary— he wanted to renew his life at some other source—moreover, he saw that either he must break with her now or accept the responsibility of a definite seduction. Her family's encouraging attitude precipitated his decision—one evening when Mr. Karger knocked discreetly at the library door to announce that he had left a bottle of old brandy in the dining-room, Anson felt that life was hemming him in. That night he wrote her a short letter in which he told her that he was going on his vacation, and that in view of all the circumstances they had better meet no more.

It was June. His family had closed up the house and gone to the country, so he was living temporarily at the Yale Club. I had heard about his affair with Dolly as it developed—accounts salted with humor, for he despised unstable women, and granted them no place in the social edifice in which he believed—and when he told me that night that he was definitely breaking with her I was glad. I had seen Dolly here and there, and each time with a feeling of pity at the hopelessness of her struggle, and of shame at knowing so much about her that I had no right to know. She was what is known as "a pretty little thing," but there was a certain recklessness which rather fascinated me. Her dedication to the goddess of waste would have been less obvious had she been less spirited—she would most certainly throw herself away, but I was glad when I heard that the sacrifice would not be consummated in my sight.

Anson was going to leave the letter of farewell at her house next morning. It was one of the few houses left open in the Fifth Avenue

district, and he knew that the Kargers, acting upon erroneous information from Dolly, had foregone a trip abroad to give their daughter her chance. As he stepped out the door of the Yale Club into
Madison Avenue the postman passed him, and he followed back
inside. The first letter that caught his eye was in Dolly's hand.

He knew what it would be—a lonely and tragic monologue, full
of the reproaches he knew, the invoked memories, the "I wonder
if's"—all the immemorial intimacies that he had communicated to
Paula Legendre in what seemed another age. Thumbing over some
bills, he brought it on top again and opened it. To his surprise it was
a short, somewhat formal note, which said that Dolly would be unable to go to the country with him for the week-end, because Perry
Hull from Chicago had unexpectedly come to town. It added that
Anson had brought this on himself: "— if I felt that you loved me
as I love you I would go with you at any time, any place, but Perry
is *so* nice, and he so much wants me to marry him——"

Anson smiled contemptuously—he had had experience with such
decoy epistles. Moreover, he knew how Dolly had labored over this
plan, probably sent for the faithful Perry and calculated the time of
his arrival—even labored over the note so that it would make him
jealous without driving him away. Like most compromises, it had
neither force nor vitality but only a timorous despair.

Suddenly he was angry. He sat down in the lobby and read it
again. Then he went to the phone, called Dolly and told her in his
clear, compelling voice that he had received her note and would call
for her at five o'clock as they had previously planned. Scarcely waiting for the pretended uncertainty of her "Perhaps I can see you for
an hour," he hung up the receiver and went down to his office. On
the way he tore his own letter into bits and dropped it in the street.

He was not jealous—she meant nothing to him—but at her pathetic ruse everything stubborn and self-indulgent in him came to
the surface. It was a presumption from a mental inferior and it could
not be overlooked. If she wanted to know to whom she belonged she
would see.

He was on the door-step at quarter past five. Dolly was dressed
for the street, and he listened in silence to the paragraph of "I can
only see you for an hour," which she had begun on the phone.

"Put on your hat, Dolly," he said, "we'll take a walk."

They strolled up Madison Avenue and over to Fifth while Anson's shirt dampened upon his portly body in the deep heat. He talked little, scolding her, making no love to her, but before they had walked six blocks she was his again, apologizing for the note, offering not to see Perry at all as an atonement, offering anything. She thought that he had come because he was beginning to love her.

"I'm hot," he said when they reached 71st Street. "This is a winter suit. If I stop by the house and change, would you mind waiting for me down-stairs? I'll only be a minute."

She was happy; the intimacy of his being hot, of any physical fact about him, thrilled her. When they came to the iron-grated door and Anson took out his key she experienced a sort of delight.

Down-stairs it was dark, and after he ascended in the lift Dolly raised a curtain and looked out through opaque lace at the houses over the way. She heard the lift machinery stop, and with the notion of teasing him pressed the button that brought it down. Then on what was more than an impulse she got into it and sent it up to what she guessed was his floor.

"Anson," she called, laughing a little.

"Just a minute," he answered from his bedroom . . . then after a brief delay: "Now you can come in."

He had changed and was buttoning his vest.

"This is my room," he said lightly. "How do you like it?"

She caught sight of Paula's picture on the wall and stared at it in fascination, just as Paula had stared at the pictures of Anson's childish sweethearts five years before. She knew something about Paula —sometimes she tortured herself with fragments of the story.

Suddenly she came close to Anson, raising her arms. They embraced. Outside the area window a soft artificial twilight already hovered, though the sun was still bright on a back roof across the way. In half an hour the room would be quite dark. The uncalculated opportunity overwhelmed them, made them both breathless, and they clung more closely. It was imminent, inevitable. Still holding one another, they raised their heads—their eyes fell together upon Paula's picture, staring down at them from the wall.

Suddenly Anson dropped his arms, and sitting down at his desk
tried the drawer with a bunch of keys.

"Like a drink?" he asked in a gruff voice.

"No, Anson."

He poured himself half a tumbler of whiskey, swallowed it, and
then opened the door into the hall.

"Come on," he said.

Dolly hesitated.

"Anson—I'm going to the country with you tonight, after all. You
understand that, don't you?"

"Of course," he answered brusquely.

In Dolly's car they rode on to Long Island, closer in their emotions than they had ever been before. They knew what would happen—not with Paula's face to remind them that something was
lacking, but when they were alone in the still, hot Long Island
night they did not care.

The estate in Port Washington where they were to spend the week-
end belonged to a cousin of Anson's who had married a Montana
copper operator. An interminable drive began at the lodge and
twisted under imported poplar saplings toward a huge, pink Spanish
house. Anson had often visited there before.

After dinner they danced at the Linx Club. About midnight Anson
assured himself that his cousins would not leave before two—then
he explained that Dolly was tired; he would take her home and return to the dance later. Trembling a little with excitement, they got
into a borrowed car together and drove to Port Washington. As they
reached the lodge he stopped and spoke to the night-watchman.

"When are you making a round, Carl?"

"Right away."

"Then you'll be here till everybody's in?"

"Yes, sir."

"All right. Listen: if any automobile, no matter whose it is, turns
in at this gate, I want you to phone the house immediately." He put
a five-dollar bill into Carl's hand. "Is that clear?"

"Yes, Mr. Anson." Being of the Old World, he neither winked
nor smiled. Yet Dolly sat with her face turned slightly away.

Anson had a key. Once inside he poured a drink for both of them
—Dolly left hers untouched—then he ascertained definitely the location of the phone, and found that it was within easy hearing distance
of their rooms, both of which were on the first floor.

Five minutes later he knocked at the door of Dolly's room.

"Anson?" He went in, closing the door behind him. She was in
bed, leaning up anxiously with elbows on the pillow; sitting beside
her he took her in his arms.

"Anson, darling."

He didn't answer.

"Anson. . . . Anson! I love you. . . . Say you love me. Say it now—
can't you say it now? Even if you don't mean it?"

He did not listen. Over her head he perceived that the picture of
Paula was hanging here upon this wall.

He got up and went close to it. The frame gleamed faintly with
thrice-reflected moonlight—within was a blurred shadow of a face
that he saw he did not know. Almost sobbing, he turned around and
stared with abomination at the little figure on the bed.

"This is all foolishness," he said thickly. "I don't know what I was
thinking about. I don't love you and you'd better wait for somebody
that loves you. I don't love you a bit, can't you understand?"

His voice broke, and he went hurriedly out. Back in the salon he
was pouring himself a drink with uneasy fingers, when the front door
opened suddenly, and his cousin came in.

"Why, Anson, I hear Dolly's sick," she began solicitously. "I hear
she's sick. . . ."

"It was nothing," he interrupted, raising his voice so that it would
carry into Dolly's room. "She was a little tired. She went to bed."

For a long time afterward Anson believed that a protective God
sometimes interfered in human affairs. But Dolly Karger, lying
awake and staring at the ceiling, never again believed in anything
at all.

VI

When Dolly married during the following autumn, Anson was
in London on business. Like Paula's marriage, it was sudden, but

it affected him in a different way. At first he felt that it was funny, and had an inclination to laugh when he thought of it. Later it depressed him—it made him feel old.

There was something repetitive about it—why, Paula and Dolly had belonged to different generations. He had a foretaste of the sensation of a man of forty who hears that the daughter of an old flame has married. He wired congratulations and, as was not the case with Paula, they were sincere—he had never really hoped that Paula would be happy.

When he returned to New York, he was made a partner in the firm, and, as his responsibilities increased, he had less time on his hands. The refusal of a life-insurance company to issue him a policy made such an impression on him that he stopped drinking for a year, and claimed that he felt better physically, though I think he missed the convivial recounting of those Celliniesque adventures which, in his early twenties, had played such a part in his life. But he never abandoned the Yale Club. He was a figure there, a personality, and the tendency of his class, who were now seven years out of college, to drift away to more sober haunts was checked by his presence.

His day was never too full nor his mind too weary to give any sort of aid to anyone who asked it. What had been done at first through pride and superiority had become a habit and a passion. And there was always something—a younger brother in trouble at New Haven, a quarrel to be patched up between a friend and his wife, a position to be found for this man, an investment for that. But his specialty was the solving of problems for young married people. Young married people fascinated him and their apartments were almost sacred to him—he knew the story of their love-affair, advised them where to live and how, and remembered their babies' names. Toward young wives his attitude was circumspect: he never abused the trust which their husbands—strangely enough in view of his unconcealed irregularities—invariably reposed in him.

He came to take a vicarious pleasure in happy marriages, and to be inspired to an almost equally pleasant melancholy by those that went astray. Not a season passed that he did not witness the collapse of an affair that perhaps he himself had fathered. When Paula was divorced and almost immediately remarried to another Bostonian, he talked about her to me all one afternoon. He would never love any one as he had loved Paula, but he insisted that he no longer cared.

"I'll never marry," he came to say; "I've seen too much of it, and I know a happy marriage is a very rare thing. Besides, I'm too old."

But he did believe in marriage. Like all men who spring from a happy and successful marriage, he believed in it passionately— nothing he had seen would change his belief, his cynicism dissolved upon it like air. But he did really believe he was too old. At twenty-eight he began to accept with equanimity the prospect of marrying without romantic love; he resolutely chose a New York girl of his own class, pretty, intelligent, congenial, above reproach—and set about falling in love with her. The things he had said to Paula with sincerity, to other girls with grace, he could no longer say at all without smiling, or with the force necessary to convince.

"When I'm forty," he told his friends, "I'll be ripe. I'll fall for some chorus girl like the rest."

Nevertheless, he persisted in his attempt. His mother wanted to see him married, and he could now well afford it—he had a seat on the Stock Exchange, and his earned income came to twenty-five thousand a year. The idea was agreeable: when his friends—he spent most of his time with the set he and Dolly had evolved—closed themselves in behind domestic doors at night, he no longer rejoiced in his freedom. He even wondered if he should have married Dolly. Not even Paula had loved him more, and he was learning the rarity, in a single life, of encountering true emotion.

Just as this mood began to creep over him a disquieting story reached his ear. His Aunt Edna, a woman just this side of forty, was carrying on an open intrigue with a dissolute, hard-drinking young man named Cary Sloane. Every one knew of it except Anson's Uncle Robert, who for fifteen years had talked long in clubs and taken his wife for granted.

Anson heard the story again and again with increasing annoyance. Something of his old feeling for his uncle came back to him, a feeling that was more than personal, a reversion toward that family solidarity on which he had based his pride. His intuition singled out the essential point of the affair, which was that his uncle shouldn't be hurt. It was his first experiment in unsolicited meddling, but with his knowledge of Edna's character he felt that he could handle the matter better than a district judge or his uncle.

His uncle was in Hot Springs. Anson traced down the sources of the scandal so that there should be no possibility of mistake and then he called Edna and asked her to lunch with him at the Plaza next day. Something in his tone must have frightened her, for she was reluctant, but he insisted, putting off the date until she had no excuse for refusing.

She met him at the appointed time in the Plaza lobby, a lovely, faded, gray-eyed blonde in a coat of Russian sable. Five great rings, cold with diamonds and emeralds, sparkled on her slender hands. It occurred to Anson that it was his father's intelligence and not his uncle's that had earned the fur and the stones, the rich brilliance that buoyed up her passing beauty.

Though Edna scented his hostility, she was unprepared for the directness of his approach.

"Edna, I'm astonished at the way you've been acting," he said in a strong, frank voice. "At first I couldn't believe it."

"Believe what?" she demanded sharply.

"You needn't pretend with me, Edna. I'm talking about Cary Sloane. Aside from any other consideration, I didn't think you could treat Uncle Robert——"

"Now look here, Anson——" she began angrily, but his peremptory voice broke through hers:

"——and your children in such a way. You've been married eighteen years, and you're old enough to know better."

"You can't talk to me like that! You——"

"Yes, I can. Uncle Robert has always been my best friend." He was tremendously moved. He felt a real distress about his uncle, about his three young cousins.

Edna stood up, leaving her crab-flake cocktail untasted.

"This is the silliest thing——"

"Very well, if you won't listen to me I'll go to Uncle Robert and tell him the whole story—he's bound to hear it sooner or later. And afterward I'll go to old Moses Sloane."

Edna faltered back into her chair.

"Don't talk so loud," she begged him. Her eyes blurred with tears. "You have no idea how your voice carries. You might have chosen a less public place to make all these crazy accusations."

He didn't answer.

"Oh, you never liked me, I know," she went on. "You're just taking advantage of some silly gossip to try and break up the only interesting friendship I've ever had. What did I ever do to make you hate me so?"

Still Anson waited. There would be the appeal to his chivalry, then to his pity, finally to his superior sophistication—when he had shouldered his way through all these there would be admissions, and he could come to grips with her. By being silent, by being impervious, by returnig constantly to his main weapon, which was his own true emotion, he bullied her into frantic despair as the luncheon hour slipped away. At two o'clock she took out a mirror and a handkerchief, shined away the marks of her tears and powdered the slight hollows where they had lain. She had agreed to meet him at her own house at five.

When he arrived she was stretched on a *chaise-longue* which was covered with cretonne for the summer, and the tears he had called up at luncheon seemed still to be standing in her eyes. Then he was aware of Cary Sloane's dark anxious presence upon the cold hearth.

"What's this idea of yours?" broke out Sloane immediately. "I understand you invited Edna to lunch and then threatened her on the basis of some cheap scandal."

Anson sat down.

"I have no reason to think it's only scandal."

"I hear you're going to take it to Robert Hunter, and to my father."

Anson nodded.

"Either you break it off—or I will," he said.

"What God damned business is it of yours, Hunter?"

"Don't lose your temper, Cary," said Edna nervously. "It's only a question of showing him how absurd——"

"For one thing, it's my name that's being handed around," interrupted Anson. "That's all that concerns you, Cary."

"Edna isn't a member of your family."

"She most certainly is!" His anger mounted. "Why—she owes this house and the rings on her fingers to my father's brains. When Uncle Robert married her she didn't have a penny."

They all looked at the rings as if they had a significant bearing on the situation. Edna made a gesture to take them from her hand.

"I guess they're not the only rings in the world," said Sloane.

"Oh, this is absurd," cried Edna. "Anson, will you listen to me? I've found out how the silly story started. It was a maid I discharged who went right to the Chilicheffs—all these Russians pump things out of their servants and then put a false meaning on them." She brought down her fist angrily on the table: "And after Robert lent them the limousine for a whole month when we were South last winter——"

"Do you see?" demanded Sloane eagerly. "This maid got hold of the wrong end of the thing. She knew that Edna and I were friends, and she carried it to the Chilicheffs. In Russia they assume that if a man and a woman——"

He enlarged the theme to a disquisition upon social relations in the Caucasus.

"If that's the case it better be explained to Uncle Robert," said Anson dryly, "so that when the rumors do reach him he'll know they're not true."

Adopting the method he had followed with Edna at luncheon he let them explain it all away. He knew that they were guilty and that presently they would cross the line from explanation into justification and convict themselves more definitely than he could ever do. By seven they had taken the desperate step of telling him the truth—Robert Hunter's neglect, Edna's empty life, the casual dalliance that had flamed up into passion—but like so many true stories it had the misfortune of being old, and its enfeebled body beat helplessly against the armor of Anson's will. The threat to go to Sloane's father

sealed their helplessness, for the latter, a retired cotton broker out
of Alabama, was a notorious fundamentalist who controlled his son
by a rigid allowance and the promise that at his next vagary the
allowance would stop forever.

They dined at a small French restaurant, and the discussion continued—at one time Sloane resorted to physical threats, a little later
they were both imploring him to give them time. But Anson was
obdurate. He saw that Edna was breaking up, and that her spirit
must not be refreshed by any renewal of their passion.

At two o'clock in a small night-club on 53d Street, Edna's nerves
suddenly collapsed, and she cried to go home. Sloane had been drinking heavily all evening, and he was faintly maudlin, leaning on the
table and weeping a little with his face in his hands. Quickly Anson
gave them his terms. Sloane was to leave town for six months, and
he must be gone within forty-eight hours. When he returned there
must be no resumption of the affair, but at the end of a year Edna
might, if she wished, tell Robert Hunter that she wanted a divorce
and go about it in the usual way.

He paused, gaining confidence from their faces for his final word.

"Or there's another thing you can do," he said slowly, "if Edna
wants to leave her children, there's nothing I can do to prevent your
running off together."

"I want to go home!" cried Edna again. "Oh, haven't you done
enough to us for one day?"

Outside it was dark, save for a blurred glow from Sixth Avenue
down the street. In that light those two who had been lovers looked
for the last time into each other's tragic faces, realizing that between
them there was not enough youth and strength to avert their eternal
parting. Sloane walked suddenly off down the street and Anson
tapped a dozing taxi-driver on the arm.

It was almost four; there was a patient flow of cleaning water
along the ghostly pavement of Fifth Avenue, and the shadows of
two night women flitted over the dark façade of St. Thomas's church.
Then the desolate shrubbery of Central Park where Anson had often
played as a child, and the mounting numbers, significant as names,
of the marching streets. This was his city, he thought, where his

name had flourished through five generations. No change could alter the permanence of its place here, for change itself was the essential substratum by which he and those of his name identified themselves with the spirit of New York. Resourcefulness and a powerful will— for his threats to weaker hands would have been less than nothing— had beaten the gathering dust from his uncle's name, from the name of his family, from even this shivering figure that sat beside him in the car.

Cary Sloane's body was found next morning on the lower shelf of a pillar of Queensboro Bridge. In the darkness and in his excitement he had thought that it was the water flowing black beneath him, but in less than a second it made no possible difference—unless he had planned to think one last thought of Edna, and call out her name as he struggled feebly in the water.

VII

Anson never blamed himself for his part in this affair—the situation which brought it about had not been of his making. But the just suffer with the unjust, and he found that his oldest and somehow his most precious friendship was over. He never knew what distorted story Edna told, but he was welcome in his uncle's house no longer.

Just before Christmas Mrs. Hunter retired to a select Episcopal heaven, and Anson became the responsible head of his family. An unmarried aunt who had lived with them for years ran the house, and attempted with helpless inefficiency to chaperone the younger girls. All the children were less self-reliant than Anson, more conventional both in their virtues and in their shortcomings. Mrs. Hunter's death had postponed the début of one daughter and the wedding of another. Also it had taken something deeply material from all of them, for with her passing the quiet, expensive superiority of the Hunters came to an end.

For one thing, the estate, considerably diminished by two inheritance taxes and soon to be divided among six children, was not a notable fortune any more. Anson saw a tendency in his youngest sisters to speak rather respectfully of families that hadn't "existed" twenty years ago. His own feeling of precedence was not echoed in them—sometimes they were conventionally snobbish, that was all. For another thing, this was the last summer they would spend on the Connecticut estate; the clamor against it was too loud: "Who wants to waste the best months of the year shut up in that dead old town?" Reluctantly he yielded—the house would go into the market in the fall, and next summer they would rent a smaller place in Westchester County. It was a step down from the expensive simplicity of his father's idea, and, while he sympathized with the revolt, it also annoyed him; during his mother's lifetime he had gone up there at least every other week-end—even in the gayest summers.

Yet he himself was part of this change, and his strong instinct for life had turned him in his twenties from the hollow obsequies of that abortive leisure class. He did not see this clearly—he still felt that there was a norm, a standard of society. But there was no norm, it was doubtful if there ever had been a true norm in New York. The few who still paid and fought to enter a particular set succeeded only to find that as a society it scarcely functioned—or, what was more alarming, that the Bohemia from which they fled sat above them at table.

At twenty-nine Anson's chief concern was his own growing loneliness. He was sure now that he would never marry. The number of weddings at which he had officiated as best man or usher was past all counting—there was a drawer at home that bulged with the official neckties of this or that wedding-party, neckties standing for romances that had not endured a year, for couples who had passed completely from his life. Scarf-pins, gold pencils, cuff-buttons, presents from a generation of grooms had passed through his jewel-box and been lost—and with every ceremony he was less and less able to imagine himself in the groom's place. Under his hearty good-will toward all those marriages there was despair about his own.

And as he neared thirty he became not a little depressed at the inroads that marriage, especially lately, had made upon his friendships. Groups of people had a disconcerting tendency to dissolve and disappear. The men from his own college—and it was upon them he had expended the most time and affection—were the most elusive of all. Most of them were drawn deep into domesticity, two were dead, one lived abroad, one was in Hollywood writing continuities for pictures that Anson went faithfully to see.

Most of them, however, were permanent commuters with an intricate family life centring around some suburban country club, and it was from these that he felt his estrangement most keenly.

In the early days of their married life they had all needed him; he gave them advice about their slim finances, he exorcised their doubts about the advisability of bringing a baby into two rooms and a bath, especially he stood for the great world outside. But now their financial troubles were in the past and the fearfully expected child had evolved into an absorbing family. They were always glad to see old Anson, but they dressed up for him and tried to impress him with their present importance, and kept their troubles to themselves. They needed him no longer.

A few weeks before his thirtieth birthday the last of his early and intimate friends was married. Anson acted in his usual rôle of best man, gave his usual silver tea-service, and went down to the usual *Homeric* to say good-by. It was a hot Friday afternoon in May, and as he walked from the pier he realized that Saturday closing had begun and he was free until Monday morning.

"Go where?" he asked himself.

The Yale Club, of course; bridge until dinner, then four or five raw cocktails in somebody's room and a pleasant confused evening. He regretted that this afternoon's groom wouldn't be along—they had always been able to cram so much into such nights: they knew how to attach women and how to get rid of them, how much consideration any girl deserved from their intelligent hedonism. A party was an adjusted thing—you took certain girls to certain places and spent just so much on their amusement; you drank a little, not much, more than you ought to drink, and at a certain time in the morning you stood up and said you were going home. You avoided college boys, sponges, future engagements, fights, sentiment, and indiscretions. That was the way it was done. All the rest was dissipation.

In the morning you were never violently sorry—you made no resolutions, but if you had overdone it and your heart was slightly out of order, you went on the wagon for a few days without saying anything about it, and waited until an accumulation of nervous boredom projected you into another party.

The lobby of the Yale Club was unpopulated. In the bar three very young alumni looked up at him, momentarily and without curiosity.

"Hello, there, Oscar," he said to the bartender. "Mr. Cahill been around this afternoon?"

"Mr. Cahill's gone to New Haven."

"Oh . . . that so?"

"Gone to the ball game. Lot of men gone up."

Anson looked once again into the lobby, considered for a moment, and then walked out and over to Fifth Avenue. From the broad window of one of his clubs—one that he had scarcely visited in five years—a gray man with watery eyes stared down at him. Anson looked quickly away—that figure sitting in vacant resignation, in supercilious solitude, depressed him. He stopped and, retracing his steps, started over 47th Street toward Teak Warden's apartment. Teak and his wife had once been his most familiar friends—it was a household where he and Dolly Karger had been used to go in the days of their affair. But Teak had taken to drink, and his wife had remarked publicly that Anson was a bad influence on him. The remark reached Anson in an exaggerated form—when it was finally cleared up, the delicate spell of intimacy was broken, never to be renewed.

"Is Mr. Warden at home?" he inquired.

"They've gone to the country."

The fact unexpectedly cut at him. They were gone to the country and he hadn't known. Two years before he would have known the date, the hour, come up at the last moment for a final drink, and planned his first visit to them. Now they had gone without a word.

Anson looked at his watch and considered a week-end with his family, but the only train was a local that would jolt through the aggressive heat for three hours. And to-morrow in the country, and Sunday—he was in no mood for porch-bridge with polite undergraduates, and dancing after dinner at a rural roadhouse, a diminutive of gaiety which his father had estimated too well.

"Oh, no," he said to himself. . . . "No."

He was a dignified, impressive young man, rather stout now, but otherwise unmarked by dissipation. He could have been cast for a pillar of something—at times you were sure it was not society, at others nothing else—for the law, for the church. He stood for a few minutes motionless on the sidewalk in front of a 47th Street apartment-house; for almost the first time in his life he had nothing whatever to do.

Then he began to walk briskly up Fifth Avenue, as if he had just been reminded of an important engagement there. The necessity of dissimulation is one of the few characteristics that we share with dogs, and I think of Anson on that day as some well-bred specimen who had been disappointed at a familiar back door. He was going to see Nick, once a fashionable bartender in demand at all private dances, and now employed in cooling non-alcoholic champagne among the labyrinthine cellars of the Plaza Hotel.

"Nick," he said, "what's happened to everything?"

"Dead," Nick said.

"Make me a whiskey sour." Anson handed a pint bottle over the counter. "Nick, the girls are different; I had a little girl in Brooklyn and she got married last week without letting me know."

"That a fact? Ha-ha-ha," responded Nick diplomatically. "Slipped it over on you."

"Absolutely," said Anson. "And I was out with her the night before."

"Ha-ha-ha," said Nick, "ha-ha-ha!"

"Do you remember the wedding, Nick, in Hot Springs where I had the waiters and the musicians singing 'God save the King'?"

"Now where was that, Mr. Hunter?" Nick concentrated doubtfully. "Seems to me that was———"

"Next time they were back for more, and I began to wonder how much I'd paid them," continued Anson.

"———seems to me that was at Mr. Trenholm's wedding."

"Don't know him," said Anson decisively. He was offended that a strange name should intrude upon his reminiscences; Nick perceived this.

"Na—aw—" he admitted, "I ought to know that. It was one of *your* crowd—Brakins . . . Baker——"

"Bicker Backer," said Anson responsively. "They put me in a hearse after it was over and covered me up with flowers and drove me away."

"Ha-ha-ha," said Nick. "Ha-ha-ha."

Nick's simulation of the old family servant paled presently and Anson went up-stairs to the lobby. He looked around—his eyes met the glance of an unfamiliar clerk at the desk, then fell upon a flower from the morning's marriage hesitating in the mouth of a brass cuspidor. He went out and walked slowly toward the blood-red sun over Columbus Circle. Suddenly he turned around and, retracing his steps to the Plaza, immured himself in a telephone-booth.

Later he said that he tried to get me three times that afternoon, that he tried every one who might be in New York—men and girls he had not seen for years, an artist's model of his college days whose faded number was still in his address book—Central told him that even the exchange existed no longer. At length his quest roved into the country, and he held brief disappointing conversations with emphatic butlers and maids. So-and-so was out, riding, swimming, playing golf, sailed to Europe last week. Who shall I say phoned?

It was intolerable that he should pass the evening alone—the private reckonings which one plans for a moment of leisure lose every charm when the solitude is enforced. There were always women of a sort, but the ones he knew had temporarily vanished, and to pass a New York evening in the hired company of a stranger never occurred to him—he would have considered that that was something shameful and secret, the diversion of a travelling salesman in a strange town.

Anson paid the telephone bill—the girl tried unsuccessfully to joke with him about its size—and for the second time that afternoon started to leave the Plaza and go he knew not where. Near the revolving door the figure of a woman, obviously with child, stood sideways to the light—a sheer beige cape fluttered at her shoulders when the door turned and, each time, she looked impatiently toward it as if she were weary of waiting. At the first sight of her a strong nervous thrill of familiarity went over him, but not until he was within five feet of her did he realize that it was Paula.

"Why, Anson Hunter!"

His heart turned over.

"Why, Paula——"

"Why, this is wonderful. I can't believe it, *Anson!*"

She took both his hands, and he saw in the freedom of the gesture that the memory of him had lost poignancy to her. But not to him— he felt that old mood that she evoked in him stealing over his brain, that gentleness with which he had always met her optimism as if afraid to mar its surface.

"We're at Rye for the summer. Pete had to come East on busi- ness—you know of course I'm Mrs. Peter Hagerty now—so we brought the children and took a house. You've got to come out and see us."

"Can I?" he asked directly. "When?"

"When you like. Here's Pete." The revolving door functioned, giving up a fine tall man of thirty with a tanned face and a trim mustache. His immaculate fitness made a sharp contrast with Anson's increasing bulk, which was obvious under the faintly tight cut-away coat.

"You oughtn't to be standing," said Hagerty to his wife. "Let's sit down here." He indicated lobby chairs, but Paula hesitated.

"I've got to go right home," she said. "Anson, why don't you— why don't you come out and have dinner with us to-night? We're just getting settled, but if you can stand that——"

Hagerty confirmed the invitation cordially.

"Come out for the night."

Their car waited in front of the hotel, and Paula with a tired gesture sank back against silk cushions in the corner.

"There's so much I want to talk to you about," she said, "it seems hopeless."

"I want to hear about you."

"Well"—she smiled at Hagerty—"that would take a long time too. I have three children—by my first marriage. The oldest is five, then four, then three." She smiled again. "I didn't waste much time having them, did I?"

"Boys?"

"A boy and two girls. Then—oh, a lot of things happened, and I got a divorce in Paris a year ago and married Pete. That's all—except that I'm awfully happy."

In Rye they drove up to a large house near the Beach Club, from which there issued presently three dark, slim children who broke from an English governess and approached them with an esoteric cry. Abstractedly and with difficulty Paula took each one into her arms, a caress which they accepted stiffly, as they had evidently been told not to bump into Mummy. Even against their fresh faces Paula's skin showed scarcely any weariness—for all her physical languor she seemed younger than when he had last seen her at Palm Beach seven years ago.

At dinner she was preoccupied, and afterward, during the homage to the radio, she lay with closed eyes on the sofa, until Anson wondered if his presence at this time was not an intrusion. But at nine o'clock, when Hagerty rose and said pleasantly that he was going to leave them by themselves for a while, she began to talk slowly about herself and the past.

"My first baby," she said—"the one we call Darling, the biggest little girl—I wanted to die when I knew I was going to have her, because Lowell was like a stranger to me. It didn't seem as though she could be my own. I wrote you a letter and tore it up. Oh, you were *so* bad to me, Anson."

It was the dialogue again, rising and falling. Anson felt a sudden quickening of memory.

"Weren't you engaged once?" she asked— "a girl named Dolly something?"

"I wasn't ever engaged. I tried to be engaged, but I never loved anybody but you, Paula."

"Oh," she said. Then after a moment: "This baby is the first one I ever really wanted. You see, I'm in love now—at last."

He didn't answer, shocked at the treachery of her remembrance. She must have seen that the "at last" bruised him, for she continued:

"I was infatuated with you, Anson—you could make me do anything you liked. But we wouldn't have been happy. I'm not smart enough for you. I don't like things to be complicated like you do." She paused. "You'll never settle down," she said.

The phrase struck at him from behind—it was an accusation that of all accusations he had never merited.

"I could settle down if women were different," he said. "If I didn't understand so much about them, if women didn't spoil you for other women, if they had only a little pride. If I could go to sleep for a while and wake up into a home that was really mine— why, that's what I'm made for, Paula, that's what women have seen in me and liked in me. It's only that I can't get through the preliminaries any more."

Hagerty came in a little before eleven; after a whiskey Paula stood up and announced that she was going to bed. She went over and stood by her husband.

"Where did you go, dearest?" she demanded.

"I had a drink with Ed Saunders."

"I was worried. I thought maybe you'd run away."

She rested her head against his coat.

"He's sweet, isn't he, Anson?" she demanded.

"Absolutely," said Anson, laughing.

She raised her face to her husband.

"Well, I'm ready," she said. She turned to Anson: "Do you want to see our family gymnastic stunt?"

"Yes," he said in an interested voice.

"All right. Here we go!"

Hagerty picked her up easily in his arms.

"This is called the family acrobatic stunt," said Paula. "He carries me up-stairs. Isn't it sweet of him?"

"Yes," said Anson.

Hagerty bent his head slightly until his face touched Paula's.

"And I love him," she said. "I've just been telling you, haven't I, Anson?"

"Yes," he said.

"He's the dearest thing that ever lived in this world; aren't you, darling? . . . Well, good night. Here we go. Isn't he strong?"

"Yes," Anson said.

"You'll find a pair of Pete's pajamas laid out for you. Sweet dreams—see you at breakfast."

"Yes," said Anson.

VIII

The older members of the firm insisted that Anson should go abroad for the summer. He had scarcely had a vacation in seven years, they said. He was stale and needed a change. Anson resisted.

"If I go," he declared, "I won't come back any more."

"That's absurd, old man. You'll be back in three months with all this depression gone. Fit as ever."

"No." He shook his head stubbornly. "If I stop, I won't go back to work. If I stop, that means I've given up—I'm through."

"We'll take a chance on that. Stay six months if you like—we're not afraid you'll leave us. Why, you'd be miserable if you didn't work."

They arranged his passage for him. They liked Anson—every one liked Anson—and the change that had been coming over him cast a sort of pall over the office. The enthusiasm that had invariably signalled up business, the consideration toward his equals and his inferiors, the lift of his vital presence—within the past four months his intense nervousness had melted down these qualities into the fussy pessimism of a man of forty. On every transaction in which he was involved he acted as a drag and a strain.

"If I go I'll never come back," he said.

Three days before he sailed Paula Legendre Hagerty died in childbirth. I was with him a great deal then, for we were crossing together, but for the first time in our friendship he told me not a word of how he felt, nor did I see the slightest sign of emotion. His chief preoccupation was with the fact that he was thirty years old—he would turn the conversation to the point where he could remind you of it and then fall silent, as if he assumed that the statement would start a chain of thought sufficient to itself. Like his partners, I was amazed at the change in him, and I was glad when the *Paris* moved off into the wet space between the worlds, leaving his principality behind.

"How about a drink?" he suggested.

We walked into the bar with that defiant feeling that characterizes the day of departure and ordered four Martinis. After one cocktail a change came over him—he suddenly reached across and slapped my knee with the first joviality I had seen him exhibit for months.

"Did you see that girl in the red tam?" he demanded, "the one with the high color who had the two police dogs down to bid her good-by."

"She's pretty," I agreed.

"I looked her up in the purser's office and found out that she's alone. I'm going down to see the steward in a few minutes. We'll have dinner with her to-night."

After a while he left me, and within an hour he was walking up and down the deck with her, talking to her in his strong, clear voice. Her red tam was a bright spot of color against the steel-green sea, and from time to time she looked up with a flashing bob of her head, and smiled with amusement and interest, and anticipation. At dinner we had champagne, and were very joyous—afterward Anson ran the pool with infectious gusto, and several people who had seen me with him asked me his name. He and the girl were talking and laughing together on a lounge in the bar when I went to bed.

I saw less of him on the trip than I had hoped. He wanted to arrange a foursome, but there was no one available, so I saw him only at meals. Sometimes, though, he would have a cocktail in the bar, and he told me about the girl in the red tam, and his adventures with her, making them all bizarre and amusing, as he had a way of doing, and I was glad that he was himself again, or at least the self that I knew, and with which I felt at home. I don't think he was ever happy unless some one was in love with him, responding to him like filings to a magnet, helping him to explain himself, promising him something. What it was I do not know. Perhaps they promised that there would always be women in the world who would spend their brightest, freshest, rarest hours to nurse and protect that superiority he cherished in his heart.

DOROTHY PARKER

Big Blonde

HAZEL MORSE was a large, fair woman of the type that
incites some men when they use the word "blonde" to click
their tongues and wag their heads roguishly. She prided herself upon
her small feet and suffered for her vanity, boxing them in snub-toed,
high-heeled slippers of the shortest bearable size. The curious things
about her were her hands, strange terminations to the flabby white
arms splattered with pale tan spots—long, quivering hands with deep
and convex nails. She should not have disfigured them with little
jewels.

She was not a woman given to recollections. At her middle thirties,
her old days were a blurred and flickering sequence, an imperfect
film, dealing with the actions of strangers.

In her twenties, after the deferred death of a hazy widowed
mother, she had been employed as a model in a wholesale dress
establishment—it was still the day of the big woman, and she was
then prettily colored and erect and high-breasted. Her job was not
onerous, and she met numbers of men and spent numbers of evenings with them, laughing at their jokes and telling them she loved
their neckties. Men liked her, and she took it for granted that the
liking of many men was a desirable thing. Popularity seemed to her

to be worth all the work that had to be put into its achievement. Men liked you because you were fun, and when they liked you they took you out, and there you were. So, and successfully, she was fun. She was a good sport. Men liked a good sport.

No othër form of diversion, simpler or more complicated, drew her attention. She never pondered if she might not be better occupied doing something else. Her ideas, or, better, her acceptances, ran right along with those of the other substantially built blondes in whom she found her friends.

When she had been working in the dress establishment some years she met Herbie Morse. He was thin, quick, attractive, with shifting lines about his shiny, brown eyes and a habit of fiercely biting at the skin around his finger nails. He drank largely; she found that entertaining. Her habitual greeting to him was with an allusion to his state of the previous night.

"Oh, what a peach you had," she used to say, through her easy laugh. "I thought I'd die, the way you kept asking the waiter to dance with you."

She liked him immediately upon their meeting. She was enormously amused at his fast, slurred sentences, his interpolations of apt phrases from vaudeville acts and comic strips; she thrilled at the feel of his lean arm tucked firm beneath the sleeve of her coat; she wanted to touch the wet, flat surface of his hair. He was as promptly drawn to her. They were married six weeks after they had met.

She was delighted at the idea of being a bride; coquetted with it, played upon it. Other offers of marriage she had had, and not a few of them, but it happened that they were all from stout, serious men who had visited the dress establishment as buyers; men from Des Moines and Houston and Chicago and, in her phrase, even funnier places. There was always something immensely comic to her in the thought of living elsewhere than New York. She could not regard as serious proposals that she share a western residence.

She wanted to be married. She was nearing thirty now, and she did not take the years well. She spread and softened, and her darkening hair turned her to inexpert dabbings with peroxide. There were times when she had little flashes of fear about her job. And she had had a couple of thousand evenings of being a good sport among her male acquaintances. She had come to be more conscientious than spontaneous about it.

Herbie earned enough, and they took a little apartment far uptown. There was a Mission-furnished dining-room with a hanging central light globed in liver-colored glass; in the living-room were an "over-stuffed suite," a Boston fern, and a reproduction of the Henner "Magdalene" with the red hair and the blue draperies; the bedroom was in gray enamel and old rose, with Herbie's photograph on Hazel's dressing-table and Hazel's likeness on Herbie's chest of drawers.

She cooked—and she was a good cook—and marketed and chatted with the delivery boys and the colored laundress. She loved the flat, she loved her life, she loved Herbie. In the first months of their marriage, she gave him all the passion she was ever to know.

She had not realized how tired she was. It was a delight, a new game, a holiday, to give up being a good sport. If her head ached or her arches throbbed, she complained piteously, babyishly. If her mood was quiet, she did not talk. If tears came to her eyes, she let them fall.

She fell readily into the habit of tears during the first years of her marriage. Even in her good sport days, she had been known to weep lavishly and disinterestedly on occasion. Her behavior at the theater was a standing joke. She could weep at anything in a play—tiny garments, love both unrequited and mutual, seduction, purity, faithful servitors, wedlock, the triangle.

"There goes Haze," her friends would say, watching her. "She's off again."

Wedded and relaxed, she poured her tears freely. To her who had laughed so much, crying was delicious. All sorrows became her sorrows; she was Tenderness. She would cry long and softly over newspaper accounts of kidnaped babies, deserted wives, unemployed men, stray cats, heroic dogs. Even when the paper was no longer before her, her mind revolved upon these things and the drops slipped rhythmically over her plump cheeks.

"Honestly," she would say to Herbie, "all the sadness there is in the world when you stop to think about it!"

"Yeah," Herbie would say.

She missed nobody. The old crowd, the people who had brought her and Herbie together, dropped from their lives, lingeringly at first. When she thought of this at all, it was only to consider it fitting. This was marriage. This was peace.

But the thing was that Herbie was not amused.

For a time, he had enjoyed being alone with her. He found the voluntary isolation novel and sweet. Then it palled with ferocious suddenness. It was as if one night, sitting with her in the steam-heated living-room, he would ask no more; and the next night he was through and done with the whole thing.

He became annoyed by her misty melancholies. At first, when he came home to find her softly tired and moody, he kissed her neck and patted her shoulder and begged her to tell her Herbie what was wrong. She loved that. But time slid by, and he found that there was never anything really, personally, the matter.

"Ah, for God's sake," he would say. "Crabbing again. All right, sit here and crab your head off. I'm going out."

And he would slam out of the flat and come back late and drunk.

She was completely bewildered by what happened to their marriage. First they were lovers; and then, it seemed without transition, they were enemies. She never understood it.

There were longer and longer intervals between his leaving his office and his arrival at the apartment. She went through agonies of picturing him run over and bleeding, dead and covered with a sheet. Then she lost her fears for his safety and grew sullen and wounded. When a person wanted to be with a person, he came as soon as possible. She desperately wanted him to want to be with her; her own hours only marked the time till he would come. It was often nearly nine o'clock before he came home to dinner. Always he had had many drinks, and their effect would die in him, leaving him loud and querulous and bristling for affronts.

He was too nervous, he said, to sit and do nothing for an eve-

ning. He boasted, probably not in all truth, that he had never read
a book in his life.

"What am I expected to do—sit around this dump on my tail
all night?" he would ask, rhetorically. And again he would slam out.

She did not know what to do. She could not manage him. She
could not meet him.

She fought him furiously. A terrific domesticity had come upon
her, and she would bite and scratch to guard it. She wanted what
she called "a nice home." She wanted a sober, tender husband,
prompt at dinner, punctual at work. She wanted sweet, comforting
evenings. The idea of intimacy with other men was terrible to her;
the thought that Herbie might be seeking entertainment in other
women set her frantic.

It seemed to her that almost everything she read—novels from
the drug-store lending library, magazine stories, women's pages in
the papers—dealt with wives who lost their husband's love. She
could bear those, at that, better than accounts of neat, companionable
marriage and living happily ever after.

She was frightened. Several times when Herbie came home in
the evening, he found her determinedly dressed—she had had to alter
those of her clothes that were not new, to make them fasten—and
rouged.

"Let's go wild tonight, what do you say?" she would hail him.
"A person's got lots of time to hang around and do nothing when
they're dead."

So they would go out, to chop houses and the less expensive cab-
arets. But it turned out badly. She could no longer find amusement in
watching Herbie drink. She could not laugh at his whimsicalities,
she was so tensely counting his indulgences. And she was unable to
keep back her remonstrances—"Ah, come on, Herb, you've had
enough, haven't you? You'll feel something terrible in the morning."

He would be immediately enraged. All right, crab; crab, crab,
crab, crab, that was all she ever did. What a lousy sport *she* was!
There would be scenes, and one or the other of them would rise and
stalk out in fury.

She could not recall the definite day that she started drinking,

herself. There was nothing separate about her days. Like drops upon
a window-pane, they ran together and trickled away. She had been
married six months; then a year; then three years.

She had never needed to drink, formerly. She could sit for most
of a night at a table where the others were imbibing earnestly and
never droop in looks or spirits, nor be bored by the doings of those
about her. If she took a cocktail, it was so unusual as to cause twenty
minutes or so of jocular comment. But now anguish was in her.
Frequently, after a quarrel, Herbie would stay out for the night, and
she could not learn from him where the time had been spent. Her
heart felt tight and sore in her breast, and her mind turned like an
electric fan.

She hated the taste of liquor. Gin, plain or in mixtures, made her
promptly sick. After experiment, she found that Scotch whisky was
best for her. She took it without water, because that was the quickest
way to its effect.

Herbie pressed it on her. He was glad to see her drink. They both
felt it might restore her high spirits, and their good times together
might again be possible.

"'Atta girl," he would approve her. "Let's see you get boiled,
baby."

But it brought them no nearer. When she drank with him, there
would be a little while of gaiety and then, strangely without beginning, they would be in a wild quarrel. They would wake in the
morning not sure what it had all been about, foggy as to what had
been said and done, but each deeply injured and bitterly resentful.
There would be days of vengeful silence.

There had been a time when they had made up their quarrels,
usually in bed. There would be kisses and little names and assurances
of fresh starts. . . . "Oh, it's going to be great now, Herb. We'll
have swell times. I was a crab. I guess I must have been tired. But
everything's going to be swell. You'll see."

Now there were no gentle reconciliations. They resumed friendly
relations only in the brief magnanimity caused by liquor, before more
liquor drew them into new battles. The scenes became more violent.
There were shouted invectives and pushes, and sometimes sharp

slaps. Once she had a black eye. Herbie was horrified next day at sight of it. He did not go to work; he followed her about, suggesting remedies and heaping dark blame on himself. But after they had had a few drinks—"to pull themselves together"—she made so many wistful references to her bruise that he shouted at her and rushed out and was gone for two days.

Each time he left the place in a rage, he threatened never to come back. She did not believe him, nor did she consider separation. Somewhere in her head or her heart was the lazy, nebulous hope that things would change and she and Herbie settle suddenly into soothing married life. Here were her home, her furniture, her husband, her station. She summoned no alternatives.

She could no longer bustle and potter. She had no more vicarious tears; the hot drops she shed were for herself. She walked ceaselessly about the rooms, her thoughts running mechanically round and round Herbie. In those days began the hatred of being alone that she was never to overcome. You could be by yourself when things were all right, but when you were blue you got the howling horrors.

She commenced drinking alone, little, short drinks all through the day. It was only with Herbie that alcohol made her nervous and quick in offense. Alone, it blurred sharp things for her. She lived in a haze of it. Her life took on a dream-like quality. Nothing was astonishing.

A Mrs. Martin moved into the flat across the hall. She was a great blonde woman of forty, a promise in looks of what Mrs. Morse was to be. They made acquaintance, quickly became inseparable. Mrs. Morse spent her days in the opposite apartment. They drank together, to brace themselves after the drinks of the nights before.

She never confided her troubles about Herbie to Mrs. Martin. The subject was too bewildering to her to find comfort in talk. She let it be assumed that her husband's business kept him much away. It was not regarded as important; husbands, as such, played but shadowy parts in Mrs. Martin's circle.

Mrs. Martin had no visible spouse; you were left to decide for yourself whether he was or was not dead. She had an admirer, Joe, who came to see her almost nightly. Often he brought several friends with him—"The Boys," they were called. The boys were big, red, good-humored men, perhaps forty-five, perhaps fifty. Mrs. Morse was glad of invitations to join the parties—Herbie was scarcely ever home at night now. If he did come home, she did not visit Mrs. Martin. An evening alone with Herbie meant inevitably a quarrel, yet she would stay with him. There was always her thin and wordless idea that, maybe, this night, things would begin to be all right.

The Boys brought plenty of liquor along with them whenever they came to Mrs. Martin's. Drinking with them, Mrs. Morse became lively and good-natured and audacious. She was quickly popular. When she had drunk enough to cloud her most recent battle with Herbie, she was excited by their approbation. Crab, was she? Rotten sport, was she? Well, there were some that thought different.

Ed was one of The Boys. He lived in Utica—had "his own business" there, was the awed report—but he came to New York almost every week. He was married. He showed Mrs. Morse the then current photographs of Junior and Sister, and she praised them abundantly and sincerely. Soon it was accepted by the others that Ed was her particular friend.

He staked her when they all played poker; sat next her and occasionally rubbed his knee against hers during the game. She was rather lucky. Frequently she went home with a twenty-dollar bill or a ten-dollar bill or a handful of crumpled dollars. She was glad of them. Herbie was getting, in her words, something awful about money. To ask him for it brought an instant row.

"What the hell do you do with it?" he would say. "Shoot it all on Scotch?"

"I try to run this house half-way decent," she would retort. "Never thought of that, did you? Oh, no, his lordship couldn't be bothered with that."

Again, she could not find a definite day, to fix the beginning of Ed's proprietorship. It became his custom to kiss her on the mouth when he came in, as well as for farewell, and he gave her little quick kisses of approval all through the evening. She liked this rather more than she disliked it. She never thought of his kisses when she was not with him.

He would run his hand lingeringly over her back and shoulders. "Some dizzy blonde, eh?" he would say. "Some doll."

One afternoon she came home from Mrs. Martin's to find Herbie in the bedroom. He had been away for several nights, evidently on a prolonged drinking bout. His face was gray, his hands jerked as if they were on wires. On the bed were two old suitcases, packed high. Only her photograph remained on his bureau, and the wide doors of his closet disclosed nothing but coat-hangers.

"I'm blowing," he said. "I'm through with the whole works. I got a job in Detroit."

She sat down on the edge of the bed. She had drunk much the night before, and the four Scotches she had had with Mrs. Martin had only increased her fogginess.

"Good job?" she said.

"Oh, yeah," he said. "Looks all right."

He closed a suitcase with difficulty, swearing at it in whispers.

"There's some dough in the bank," he said. "The bank book's in your top drawer. You can have the furniture and stuff."

He looked at her, and his forehead twitched.

"God damn it, I'm through, I'm telling you," he cried. "I'm through."

"All right, all right," she said. "I heard you, didn't I?"

She saw him as if he were at one end of a cannon and she at the other. Her head was beginning to ache bumpingly, and her voice had a dreary, tiresome tone. She could not have raised it.

"Like a drink before you go?" she asked.

Again he looked at her, and a corner of his mouth jerked up.

"Cockeyed again for a change, aren't you?" he said. "That's nice. Sure, get a couple of shots, will you?"

She went to the pantry, mixed him a stiff highball, poured herself a couple of inches of whisky and drank it. Then she gave herself another portion and brought the glasses into the bedroom. He had strapped both suitcases and had put on his hat and overcoat.

He took his highball.

"Well," he said, and he gave a sudden, uncertain laugh. "Here's mud in your eye."

"Mud in your eye," she said.

They drank. He put down his glass and took up the heavy suitcases.

"Got to get a train around six," he said.

She followed him down the hall. There was a song, a song that Mrs. Martin played doggedly on the phonograph, running loudly through her mind. She had never liked the thing.

> *"Night and daytime,*
> *Always playtime.*
> *Ain't we got fun?"*

At the door he put down the bags and faced her.

"Well," he said. "Well, take care of yourself. You'll be all right, will you?"

"Oh, sure," she said.

He opened the door, then came back to her, holding out his hand.

" 'By Haze," he said. "Good luck to you."

She took his hand and shook it.

"Pardon my wet glove," she said.

When the door had closed behind him, she went back to the pantry.

She was flushed and lively when she went in to Mrs. Martin's that evening. The Boys were there, Ed among them. He was glad to be in town, frisky and loud and full of jokes. But she spoke quietly to him for a minute.

"Herbie blew today," she said. "Going to live out west."

"That so?" he said. He looked at her and played with the fountain pen clipped to his waistcoat pocket.

"Think he's gone for good, do you?" he asked.

"Yeah," she said. "I know he is. I know. Yeah."

"You going to live on across the hall just the same?" he said. "Know what you're going to do?"

"Gee, I don't know," she said. "I don't give much of a damn."

"Oh, come on, that's no way to talk," he told her. "What you need —you need a little snifter. How about it?"

"Yeah," she said. "Just straight."

She won forty-three dollars at poker. When the game broke up, Ed took her back to her apartment.

"Got a little kiss for me?" he asked.

He wrapped her in his big arms and kissed her violently. She was entirely passive. He held her away and looked at her.

"Little tight, honey?" he asked, anxiously. "Not going to be sick, are you?"

"Me?" she said. "I'm swell."

II

When Ed left in the morning, he took her photograph with him. He said he wanted her picture to look at, up in Utica. "You can have that one on the bureau," she said.

She put Herbie's picture in a drawer, out of her sight. When she could look at it, she meant to tear it up. She was fairly successful in keeping her mind from racing around him. Whisky slowed it for her. She was almost peaceful, in her mist.

She accepted her relationship with Ed without question or enthusiasm. When he was away, she seldom thought definitely of him. He was good to her; he gave her frequent presents and a regular allowance. She was even able to save. She did not plan ahead of any day, but her wants were few, and you might as well put money in the bank as have it lying around.

When the lease of her apartment neared its end, it was Ed who suggested moving. His friendship with Mrs. Martin and Joe had become strained over a dispute at poker; a feud was impending.

"Let's get the hell out of here," Ed said. "What I want you to have is a place near the Grand Central. Make it easier for me."

So she took a little flat in the Forties. A colored maid came in every day to clean and to make coffee for her—she was "through with that housekeeping stuff," she said, and Ed, twenty years married to a passionately domestic woman, admired this romantic uselessness and felt doubly a man of the world in abetting it.

The coffee was all she had until she went out to dinner, but alcohol kept her fat. Prohibition she regarded only as a basis for jokes. You could always get all you wanted. She was never noticeably drunk and seldom nearly sober. It required a larger daily allowance to keep her misty-minded. Too little, and she was achingly melancholy.

Ed brought her to Jimmy's. He was proud, with the pride of the transient who would be mistaken for a native, in his knowledge of small, recent restaurants occupying the lower floors of shabby brownstone houses; places where, upon mentioning the name of an habitué friend, might be obtained strange whisky and fresh gin in many of their ramifications. Jimmy's place was the favorite of his acquaintances.

There, through Ed, Mrs. Morse met many men and women, formed quick friendships. The men often took her out when Ed was in Utica. He was proud of her popularity.

She fell into the habit of going to Jimmy's alone when she had no engagement. She was certain to meet some people she knew, and join them. It was a club for her friends, both men and women.

The women at Jimmy's looked remarkably alike, and this was curious, for through feuds, removals, and opportunities of more profitable contacts, the personnel of the group changed constantly. Yet always the newcomers resembled those whom they replaced. They were all big women and stout, broad of shoulder and abundantly breasted, with faces thickly clothed in soft, high-colored flesh. They laughed loud and often, showing opaque and lusterless teeth like squares of crockery. There was about them the health of the big, yet a slight, unwholesome suggestion of stubborn preservation. They might have been thirty-six or forty-five or anywhere between.

They composed their titles of their own first names with their husbands' surnames—Mrs. Florence Miller, Mrs. Vera Riley, Mrs. Lilian Block. This gave at the same time the solidity of marriage and the glamour of freedom. Yet only one or two were actually divorced. Most of them never referred to their dimmed spouses; some, a shorter time separated, described them in terms of great biological interest. Several were mothers, each of an only child—a boy at school somewhere, or a girl being cared for by a grandmother. Often, well on toward morning, there would be displays of kodak portraits

They were comfortable women, cordial and friendly and irrepressibly matronly. Theirs was the quality of ease. Become fatalistic, especially about money matters, they were unworried. Whenever their funds dropped alarmingly, a new donor appeared; this had always happened. The aim of each was to have one man, permanently, to pay all her bills, in return for which she would have immediately given up other admirers and probably would have become exceedingly fond of him; for the affections of all of them were, by now, unexacting, tranquil, and easily arranged. This end, however, grew increasingly difficult yearly. Mrs. Morse was regarded as fortunate.

Ed had a good year, increased her allowance and gave her a sealskin coat. But she had to be careful of her moods with him. He insisted on gaiety. He would not listen to admissions of aches or weariness.

"Hey, listen," he would say, "I got worries of my own, and plenty. Nobody wants to hear other people's troubles, sweetie. What you got to do, you got to be a sport and forget it. See? Well, slip us a little smile, then. That's my girl."

She never had enough interest to quarrel with him as she had with Herbie, but she wanted the privilege of occasional admitted sadness. It was strange. The other women she saw did not have to fight their moods. There was Mrs. Florence Miller who got regular crying jags, and the men sought only to cheer and comfort her. The others spent whole evenings in grieved recitals of worries and ills; their escorts paid them deep sympathy. But she was instantly undesirable when she was low in spirits. Once, at Jimmy's, when she could not make herself lively, Ed had walked out and left her.

"Why the hell don't you stay home and not go spoiling everybody's evening?" he had roared.

Even her slightest acquaintances seemed irritated if she were not conspicuously light-hearted.

"What's the matter with you, anyway?" they would say. "Be your age, why don't you? Have a little drink and snap out of it."

When her relationship with Ed had continued nearly three years, he moved to Florida to live. He hated leaving her; he gave her a large check and some shares of a sound stock, and his pale eyes were wet when he said good-by. She did not miss him. He came to New York infrequently, perhaps two or three times a year, and hurried directly from the train to see her. She was always pleased to have him come and never sorry to see him go.

Charley, an acquaintance of Ed's that she had met at Jimmy's, had long admired her. He had always made opportunities of touching her and leaning close to talk to her. He asked repeatedly of all their friends if they had ever heard such a fine laugh as she had. After Ed left, Charley became the main figure in her life. She classified him and spoke of him as "not so bad." There was nearly a year of Charley; then she divided her time between him and Sydney, another frequenter of Jimmy's; then Charley slipped away altogether.

Sydney was a little, brightly dressed, clever Jew. She was perhaps nearest contentment with him. He amused her always; her laughter was not forced.

He admired her completely. Her softness and size delighted him. And he thought she was great, he often told her, because she kept gay and lively when she was drunk.

"Once I had a gal," he said, "used to try and throw herself out of the window every time she got a can on. Jee-*zuss*," he added, feelingly.

Then Sydney married a rich and watchful bride, and then there was Billy. No—after Sydney came Ferd, then Billy. In her haze, she never recalled how men entered her life and left it. There were no surprises. She had no thrill at their advent, nor woe at their departure. She seemed to be always able to attract men. There was never another as rich as Ed, but they were all generous to her, in their means.

Once she had news of Herbie. She met Mrs. Martin dining at Jimmy's, and the old friendship was vigorously renewed. The still admiring Joe, while on a business trip, had seen Herbie. He had settled in Chicago, he looked fine, he was living with some woman— seemed to be crazy about her. Mrs. Morse had been drinking vastly that day. She took the news with mild interest, as one hearing of the sex peccadilloés of somebody whose name is, after a moment's groping, familiar.

"Must be damn near seven years since I saw him," she commented. "Gee. Seven years."

More and more, her days lost their individuality. She never knew dates, nor was sure of the day of the week.

"My God, was that a year ago!" she would exclaim, when an event was recalled in conversation.

She was tired so much of the time. Tired and blue. Almost everything could give her the blues. Those old horses she saw on Sixth Avenue—struggling and slipping along the car-tracks, or standing at the curb, their heads dropped level with their worn knees. The tightly stored tears would squeeze from her eyes as she teetered past on her aching feet in the stubby, champagne-colored slippers.

The thought of death came and stayed with her and lent her a sort of drowsy cheer. It would be nice, nice and restful, to be dead.

There was no settled, shocked moment when she first thought of killing herself; it seemed to her as if the idea had always been with her. She pounced upon all the accounts of suicides in the newspapers. There was an epidemic of self-killings—or maybe it was just that she searched for the stories of them so eagerly that she found many. To read of them roused reassurance in her; she felt a cozy solidarity with the big company of the voluntary dead.

She slept, aided by whisky, till deep in the afternoons, then lay abed, a bottle and glass at her hand, until it was time to dress and go out for dinner. She was beginning to feel toward alcohol a little puzzled distrust, as toward an old friend who has refused a simple favor. Whisky still soothed her for most of the time, but there were sudden, inexplicable moments when the cloud fell treacherously away from her, and she was sawed by the sorrow and bewilderment and nuisance of all living. She played voluptuously with the thought of cool, sleepy retreat. She had never been troubled by religious belief and no vision of an after-life intimidated her. She dreamed by day of never again putting on tight shoes, of never having to laugh and listen and admire, of never more being a good sport. Never.

But how would you do it? It made her sick to think of jumping from heights. She could not stand a gun. At the theater, if one of the actors drew a revolver, she crammed her fingers into her ears and could not even look at the stage until after the shot had been fired. There was no gas in her flat. She looked long at the bright blue veins in her slim wrists—a cut with a razor blade, and there you'd be. But it would hurt, hurt like hell, and there would be blood to see. Poison —something tasteless and quick and painless—was the thing. But they wouldn't sell it to you in drugstores, because of the law.

She had few other thoughts.

There was a new man now—Art. He was short and fat and exacting and hard on her patience when he was drunk. But there had been only occasionals for some time before him, and she was glad of a little stability. Too, Art must be away for weeks at a stretch, selling silks, and that was restful. She was convincingly gay with him, though the effort shook her.

"The best sport in the world," he would murmur, deep in her neck. "The best sport in the world."

One night, when he had taken her to Jimmy's, she went into the dressing-room with Mrs. Florence Miller. There, while designing curly mouths on their faces with lip-rouge, they compared experiences of insomnia.

"Honestly," Mrs. Morse said, "I wouldn't close an eye if I didn't go to bed full of Scotch. I lie there and toss and turn and toss and turn. Blue! Does a person get blue lying awake that way!"

"Say, listen, Hazel," Mrs. Miller said, impressively, "I'm telling you I'd be awake for a year if I didn't take veronal. That stuff makes you sleep like a fool."

"Isn't it poison, or something?" Mrs. Morse asked.

"Oh, you take too much and you're out for the count," said Mrs. Miller. "I just take five grains—they come in tablets. I'd be scared to fool around with it. But five grains, and you cork off pretty."

"Can you get it anywhere?" Mrs. Morse felt superbly Machiavellian.

"Get all you want in Jersey," said Mrs. Miller. "They won't give it to you here without you have a doctor's prescription. Finished? We'd better go back and see what the boys are doing."

That night, Art left Mrs. Morse at the door of her apartment; his mother was in town. Mrs. Morse was still sober, and it happened that there was no whisky left in her cupboard. She lay in bed, looking up at the black ceiling.

She rose early, for her, and went to New Jersey. She had never taken the tube, and did not understand it. So she went to the Pennsylvania Station and bought a railroad ticket to Newark. She thought of nothing in particular on the trip out. She looked at the uninspired hats of the women about her and gazed through the smeared window at the flat, gritty scene.

In Newark, in the first drugstore she came to, she asked for a tin of talcum powder, a nailbrush, and a box of veronal tablets. The powder and the brush were to make the hypnotic seem also a casual need. The clerk was entirely unconcerned. "We only keep them in bottles," he said, and wrapped up for her a little glass vial containing ten white tablets, stacked one on another.

She went to another drugstore and bought a face-cloth, an orangewood stick, and a bottle of veronal tablets. The clerk was also uninterested.

"Well, I guess I got enough to kill an ox," she thought, and went back to the station.

At home, she put the little vials in the drawer of her dressing-table and stood looking at them with a dreamy tenderness.

"There they are, God bless them," she said, and she kissed her finger-tip and touched each bottle.

The colored maid was busy in the living-room.

"Hey, Nettie," Mrs. Morse called. "Be an angel, will you? Run around to Jimmy's and get me a quart of Scotch."

She hummed while she awaited the girl's return.

During the next few days, whisky ministered to her as tenderly as it had done when she first turned to its aid. Alone, she was soothed and vague, at Jimmy's she was the gayest of the groups. Art was delighted with her.

Then, one night, she had an appointment to meet Art at Jimmy's for an early dinner. He was to leave afterward on a business excursion, to be away for a week. Mrs. Morse had been drinking all the afternoon; while she dressed to go out, she felt herself rising pleasurably from drowsiness to high spirits. But as she came out into the street the effects of the whisky deserted her completely, and she was filled with a slow, grinding wretchedness so horrible that she stood swaying on the pavement, unable for a moment to move forward. It was a gray night with spurts of mean, thin snow, and the streets shone with dark ice. As she slowly crossed Sixth Avenue, consciously dragging one foot past the other, a big, scarred horse pulling a rickety express-wagon crashed to his knees before her. The driver swore and screamed and lashed the beast insanely, bringing the whip back over his shoulder for every blow, while the horse struggled to get a footing on the slippery asphalt. A group gathered and watched with interest.

Art was waiting, when Mrs. Morse reached Jimmy's.

"What's the matter with you, for God's sake?" was his greeting to her.

"I saw a horse," she said. "Gee, I—a person feels sorry for horses. I—it isn't just horses. Everything's kind of terrible, isn't it? I can't help getting sunk."

"Ah, sunk, me eye," he said. "What's the idea of all the belly-aching? What have you got to be sunk about?"

"I can't help it," she said.

"Ah, help it, me eye," he said. "Pull yourself together, will you? Come on and sit down, and take that face off you."

She drank industriously and she tried hard, but she could not overcome her melancholy. Others joined them and commented on her gloom, and she could do no more for them than smile weakly. She made little dabs at her eyes with her handkerchief, trying to time her movements so they would be unnoticed, but several times Art caught her and scowled and shifted impatiently in his chair.

When it was time for him to go to his train, she said she would leave, too, and go home.

"And not a bad idea, either," he said. "See if you can't sleep yourself out of it. I'll see you Thursday. For God's sake, try and cheer up by then, will you?"

"Yeah," she said. "I will."

In her bedroom, she undressed with a tense speed wholly unlike her usual slow uncertainty. She put on her nightgown, took off her hair-net and passed the comb quickly through her dry, vari-colored hair. Then she took the two little vials from the drawer and carried them into the bathroom. The splintering misery had gone from her, and she felt the quick excitement of one who is about to receive an anticipated gift.

She uncorked the vials, filled a glass with water and stood before the mirror, a tablet between her fingers. Suddenly she bowed graciously to her reflection, and raised the glass to it.

"Well, here's mud in your eye," she said.

The tablets were unpleasant to take, dry and powdery and sticking obstinately half-way down her throat. It took her a long time to swallow all twenty of them. She stood watching her reflection with deep, impersonal interest, studying the movements of the gulping throat. Once more she spoke aloud.

"For God's sake, try and cheer up by Thursday, will you?" she said. "Well, you know what he can do. He and the whole lot of them."

She had no idea how quickly to expect effect from the veronal. When she had taken the last tablet, she stood uncertainly, wondering, still with a courteous, vicarious interest, if death would strike her down then and there. She felt in no way strange, save for a slight stirring of sickness from the effort of swallowing the tablets, nor did her reflected face look at all different. It would not be immediate, then; it might even take an hour or so.

She stretched her arms high and gave a vast yawn.

"Guess I'll go to bed," she said. "Gee, I'm nearly dead."

That struck her as comic, and she turned out the bathroom light and went in and laid herself down in her bed, chuckling softly all the time.

"Gee, I'm nearly dead," she quoted. "That's a hot one!"

III

Nettie, the colored maid, came in late the next afternoon to clean the apartment, and found Mrs. Morse in her bed. But then, that was not unusual. Usually, though, the sounds of cleaning waked her, and she did not like to wake up. Nettie, an agreeable girl, had learned to move softly about her work.

But when she had done the living-room and stolen in to tidy the little square bedroom, she could not avoid a tiny clatter as she arranged the objects on the dressing-table. Instinctively, she glanced over her shoulder at the sleeper, and without warning a sickly uneasiness crept over her. She came to the bed and stared down at the woman lying there.

Mrs. Morse lay on her back, one flabby, white arm flung up, the wrist against her forehead. Her stiff hair hung untenderly along her face. The bed covers were pushed down, exposing a deep square of soft neck and a pink nightgown, its fabric worn uneven by many launderings; her great breasts, freed from their tight confiner, sagged beneath her arm-pits. Now and then she made knotted, snoring sounds, and from the corner of her opened mouth to the blurred turn of her jaw ran a lane of crusted spittle.

"Mis' Morse," Nettie called. "Oh, Mis' Morse! It's terrible late."

Mrs. Morse made no move.

"Mis' Morse," said Nettie. "Look, Mis' Morse. How'm I goin' get this bed made?"

Panic sprang upon the girl. She shook the woman's hot shoulder. "Ah, wake up, will yuh?" she whined. "Ah, please wake up."

Suddenly the girl turned and ran out in the hall to the elevator door, keeping her thumb firm on the black, shiny button until the elderly car and its Negro attendant stood before her. She poured a jumble of words over the boy, and led him back to the apartment. He tiptoed creakingly in to the bedside; first gingerly, then so lustily that he left marks in the soft flesh, he prodded the unconscious woman.

"Hey, there!" he cried, and listened intently, as for an echo.

"Jeez. Out like a light," he commented.

At his interest in the spectacle, Nettie's panic left her. Importance was big in both of them. They talked in quick, unfinished whispers, and it was the boy's suggestion that he fetch the young doctor who lived on the ground floor. Nettie hurried along with him. They

looked forward to the limelit moment of breaking their news of
something untoward, something pleasurably unpleasant. Mrs. Morse
had become the medium of drama. With no ill wish to her, they
hoped that her state was serious, that she would not let them down
by being awake and normal on their return. A little fear of this
determined them to make the most, to the doctor, of her present
condition. "Matter of life and death," returned to Nettie from her
thin store of reading. She considered startling the doctor with the
phrase.

The doctor was in and none too pleased at interruption. He wore
a yellow and blue striped dressing-gown, and he was lying on his
sofa, laughing with a dark girl, her face scaly with inexpensive
powder, who perched on the arm. Half-emptied highball glasses
stood beside them, and her coat and hat were neatly hung up with
the comfortable implication of a long stay.

Always something, the doctor grumbled. Couldn't let anybody
alone after a hard day. But he put some bottles and instruments into
a case, changed his dressing-gown for his coat and started out with
the Negroes.

"Snap it up there, big boy," the girl called after him. "Don't be
all night."

The doctor strode loudly into Mrs. Morse's flat and on to the bedroom, Nettie and the boy right behind him. Mrs. Morse had not
moved; her sleep was as deep, but soundless, now. The doctor looked
sharply at her, then plunged his thumbs into the lidded pits above
her eyeballs and threw his weight upon them. A high, sickened cry
broke from Nettie.

"Look like he tryin' to push her right on th'ough the bed," said
the boy. He chuckled.

Mrs. Morse gave no sign under the pressure. Abruptly the doctor
abandoned it, and with one quick movement swept the covers down
to the foot of the bed. With another he flung her nightgown back
and lifted the thick, white legs, cross-hatched with blocks of tiny,
iris-colored veins. He pinched them repeatedly, with long, cruel nips,
back of the knees. She did not awaken.

"What's she been drinking?" he asked Nettie, over his shoulder.

With the certain celerity of one who knows just where to lay hands on a thing, Nettie went into the bathroom, bound for the cupboard where Mrs. Morse kept her whisky. But she stopped at the sight of the two vials, with their red and white labels, lying before the mirror. She brought them to the doctor.

"Oh, for the Lord Almighty's sweet sake!" he said. He dropped Mrs. Morse's legs, and pushed them impatiently across the bed. "What did she want to go taking that tripe for? Rotten yellow trick, that's what a thing like that is. Now we'll have to pump her out, and all that stuff. Nuisance, a thing like that is; that's what it amounts to. Here, George, take me down in the elevator. You wait here, maid. She won't do anything."

"She won't die on me, will she?" cried Nettie.

"No," said the doctor. "God, no. You couldn't kill her with an ax."

IV

After two days, Mrs. Morse came back to consciousness, dazed at first, then with a comprehension that brought with it the slow, saturating wretchedness.

"Oh, Lord, oh, Lord," she moaned, and tears for herself and for life striped her cheeks.

Nettie came in at the sound. For two days she had done the ugly, incessant tasks in the nursing of the unconscious, for two nights she had caught broken bits of sleep on the living-room couch. She looked coldly at the big, blown woman in the bed.

"What you been tryin' to do, Mis' Morse?" she said. "What kine o' work is that, takin' all that stuff?"

"Oh, Lord," moaned Mrs. Morse, again, and she tried to cover her eyes with her arms. But the joints felt stiff and brittle, and she cried out at their ache.

"Tha's no way to ack, takin' them pills," said Nettie. "You can thank you' stars you heah at all. How you feel now?"

"Oh, I feel great," said Mrs. Morse. "Swell, I feel."

Her hot, painful tears fell as if they would never stop.

"Tha's no way to take on, cryin' like that," Nettie said. "After what you done. The doctor, he says he could have you arrested, doin' a thing like that. He was fit to be tied, here."

"Why couldn't he let me alone?" wailed Mrs. Morse. "Why the hell couldn't he have?"

"Tha's terr'ble, Mis' Morse, swearin' an' talkin' like that," said Nettie, "after what people done for you. Here I ain' had no sleep at all for two nights, an' had to give up goin' out to my other ladies!"

"Oh, I'm sorry, Nettie," she said. "You're a peach. I'm sorry I've given you so much trouble. I couldn't help it. I just got sunk. Didn't you ever feel like doing it? When everything looks just lousy to you?"

"I wouldn' think o' no such thing," declared Nettie. "You got to cheer up. Tha's what you got to do. Everybody's got their troubles."

"Yeah," said Mrs. Morse. "I know."

"Come a pretty picture card for you," Nettie said. "Maybe that will cheer you up."

She handed Mrs. Morse a post-card. Mrs. Morse had to cover one eye with her hand, in order to read the message; her eyes were not yet focusing correctly.

It was from Art. On the back of a view of the Detroit Athletic Club he had written: "Greeting and salutations. Hope you have lost that gloom. Cheer up and don't take any rubber nickels. See you on Thursday."

She dropped the card to the floor. Misery crushed her as if she were between great smooth stones. There passed before her a slow, slow pageant of days spent lying in her flat, of evenings at Jimmy's being a good sport, making herself laugh and coo at Art and other Arts; she saw a long parade of weary horses and shivering beggars and all beaten, driven, stumbling things. Her feet throbbed as if she had crammed them into the stubby champagne-colored slippers. Her heart seemed to swell and harden.

"Nettie," she cried, "for heaven's sake pour me a drink, will you?"

The maid looked doubtful.

"Now you know, Mis' Morse," she said, "you been near daid. I don' know if the doctor he let you drink nothin' yet."

"Oh, never mind him," she said. "You get me one, and bring in the bottle. Take one yourself."

"Well," said Nettie.

She poured them each a drink, deferentially leaving hers in the bathroom to be taken in solitude, and brought Mrs. Morse's glass in to her.

Mrs. Morse looked into the liquor and shuddered back from its odor. Maybe it would help. Maybe, when you had been knocked cold for a few days, your very first drink would give you a lift. Maybe whisky would be her friend again. She prayed without addressing a God, without knowing a God. Oh, please, please, let her be able to get drunk, please keep her always drunk.

She lifted the glass.

"Thanks, Nettie," she said. "Here's mud in your eye."

The maid giggled. "Tha's the way, Mis' Morse," she said. "You cheer up, now."

"Yeah," said Mrs. Morse. "Sure."

CONRAD AIKEN

The Dark City

HIS greatest pleasure in life came always at dusk. Its prelude was the reading of the evening paper in the train that took him out of the city. By long association the very unfolding of the grimy ink-smelling sheets was part of the ritual: his dark eyes dilated, he felt himself begin to "grin," the staggering load of business detail, under which he had struggled all day in the office, was instantly forgotten. He read rapidly, devoured with rapacious eyes column after column—New York, London, Paris, Lisbon—wars, revolutions, bargains in umbrellas, exhibitions of water colors. This consumed three-quarters of the journey. After that he watched the procession of houses, walls, trees, reeling past in the mellow slant light, and began already to feel his garden about him. He observed the flight of the train unconsciously, and it was almost automatically, at the unrealized sight of a certain group of trees, oddly leaning away from each other, like a group of ballet dancers expressing an extravagance of horror, that he rose and approached the door.

The sense of escape was instant. Sky and earth generously took him, the train fled shrieking into the vague bright infinity of afternoon. The last faint wail of it, as it plunged into a tunnel, always

Reprinted by permission of the publishers, Duell, Sloan & Pearce, Inc. From the book *The Short Stories of Conrad Aiken*. Copyright, 1922, 1950, by Conrad Aiken.

seemed to him to curl about his head like a white tentacle, too weak
to be taken seriously. Then, in the abrupt silence, he began climbing
the long hill that led to his house. He walked swiftly, blowing
tattered blue clouds of smoke over his shoulders, revolving in his
mind the items of news amusing enough to be reported to Hilda;
such as that Miss Green, the stenographer, who had for some time
been manifesting a disposition to flirt with him, today, just after
closing, when everybody else had gone out, had come to him, blush-
ing, and asked him to fasten the sleeve of her dress. A delicious
scene! He smiled about the stem of his pipe, but exchanged his
smile for a laugh when, looking in through a gap in his neighbor's
hedge, he found himself staring into the depraved eyes of a goat.
This would add itself to the episode of Miss Green, for these eyes
were precisely hers. He turned the corner and saw his house before
him, riding on the hill like a small ship on a long green wave. The
three children were playing a wild game of croquet, shrieking.
Louder sounds arose at his appearance, and as he strode across the
lawn they danced about him chattering and quarreling.

"Daddy, Martha won't play in her turn, and I say——"

"Majorie takes the heavy mallet——"

The chorus rose shrill about him, but he laughed and went into
the house, shouting only, "Out of the way! I'm in a hurry! The
beans are dying, the tomatoes are clamoring for me, the peas are
holding out their hands!"

"Daddy says the beans are dying. Isn't he silly?"

"Let's get to the garden before daddy does."

As he closed the door he heard the shrieks trailing off round the
corner of the house, diminuendo. He hung up coat and hat with a
rapid gesture and hurried to the kitchen. Hilda, stirring the cocoa
with a long spoon, looked round at him laconically.

"Chocolate!" he shouted, and pulled a cake of chocolate out of his
pocket. He was astonished, he rolled his eyes, for it appeared to have
been sat upon—"in the train." Hilda shrieked with laughter. He
thrust it into her apron pocket and fled up the stairs to change.

He could not find his old flannel trousers. Not in the cupboard—
not in the bureau. He surrendered to an impulse to comic rage. "Not

under the bed!" he cried. He thrust his head out of the window that overlooked the garden and addressed his children.

"Martha! Bring my trousers here this instant!"

He drew in his head again from the shower of replies that flew up at him like missiles and going to the door roared down to his wife.

"I've lost my trousers!"

Then he found them in the closet behind the door and, laughing, put them on.

II

He ran out of the side door, under the wistaria-covered trellis, and down the slippery stone steps to the vegetable garden.

"Here comes daddy, now," shrilled to him from Martha.

He lighted his pipe, shutting his left eye, and stood in profound meditation before the orderly, dignified, and extraordinarily vigorous rows of beans. They were in blossom—bees were tumbling the delicate lilac-pink little hoods. Clouds of fragrance came up from them. The crickets were beginning to tune up for the evening. The sun was poised above the black water-tower on the far hill.

Martha and Marjorie began giggling mysteriously behind the lilacs.

"My hoe!" he wailed.

The hoe was thrust out from behind the lilacs.

"If anybody should drive up in a scarlet taxi," he said to Martha, accepting the hoe, "and inform you that your soul is free, don't believe him. Tell him he's a liar. Point me out to him as a symbol of the abject slavery that all life is. Say that I'm a miserable thrall to wife, children, and beans—particularly beans. I spend my days on my knees before my beans."

"I'll do nothing of the sort," said Martha.

He held his hoe under his arm and walked solemnly among the beans. The two girls followed him.

"Here's a caterpillar, daddy!"

"Kill him!"

"Here's another—a funny green one with red sparkles on his back. Oh, look at him!"

"Don't look at him! Kill him!"

"He squirts out like green tooth-paste."

"Don't, Martha!" he cried, pained. "Don't say such things! Spare your neurotic father."

He shrank visibly and strode off to the corner where his peas were planted and started methodically hoeing the rows, turning the rich loam up about the pale stalks. Now and again a pebble clinked, he stooped and threw it off into the meadow. Mary, the youngest, came to the top of the steps and cried. Martha and Marjorie went to her, and he forgot them. The rising and falling of the hoe-blade, shiny with much polishing in the brown soil, hypnotized him, and his thoughts fell into a sort of rhythm, came and went without his interference. "Ridiculous!" he thought, "that this solemn singular biped, whom other bipeds for convenience call Andrew, should stand here with a stick and scratch the skin of this aged planet. What does he expect to get for it? It pleases the aged planet. She stretches herself in the twilight, purrs like an old cat, and expresses her pleasure in the odd and useful effluvium we call peas. And this biped wears clothes. Think of it! He wears clothes; things made out of plant-fibre and sheep's wool cunningly and hideously made to fit his arms and legs. He has in his pocket—a small pouch made in these singular garments—a watch, a small shiny round object in which he has reduced to feeble but regular iambics the majestic motions of the sun, earth and stars. He takes it out and looks at it with an air of comprehension and puts it back again. Why doesn't he laugh at himself?" . . . He chuckled . . . "This object tells him that he has time for two more rows before dinner. Clink, clink. Damn these pebbles. My antediluvian anthropoid ape of an ancestor had to walk round them, they were so huge. He sat on them, cracked nuts against them, chattered with his family. He had no watch, and his trousers grew like grass . . . Thank the Lord they've become pebbles."

He sighed, and for a moment rested his chin on the hoe-handle, peering out towards the tree-encircled swamp. The hylas were beginning to jingle their elfin bells. A red-winged blackbird sailed in the last sunlight from one apple-tree to another.

"All a vicious circle—and all fascinating. Utterly preposterous and futile, but fascinating."

He dropped the hoe and trundled the wheelbarrow to the edge of the strawberry-bed.

"Why can't you stay where you're put?" he said. "Why do you grow all over the place like this?"

With a trowel he began digging up the runners and placing them on the wheelbarrow. It delighted him to part the soft cool soil with his fingers, to thrust them sensitively among the finely filamented roots. The delicate snap, subterranean, of rootlets gave him a delicious pang. "Blood flows—but it's all for the best; in the best of all possible worlds. Yield to me, strawberries, and you shall bear. I am the resurrection and the life." When he had a sufficient pile of plants, he trundled the wheelbarrow to the new bed, exquisitely prepared, rich, warm, inviting. With the hoe he made a series of holes, and then, stooping, thrust the hairy roots back into the earth, pressing the soil tenderly about them. Then he rose, stretched his back, and lighted his pipe, shutting his left eye, and enshrining the flame, which danced, in the hollow of his stained hands. The cloud of smoke went up like incense.

"Water!" he cried. "Water! Water!"

Martha appeared, after a moment, bringing the watering-pot. She held it in front of her with both hands.

"Quick, Martha, before they die. Their tongues are turning black."

"Silly!" Martha replied.

The earth about each plant was darkened with the tilted water, and the soiled leaves and stems were brightened.

"Listen, daddy! They're smacking their lips."

"They are pale, they have their eyes shut, they are reaching desperately down into the darkness for something to hold on to. They grope and tickle at atoms of soil, they shrink away from pebbles, they sigh and relax."

"When the dew falls, they'll sing."

"Ha! ha! what fools we are."

He flung the hoe across the wheelbarrow and started wheeling it towards the toolhouse.

"Bring the watering-pot."

Martha ran after him and put it in the wheelbarrow.

"That's right—add to my burden—never do anything that you can make somebody else do."

Martha giggled in response and skipped towards the house. When she reached the stone steps she put her feet close together and with dark seriousness hopped up step after step in that manner. He watched her and smiled.

"O Lord, Lord," he said, "what a circus we are."

He trundled the bumping wheelbarrow and whistled. The red sun, enormous in the slight haze, was gashing itself cruelly on a black pine-tree. The hylas, by now, had burst into full shrill-sweet chorus in the swamp, and of the birds all but a few scraping grackles were still. "Peace—peace—peace," sang the hylas, a thousand at once. Silver bells, frailer than thimbles, ringing under a still and infinite sea of ether . . . "Peace—peace," he murmured. Then he dropped the wheelbarrow in horror, and put his hands to his ears. "The enemy!" he cried. "Martha! hurry! Martha!" This time Martha seemed to be out of earshot, so he was obliged to circumvent the enemy with great caution. The enemy was a toad who sat by preference near the toolhouse door: obese, sage, and wrinkled like a Chinese god. "Toad that under cold stone." Marvelous compulsion of rhythm . . . He thrust the wheelbarrow into the cool pleasant-smelling darkness of the toolhouse, and walked towards the kitchen door, which just at that moment Hilda opened.

"Hurry up," she said. Her voice had a delicious mildness in the still air and added curiously to his already overwhelming sense of luxury. He had, for a moment, an extraordinarily satisfying sense of space.

III

He lifted his eyes from the pudding to the Hokusai print over the mantel.

"Think of it with shame! We sit here again grossly feeding our insatiable bellies, while Fujiyama, there, thrusts his copper-colored cone into a cobalt sky among whipped-cream clouds! Pilgrims, in the dusk, toil up his sides with staves. Pilgrims like ants. They struggle upwards in the darkness for pure love of beauty."

"I don't like bread-pudding!" ejaculated Mary solemnly, "it's beany."

Martha and Marjorie joined in a silvery cascade of giggles.

"Where *did* she get that awful word!" said Hilda.

"Tom says it, mother."

"Well, for goodness' sake forget it."

Mary stared gravely about the table, spoon in mouth, and then, removing the spoon, repeated, "It's beany."

He groaned, folding his napkin.

"What an awful affliction a family is. Why did we marry, Hilda? Life is a trap."

"Mrs. Ferguson called this afternoon and presented me with a basket of green strawberries. I'm afraid she thought I wasn't very appreciative. I hate to be interrupted when I'm sewing. Why under the sun does she pick them before they're ripe?"

"That's a nice way to treat a neighbor who gives you a present! . . . You *are* an ungrateful creature."

Hilda was languid.

"Well, I didn't ask her for them."

Her eyes gleamed with a slow provocative amusement.

"They're beany," said Mary.

He rolled his eyes at Mary.

> "Our kids are too much with us. Bib and spoon,
> Feeding and spanking, we lay waste our powers!"

They all pushed back their chairs, laughing, and a moment later, as he lighted his cigar, he heard, from the music-room, Hilda's violin begin with tremulous thin notes, oddly analogous to the sound of her voice when she sang, playing Bach to a methodical loud piano accompaniment by Martha. Melancholy came like a blue wave out of the dusk, lifted him, and broke slowly and deliciously over him. He stood for a moment, made motionless by the exquisite, intricate melody, stared, as if seeking with his eyes for the meaning of the silvery algebra of sound, and then went out.

The sun had set, darkness was at hand. He walked to the top of the stone steps and looked across the shallow valley towards the fading hill and the black water-tower. The trees on the crest, sharply silhouetted against a last band of pale light, looked like marching men. Lights winked at the base of the hill. And now, as hill and water-tower and trees became obscure, he began to see once more the dim phantasmal outlines of the dark city, the city submerged under the infinite sea, the city not inhabited by mortals. Immense, sinister and black, old and cold as the moon, were the walls that surrounded it. No gate gave entrance to it. Of a paler stone were the houses upon houses, tiers upon tiers of shadowy towers, which surmounted the walls. Not a light was to be seen in it, not a motion: it was still. He stared and stared at it, following with strained eyes the faint lines which might indicate its unlighted streets, seeking in vain, as always, to discover in the walls of it any sign of any window. It grew darker, it faded, a profound and vast secret, an inscrutable mystery.

"She is older than the rocks," he murmured.

He turned away and walked over the lawn in the darkness, listening to the hylas, who seemed now to be saturating the hushed night with sound. "Peace—peace—peace—" they sang. *Pax vobiscum.* He gathered the croquet mallets and leaned them against the elm-tree, swearing when he tripped over an unseen wicket. This done, he walked down the pale road, blowing clouds of smoke above him with uplifted face, and luxuriated in the sight of the dark tops of trees motionless against the stars. A soft skipping sound in the leaves at the road's edge made him jump. He laughed to himself . . . "He had no watch, and his trousers grew like grass . . ." He took out his watch and peered closely at it. The children were in bed, and Hilda was waiting for a game of chess. He walked back with his hands deep in his pockets. Pawn to king-four.

"Hilda! Wake up!"

Hilda opened her candid eyes without astonishment and sat up over the chess-board, on which the tiny men were already arranged.

"Goodness! How you scared me. What took you so long? I've been dreaming about Bluebeard."

"Bluebeard! Good Heavens! I hope he didn't look like me."

"He did—remarkably!"

"A *nice* thing to say to your husband . . . Move! Hurry up! . . . I'm going to capture your king. Queens die young and fair."

He smoked his pipe. Hilda played morosely. Delicious, she was when she was half asleep like this! She leaned her head on one hand, her elbow on the table . . . When she had been checkmated at the end of half an hour she sank back wearily in her chair. She looked at him intently for a moment and began to smile.

"And how about the dark city tonight?" she asked. He took slow puffs at his pipe and stared meditatively at the ceiling.

"Ah—the dark city, Hilda! The city submerged under an infinite sea, the city not inhabited by mortals! . . . It was there again—would you believe it? . . . It was there. . . . I went out to the stone steps, smoking my cigar, while you played Bach. I hardly dared to look— I watched the hill out of the corner of my eyes and pretended to be listening to the music . . . And suddenly, at the right moment of dusk, just after the street lamps had winked along the base of the hill, I saw it. The hill that we see there in the daylight, with its water-tower and marching trees, its green sloping fields and brook that flashes in the sun, is unreal, an illusion, the thinnest of disguises —a cloak of green velvet which the dark city throws over itself at the coming of the first ray of light . . . I saw it distinctly. Immense, smooth and black, old and cold as the moon, are the walls that surround it. No gate gives entrance to it. Of a paler stone are the houses upon houses, tiers upon tiers of shadowy towers that surmount those sepulchral walls. No motion was perceptible there—no lights gleamed there—no sound, no whisper rose from it. I thought: perhaps it is a city of the dead. The walls of it have no windows, and its inhabitants must be blind . . . And then I seemed to see it more closely, in a twilight which appeared to be its own, and this closer perception gave way in turn to a vision. For first I saw that all the walls of it are moist, dripping, slippery, as if it were bathed in a deathlike dew; and then I saw its people. Its people are maggots—maggots of perhaps the size of human children; their heads are small and wedge-shaped, and glow with a faint bluish light. Masses of them swarm within those walls. Masses of them pour through the streets, glisten on the buttresses and parapets. They are intelligent. What horrible feast is it that nightly they celebrate there in silence? On what carrion do they feed? It is the universe that they devour; and they build above it, as they devour it, their dark city like a hollow tomb . . . Extraordinary that this city, which seen from here at dusk has so supernatural a beauty, should hide at the core so vile a secret . . ."

Hilda stared at him.

"Really, Andrew, I think you're going mad."

"Going? I'm gone! My brain is maggoty."

They laughed and rattled the chessmen into their wooden box. Then they began locking the doors and windows for the night.

JAMES THURBER

Menaces in May

THE lights of the Hotel Belgium's lank electric sign in West Forty-seventh Street go out at one o'clock. The side of the Palace Theatre across the street looms up then like a dark hill. Two doors away glow the lights of the Somerset delicatessen, open all night. Farther toward Sixth Avenue a little green door swings open and shut incessantly and men bustle in and other men stumble out. Across Sixth Avenue Brentano's and its neighbors are chastely asleep and the street is as tranquil as a road in a suburb.

To the man standing at a window on the fifth floor of the Belgium, the prospect is new and interesting. He watches the vaudeville people coming out of the Somerset, their sharp pantomime blurred by a steady rain. The chap in the very gray suit is obviously mimicking Ted Lewis. A girl takes his gesticulating arm and laughs. Four men stand in a group by the curb, talking loudly, waving their hands: probably dismissing someone as lousy—a noted performer perhaps, or all stage managers.

The sound of a quartet singing on a phonograph record, "Dear, on a Night Like This," comes from the room the man is in, and he turns away from the window. Joe is muffling the Victrola by stuffing a towel into it, because it is so late. Julia is sitting on the edge of the bed. She doesn't say anything when Joe asks her where the devil the fibre needles are. Joe, the man notices, has become a little fat and his hair is thinning. Julia is exactly the same as eighteen years ago. The man ponders the little miracle of their meeting tonight. He had turned an unfamiliar corner and there they were. Julia, as lovely as ever, laughing in the rain. Once they had all been in an Ohio grammar school together. Now they had met on a silly corner in New York, in the rain, at midnight. Perfectly swell the way things happen. Probably everything in life is arranged that way: precise, ineluctable, like a Jed Harris play. "What a day was yes-ter-day for yes-ter-day gave me you-u-u." Joe admires the way Gene Austin sings. He's marvellous, isn't he? What? Oh, yes, wonderful. Isn't he now? Marvellous. Joe is hunting for something again. Where the devil is "Mary Ann"—you got to hear the saxophone in that. The man remembers that Joe had always been importunate, restless like this. The man had been shy, "smart at his lessons." One doesn't win Julias that way. Is one sorry about that? The man looks down into the street again. Funny, now he is writing plays and Joe and Julia are dancing together. Vaudeville. What would that be like? A blonde lady comes out of the Somerset finishing a sandwich. Swiss cheese with lotsa mustard probably. How the devil could Julia be so untouched by all that sort of thing? Was she? Well, what if she wasn't? "And then—my heart—stood—still . . ."

His heart too stands still. Does something, anyway. When she puts her hand to her hair like that. The first gesture he had ever been stricken forlorn by. His mother used to laugh about it. Puppy love. How he had hated that! "Deep as first love and wild with all re-gret. . . ." What? Oh, yes, swell saxophone. That's Red Nichols—great, isn't he? Great. How the mechanics of music affects Joe! He doesn't seem to hear the words. "We'll always be-e-e to-geth-er . . ." Julia rises and lifts the needle. What's the matter with that? Oh, play something lively, Joe. That's lively. Wonder what Julia's life with him is like. Wonder what his own life with Julia would have been. Hers with him. "Every daisy—in the dell—seems to know— but they won't tell—Mary Ann . . ." Joe sings with the record. He can sing. "I'll be yours—say you'll be mine—Mary Ann." Joe goes over and kisses her. The man stirs quickly. Joe keeps his arm around

her. The man moves about. It's terribly late. He must go. It's three
o'clock. One more drink. Well, all right. Here's Happiness . . .

The man leaves, goes down in the elevator, out into the street.
Happiness . . . What a nice thing life is. He sees his image in the
elevator mirrors grinning at him. Good Lord, he's acting like a
youngster in love. Well, what of it? It's wonderful. He starts to
hum ". . . for yes-ter-day gave me you-u-u." On the way out of the
hotel he notices the sign he had laughed about when they came in:
Permanent-Transient. One word. Lot in that. Or is there? Permanent.
Odd, the word seems strange and meaningless when you study it. He
thinks abruptly of Lydia. Lydia is away . . . Lydia has been away a
long time . . . Lydia . . . Funny, that name sounds unfamiliar too
when you keep saying it. He remembers how he used to do that
when he was a boy, keep saying words till they sounded crazy. Wife.
Wife. *That* sounds crazy. Husband. Meals. All that sounds crazy
. . . "What a day was yes-ter-day . . ."

More lights go out in the street. Stragglers march by like worn
soldiers bringing up the frayed and awful edge of battle. Someone
shouts a tremendous curse that rolls down the street like an iron
wheel. Someone else falls sprawling, his overcoat flapping out on
both sides. "Hey, buddy! Hey! cops!" "Ta hell with tha cops fa cry
sake, what da hell's a cop mean to me, what's he got on me—nothin',
see?" It is dark and a little cold and the rain is relentless. There is
the dull morose thunder of ashcans being shoved and rolled and
dropped, the ponderous noises of after three o'clock. They are pulling
the stupid sleepy city onto its feet for another day. A taxi rides up
with its melancholy clacking rhythms, shrieks as it slows down,
groans and rides on.

A sharp sense of menace strikes the man as he turns into Times
Square. Men walk with a creeping tread at three o'clock on a wet
morning along Broadway. They lurch toward you with sinister
suddenness and no word. The sound of a scuffle comes out of a doorway and a choking curse: two cops appear dragging a young fellow
between them. His hat is smashed on his head, his face leers up all
covered with blood. The cops are breathing hard and grinning
grimly. The young fellow gasps short horrible words. "Ya want

another sock in the eye, don't ya?" "Yeh, ya ga—" "Well, by—" They hit him and go on around a corner, dragging him.

In their wake a cluster of men pronounce judgment in wisecracks. Jackals attracted by a crumbling person. One of them wears a strangely prim pair of nose glasses. "The poor son of a—" . . . "Guy's crazy is all" . . . "Yeh, like an Airedale" . . . "Damn clever, these cops" . . . "Sure, two of 'em can beat a guy up easy." The man is haunted by an abrupt feeling of groping at and touching chaos with his hands.

Times Square is a deserted circus ground. The splendor of lights and the fifty thousand people have passed in a few ticks of the clock. A dozen wanderers move about like sick clowns left behind. Two men, dressed too neatly in clothes that are too light, walk past close to the man. One talks without moving his lips. "By god I bin gettin' somethin' on this bird for two years and now by god I'm goin' t' get him." "Pipe down fa cry sake, ya wanta tell the world about it?" They glance at the man. Their eyes are the points of revolvers. The whole pattern of one's life could be destroyed by a stranger's finger on an iron thing. Thank God he didn't overhear them name anyone. Mike Zerrelli—it would have been some meaningless name like that. He shudders and passes along quickly. "Good Lord, I'm nervous as a girl."

Stalking figures clack out a death watch waiting for the express at Times Square. Someone plays the chocolate and Spearmint machines with all the pennies he has. A girl laughs loudly under a sailor's jaw. In New York you never see sailors where sailors belong. Sailors are always in the subway. She stares incessantly at the sailor's eyes, fingering his blouse. He doesn't look at her and his small grin is fixed. Like a prize fight: she's trying to fall into a clinch, he's beating her off with quick, hard body punches and he isn't moving a muscle. He'll probably slip out at Seventy-second Street just as the door starts to close and she'll ride on a dozen stops farther, bitterly silent, chewing gum.

The downtown local gets to Times Square first. The local is asprawl with sleeping men. Incongruously upright men are fascinated by the decay of sleep, mouths drop agape, a hat rolls dustily onto the floor, a man's jaw hits his knee and he sits up with an impossibly quick regaining of his senses. In an impossibly brief while he sags again. A lean man, very drunk, gets on at the Pennsylvania Station. He is as menacing as a flung knife. He kicks the hat that lies on the floor, sits down too quickly beside a drowsing workman, cuffs off the workman's hat. "Whatta hell's matta you?" the insulted one mumbles. "Yeah, whatta hell's matta *you?*" says the drunken one. "Ya ever bin in love ya ever bin in love the hell ya ever bin in love the hell ya have . . ."

The man gets off at Fourteenth, goes out the Thirteenth Street exit. He steps around a puddle of dark water and shivers. He remembers that a month ago a Cuban robbed a poolroom nearby, fled with eight dollars, shot a man through the heart, killed him, ran madly down into the subway, into the exit, beat against the spiked iron gate. "Hey! You can't get through that way, mister!" a youngster cried. A cop loomed at the top stair. The Cuban shot himself through the head. He had killed a man. The morning papers told how the man he had killed wasn't killed at all because he carried a Columbian half dollar for luck in his vest pocket and that saved him. Someone is whistling at the top of the steps tonight. "Spare a guy a dime, brother?" The man gives him a handful of coins and hurries on. His heart is beating fast. "I'm a damn coward." He remembers Lord Jim and how bravely he died. Well, Lord Jim had a reason to die. People cried about Lord Jim, he supposed. What the devil, it was a perfect death, his own inevitable end. Nothing hard about that. It's the dread of your life being ended for no reason—for no reason "On a Night Like This." That was it. Take Cyrano. Someone hit Cyrano on the head with a chimney brick or something. "I have missed everything, even my own death," Cyrano said. That's the menace, missing your own end—your own third act. "I'm not a coward." The man goes on whistling.

He clicks the door of his room behind him and leans heavily against the door. What the devil has been the matter with him? It was because of meeting Julia. That was it. Chaos had threatened a perfectly directed evening. Maybe his life even. Anyway, his second act with Julia. He would put it all in a play.

How would it be to end a play in the first act by having the hero killed by a Mack truck? Lord, he had never had such crazy thoughts before about death . . . He finds himself abruptly standing in front of one of the old bronze candelabra Lydia brought home from France. A breeze from an open window stirs in the room. He can see Lydia's fingers moving in and out of the tinkling crystal pendants, arranging the slim pink candles. What was that poem of Lizette Reese's? "Lydia's been gone this many a year, but the house is full of her." Something like that. The house is full of her. It always is. Even this long while she's been gone. She'll be back in a week now . . .

Suddenly he is getting out some pictures. Here is Lydia in April sunlight, when she is eighteen. Lydia in college, Lydia feeding the silly gulls at Nice, Lydia in a snow of lavender crocuses at Saint Martin Vésubie—that had been in May—two, Lord, three years ago. Lydia on a hillside across from Saint Paul du Var that Sunday when they listened to the ancient bells of the town over the valley. What a finely wrought thing they had made of life. Lovely as a design in crystal, but strong as life. How strong was that? Supposing that sailor in the subway had started to choke the girl. You'd be a coward if you didn't do something, wouldn't you? It's heroic to try to save a life; any life, a sordid, senseless, alien life. A man doesn't run. No, he would have to stick it out and be stabbed by a lecherous sailor. The papers would have run his picture and said what he did was fine. Fine! Lydia would have come home to *that*. But what a swell thing it was after all to walk on the high thin edge of irony and snap your fingers at an alien and nameless terror. Snap your fingers. He hadn't snapped his fingers. He had been scared to death. Because of Lydia. He smiles, not knowing just why.

He gets undressed and goes to bed. The thunder of cans being dropped and the flash of bitter phrases ring through his mind. He tries to keep his mind fixed on the dark sheen of a whirling Victrola record. "What a day was yes-ter-day for yes-ter-day gave me you-u-u . . . the hell ya ever bin in love the hell ya bin in love the hell ya have . . ."

RUTH SUCKOW

Four Generations

"MOVE just a little closer together—the little girl more toward the center—that's good. Now I think we'll get it."

The photographer dived once more under the black cloth.

"Stand back, Ma," a husky voice said. "You'll be in the picture."

Aunt Em stepped hastily back with a panicky look. Mercy, she didn't want to show! She hadn't had time to get her dress changed yet, had come right out of the kitchen where she was baking pies to see the photograph taken. She was in her old dark blue kitchen dress and had her hair just wadded up until she could get time to comb it. It didn't give her much time for dressing up, having all this crowd to cook for.

The boys, and Uncle Chris, standing away back on the edges, grinned appreciatively. Fred whispered to Clarence, "Laugh if Ma got in it." The way she jumped back, and her unconsciousness of the ends sticking up from her little wad of hair, delighted the boys. When they looked at each other, a little remembering glint came into their eyes.

There was quite a crowd of onlookers. Aunt Em. Uncle Chris in his good trousers, and his shirt-sleeves, his sunburned face dark brown above the white collar that Aunt Em had made him put on

Reprinted by permission from *The American Mercury*, January 1924. Copyright 1924 and 1952, The American Mercury.

because of Charlie's. Uncle Gus and Aunt Sophie Spfierschlage had come over to dinner, and stood back against the white house wall, Aunt Sophie mountainous in her checked gingham. The boys, of course, and Bernie Schuldt, who was working for Chris; and another fellow who had come to look at some hogs and who was standing there, conscious of his old overalls and torn straw hat, mumbling, "Well, didn't know I was gona find anything like this goin' on." . . . Charlie's wife, Ella, had been given a chair where she could have a good view of the proceedings. She tried to smile and wave her handkerchief when little Phyllis looked around at her. Then she put her handkerchief to her eyes, lifting up her glasses with their narrow light shell rims, still smiling a little painfully. She had to think from how far Katherine had come.

Aunt Em and Aunt Sophie were whispering: "Ain't it a shame Edna couldn't get over! They coulda took one of Chris and her, and Marine and Merle, with Grandpa, too. . . . That little one looks awful cute, don't she? . . . Well, what takes him so long? Grandpa won't sit there much longer. I should think they coulda had it taken by this time a'ready."

They all watched the group on the lawn. They had decided that the snowball bushes would "make a nice background." The blossoms were gone, but the leaves were dark green, and thick. What a day for taking a picture! It would be so much better out here than in the house. Katherine had made them take it right after dinner, so that little Phyllis would not be late for her nap—nothing must ever interfere with that child's nap. It was the brightest, hottest time of the day. The tall orange summer lilies seemed to open and shimmer in the heat. Things were so green—the country lawn with its thick grass, the heavy foliage of the maple trees against the blue, summery sky of July. The thin varnished supports of the camera stand glittered yellow and sticky. The black cloth of the lens looked thick, dense, hot. The photographer's shirt was dazzling white in the sun, and when he drew his head out from under the cloth his round face shone pink. His coat made a black splotch tossed on the grass.

"The little girl more toward the center."

All three of the others tried anxiously to make little Phyllis more

conspicuous. "Here, we've got to have you showing—my, my!—
whether the rest of us do or not," Charlie said jovially. Grandpa's
small, aged, frail hand moved a little as if he were going to draw
the child in front of him—but, with a kind of delicacy, did not
quite touch her little arm.

They had to wait while a little fleecy cloud crossed the sun, putting a brief, strange, cool shadow over the vivid lawn. In that moment the onlookers were aware of the waiting group. Four generations!
Great-grandfather, grandfather, mother, daughter. It was all the
more impressive when they thought of Katherine and Phyllis having
come from so many miles away. The snowball bushes were densely
green behind them—almost dusky in the heat. Grandpa's chair had
been placed out there—a homemade chair of willow branches. To
think that these four belonged together!

Grandpa, sitting in the chair, might have belonged to another
world. Small, bent like a little old troll, foreign with his black cam-
bric skullcap, his blue, far-apart peasant eyes with their still gaze,
his thin, silvery beard. His hands, gnarled from years of farm work
in a new country, clasped the homemade knotted stick that he held
between his knees. His feet, in old felt slippers with little tufted
wool flowers, were set flat on the ground. He wore the checked
shirt of an old farmer. . . . It hardly seemed that Charlie was his son.
Plump and soft, dressed in the easy garments, of good quality and
yet a trifle careless, of Middle Western small-town prosperity. His
shaven face, paler now than it used to be and showing his age in the
folds that had come about his chin; his glasses with shell rims and
gold bows; the few strands of grayish hair brushed across his pale,
luminous skull. A small-town banker. Now he looked both impressed
and shamefaced at having the photograph taken. . . . And then
Katherine, taking after no one knew whom. Slender, a little hag-
gard and worn, still young, her pale, delicate face and the cords in
her long, soft throat, her little collar bones, her dark, intelligent
weak eyes behind her thick black-rimmed glasses. Katherine had always been like that. Refined, "finicky," studious, thoughtful. Her
hand, slender and a trifle sallow, lay on Phyllis's shoulder.

Phyllis. . . . Her little yellow frock made her vivid as a canary

bird against the dark green of the foliage. Yellow—the relatives did
not know whether they liked that, bright yellow. Still, she did look
sweet. They hadn't thought Katherine's girl would be so pretty. Of
course the care that Katherine took of her—everything had to re-
volve around that child. There was something faintly exotic about
her liquid brown eyes with their jet-black lashes, the shining straight
gold-brown hair, the thick bangs that lay, parted a little and damp
with the heat, on the pure white of her forehead. Her little precise
"Eastern accent." . . . Grandpa looked wonderingly at the bare
arms, round and soft and tiny, white and moist in the heat. Fragile
blue veins made a flowerlike tracery of indescribable purity on the
white skin. Soft, tender, exquisite . . . ach, what a little girl was
here, like a princess!

The cloud passed. Katherine's white and Phyllis's yellow shone
out again from the green. The others stood back watching, a heavy
stolid country group against the white wall of the farmhouse that
showed bright against the farther green of the grove. Beyond lay
the orchard and the rank green spreading cornfields where little
silvery clouds of gnats went shimmering over the moist richness of
the leaves.

"Watch—he's taking it now!"

In the breathless silence they could hear the long whirr and rush
of a car on the brown country road beyond the grove.

Well, the picture was taken. Everyone was glad to be released
from the strain.

Grandpa's chair had been placed nearer the house, under some
maple trees. Charlie stayed out there with him a while. It was his
duty, he felt, to talk to the old man a while, when he was here at
the farm. He didn't get over very often—well, it was a hundred
miles from Rock River, and the road's weren't very good up here
in Sac township. His car stood out at the edge of the grove in the
shade. The new closed car that he had lately bought, a "coach," opulent, shining, with its glass and upholstery and old-blue drapes,
there against the background of the evergreen grove with its fallen

branches and pieces of discarded farm machinery half visible in the deepest shade.

It wasn't really very hard to get away from Rock River and the bank. He and Ella took plenty of trips. He ought to come and see his father more than he did. But he seemed to have nothing to say to Grandpa. The old man had scarcely been off the place for years.

"Well, Pa, you keep pretty well, do you?"

"Ja, pretty goot . . . ja, for so old as I am——"

"Oh, now, you mustn't think of yourself as so old."

Charlie yawned, re-crossed his legs. He lighted a cigar.

"Chris's corn doing pretty well this season?"

"Ach, dot I know nuttings about. Dey don't tell me nuttings."

"Well, you've had your day at farming, Pa."

"Ja . . . ja, ja . . ."

He fumbled in the pocket of his coat, drew out an ancient black pipe.

Charlie said cheerfully, "Have some tobacco?" He held out a can.

The old man peered into it, sniffed. "Ach, dot stuff? No, no, dot is shust like shavings. I smoke de real old tobacco."

"Like it strong, hey?"

They both puffed away.

Grandpa sat in the old willow chair. His blue eyes had a look half wistful, half resentful. Charlie was his oldest child. He would have liked to talk with Charlie. He was always wishing that Charlie would come, always planning how he would tell him things—about how the old ways were going and how the farmers did now, how none of them told him things—but when Charlie came, then that car was always standing ready there to take him right back home again, and there seemed nothing to be said. He always remembered Charlie as the young man, the little boy who used to work beside him in the field—and then when Charlie came, he was this stranger. Charlie was a town man now. He owned a bank! He had forgotten all about the country, and the old German ways. To think of Charlie, their son, being a rich banker, smoking cigars, riding round in a fine carriage with glass windows. . . .

"Dot's a fine wagon you got dere."

Charlie laughed. "That's a coach, Pa."

"So? Coach, is dot what you call it? Like de old kings, like de emperors, de kaisers, rode around in. Ja, you can live in dot. Got windows and doors, curtains—is dere a table, too, stove—no? Ja, dot's a little house on wheels."

He pursed out his lips comically. But ach, such a carriage! He could remember when he was glad enough to get to town in a lumber wagon. Grandma and the children used to sit in the back on the grain sacks. His old hands felt of the smooth knots of his stick. He went back, back, into reverie. . . . He muttered just above his breath, "Ach, ja, ja, ja . . . dot was all so long ago. . . ."

Charlie was silent, too. He looked at the car, half drew out his watch, put it back again. . . . Katherine crossed the lawn. His eyes followed her. Bluish-gray, a little faded behind his modern glasses—there was resentment, bewilderment, wistfulness in them at the same time, and loneliness. He was thinking of how he used to bring Kittie out here to the farm when she was a little girl, when Chris used to drive to Germantown and get them with a team and two-seated buggy. They had come oftener than now when they had the car. . . . "Papa, *really* did you live out here—on this farm?" He had been both proud and a little jealous because she wasn't sunburned and wiry, like Chris's children. A little, slim, long-legged, soft-skinned, dark-eyed girl. "Finicky" about what she ate and what she did—he guessed he and Ella had encouraged her in that. Well, he hadn't had much when he was a child, and he'd wanted his little girl to have the things he'd missed. He wanted her to have more than his brothers' and sisters' children. He was Charlie, the one who lived in town, the successful one. Music lessons, drawing lessons, college . . . and here she had grown away from her father and mother. Chris's children lived close around him, but it sometimes seemed to him that he and Ella had lost Kittie. Living away off there in the East. And when she came home, although she was carefully kind and dutiful and affectionate, there was something aloof. He thought jealously, maybe it would have been better if they hadn't given her all those things, had kept her right at home with them. . . . It hadn't been as much pleasure as he had anticipated having his little grandchild there. There was her "schedule" that Kittie was so pernickety about. He'd been proud to have people in Rock River see her beauty and perfection, but he hadn't been able to take her around and show her off as he'd hoped.

All day he had been seeing a little slim, fastidious girl in a white dress and white hair ribbons and black patent-leather slippers, clinging to his hand with little soft fingers when he took her out to see the cows and pigs. . . . "Well, Kittie, do you wish we lived out here instead of in town?" She shook her head, and her small underlip curled just a little. . . .

He saw Chris and Gus off near the house. They could talk about how crops were coming, and he could tell them, with a banker's authority, about business conditions. He stirred uneasily, got up, yawned, stretched his arms, said with a little touch of shame:

"Well, Pa, I guess I'll go over and talk to Chris a while. I'll see you again before we leave."

"Ja——" The old man did not try to keep him. He watched Charlie's plump figure cross the grass. Ja, he had more to say to the young ones.

Aunt Em was through baking. She had gone into the bedroom to "get cleaned up." She brought out chairs to the front porch. "Sit out here. Here's a chair, Ella—here, Katherine. Ach, Sophie, take a better chair than that."—"Naw, this un'll do for me, Em."

"The womenfolks"—Katherine shuddered away from that phrase. She had always, ever since she was a little girl, despised sitting about this way with "the womenfolks." Planted squat in their chairs, rocking, yawning, telling over and over about births and deaths and funerals and sicknesses. There was a kind of feminine grossness about it that offended what had always been called her "finickiness."

Her mother enjoyed it. She was different from Aunt Em and Aunt Sophie, lived in a different way—a small, plump, elderly woman with waved grayish-silvery hair and a flowered voile dress with little fussy laces, feminine strapped slippers. But still there was something that she liked about sitting here in the drowsy heat and going over and over things with the other women. Sometimes, to Katherine's suffering disgust, she would add items about the birth of Katherine herself—"Well, I thought sure Kittie was going to be a boy. She kicked so hard——" "Oh, Mother, spare us!" Aunt Em would give a fat, comfortable laugh—"Don't look so rambunctious now, does she? Kittie, ain't you ever gona get a little flesh on your bones? You study too hard. She oughta get out and ride the horses like Edna does."

Aunt Sophie Spfierschlage—that was the way she sat rocking, her feet flat on the floor, her stomach comfortably billowing, beads of sweat on her heavy chin and lips and around the roots of her stiff, dull hair. Well, thank goodness she was only Aunt Em's sister, she wasn't really related to the Kleins. Aunt Em was bad enough.

They used to laugh over her fastidious disgust, when she sat here, a delicate, critical little girl who didn't want to get on one of the horses or jump from rafters into the hay. "Kittie thinks that's terrible. Well, Kittie, that's the way things happen." "Ach, she won't be so squeamish when she grows up and has three or four of her own." Now she sat beside them, delicate, still too thin, to Aunt Em's amazement. "Ain't you got them ribs covered up yet? What's the matter? Don't that man of yours give you enough to eat?"—her soft skin pale and her eyes dark from the heat, dressed with a kind of fastidious precision, an ultra-refinement. A fragile bar pin holding the soft white silk of her blouse, her fine dark hair drooping about her face. "Well, you ain't changed much since you got married!" Aunt Em had said. They expected to admit her now to their freemasonry, to have *her* add interesting items about the birth of Phyllis.

Phyllis—her little darling! As if the exquisite miracle of Phyllis could have anything in common with these things! Katherine suffered just as she had always suffered from even small vulgarities. But she sat courteous and ladylike now, a slight dutiful smile on her lips.

"Where does she get them brown eyes? They ain't the color of yours, are they? Turn around and let's have a look at you—no, I thought yours was kinda darker."

Aunt Em had come out now, had squatted down into another chair. "I guess her papa's got the brown eyes."

"Yes, I think she looks a little like Willis."

Ella said almost resentfully, "Well, I don't know whether she takes after Willis's folks or not, but I can't see that she looks one bit like Kittie or any of us."

"Well," Aunt Em said, "but look at Kittie. She don't look like you or Charlie neither. But I guess she's yours just the same, ain't she, Ella? . . . Say, you remember that Will Fuchs? Ja, his girl's got one they say don't belong to who it ought to. Her and that young Bender from over South——"

Katherine did not listen. How long before they could leave? She had thought it right to bring Phyllis over here where her great-grandfather lived, as her father had wished. But it seemed worse to her than ever. She knew that Aunt Em wouldn't let them go without something more to eat, another of her great heavy meals with pie and cake and coffee. Her mother had always said, as if in extenuation of her visible enjoyment of the visit and the food: "Well, Aunt Em means well. Why don't you try and talk with her? She wants to talk with you." But Aunt Em and the Spfierschlages and the whole place seemed utterly alien and horrible to Katherine. For a moment, while they had been taking the photograph out on the lawn, she had felt touched with a sense of beauty. But she had never belonged here. She felt at home in Willis's quiet old frame house in New England, with his precise, elderly New England parents—"refinement," "culture," Willis's father reading "the classics," taking the *Atlantic Monthly* ever since their marriage. She had always felt that those were the kind of people she ought to have had, the kind of home. Of course she loved Father and Mother and was loyal to them. They depended upon her as their only child.

This porch! It seemed to express the whole of her visits to the farm. It was old-fashioned now—a long, narrow porch with a fancy railing, the posts trimmed with red. Her ancestral home! It was utterly alien to her.

They were talking to her again.

"Where's the girl—in taking her nap yet?"

"Yes, she's sleeping."

"Ach, you hadn't ought to make her sleep all the time when she's off visiting. I baked a little piece of piecrust for her. I thought I'd give it to her while it was nice and warm."

"Oh, better not try to give her piecrust," Ella said warningly.

"Ach, that ain't gona hurt her—nice homemade pie. Mine always et that."

"Ja, mine did too."

Katherine's lips closed firmly. She couldn't hurry and hurt Father and Mother—but oh, to get Phyllis home! Father—he was always trying to give the child something she shouldn't have, he wanted to spoil her as he had tried to spoil Katherine herself. . . . She shut her lips tight to steel herself against the pitifulness of the sudden vision of Father—getting so much older these last few years—looking like a child bereft of his toy when she had firmly taken away the things with which he had come trotting happily home for his grandchild. He had gradually drawn farther and farther away. Once he had hurt her by saying significantly, when Phiyllis had wanted a pink blotter in the bank: "You'll have to ask your mother. Maybe there's something in it to hurt you. *Grandpa* don't know." He had wanted to take Phyllis to a little cheap circus that had come to town, to show her off and exhibit her. Mother was more sympathetic, even a little proud of retailing to the other "ladies" how careful Katherine was in bringing up the child, what a "nice family" Willis had. But even she was plaintive and didn't understand. Both she and Father thought that Katherine and Willis were "carrying it too far" when they decided to have Willis teach the child until they could find the proper school for her.

She heard a little sleepy, startled voice from within the house— "Moth-uh!"

"Uh-huh! There's somebody!" Aunt Em exclaimed delightedly.

Katherine hurried into the darkened bedroom where Phyllis lay on Aunt Em's best bedspread. The shades were down, but there was the feeling of the hot sunlight back of them. Phyllis's bare arms and legs were white and dewy. Her damp golden-brown bangs were pushed aside. Katherine knelt adoring. She began to whisper.

"Is Mother's darling awake? . . . Shall we go home soon—see Father? Sleep in her own little room?" . . . Her throat tightened with a homesick vision of the little room with the white bed and the yellow curtains.

They had left Grandpa alone again. Charlie and the other men were standing out beside the car, bending down and examining it, feeling of the tires, trying the handles of the doors.

Grandpa had left his chair in the yard and gone to the old wooden rocker that stood just inside the door of his room. His room was part of the old house, the one that he and Grandma had had here on the farm. It opened out upon the back yard, with a little worn, narrow plank out from the door. It looked out upon the mound of the old cyclone cellar, with its wooden door, where now Aunt Em kept her vegetables in sacks on the damp, cool floor, with moist earthen jars of plum and apple butter on the shelf against the cob-webbed wall. The little triangular chicken houses were scattered about in the back yard, and beyond them was the orchard where now small apples were only a little lighter than the vivid summer green of the heavy foliage and where little, dark, shiny bubbles of aromatic sap had oozed out from the rough, crusty bark.

The shadows in the orchard were drawing out long toward the east, and the aisles of sunlight, too, looked longer. The groups of people moved about more. Everything had the freshened look of late afternoon. Grandpa rocked a little. He puffed on his pipe, took it out and held it between his fingers. It left his lower lip moist and shining above the fringe of silvery beard. His blue eyes kept looking toward the orchard, in a still, fathomless gaze. His lips moved at times.

"Ach, ja, ja, ja. . . ." A kind of mild, sighing groan. It had pleased him that they had wanted the photograph taken, with the little great-grandchild. But that was over now. They had left him alone. And again, with a movement of his head, "Ja, dot was all so long ago."

Beyond the orchard, beyond the dark green cornfields that lay behind it, beyond the river and the town, beyond all the wide western country, and the ocean . . . what were his fixed blue eyes, intent and inward and sad, visioning now?

The rocker was framed in the doorway of his room. Even the odor of the room was foreign. His bed with a patchwork quilt, a little dresser, a chest of drawers. The ancient wallpaper had been torn off and the walls calcimined a sky-blue. Against the inner one hung his big silver watch, slowly ticking. . . . His eyes, blue, and his hair under the little black cap, his beard, were silvery. . . . A German text with gaudy flowers hung on a woolen cord above the bed, *"Der Herr ist mein Hirte."*

He started. "Nun—who is dot?"

He did not know that little Phyllis had been watching him. Standing outside the door, in her bright canary yellow, her beautiful liquid brown eyes solemnly studying him. She was half afraid. She had never seen anything so old as "Great-grandfather." The late afternoon sunlight shimmered in the fine texture of his thin silvery beard. It brought out little frostings and marks and netted lines on his old face in which the eyes were so blue. One hand lay upon his knee. She stared wonderingly at the knots that the knuckles made, the brownish spots, the thick veins, the queer, stretched, shiny look of the skin between the bones. She looked at his black pipe, his funny little cap, his slippers with the tufted flowers. . . .

"Ach, so? You t'ink Grandpa is a funny old man, den? You want to look at him? So?"

He spoke softly. A kind of pleased smiling look came upon his face. He stretched out his hand slowly and cautiously, as if it were a butterfly poised just outside his door. A sudden longing to get this small, pretty thing nearer, an ingenuous delight, possessed him now that he was alone with her. He spoke as one speaks to a bird toward which one is carefully edging nearer, afraid that a sudden motion will startle its bright eyes and make it take wing.

"Is dis a little yellow bird? Can it sing a little song?"

A faint smile dawned on the serious parted lips. He nodded at her. She seemed to have come a little closer. He, too, looked in wonderment, as he had done before, at the shining hair, the fragile blue veins on the white temples, the moist, pearly white of the little neck, marveling as he would have marveled at some beautiful strange bird that might have alighted a moment on his doorstep. . . .

"Can't sing a little song? No? Den Grandpa will have to sing one to you."

He had been thinking of songs as he sat here, they had been murmuring somewhere in his mind. Old, old songs that he had known long ago in the old country. . . His little visitor stood quite still as his faint, quavering voice sounded with a kind of dim sweetness in the sunshine. . . .

> "Du, du liegst mir im Herzen,
> Du, du liegst mir im Sinn,
> Du, du machst mir viel Schmerzen,
> Weist nicht wie gut ich dir bin—
> Ja, ja, ja, ja, weist nicht wie gut ich dir bin."

The gaze of her brown, shining eyes never wavered, and a soft glow of fascinated interest grew in them as the sad wailing simplicity of the old tune quavered on the summer air. For a moment she was quite near, they understood each other.

"You like dot? Like Grandpa's song?"

She nodded. A tiny pleased smile curved her fresh lips.

Then suddenly, with a little delicate scared movement, as if after all she had discovered that the place was strange, she flitted away to her mother.

POETRY

AMY LOWELL

Meeting-House Hill

I must be mad, or very tired,
When the curve of a blue bay beyond a railroad track
Is shrill and sweet to me like the sudden springing of a tune,
And the sight of a white church above thin trees in a city square
Amazes my eyes as though it were the Parthenon.
Clear, reticent, superbly final,
With the pillars of its portico refined to a cautious elegance,
It dominates the weak trees,
And the shot of its spire
Is cool and candid,
Rising into an unresisting sky.

Strange meeting-house
Pausing a moment upon a squalid hill-top.
I watch the spire sweeping the sky,
I am dizzy with the movement of the sky;
I might be watching a mast
With its royals set full
Straining before a two-reef breeze.
I might be sighting a tea-clipper,

Tacking into the blue bay,
Just back from Canton
With her hold full of green and blue porcelain
And a Chinese coolie leaning over the rail
Gazing at the white spire
With dull, sea-spent eyes.

ROBERT FROST

Stopping by Woods on a Snowy Evening

Whose woods these are I think I know.
His house is in the village though;
He will not see me stopping here
To watch his woods fill up with snow.

My little horse must think it queer
To stop without a farmhouse near
Between the woods and frozen lake
The darkest evening of the year.

He gives his harness bells a shake
To ask if there is some mistake.
The only other sound's the sweep
Of easy wind and downy flake.

The woods are lovely, dark and deep,
But I have promises to keep,
And miles to go before I sleep,
And miles to go before I sleep.

CARL SANDBURG

Jazz Fantasia

Drum on your drums, batter your banjoes,
sob on the long cool winding saxophones.
Go to it, O jazzmen.

Sling your knuckles on the bottoms of the happy
tin pans, let your trombones ooze, and go husha-
husha-hush with the slippery sand-paper.

Moan like an autumn wind high in the lonesome treetops, moan soft
like you wanted somebody terrible, cry like a racing car slipping away
from a motorcycle cop, bang-bang! you jazzmen, bang altogether
drums, traps, banjoes, horns, tin cans—make two people fight on
the top of a stairway and scratch each other's eyes in a clinch tumbling down the stairs.

Can the rough stuff . . . now a Mississippi steamboat pushes up the
night river with a hoo-hoo-hoo-oo . . . and the green lanterns calling
to the high soft stars . . . a red moon rides on the humps of the low
river hills . . . go to it, O jazzmen.

Accomplished Facts

Every year Emily Dickinson sent one friend
the first arbutus bud in her garden.

In a last will and testament Andrew Jackson
remembered a friend with the gift of George
Washington's pocket spy-glass.

Napoleon too, in a last testament, mentioned a silver
watch taken from the bedroom of Frederick the Great,
and passed along this trophy to a particular friend.

O. Henry took a blood carnation from his coat lapel
and handed it to a country girl starting work in a
bean bazaar, and scribbled: "Peach blossoms may or
may not stay pink in city dust."

So it goes. Some things we buy, some not.
Tom Jefferson was proud of his radishes, and Abe
Lincoln blacked his own boots, and Bismarck called
Berlin a wilderness of brick and newspapers.

So it goes. There are accomplished facts.
Ride, ride, ride on in the great new blimps—
Cross unheard-of oceans, circle the planet.
When you come back we may sit by five hollyhocks.
We might listen to boys fighting for marbles.
The grasshopper will look good to us.

So it goes . . .

STEPHEN VINCENT BENÉT

John Brown's Body

He was a farmer, he didn't think much of towns,
The wheels, the vastness.
He liked the wide fields, the yellows, the lonely browns,
The black ewe's fastness.

Out of his body grows revolving steel,
Out of his body grows the spinning wheel
Made up of wheels, the new, mechanic birth,
No longer bound by toil
To the unsparing soil
Or the old furrow-line,
The great, metallic beast
Expanding West and East,
His heart a spinning coil,
His juices burning oil,
His body serpentine.
Out of John Brown's strong sinews the tall skyscrapers grow,
Out of his heart the chanting buildings rise,
Rivet and girder, motor and dynamo,
Pillar of smoke by day and fire by night,

The steel-faced cities reaching at the skies,
The whole enormous and rotating cage
Hung with hard jewels of electric light,
Smoky with sorrow, black with splendor, dyed
Whiter than damask for a crystal bride
With metal suns, the engine-handed Age,
The genie we have raised to rule the earth,
Obsequious to our will
But servant-master still,
The tireless serf already half a god—

Touch the familiar sod
Once, then gaze at the air
And see the portent there,
With eyes for once washed clear
Of worship and of fear:
There is its hunger, there its living thirst,
There is the beating of the tremendous heart
You cannot read for omens.
                              Stand apart
From the loud crowd and look upon the flame
Alone and steadfast, without praise or blame.
This is the monster and the sleeping queen
And both have roots struck deep in your own mind,
This is reality that you have seen,
This is reality that made you blind.

So, when the crowd gives tongue
And prophets, old or young,
Bawl out their strange despair
Or fall in worship there,
Let them applaud the image or condemn
But keep your distance and your soul from them.
And, if the heart within your breast must burst
Like a cracked crucible and pour its steel
White-hot before the white heat of the wheel,
Strive to recast once more

That attar of the ore
In the strong mold of pain
Till it is whole again,
And while the prophets shudder or adore
Before the flame, hoping it will give ear,
If you at last must have a word to say,
Say neither, in their way,
"It is a deadly magic and accursed,"
Nor "It is blest," but only "It is here."

E. E. CUMMINGS

All in Green Went My Love Riding

All in green went my love riding
on a great horse of gold
into the silver dawn.

four lean hounds crouched low and smiling
the merry deer ran before.

Fleeter be they than dappled dreams
the swift sweet deer
the red rare deer.

Four red roebuck at a white water
the cruel bugle sang before.

Horn at hip went my love riding
riding the echo down
into the silver dawn.

four lean hounds crouched low and smiling
the level meadows ran before.

Softer be they than slippered sleep
the lean lithe deer
the fleet flown deer.

Four fleet does at a gold valley
the famished arrow sang before.

Bow at belt went my love riding
riding the mountain down
into the silver dawn.

four lean hounds crouched low and smiling
the sheer peaks ran before.

Paler be they than daunting death
the sleek slim deer
the tall tense deer.

Four tall stags at a green mountain
the lucky hunter sang before.

All in green went my love riding
on a great horse of gold
into the silver dawn.

four lean hounds crouched low and smiling
my heart fell dead before.

HART CRANE

At Melville's Tomb

Often beneath the wave, wide from this ledge
The dice of drowned men's bones he saw bequeath
An embassy. Their numbers as he watched,
Beat on the dusty shore and were obscured.

And wrecks passed without sound of bells,
The calyx of death's bounty giving back
A scattered chapter, lived hieroglyph,
The portent wound in corridors of shells.

Then in the circuit calm of one vast coil,
Its lashings charmed and malice reconciled,
Forested eyes there were that lifted altars;
And silent answers crept across the stars.

Compass, quadrant and sextant contrive
No farther tides . . . High in the azure steeps
Monody shall not wake the mariner.
This fabulous shadow only the sea keeps.

WALLACE STEVENS

The Bird with the Coppery, Keen Claws

Above the forest of the parakeets,
A parakeet of parakeets prevails,
A pip of life amid a mort of tails

(The rudiments of tropics are around,
Aloe of ivory, pear of rusty rind.)
His lids are white because his eyes are blind.

He is not paradise of parakeets,
Of his gold ether, golden alguazil.
Except because he broods there and is still,

Panache upon panache, his tails deploy
Upward and outward, in green-vented forms,
His tip a drop of water full of storms.

But though the turbulent tinges undulate
As his pure intellect applies its laws,
He moves not on his coppery, keen claws.

He munches a dry shell while he exerts
His will, yet never ceases, perfect cock,
To flare, in the sun-pallor of his rock.

Reprinted from *Harmonium* by Wallace Stevens, by permission of Alfred A. Knopf, Inc. Copyright 1923, 1931 by Alfred A. Knopf, Inc.

T. S. ELIOT

Gerontion

*Thou hast nor youth nor age
But as it were an after dinner sleep
Dreaming of both.*

Here I am, an old man in a dry month,
Being read to by a boy, waiting for rain.
I was neither at the hot gates
Nor fought in the warm rain
Nor knee deep in the salt marsh, heaving a cutlass,
Bitten by flies, fought.
My house is a decayed house,
And the Jew squats on the window sill, the owner,
Spawned in some estaminet of Antwerp,
Blistered in Brussels, patched and peeled in London.
The goat coughs at night in the field overhead;
Rocks, moss, stonecrop, iron, merds.
The woman keeps the kitchen, makes tea,
Sneezes at evening, poking the peevish gutter.
                                     I am an old man,
A dull head among windy spaces.

Signs are taken for wonders. "We would see a sign!"
The word within a word, unable to speak a word,
Swaddled with darkness. In the juvescence of the year
Came Christ the tiger.

In depraved May, dogwood and chestnut, flowering judas,
To be eaten, to be divided, to be drunk
Among whispers; by Mr. Silvero
With caressing hands, at Limoges
Who walked all night in the next room;

By Hakagawa, bowing among the Titians;
By Madame de Tornquist, in the dark room
Shifting the candles; Fraülein von Kulp
Who turned in the hall, one hand on the door.
    Vacant shuttles
Weave the wind. I have no ghosts,
An old man in a draughty house
Under a windy knob.

After such knowledge, what forgiveness? Think now
History has many cunning passages, contrived corridors
And issues, deceives with whispering ambitions,
Guides us by vanities. Think now
She gives when our attention is distracted
And what she gives, gives with such supple confusions
That the giving famishes the craving. Gives too late
What's not believed in, or if still believed,
In memory only, reconsidered passion. Gives too soon
Into weak hands, what's thought can be dispensed with
Till the refusal propagates a fear. Think
Neither fear nor courage saves us. Unnatural vices
Are fathered by our heroism. Virtues
Are forced upon us by our impudent crimes.
These tears are shaken from the wrath-bearing tree.

The tiger springs in the new year. Us he devours. Think at last
We have not reached conclusion, when I

Stiffen in a rented house. Think at last
I have not made this show purposelessly
And it is not by any concitation
Of the backward devils.
I would meet you upon this honestly.
I that was near your heart was removed therefrom
To lose beauty in terror, terror in inquisition.
I have lost my passion: why should I need to keep it
Since what is kept must be adulterated?
I have lost my sight, smell, hearing, taste and touch:
How should I use it for your closer contact?

These with a thousand small deliberations
Protract the profit, of their chilled delirium,
Excite the membrane, when the sense has cooled,
With pungent sauces, multiply variety
In a wilderness of mirrors. What will the spider do,
Suspend its operations, will the weevil
Delay? De Bailhache, Fresca, Mrs. Cammell, whirled
Beyond the circuit of the shuddering Bear
In fractured atoms. Gull against the wind, in the windy straits
Of Belle Isle, or running on the Horn,
White feathers in the snow, the Gulf claims,
And an old man driven by the Trades
To a sleepy corner.

        Tenants of the house,
Thoughts of a dry brain in a dry season.

MARIANNE MOORE

A Talisman

Under a splintered mast,
torn from the ship and cast
      near her hull,

a stumbling shepherd found,
embedded in the ground,
      a sea gull

of lapis lazuli,
a scarab of the sea,
      with wings spread—

curling its coral feet
parting its beak to greet
      men long dead.

ELINOR WYLIE

The Eagle and the Mole

Avoid the reeking herd,
Shun the polluted flock,
Live like that stoic bird,
The eagle of the rock.

The huddled warmth of crowds
Begets and fosters hate;
He keeps, above the clouds,
His cliff inviolate.

When flocks are folded warm,
And herds to shelter run,
He sails above the storm,
He stares into the sun.

If in the eagle's track
Your sinews cannot leap,
Avoid the lathered pack,
Turn from the steaming sheep.

If you would keep your soul
From spotted sight or sound,

Live like a velvet mole;
Go burrow underground.

And there hold intercourse
With roots of trees and stones,
With rivers at their source,
And disembodied bones.

EDNA ST. VINCENT MILLAY

Euclid Alone Has Looked—

Euclid alone has looked on Beauty bare.
Let all who prate of Beauty hold their peace,
And lay them prone upon the earth and cease
To ponder on themselves, the while they stare
At nothing, intricately drawn nowhere
In shapes of shifting lineage; let geese
Gabble and hiss, but heroes seek release
From dusty bondage into luminous air.

O blinding hour, O holy, terrible day,
When first the shaft into his vision shone
Of light anatomized! Euclid alone
Has looked on Beauty bare. Fortunate they
Who, though once only and then but far away,
Have heard her massive sandal set on stone.

"Euclid Alone Has Looked On Beauty Bare" from *The Harp-Weaver and Other Poems* published by Harper & Brothers, Copyright 1920, 1948 by Edna St. Vincent Millay.

H. D.

Song

You are as gold
as the half-ripe grain
that merges to gold again,
as white as the white rain
that beats through
the half-opened flowers
of the great flower tufts
thick on the black limbs
of an Illyrian apple bough.

Can honey distill such fragrance
as your bright hair—
for your face is as fair as rain;
yet as rain that lies clear
on white honey-comb
lends radiance to the white wax,
so your hair on your brow
casts light for a shadow.

CONRAD AIKEN

When Trout Swim Down Great Ormond Street

When trout swim down Great Ormond Street,
And sea-gulls cry above them lightly,
And hawthorns heave cold flagstones up
To blossom whitely,

Against old walls of houses there,
Gustily shaking out in moonlight
Their country sweetness on sweet air;
And in the sunlight,

By the green margin of that water,
Children dip white feet and shout,
Casting nets in the braided water
To catch the trout:

Then I will hold my breath and die,
Swearing I never loved you; no,
'You were not lovely!' I shall cry,
'I never loved you so.'

From *Priapus and the Pool,* published by Boni & Liveright. Copyright 1925 by Conrad Aiken.

EXCERPTS FROM NOVELS

SINCLAIR LEWIS

Babbitt

O N the morning of the dinner, Mrs. Babbitt was restive.
"Now, George, I want you to be sure and be home early to-
night. Remember, you have to dress."

"Uh-huh. I see by the *Advocate* that the Presbyterian General Assembly has voted to quit the Interchurch World Movement. That—"

"George! Did you hear what I said? You must be home in time to
dress to-night."

"Dress? Hell! I'm dressed now! Think I'm going down to the office in my B.V.D.'s?"

"I will not have you talking indecently before the children! And
you do have to put on your dinner-jacket!"

"I guess you mean my Tux. I tell you, of all the doggone nonsensical nuisances that was ever invented—"

Three minutes later, after Babbitt had wailed, "Well, I don't know
whether I'm going to dress or *not*" in a manner which showed that
he was going to dress, the discussion moved on.

"Now, George, you mustn't forget to call in at Vecchia's on the
way home and get the ice cream. Their delivery-wagon is broken
down, and I don't want to trust them to send it by—"

"All right! You told me that before breakfast!"

"Well, I don't want you to forget. I'll be working my head off all day long, training the girl that's to help with the dinner—"

"All nonsense, anyway, hiring an extra girl for the feed. Matilda could perfectly well—"

"—and I have to go out and buy the flowers, and fix them, and set the table, and order the salted almonds, and look at the chickens, and arrange for the children to have their supper upstairs and— And I simply must depend on you to go to Vecchia's for the ice cream."

"All riiiiiight! Gosh, I'm going to get it!"

"All you have to do is to go in and say you want the ice cream that Mrs. Babbitt ordered yesterday by 'phone, and it will be all ready for you."

At ten-thirty she telephoned to him not to forget the ice cream from Vecchia's.

He was surprised and blasted then by a thought. He wondered whether Floral Heights dinners were worth the hideous toil involved. But he repented the sacrilege in the excitement of buying the materials for cocktails.

Now this was the manner of obtaining alcohol under the reign of righteousness and prohibition:

He drove from the severe rectangular streets of the modern business center into the tangled byways of Old Town—jagged blocks filled with sooty warehouses and lofts; on into The Arbor, once a pleasant orchard but now a morass of lodging-houses, tenements, and brothels. Exquisite shivers chilled his spine and stomach, and he looked at every policeman with intense innocence, as one who loved the law, and admired the Force, and longed to stop and play with them. He parked his car a block from Healey Hanson's saloon, worrying, "Well, rats, if anybody did see me, they'd think I was here on business."

He entered a place curiously like the saloons of ante-prohibition days, with a long greasy bar with sawdust in front and streaky mirror behind, a pine table at which a dirty old man dreamed over a glass of something which resembled whisky and with two men at the bar, drinking something which resembled beer, and giving that

impression of forming a large crowd which two men always give in
a saloon. The bartender, a tall pale Swede with a diamond in his
lilac scarf, stared at Babbitt as he stalked plumply up to the bar and
whispered, "I'd, uh— Friend of Hanson's sent me here. Like to get
some gin."

The bartender gazed down on him in the manner of an outraged
bishop. "I guess you got the wrong place, my friend. We sell nothing
but soft drinks here." He cleaned the bar with a rag which would
itself have done with a little cleaning, and glared across his mechanically moving elbow.

The old dreamer at the table petitioned the bartender, "Say, Oscar,
listen."

Oscar did not listen.

"Aw, say, Oscar, listen, will yuh? Say, lis-sen!"

The decayed and drowsy voice of the loafer, the agreeable stink
of beer-dregs, threw a spell of inanition over Babbitt. The bartender moved grimly toward the crowd of two men. Babbitt followed him as delicately as a cat, and wheedled, "Say, Oscar, I want
to speak to Mr. Hanson."

"Whajuh wanta see him for?"

"I just wanted to talk to him. Here's my card."

It was a beautiful card, an engraved card, a card in the blackest
black and the sharpest red, announcing that Mr. George F. Babbitt
was Estates, Insurance, Rents. The bartender held it as though it
weighed ten pounds, and read it as though it were a hundred words
long. He did not bend from his episcopal dignity, but he growled,
"I'll see if he's around."

From the back room he brought an immensely old young man,
a quiet sharp-eyed man, in tan silk shirt, checked vest hanging open,
and burning brown trousers—Mr. Healey Hanson. Mr. Hanson said
only "Yuh?" but his implacable and contemptuous eyes queried Babbitt's soul, and he seemed not at all impressed by the new dark-gray
suit for which (as he had admitted to every acquaintance at the
Athletic Club) Babbitt had paid a hundred and twenty-five dollars.

"Glad meet you, Mr. Hanson. Say, uh— I'm George Babbitt of

the Babbitt-Thompson Realty Company. I'm a great friend of Jake Offutt's."

"Well, what of it?"

"Say, uh, I'm going to have a party, and Jake told me you'd be able to fix me up with a little gin." In alarm, in obsequiousness, as Hanson's eyes grew more bored, "You telephone to Jake about me, if you want to."

Hanson answered by jerking his head to indicate the entrance to the back room, and strolled away. Babbitt melodramatically crept into an apartment containing four round tables, eleven chairs, a brewery calendar, and a smell. He waited. Thrice he saw Healey Hanson saunter through, humming, hands in pockets, ignoring him.

By this time Babbitt had modified his valiant morning vow, "I won't pay one cent over seven dollars a quart" to "I might pay ten." On Hanson's next weary entrance he besought, "Could you fix that up?" Hanson scowled, and grated, "Just a minute—Pete's sake—just a min-ute!" In growing meekness Babbitt went on waiting till Hanson casually reappeared with a quart of gin—what is euphemistically known as a quart—in his disdainful long white hands.

"Twelve bucks," he snapped.

"Say, uh, but say, cap'n, Jake thought you'd be able to fix me up for eight or nine a bottle."

"Nup. Twelve. This is the real stuff, smuggled from Canada. This is none o' your neutral spirits with a drop of juniper extract," the honest merchant said virtuously. "Twelve bones—if you want it. Course y' understand I'm just doing this anyway as a friend of Jake's."

"Sure! Sure! I understand!" Babbitt gratefully held out twelve dollars. He felt honored by contact with greatness as Hanson yawned, stuffed the bills, uncounted, into his radiant vest, and swaggered away.

He had a number of titillations out of concealing the gin-bottle under his coat and out of hiding it in his desk. All afternoon he snorted and chuckled and gurgled over his ability to "give the Boys a real shot in the arm to-night." He was, in fact, so exhilarated that he was within a block of his house before he remembered that there

was a certain matter, mentioned by his wife, of fetching ice cream
from Vecchia's. He explained, "Well, darn it—" and drove back.

Vecchia was not a caterer, he was The Caterer of Zenith. Most
coming-out parties were held in the white and gold ballroom of the
Maison Vecchia; at all nice teas the guests recognized the five kinds
of Vecchia sandwiches and the seven kinds of Vecchia cakes; and
all really smart dinners ended, as on a resolving chord, in Vecchia
Neapolitan ice cream in one of the three reliable molds—the melon
mold, the round mold like a layer cake, and the long brick.

Vecchia's shop had pale blue woodwork, tracery of plaster roses,
attendants in frilled aprons, and glass shelves of "kisses" with all
the refinement that inheres in whites of eggs. Babbitt felt heavy and
thick amid this professional daintiness, and as he waited for the ice
cream he decided, with hot prickles at the back of his neck, that a
girl customer was giggling at him. He went home in a touchy temper. The first thing he heard was his wife's agitated:

"George! *Did* you remember to go to Vecchia's and get the ice
cream?"

"Say! Look here! Do I ever forget to do things?"

"Yes! Often!"

"Well now, it's darn seldom I do, and it certainly makes me
tired, after going into a pink-tea joint like Vecchia's and having to
stand around looking at a lot of half-naked young girls, all rouged up
like they were sixty and eating a lot of stuff that simply ruins their
stomachs—"

"Oh, it's too bad about you! I've noticed how you hate to look at
pretty girls!"

With a jar Babbitt realized that his wife was too busy to be impressed by that moral indignation with which males rule the world,
and he went humbly up-stairs to dress. He had an impression of a
glorified dining-room, of cut-glass, candles, polished wood, lace,
silver, roses. With the awed swelling of his heart suitable to so grave
a business as giving a dinner, he slew the temptation to wear his
plaited dress-shirt for a fourth time, took out an entirely fresh one,
tightened his black bow, and rubbed his patent-leather pumps with
a handkerchief. He glanced with pleasure at his garnet and silver

studs. He smoothed and patted his ankles, transformed by silk socks from the sturdy shanks of George Babbitt to the elegant limbs of what is called a Clubman. He stood before the pier-glass, viewing his trim dinner-coat, his beautiful triple-braided trousers; and murmured in lyric beatitude, "By golly, I don't look so bad. I certainly don't look like Catawba. If the hicks back home could see me in this rig, they'd have a fit!"

He moved majestically down to mix the cocktails. As he chipped ice, as he squeezed oranges, as he collected vast stores of bottles, glasses, and spoons at the sink in the pantry, he felt as authoritative as the bartender at Healey Hanson's saloon. True, Mrs. Babbitt said he was under foot, and Matilda and the maid hired for the evening brushed by him, elbowed him, shrieked "Pleasopn door," as they tottered through with trays, but in this high moment he ignored them.

Besides the new bottle of gin, his cellar consisted of one half-bottle of Bourbon whisky, a quarter of a bottle of Italian vermouth, and approximately one hundred drops of orange bitters. He did not possess a cocktail-shaker. A shaker was proof of dissipation, the symbol of a Drinker, and Babbitt disliked being known as a Drinker even more than he liked a Drink. He mixed by pouring from an ancient gravy-boat into a handleless pitcher; he poured with a noble dignity, holding his alembics high beneath the powerful Mazda globe, his face hot, his shirt-front a glaring white, the copper sink a scoured red-gold.

He tasted the sacred essence. "Now, by golly, if that isn't pretty near one fine old cocktail! Kind of a Bronx, and yet like a Manhattan. Ummmmmm! Hey, Myra, want a little nip before the folks come?"

Bustling into the dining-room, moving each glass a quarter of an inch, rushing back with resolution implacable on her face, her gray and silver-lace party frock protected by a denim towel, Mrs. Babbitt glared at him, and rebuked him, "Certainly not!"

"Well," in a loose, jocose manner, "I think the old man will!"

The cocktail filled him with a whirling exhilaration behind which he was aware of devastating desires—to rush places in fast motors,

to kiss girls, to sing, to be witty. He sought to regain his lost dignity
by announcing to Matilda:

"I'm going to stick this pitcher of cocktails in the refrigerator.
Be sure you don't upset any of 'em."

"Yeh."

"Well, be sure now. Don't go putting anything on this top shelf."

"Yeh."

"Well, be—" He was dizzy. His voice was thin and distant.
"Whee!" With enormous impressiveness he commanded, "Well, be
sure now," and minced into the safety of the living-room. He wondered whether he could persuade "as slow a bunch as Myra and the
Littlefields to go some place aft' dinner and raise Cain and maybe
dig up smore booze." He perceived that he had gifts of profligacy
which had been neglected.

By the time the guests had come, including the inevitable late
couple for whom the others waited with painful amiability, a great
gray emptiness had replaced the purple swirling in Babbitt's head,
and he had to force the tumultuous greetings suitable to a host on
Floral Heights.

The guests were Howard Littlefield, the doctor of philosophy who
furnished publicity and comforting economics to the Street Traction
Company; Vergil Gunch, the coal-dealer, equally powerful in the
Elks and in the Boosters' Club; Eddie Swanson, the agent for the
Javelin Motor Car, who lived across the street; and Orville Jones,
owner of the Lily White Laundry, which justly announced itself
"the biggest, busiest, bulliest cleanerie shoppe in Zenith." But, naturally, the most distinguished of all was T. Cholmondeley Frink,
who was not only the author of "Poemulations," which, syndicated
daily in sixty-seven leading newspapers, gave him one of the largest
audiences of any poet in the world, but also an optimistic lecturer
and the creator of "Ads that Add." Despite the searching philosophy
and high morality of his verses, they were humorous and easily understood by any child of twelve; and it added a neat air of pleasantry
to them that they were set not as verse but as prose. Mr. Frink was
known from Coast to Coast as "Chum."

With them were six wives, more or less—it was hard to tell, so early in the evening, as at first glance they all looked alike, and as they all said, "Oh, *isn't* this nice!" in the same tone of determined liveliness. To the eye, the men were less similar: Littlefield, a hedge-scholar, tall and horse-faced; Chum Frink, a trifle of a man with soft and mouse-like hair, advertising his profession as poet by a silk cord on his eye-glasses; Vergil Gunch, broad, with coarse black hair *en brosse;* Eddie Swanson, a bald and bouncing young man who showed his taste for elegance by an evening waistcoat of figured black silk with glass buttons; Orville Jones, a steady-looking, stubby, not very memorable person, with a hemp-colored toothbrush mustache. Yet they were all so well fed and clean, they all shouted " 'Evenin', Georgie!" with such robustness, that they seemed to be cousins, and the strange thing is that the longer one knew the women, the less alike they seemed while the longer one knew the men, the more alike their bold patterns appeared.

The drinking of the cocktails was as canonical a rite as the mixing. The company waited, uneasily, hopefully, agreeing in a strained manner that the weather had been rather warm and slightly cold, but still Babbitt said nothing about drinks. They became despondent. But when the late couple (the Swansons) had arrived, Babbitt hinted, "Well, folks, do you think you could stand breaking the law a little?"

They looked at Chum Frink, the recognized lord of language. Frink pulled at his eye-glass cord as at a bell-rope, he cleared his throat and said that which was the custom:

"I'll tell you, George: I'm a law-abiding man, but they do say Verg Gunch is a regular yegg, and of course he's bigger 'n I am, and I just can't figure out what I'd do if he tried to force me into anything criminal!"

Gunch was roaring, "Well, I'll take a chance—" when Frink held up his hand and went on, "So if Verg and you insist, Georgie, I'll park my car on the wrong side of the street, because I take it for granted that's the crime you're hinting at!"

There was a great deal of laughter. Mrs. Jones asserted, "Mr. Frink is simply too killing! You'd think he was so innocent!"

Babbitt clamored, "How did you guess it, Chum? Well, you-all

just wait a moment while I go out and get the—keys to your cars!"
Through a froth of merriment he brought the shining promise, the
mighty tray of glasses with the cloudy yellow cocktails in the glass
pitcher in the center. The men babbled, "Oh, gosh, have a look!"
and "This gets me right where I live!" and "Let me at it!" But Chum
Frink, a traveled man and not unused to woes, was stricken by the
thought that the potion might be merely fruit-juice with a little neutral spirits. He looked timorous as Babbitt, a moist and ecstatic
almoner, held out a glass, but as he tasted it he piped, "Oh, man,
let me dream on! It ain't true, but don't waken me! Jus' lemme
slumber!"

Two hours before, Frink had completed a newspaper lyric beginning:

*I sat alone and groused and thunk, and scratched my head and
sighed and wunk, and groaned, "There still are boobs, alack, who'd
like the old-time gin-mill back; that den that makes a sage a loon,
the vile and smelly old saloon!" I'll never miss their poison booze,
whilst I the bubbling spring can use, that leaves my head at merry
morn as clear as any babe new-born!*

Babbit drank with the others; his moment's depression was gone;
he perceived that these were the best fellows in the world; he wanted
to give them a thousand cocktails. "Think you could stand another?"
he cried. The wives refused, with giggles, but the men, speaking in
a wide, elaborate, enjoyable manner, gloated, "Well, sooner than
have you get sore at me, Georgie—"

"You got a little dividend coming," said Babbitt to each of them,
and each intoned, "Squeeze it, Georgie, squeeze it!"

When, beyond hope, the pitcher was empty, they stood and talked
about prohibition. The men leaned back on their heels, put their
hands in their trousers-pockets, and proclaimed their views with the
booming profundity of a prosperous male repeating a thoroughly
hackneyed statement about a matter of which he knows nothing
whatever.

"Now, I'll tell you," said Vergil Gunch; "way I figure it is this,
and I can speak by the book, because I've talked to a lot of doctors
and fellows that ought to know, and the way I see it is that it's a

good thing to get rid of the saloon, but they ought to let a fellow have beer and light wines."

Howard Littlefield observed, "What isn't generally realized is that it's a dangerous prop'sition to invade the rights of personal liberty. Now, take this for instance: The King of—Bavaria? I think it was Bavaria—yes, Bavaria, it was—in 1862, March, 1862, he issued a proclamation against public grazing of live-stock. The peasantry had stood for overtaxation without the slightest complaint, but when this proclamation came out, they rebelled. Or it may have been Saxony. But it just goes to show the dangers of invading the rights of personal liberty."

"That's it—no one got a right to invade personal liberty," said Orville Jones.

"Just the same, you don't want to forget prohibition is a mighty good thing for the working-classes. Keeps 'em from wasting their money and lowering their productiveness," said Vergil Gunch.

"Yes, that's so. But the trouble is the manner of enforcement," insisted Howard Littlefield. "Congress didn't understand the right system. Now, if I'd been running the thing, I'd have arranged it so that the drinker himself was licensed, and then we could have taken care of the shiftless workman—kept him from drinking—and yet not've interfered with the rights—with the personal liberty—of fellows like ourselves."

They bobbed their heads, looked admiringly at one another, and stated, "That's so, that would be the stunt."

"The thing that worries me is that a lot of these guys will take to cocaine," sighed Eddie Swanson.

They bobbed more violently, and groaned, "That's so, there is a danger of that."

Chum Frink chanted, "Oh, say, I got hold of a swell new receipt for home-made beer the other day. You take—"

Gunch interrupted, "Wait! Let me tell you mine!" Littlefield snorted, "Beer! Rats! Thing to do is to ferment cider!" Jones insisted, "I've got the receipt that does the business!" Swanson begged, "Oh, say, lemme tell you the story—" But Frink went on resolutely,

"You take and save the shells from peas, and pour six gallons of water on a bushel of shells and boil the mixture till—"

Mrs. Babbitt turned toward them with yearning sweetness; Frink hastened to finish even his best beer-recipe; and she said gaily, "Dinner is served."

There was a good deal of friendly argument among the men as to which should go in last, and while they were crossing the hall from the living-room to the dining-room Vergil Gunch made them laugh by thundering, "If I can't sit next to Myra Babbitt and hold her hand under the table, I won't play—I'm goin' home." In the dining-room they stood embarrassed while Mrs. Babbitt fluttered, "Now, let me see— Oh, I was going to have some nice hand-painted place-cards for you but— Oh, let me see; Mr. Frink, you sit there."

The dinner was in the best style of women's-magazine art, whereby the salad was served in hollowed apples, and everything but the invincible fried chicken resembled something else.

Ordinarily the men found it hard to talk to the women; flirtation was an art unknown on Floral Heights, and the realms of offices and of kitchens had no alliances. But under the inspiration of the cocktails, conversation was violent. Each of the men still had a number of important things to say about prohibition, and now that each had a loyal listener in his dinner-partner he burst out:

"I found a place where I can get all the hooch I want at eight a quart—"

"Did you read about this fellow that went and paid a thousand dollars for ten cases of red-eye that proved to be nothing but water? Seems this fellow was standing on the corner and fellow comes up to him—"

"They say there's a whole raft of stuff being smuggled across at Detroit—"

"What I always say is—what a lot of folks don't realize about prohibition—"

"And then you get all this awful poison stuff—wood alcohol and everything—"

"Course I believe in it on principle, but I don't propose to have anybody telling me what I got to think and do. No American'll ever stand for that!"

But they all felt that it was rather in bad taste for Orville Jones— and he not recognized as one of the wits of the occasion anyway— to say, "In fact, the whole thing about prohibition is this: it isn't the initial cost, it's the humidity."

Not till the one required topic had been dealt with did the conversation become general.

It was often and admiringly said of Vergil Gouch, "Gee, that fellow can get away with murder! Why, he can pull a Raw One in mixed company and all the ladies'll laugh their heads off, but me, gosh, if I crack anything that's just the least bit off color I get the razz for fair!" Now Gunch delighted them by crying to Mrs. Eddie Swanson, youngest of the women, "Louetta! I managed to pinch Eddie's doorkey out of his pocket, and what say you and me sneak across the street when the folks aren't looking? Got something," with a gorgeous leer, "awful important to tell you!"

The women wriggled, and Babbitt was stirred to like naughtiness. "Say, folks, I wished I dared show you a book I borrowed from Doc Patten!"

"Now, George! The idea!" Mrs. Babbitt warned him.

"This book—racy isn't the word! It's some kind of an anthropological report about—about Customs, in the South Seas, and what it doesn't *say!* It's a book you can't buy. Verg, I'll lend it to you."

"Me first!" insisted Eddie Swanson. "Sounds spicy!"

Orville Jones announced, "Say, I heard a Good One the other day about a couple of Swedes and their wives," and, in the best Jewish accent, he resolutely carried the Good One to a slightly disinfected ending. Gunch capped it. But the cocktails waned, the seekers dropped back into cautious reality.

Chum Frink had recently been on a lecture-tour among the small towns, and he chuckled, "Awful good to get back to civilization! I certainly been seeing some hick towns! I mean— Course the folks there are the best on earth, but, gee whiz, those Main Street burgs are slow, and you fellows can't hardly appreciate what it means to be here with a bunch of live ones!"

"You bet!" exulted Orville Jones. "They're the best folks on earth, those small-town folks, but, oh, mama! what conversation! Why, say, they can't talk about anything but the weather and the ne-oo Ford, by heckalorum!"

"That's right. They all talk about just the same things," said Eddie Swanson.

"Don't they, though! They just say the same things over and over," said Vergil Gunch.

"Yes, it's really remarkable. They seem to lack all power of looking at things impersonally. They simply go over and over the same talk about Fords and the weather and so on," said Howard Littlefield.

"Still, at that, you can't blame 'em. They haven't got any intellectual stimulus such as you get up here in the city," said Chum Frink.

"Gosh, that's right," said Babbitt. "I don't want you highbrows to get stuck on yourselves but I must say it keeps a fellow right up on his toes to sit in with a poet and with Howard, the guy that put the con in economics! But these small-town boobs, with nobody but each other to talk to, no wonder they get so sloppy and uncultured in their speech, and so balled-up in their thinking!"

Orville Jones commented, "And, then take our other advantages— the movies, frinstance. These Yapville sports think they're all-get-out if they have one change of bill a week, where here in the city you got your choice of a dozen diff'rent movies any evening you want to name!"

"Sure, and the inspiration we get from rubbing up against high-class hustlers every day and getting jam full of ginger," said Eddie Swanson.

"Same time," said Babbitt, "no sense excusing these rube burgs too easy. Fellow's own fault if he doesn't show the initiative to up and beat it to the city, like we done—did. And, just speaking in confidence among friends, they're jealous as the devil of a city man. Every time I go up to Catawba I have to go around apologizing to the fellows I was brought up with because I've more or less succeeded and they haven't. And if you talk natural to 'em, way we do here, and show finesse and what you might call a broad point of view, why, they think you're putting on side. There's my own half-brother Martin—runs the little ole general store my Dad used to keep. Say, I'll bet he don't know there is such a thing as a Tux—as a dinner-jacket. If he was to come in here now, he'd think we were a bunch of—of— Why, gosh, I swear, he wouldn't know what to think! Yes, sir, they're jealous!"

Chum Frink agreed. "That's so. But what I mind is their lack of culture and appreciation of the Beautiful—if you'll excuse me for being highbrow. Now, I like to give a high-class lecture, and read some of my best poetry—not the newspaper stuff but the magazine things. But say, when I get out in the tall grass, there's nothing will take but a lot of cheesy old stories and slang and junk that if any of us were to indulge in it here, he'd get the gate so fast it would make his head swim."

Vergil Gunch summed it up: "Fact is, we're mighty lucky to be living among a bunch of city-folks, that recognize artistic things and business-punch equally. We'd feel pretty glum if we got stuck in some Main Street burg and tried to wise up the old codgers to the kind of life we're used to here. But, by golly, there's this you got to say for 'em: Every small American town is trying to get population and modern ideals. And darn if a lot of 'em don't put it across! Somebody starts panning a rube crossroads, telling how he was there in 1900 and it consisted of one muddy street, count 'em, one, and nine hundred human clams. Well, you go back there in 1920, and you find pavements and a swell little hotel and a first-class ladies' ready-to-wear shop—real perfection, in fact! You don't want to just look at what these small towns are, you want to look at what they're aiming to become, and they all got an ambition that in the long run is going to make 'em the finest spots on earth—they all want to be just like Zenith!"

*　*　*

Babbitt was fond of his friends, he loved the importance of being host and shouting, "Certainly, you're going to have smore chicken— the idea!" and he appreciated the genius of T. Cholmondeley Frink, but the vigor of the cocktails was gone, and the more he ate the less joyful he felt. Then the amity of the dinner was destroyed by the nagging of the Swansons.

In Floral Heights and the other prosperous sections of Zenith, especially in the "young married set," there were many women who had nothing to do. Though they had few servants, yet with gas stoves, electric ranges and dish-washers and vacuum cleaners, and tiled kitchen walls, their houses were so convenient that they had little housework, and much of their food came from bakeries and delicatessens. They had but two, one, or no children; and despite the myth that the Great War had made work respectable, their husbands objected to their "wasting time and getting a lot of crank ideas" in unpaid social work, and still more to their causing a rumor, by earning money, that they were not adequately supported. They worked perhaps two hours a day, and the rest of the time they ate chocolates, went to the motion-pictures, went window-shopping, went in gossiping twos and threes to cardparties, read magazines, thought timorously of the lovers who never appeared, and accumulated a splendid restlessness which they got rid of by nagging their husbands. The husbands nagged back.

Of these naggers the Swansons were perfect specimens.

Throughout the dinner Eddie Swanson had been complaining, publicly, about his wife's new frock. It was, he submitted, too short, too low, too immodestly thin, and much too expensive. He appealed to Babbitt:

"Honest, George, what do you think of that rag Louetta went and bought? Don't you think it's the limit?"

"What's eating you, Eddie? I call it a swell little dress."

"Oh, it is, Mr. Swanson. It's a sweet frock," Mrs. Babbitt protested.

"There now, do you see, smarty! You're such an authority on clothes!" Louetta raged, while the guests ruminated and peeped at her shoulders.

"That's all right now," said Swanson. "I'm authority enough so I know it was a waste of money, and it makes me tired to see you not wearing out a whole closetful of clothes you got already. I've expressed my idea about this before, and you know good and well you

didn't pay the least bit of attention. I have to camp on your trail to
get you to do anything—"

There was much more of it, and they all assisted, all but Babbitt.
Everything about him was dim except his stomach, and that was a
bright scarlet disturbance. "Had too much grub; oughtn't to eat this
stuff," he groaned—while he went on eating, while he gulped down
a chill and glutinous slice of the ice-cream brick, and cocoanut cake
as oozy as shaving-cream. He felt as though he had been stuffed with
clay; his body was bursting, his throat was bursting, his brain was
hot mud; and only with agony did he continue to smile and shout as
became a host on Floral Heights.

He would, except for his guests, have fled outdoors and walked
off the intoxication of food, but in the haze which filled the room
they sat forever, talking, talking, while he agonized, "Darn fool to
be eating all this—not 'nother mouthful," and discovered that he
was again tasting the sickly welter of melted ice cream on his plate.
There was no magic in his friends; he was not uplifted when Howard
Littlefield produced from his treasure-house of scholarship the information that the chemical symbol for raw rubber is $C_{10}H_{16}$, which
turns into isoprene, or $2C_5H_8$. Suddenly, without precedent, Babbitt
was not merely bored but admitting that he was bored. It was ecstasy
to escape from the table, from the torture of a straight chair, and
loll on the davenport in the living-room.

The others, from their fitful unconvincing talk, their expressions
of being slowly and painfully smothered, seemed to be suffering
from the toil of social life and the horror of good food as much as
himself. All of them accepted with relief the suggestion of bridge.

Babbitt recovered from the feeling of being boiled. He won at
bridge. He was again able to endure Vergil Gunch's inexorable
heartiness. But he pictured loafing with Paul Riesling beside a lake
in Maine. It was as overpowering and imaginative as homesickness.
He had never seen Maine, yet he beheld the shrouded mountains,
the tranquil lake of evening. "That boy Paul's worth all these bally-
hooing highbrows put together," he muttered; and, "I'd like to get
away from—everything."

Even Louetta Swanson did not rouse him.

Mrs. Swanson was pretty and pliant. Babbitt was not an analyst of women, except as to their tastes in Furnished Houses to Rent. He divided them into Real Ladies, Working Women, Old Cranks, and Fly Chickens. He mooned over their charms but he was of opinion that all of them (save the women of his own family) were "different" and "mysterious." Yet he had known by instinct that Louetta Swanson could be approached. Her eyes and lips were moist. Her face tapered from a broad forehead to a pointed chin, her mouth was thin but strong and avid, and between her brows were two outcurving and passionate wrinkles. She was thirty, perhaps, or younger. Gossip had never touched her, but every man naturally and instantly rose to flirtatiousness when he spoke to her, and every woman watched her with stilled blankness.

Between games, sitting on the davenport, Babbitt spoke to her with the requisite gallantry, that sonorous Floral Heights gallantry which is not flirtation but a terrified flight from it:

"You're looking like a new soda-fountain to-night, Louetta."

"Am I?"

"Ole Eddie kind of on the rampage."

"Yes. I get so sick of it."

"Well, when you get tired of hubby, you can run off with Uncle George."

"If I ran away— Oh, well—"

"Anybody ever tell you your hands are awful pretty?"

She looked down at them, she pulled the lace of her sleeves over them, but otherwise she did not heed him. She was lost in unexpressed imaginings.

Babbitt was too languid this evening to pursue his duty of being a captivating (though strictly moral) male. He ambled back to the bridge-tables. He was not much thrilled when Mrs. Frink, a small twittering woman, proposed that they "try and do some spiritualism and table-tipping—you know Chum can make the spirits come—honest, he just scares me!"

The ladies of the party had not emerged all evening, but now, as the sex given to things of the spirit while the men warred against base things material, they took command and cried, "Oh, let's!" In the dimness the men were rather solemn and foolish, but the good-wives quivered and adored as they sat about the table. They laughed, "Now, you be good or I'll tell!" when the men took their hands in the circle.

Babbitt tingled with a slight return of interest in life as Louetta Swanson's hand closed on his with quiet firmness.

All of them hunched over, intent. They startled as some one drew a strained breath. In the dusty light from the hall they looked unreal, they felt disembodied. Mrs. Gunch squeaked, and they jumped with unnatural jocularity, but at Frink's hiss they sank into subdued awe. Suddenly, incredibly, they heard a knocking. They stared at Frink's half-revealed hands and found them lying still. They wiggled, and pretended not to be impressed.

Frink spoke with gravity: "Is some one there?" A thud. "Is one knock to be the sign for 'yes'?" A thud. "And two for 'no'?" A thud.

"Now, ladies and gentlemen, shall we ask the guide to put us into communication with the spirit of some great one passed over?" Frink mumbled.

Mrs. Orville Jones begged, "Oh, let's talk to Dante! We studied him at the Reading Circle. You know who he was, Orvy."

"Certainly I know who he was! The Wop poet. Where do you think I was raised?" from her insulted husband.

"Sure—the fellow that took the Cook's Tour to Hell. I've never waded through his po'try, but we learned about him in the U.," said Babbitt.

"Page Mr. Dannnnnty!" intoned Eddie Swanson.

"You ought to get him easy, Mr. Frink, you and he being fellow-poets," said Louetta Swanson.

"Fellow-poets, rats! Where d' you get that stuff?" protested Vergil Gunch. "I suppose Dante showed a lot of speed for an old-timer—not that I've actually read him, of course—but to come right down to hard facts, he wouldn't stand one-two-three if he had to buckle down to practical literature and turn out a poem for the newspaper-syndicate every day, like Chum does!"

"That's so," from Eddie Swanson. "Those old birds could take their time. Judas Priest, I could write poetry myself if I had a whole

year for it, and just wrote about that old-fashioned junk like Dante
wrote about."

Frink demanded, "Hush, now! I'll call him. . . . O, Laughing Eyes,
emerge forth into the, uh, the ultimates and bring hither the spirit
of Dante, that we mortals may list to his words of wisdom."

"You forgot to give um the address: 1658 Brimstone Avenue,
Fiery Heights, Hell," Gunch chuckled, but the others felt that this
was irreligious. And besides—"probably it was just Chum making
the knocks, but still, if there did happen to be something to all this,
be exciting to talk to an old fellow belonging to—way back in early
times—"

A thud. The spirit of Dante had come to the parlor of George F.
Babbitt.

He was, it seemed, quite ready to answer their questions. He was
"glad to be with them, this evening."

Frink spelled out the messages by running through the alphabet
till the spirit interpreter knocked at the right letter.

Littlefield asked, in a learned tone, "Do you like it in the Paradiso,
Messire?"

"We are very happy on the higher plane, Signor. We are glad
that you are studying this great truth of spiritualism," Dante replied.

The circle moved with an awed creaking of stays and shirtfronts.
"Suppose—suppose there were something to this?"

Babbitt had a different worry. "Suppose Chum Frink was really
one of these spiritualists! Chum had, for a literary fellow, always
seemed to be a Regular Guy; he belonged to the Chatham Road
Presbyterian Church and went to the Boosters' lunches and liked
cigars and motors and racy stories. But suppose that secretly— After
all, you never could tell about these darn highbrows; and to be an
out-and-out spiritualist would be almost like being a socialist!"

No one could long be serious in the presence of Vergil Gunch.
"Ask Dant' how Jack Shakespeare and old Verg'—the guy they
named after me—are gettin' along, and don't they wish they could
get into the movie game!" he blared, and instantly all was mirth.
Mrs. Jones shrieked, and Eddie Swanson desired to know whether
Dante didn't catch cold with nothing on but his wreath.

The pleased Dante made humble answer.

But Babbitt—the curst discontent was torturing him again, and heavily, in the impersonal darkness, he pondered, "I don't— We're all so flip and think we're so smart. There'd be— A fellow like Dante— I wish I'd read some of his pieces. I don't suppose I ever will, now."

He had, without explanation, the impression of a slaggy cliff and on it, in silhouette against menacing clouds, a lone and austere figure. He was dismayed by a sudden contempt for his surest friends. He grasped Louetta Swanson's hand, and found the comfort of human warmth. Habit came, a veteran warrior; and he shook himself. "What the deuce is the matter with me, this evening?"

He patted Louetta's hand, to indicate that he hadn't meant anything improper by squeezing it, and demanded of Frink, "Say, see if you can get old Dant' to spiel us some of his poetry. Talk up to him. Tell him, *'Buena giorna, señor, com sa va, wie geht's? Keskersaykersa* a little pome, *señor?'* "

The lights were switched on; the women sat on the fronts of their chairs in that determined suspense whereby a wife indicates that as soon as the present speaker has finished, she is going to remark brightly to her husband, "Well, dear, I think per-*haps* it's about time for us to be saying good-night." For once Babbitt did not break out in blustering efforts to keep the party going. He had—there was something he wished to think out— But the psychical research had started them off again. ("Why didn't they go home! Why didn't they go home!") Though he was impressed by the profundity of the statement, he was only half-enthusiastic when Howard Littlefield lectured, "The United States is the only nation in which the government is a Moral Idea and not just a social arrangement." ("True—true—weren't they *ever* going home?") He was usually delighted to have an "inside view" of the momentous world of motors but to-night he scarcely listened to Eddie Swanson's revelation: "If you want to go above the Javelin class, the Zeeco is a mighty good buy. Couple weeks ago, and mind you, this was a fair, square test, they took a Zeeco stock touring-car and they slid up the Tonawanda hill on high, and fellow told me—" ("Zeeco—good boat but— Were they planning to stay all night?")

They really were going, with a flutter of "We did have the best time!"

Most aggressively friendly of all was Babbitt, yet as he burbled he was reflecting, "I got through it, but for a while there I didn't hardly think I'd last out." He prepared to taste that most delicate pleasure of the host: making fun of his guests in the relaxation of midnight. As the door closed he yawned voluptuously, chest out, shoulders wriggling, and turned cynically to his wife.

She was beaming. "Oh, it was nice, wasn't it! I know they enjoyed every minute of it. Don't you think so?"

He couldn't do it. He couldn't mock. It would have been like sneering at a happy child. He lied ponderously: "You bet! Best party this year, by a long shot."

"Wasn't the dinner good! And honestly I thought the fried chicken was delicious!"

"You bet! Fried to the Queen's taste. Best fried chicken I've tasted for a coon's age."

"Didn't Matilda fry it beautifully! And don't you think the soup was simply delicious?"

"It certainly was! It was corking! Best soup I've tasted since Heck was a pup!" But his voice was seeping away. They stood in the hall, under the electric light in its square box-like shade of red glass bound with nickel. She stared at him.

"Why, George, you don't sound—you sound as if you hadn't really enjoyed it."

"Sure I did! Course I did!"

"George! What is it?"

"Oh, I'm kind of tired, I guess. Been pounding pretty hard at the office. Need to get away and rest up a little."

"Well, we're going to Maine in just a few weeks now, dear."

"Yuh—" Then he was pouring it out nakedly, robbed of reticence. "Myra: I think it'd be a good thing for me to get up there early."

"But you have this man you have to meet in New York about business."

"What man? Oh, sure. Him. Oh, that's all off. But I want to hit Maine early—get in a little fishing, catch me a big trout, by golly!" A nervous, artificial laugh.

"Well, why don't we do it? Verona and Matilda can run the house between them, and you and I can go any time, if you think we can afford it."

"But that's— I've been feeling so jumpy lately, I thought maybe it might be a good thing if I kind of got off by myself and sweat it out of me."

"George! Don't you *want* me to go along?" She was too wretchedly in earnest to be tragic, or gloriously insulted, or anything save dumpy and defenseless and flushed to the red steaminess of a boiled beet.

"Of course I do! I just meant—" Remembering that Paul Riesling had predicted this, he was as desperate as she. "I mean, sometimes it's a good thing for an old grouch like me to go off and get it out of his system." He tried to sound paternal. "Then when you and the kids arrive—I figured maybe I might skip up to Maine just a few days ahead of you—I'd be ready for a real bat, see how I mean?" He coaxed her with large booming sounds, with affable smiles, like a popular preacher blessing an Easter congregation, like a humorous lecturer completing his stint of eloquence, like all perpetrators of masculine wiles.

She stared at him, the joy of festival drained from her face. "Do I bother you when we go on vacations? Don't I add anything to your fun?"

He broke. Suddenly, dreadfully, he was hysterical, he was a yelping baby. "Yes, yes, yes! Hell, yes! But can't you understand I'm shot to pieces? I'm all in! I got to take care of myself! I tell you, I got to— I'm sick of everything and everybody I got to—"

It was she who was mature and protective now. "Why, of course! You shall run off by yourself! Why don't you get Paul to go along, and you boys just fish and have a good time?" She patted his shoulder—reaching up to it—while he shook with palsied helplessness, and in that moment was not merely by habit fond of her but clung to her strength.

She cried cheerily, "Now up-stairs you go, and pop into bed. We'll fix it all up. I'll see to the doors. Now skip!"

For many minutes, for many hours, for a bleak eternity, he lay awake, shivering, reduced to primitive terror, comprehending that he had won freedom, and wondering what he could do with anything so unknown and so embarrassing as freedom.

ELLEN GLASGOW

They Stooped to Folly

MRS. DALRYMPLE was alone when he entered, and while she
rose from her inviting sofa and trailed toward him in a tea-
gown of pale yellow chiffon, he breathed in the intoxicating perfume
of her emotion. Ah, if only woman had consented to remain the
delight and the relaxation of man! Everything in the room was soft,
restful, flattering to masculine vanity, and kind to the tarnishing flight
of the years. In that fire-coloured glamour, Mrs. Dalrymple's charm
was still magical. While he held her large white hand, which was a
trifle too plump, but as soft as a flower, he heard, above the tumult
in his heart, the restless flames murmuring like a far-off cluster of
honeybees. A burning sweetness, an effervescent delight, rippled
from his touch to his senses. From the harsh complexities of modern
life, from the fleshless bones of moral problems, he was sinking back
deliciously into the dreamless slumber of pleasures that are not too
important. It was agreeable to discover that nothing, least of all the
bidding of conscience, which decreed that his duty was elsewhere,
had altered in Mrs. Dalrymple's company. For the hour, he was
living again in a man's world. Mrs. Dalrymple, notwithstanding her
war record, was still a woman whom one desired but did not respect.
What a help, what a support are definite classifications, he reflected,

as he sat down beside her, and defended his masculine courage from his legal precaution. Had Mrs. Dalrymple been a good woman, had she been even a perfect lady, serious complications might have ensued. Not only might a sense of duty have preceded him in her affections, but the solid burden of responsibility might have dampened, if it had not extinguished, the pure delight of his senses. It was encouraging to remember (though he was chivalrous at heart) that he was not responsible for what happened, that he was not even involved, except remotely, as the husband of some other woman. For, as every gentleman of the Victorian era was well aware, he could not become involved, except remotely, with a woman who had first forgotten herself with somebody else. All that was expected of a man, if he were profligate, was to enjoy and forget, or, after the habit of Mr. Littlepage, if he were temperate, was to enjoy and regret.

Sitting there in that rosy glamour, he found that instead of profiting by the occasion in a way which would meet the requirements of contemporary fiction, he was seduced into a meditation upon the perishable nature of woman's attraction. At a distance, he had longed passionately, with all the heated fervour of youth, for this moment; but basking now in the warm firelight, he told himself that he had no intention of being faithless to his vows of monogamy. Once again, in spite of his vehement desires, he found that habit, as a controlling motive, is superior to impulse. Once again, he said to himself, with his sombre eyes on the ripened fruit of Mrs. Dalrymple's bosom, he was doomed to hesitate and fail on the very brink of fulfilment.

While he hesitated, Mrs. Dalrymple, who had decided long ago that the tastes of Southern gentlemen are languishing, raised her eyes to his flushed features and began to coo in her most mellifluous notes. "If only I could make you realize how much you have helped me."

"I wish I could have done more," he responded sincerely. "Anybody could have given you that advice."

She bowed her head, and the firelight danced over all the amber waves, from the gleaming crown to the fluffy little curls that pro-

tected her ears. "I believe I'd rather have them too fast than too
slow," she was thinking, "slowness always makes me so nervous;
but it is perfectly true that the faster they are, the quicker you lose
them. No matter what anybody tells you," she mused more deeply,
since Mr. Littlepage showed no signs of hurrying his impulses, "no
matter what anybody tells you, nothing compares with stinginess
when it comes to holding a man. No sooner have you bound one to
you with ties of generosity or pleasure or gratitude, than some woman
with real stinginess appears, and all your labour goes for naught.
The trouble with me is that I've cheapened myself from the most
generous motives. It has taken all these years to teach me that no
man ever put the proper value upon a bargain." Sighing, she continued presently to herself, after a glance at her companion, "If I
had my life to live over again, I'd make it a rule to give away nothing. Nothing! Not an old dress, not a bad penny, not even a kiss."

"Anybody could have given you that advice," Mr. Littlepage repeated suddenly, which was exactly what he had said five minutes
before. Slowness had been always, she told herself, the peculiar flaw
in this kind of love-making. Well, perhaps, for all she had heard to
the contrary, this might prove in the end to be merely another blessing in disguise. If he had not been so slow in the past, this affair
might be already over and done with, and then, in the hour of her
greatest necessity, she might have been left stranded for lovers. Slow
but sure! Had not those restful traits been paired off in a proverb?
And after fifty, no matter how well-preserved, a woman knows how
to appreciate staying power in a lover.

Cheered but not enlivend by these reflections, she said aloud in
her softest accents, "You can't imagine how much it has meant to
me. Even more than your advice, your wonderful sympathy has
helped me to hold up my head."

"Well, you must keep it up now, my dear lady. There isn't any
reason you shouldn't. The world isn't so harsh as it used to be."

"But I never forget. No one to look at me would dream I have a
deep nature. People think that I am volatile because I dance and go
to the movies. They don't understand that I am only trying to escape
from myself."

Indeed, indeed. He looked down at her compassionately while he patted her hand. Such sensibility, no doubt, was old-fashioned, but it was also very feminine. Even though he preferred the light to the heavy touch in love-making that involved no serious responsibility, he was genuinely moved by Mrs. Dalrymple's confession. Strange, how he had misjudged her! Strange, how he had misjudged anything so obvious as her old affection for him!

"You have been very brave, I know," he said gently, while pity broke out in a moist heat over his forehead.

"I can't tell you," she murmured presently, "how much it means to me to find that you haven't forgotten."

"No, I haven't forgotten." After all, he thought as he looked at her primrose-coloured draperies, women are more graceful in tea-gowns.

"When I went away twelve years ago," she said caressingly, while she insisted in an inaudible but more positive tone that you frightened men away if you began to talk about yourself, "I thought that you no longer respected me."

He shook his head in denial. "I am sorry. I feared that we had made a mistake, but I blamed only myself."

She sighed and wiped a tear from her lashes. "I was weak, I know, but I felt that you were so strong." Was that really too serious? she wondered. Or would the epithet "strong," which she had found so efficacious in turning rabbit souls into lion hearts, quiet the moral scruples that were now making trouble?

"I blamed only myself," he repeated, which was true as far as it went. A pleasant fire ran through his veins and flickered out in that obscure region where conscience resides. More years than he liked to remember had flown since a woman had sighed because he was too strong for her; and Mr. Littlepage, who knew his own weakness, felt that strength was the attribute in which he preferred to excel. Looking down, in fear rather than reproach, on Mrs. Dalrymple's curls, and listening to the soft, irregular pulse in her throat, he found himself regretting the lost capacity of youth to yield to temptation. "I suppose I'm not cut out for a philanderer," some detached, ironic spectator in his mind thought as clearly as if it occupied a box at a concert. "After all, few natural bents are harder to overcome than a fixed habit of fidelity." In his private office, or between the cool linen sheets of his twin bed, he had believed himself to be a match for any occasion. But here, in this rosy enchantment, where temptation, as it seemed to him, was almost too free and bold to be tempting, he admitted reluctantly that he was inadequate to the exacting, if silent, demands of a guilty passion. Though he still desired Mrs. Dalrymple, he was content, at least for the present, to desire her less as a happy lover than as a disappointed idealist. For, in common with the best masculine taste of the great tradition, he preferred sin on the stage and elsewhere when it was treated in the grand manner, with an orchestral accompaniment. Without musical or at least dramatic support, he felt that it left one entirely too much at the mercy of one's appetites; and appetites, though useful in evolution, are superfluous in the finished product of a Southern gentleman.

While he reclined there in the firelight, stroking Mrs. Dalrymple's hand, which reminded him of a particularly large and fine magnolia blossom, the idea dawned slowly upon him that his respectful manner of love-making was not giving complete satisfaction. Though the last thing he wished for was a costly, or even a complimentary, affair in his life (having too often arranged the fruits of such intrigues), he was still as sensitive as other men in his vanity, and it wounded him to have any woman imagine that he was deficient in a lower nature. For the first time, it occurred to him to regret that a woman with a past, however stimulating to the emotions, could so seldom be anything else. The changeable moods of man were familiar to him; but he told himself now that the failure of the *grande amoureuse* was in variety. He had never known a woman with a past (except the unwomanly Milly) who seemed to him to have even the weakest grasp upon either the present or the future. Frailty was, no doubt, very attractive; a broken heart made an irresistible appeal to a chivalrous mind; but, since change is the only permanent law of our nature, Mr. Littlepage reflected that even frailty might be expected to harden and broken hearts to become whole again. Certainly, such a sanguine view of tragedy was more American, if less romantic. A passive attitude, even in repentance, he told himself, was not only out of place in a march of progress, but impressed the citizens of our Republic as antiquated and incompetent.

"If only I could see more of you." Mrs. Dalrymple's inviting tone broke in upon his meditations like the amorous note of a dove in the spring. Had she, once again, she questioned mutely, lost sight in her folly of the timid nature of lovers? Had her restless vitality overleaped her discretion and her expert knowledge of men? Well, after all, even if he were the only one on her hook, she reminded herself, with robust but homely wisdom, there are as good fish in the sea as have ever come out of it. Though she told herself that she was prepared to fall in love with him, if the prospect appeared sufficiently promising, she was under no delusion as to what the venture might hold for her. For she had observed that the law of diminishing returns rules in love as in everything else. Like most of her married lovers, Mr. Littlepage, she surmised, would probably prove to be just rather than generous in illicit relations, and as careful as other unfaithful husbands to keep the more durable presents within the family. Yet, knowing these things, she sighed again, in obedience to some deep instinct that was older and wiser than knowledge, "If only I could see more of you, I should have something to look forward to."

"Couldn't you," he asked gently, "take an interest in some good work? In some—cause or charity?" Much as he disliked philanthropists, there were situations, he felt, in which one was compelled to resort to desperate remedies.

She shook her perfectly arranged head, which had been arranged, she reminded herself, not for philanthropy but for adventure. "I never took any interest in such things."

"Nor do I. I don't like reformers, but, after all, you need something to occupy your time. As Duncan says, we cannot have a world war every day."

A sigh escaped her. "Ah, I haven't any life now. I live entirely in the past."

"But that's a mistake, my dear lady. The past, however painful, is over and done with. You are young yet. You are as attractive as you ever were. You look every whit as handsome to me as you did the first time I saw you."

Turning slightly, she enveloped him in one of the celebrated smiles of the 'nineties. "I was a beauty—why shouldn't I say it?—in another period. We had hearts in those days."

"And they were broken," he answered in a troubled tone, while the moist heat cooled to chill dampness on his forehead.

Her eyes, as glimmering as twilight, dwelt on him tenderly. "What else, my dear, are hearts for?" she asked, with a delicious revival of last-century archness.

"What else?" he repeated daringly; and reflected that if only she could sustain her sprightly mood, the evening might become more agreeable. Smiling into her dangerous eyes, he thought of all the ballroom floors and other public places where Mrs. Dalrymple had held court, as a crowned queen, in the early 'nineties, and he thought also, though less cheerfully, of the long procession of Southern gentlemen who had vied with one another for the honour of holding her bouquet when she danced. That was, he hastened to recall, before the noisy scandal of her divorce; for, after the judicious retreat of her first lover, Southern gentlemen had flocked to her not in processions but in single combat, and had shown a disposition to seek quiet corners rather than crowded ballrooms. And then, gradually and imperceptibly, tastes had altered, and the late-Victorian ideal of beauty had gone out of fashion. Vanished also, or surviving with a faded splendour, was the brilliant archness, the irresistible coquetry, which had turned the more nimble or less solid wits of the nineteenth century. Yes, the truth was (he perceived this in the very act of denying it) that she had had her long and glorious day and was now ending. Never again, except in the delusive pages of fiction, would the great Victorian ideal inflame the emotions and the imaginations of men.

"I thought once you might teach me that." Her upraised eyes challenged him while the playful tone of her voice smoothed away his alarm. "If only I could see you now and then."

"Of course, you must see me. It is always," he added, fearful yet resigned, "a pleasure to see you."

"Queenborough has changed so much that I feel like a stranger. So few of my old friends appear to remember me."

"Then you must make new ones. I told you how highly my daughter praises your war record."

"Yes, she was kind to me when we were in the Balkans together. But I wasn't thinking of the younger generation. That is friendly enough. Only the women I used to know have never forgiven me."

He smiled consolingly. "They will when you begin to look as old as they do." This was the kind of thing, he told himself, that every woman of her age and experience expected. For the conversation was flowing again into the old channels, and nothing more, he knew, was required of him than a willing surrender to the warm and slow-moving current. "After all," he continued, with his whimsical humour, "you must confess that you never cared much for women."

"No, they didn't seem worth bothering about. I suppose you would call me a man's woman. That may be the reason," she added gravely, visited by a flash of penetration, "why I had so few friends when I needed them."

"But men still befriended you." Though he tried to make his voice steady, he could not subdue the nervous tremor that afflicted his mind. After a quarter of a century, his conscience still accused him when he remembered her loneliness while the storm broke over her head. Such a lovely head it was then and even to-day; so high, so proud, so like a golden rose in its airy grace. To be sure, he had done more than the rest to protect her; but had he, in the face of his accusing conscience, done all that he could? While her guilty lover had dashed for the stormproof shelter of marriage, the beauty that allured men for pleasure had failed to hold them, Mr. Littlepage mused, in the hour of adversity.

"Are men ever more than fair-weather friends to a man's woman?" she asked, with the capricious gaiety he had never forgotten.

"You know that is not true," he answered, while his reverie warmed and melted beneath her sprightliness. "You know that is not true." Something—was it the transforming glow of the flames or the misty radiance in her eyes?—awakened the living memory of that August evening. As he lost himself in that summer darkness, the old desire and the old ecstasy drummed again in his pulses. "You know that is not true, Amy," he repeated heavily, as if he were in a trance or asleep.

In another instant he would have embraced his illusion. In another instant he would have held out his arms to that misty radiance, to that startled surprise, which tempted and eluded him in her face. But, while he reached toward her, in the very flash and pause with which she surrendered, a trivial incident, as insignificant as the turning on of a light in the hall, shattered the crystal globe of the moment. A bell rang; a step passed; and he heard a messenger asking a question.

Collecting himself with an effort, he looked at his watch. "It is late. I must go," he said, but his voice was thick and clotted with longing.

With a gesture, she seemed to put herself in order, to smooth her shining hair, to reassemble her faculties. "Must you really go?"

"What else can I do?"

"But you'll come again?"

"Oh, yes, I'll come again. Haven't I," he asked, with playful evasion, "always come again?"

"After twelve years?" she sighed, and he thought that she looked suddenly older and more tarnished. The glow had wavered down in her eyes, but they were still dark and unfathomable.

"Oh, it won't be twelve years this time!" he exclaimed in a mood that was more tender than thunderous. "It may be to-night."

"If you cared, you wouldn't go," she said breathlessly. How intense women were, even the lightest, the loosest! Why were they never satisfied to turn from one thing to another, as every man in the world was able to do?

"But I can't stay. Amy, you know I can't stay."

Her eyes were wet as she looked at him. "Will you promise me to come back to-night?"

"If I can, if I can possibly arrange it, I will come back to-night." Did she really care for him, he wondered, oppressed by the responsibility, or was she obeying some general law of woman's impulse to cling? What illogical memories women possessed! What disastrous loyalties! True, he craved the lost flavour of youth; true, he longed, in safe places, for the perilous fires of romance. But he knew now, beyond any doubt, that the only romance he needed was the kind that did not give serious trouble. Prudent rather than possessive, he kissed her clinging lips, and turned quickly away.

As the door closed behind him, Mrs. Dalrymple gazed pensively into her most becoming mirror, which hung over a vase of yellow roses on a graceful Heppelwhite table. While his steps still echoed from the flagged walk to the gate, she sighed with weary resignation. "I shall probably never see him again." Then, more in pity than in resentment, she added sorrowfully, "I don't believe he has a spark of true manhood."

JOHN DOS PASSOS

Manhattan Transfer

Ferryslip

THREE gulls wheel above the broken boxes, orangerinds, spoiled cabbage heads that heave between the splintered plank walls, the green waves spume under the round bow as the ferry, skidding on the tide, crashes, gulps the broken water, slides, settles slowly into the slip. Handwinches whirl with jingle of chains. Gates fold upwards, feet step out across the crack, men and women press through the manuresmelling wooden tunnel of the ferry-house, crushed and jostling like apples fed down a chute into a press.

Metropolis

There were Babylon and Nineveh; they were built of brick. Athens was gold marble columns. Rome was held up on broad arches of rubble. In Constantinople the minarets flame like great candles round the Golden Horn . . . Steel, glass, tile, concrete will be the materials of the skyscrapers. Crammed on the narrow island the millionwindowed buildings will jut glittering, pyramid on pyramid like the white cloudhead above a thunderstorm.

Tracks

The rumpetybump rumpetybump spaced out, slackened; bumpers banged all down the train. The man dropped off the rods. He couldn't move for stiffness. It was pitchblack. Very slowly he crawled out, hoisted himself to his knees, to his feet until he leaned panting against the freightcar. His body was not his own; his muscles were smashed wood, his bones were twisted rods. A lantern burst his eyes.

"Get outa here quick yous. Company detectives is beatin through de yards."

"Say feller, is this New York?"

"You're goddam right it is. Juss foller my lantern; you kin git out along de waterfront."

His feet could barely stumble through the long gleaming v's and crisscrossed lines of tracks, he tripped and fell over a bundle of signal rods. At last he was sitting on the edge of a wharf with his head in his hands. The water made a soothing noise against the piles like the lapping of a dog. He took a newspaper out of his pocket and unwrapped a hunk of bread and a slice of gristly meat. He ate them dry, chewing and chewing before he could get any moisture in his mouth. Then he got unsteadily to his feet, brushed the crumbs off his knees, and looked about him. Southward beyond the tracks the murky sky was drenched with orange glow.

"The Gay White Way," he said aloud in a croaking voice. "The Gay White Way."

Great Lady on a White Horse

Morning clatters with the first L train down Allen Street. Daylight rattles through the windows, shaking the old brick houses, splatters the girders of the L structure with bright confetti.

The cats are leaving the garbage cans, the chinches are going back into the walls, leaving sweaty limbs, leaving the grimetender necks of little children asleep. Men and women stir under blankets and bedquilts on mattresses in the corners of rooms, clots of kids begin to untangle and to scream and kick.

At the corner of Riverton the old man with the hempen beard who sleeps where nobody knows is putting out his picklestand. Tubs of gherkins, pimentos, melonrind, piccalilli give out twining vines and cold tendrils of dank pepperyfragrance that grow like a marshgarden out of the musky bedsmells and the rancid clangor of the cobbled awakening street.

The old man with the hempen beard who sleeps where nobody knows sits in the midst of it like Jonah under his gourd.

Nine Days' Wonder

The sun's moved to Jersey, the sun's behind Hoboken.

Covers are clicking on typewriters, rolltop desks are closing; elevators go up empty come down jammed. It's ebbtide in the downtown district, flood in Flatbush, Woodlawn, Dyckman Street, Sheepshead Bay, New Lots Avenue, Canarsie.

Pink sheets, green sheets, gray sheets. FULL MARKET REPORTS, FINALS ON HAVRE DE GRACE. Print squirms among the shopworn officeworn sagging faces, sore fingertips, aching insteps, strongarm men cram into subway expresses. SENATORS 8, GIANTS 2, DIVA RECOVERS PEARLS, $800,000 ROBBERY.

It's ebbtide on Wall Street, floodtide in the Bronx.

The sun's gone down in Jersey.

Rejoicing City That Dwelt Carelessly

There are flags on all the flagpoles up Fifth Avenue. In the shrill wind of history the great flags flap and tug at their lashings on the creaking goldknobbed poles up Fifth Avenue. The stars jiggle sedately against the slate sky, the red and white stripes writhe against the clouds.

In the gale of brassbands and trampling horses and rumbling clatter of cannon, shadows like the shadows of claws grasp at the taut flags, the flags are hungry tongues licking twisting curling.

Oh it's a long way to Tipperary . . . Over there! Over there!

The harbor is packed with zebrastriped skunkstriped piebald steamboats, the Narrows are choked with bullion, they're pulling gold sovereigns up to the ceilings in the Subtreasury. Dollars whine on the radio, all the cables tap out dollars.

There's a long long trail awinding . . . Over there! Over there!

In the subway their eyes pop as they spell out APOCALYPSE, typhus, cholera, shrapnel, insurrection, death in fire, death in water, death in hunger, death in mud.

Oh it's a long way to Madymosell from Armenteers, over there! The Yanks are coming, the Yanks are coming. Down Fifth Avenue the bands blare for the Liberty Loan drive, for the Red Cross drive. Hospital ships sneak up the harbor and unload furtively at night in old docks in Jersey. Up Fifth Avenue the flags of the seventeen nations are flaring curling in the shrill hungry wind.

O the oak and the ash and the weeping willow tree
And green grows the grass in God's country.

The great flags flap and tug at their lashings on the creaking goldknobbed poles up Fifth Avenue.

Nickelodeon

A nickel before midnight buys tomorrow . . . holdup headlines, a cup of coffee in the automat, a ride to Woodlawn, Fort Lee, Flatbush . . . A nickel in the slot buys chewing gum. Somebody Loves Me, Baby Divine, You're in Kentucky Juss Shu' As You're Born . . . bruised notes of foxtrots go limping out of doors, blues, waltzes (We'd Danced the Whole Night Through) trail gyrating tinsel memories . . . On Sixth Avenue on Fourteenth there are still flyspecked stereopticons where for a nickel you can peep at yellowed yesterdays. Beside the peppering shooting gallery you stoop into the flicker A HOT TIME, THE BACHELOR'S SURPRISE, THE STOLEN GARTER . . . wastebasket of tornup daydreams . . . A nickel before midnight buys our yesterdays.

Skyscraper

The young man without legs has stopped still in the middle of the south sidewalk of Fourteenth Street. He wears a blue knitted sweater and a blue stocking cap. His eyes staring up widen until they fill the paperwhite face. Drifts across the sky a dirigible, bright tinfoil cigar misted with height, gently prodding the rainwashed sky and the soft clouds. The young man without legs stops still propped on his arms in the middle of the south sidewalk of Fourteenth Street. Among striding legs, lean legs, waddling legs, legs in skirts and pants and knickerbockers, he stops perfectly still, propped on his arms, looking up at the dirigible.

THOMAS WOLFE

Look Homeward, Angel

EUGENE was loose now in the limitless meadows of sensation: his sensory equipment was so complete that at the moment of perception of a single thing, the whole background of color, warmth, odor, sound, taste established itself, so that later, the breath of hot dandelion brought back the grass-warm banks of Spring, a day, a place, the rustling of young leaves, or the page of a book, the thin exotic smell of tangerine, the wintry bite of great apples; or, as with *Gulliver's Travels,* a bright windy day in March, the spurting moments of warmth, the drip and reek of the earth-thaw, the feel of the fire.

He had won his first release from the fences of home—he was not quite six, when, of his own insistence, he went to school. Eliza did not want him to go, but his only close companion, Max Isaacs, a year his senior, was going, and there was in his heart a constricting terror that he would be left alone again. She told him he could not go: she felt, somehow, that school began the slow, the final loosening of the cords that held them together, but as she saw him slide craftily out the gate one morning in September and run at top speed to the corner where the other little boy was waiting, she did nothing to bring him back. Something taut snapped in her: she remembered his furtive backward glance, and she wept. And she did not weep for herself, but for him: the hour after his birth she had looked in his dark eyes and had seen something that would brood there eternally, she knew, unfathomable wells of remote and intangible loneliness: she knew that in her dark and sorrowful womb a stranger had come to life, fed by the lost communications of eternity, his own ghost, haunter of his own house, lonely to himself and to the world. O lost.

Busy with the ache of their own growing-pains, his brothers and sisters had little time for him: he was almost six years younger than Luke, the youngest of them, but they exerted over him the occasional small cruelties, petty tormentings by elder children of a younger, interested and excited by the brief screaming insanity of his temper when, goaded and taunted from some deep dream, he would seize a carving knife and pursue them, or batter his head against the walls.

They felt that he was "queer"—the other boys preached the smug cowardice of the child-herd, defending themselves, when their persecutions were discovered, by saying they would make a "real boy" of him. But there grew up in him a deep affection for Ben who stalked occasionally and softly through the house, guarding even then with scowling eyes, and surly speech, the secret life. Ben was a stranger: some deep instinct drew him to his child-brother, a portion of his small earnings as a paper-carrier he spent in gifts and amusement for Eugene, admonishing him sullenly, cuffing him occasionally, but defending him before the others.

Gant, as he watched his brooding face set for hours before a fire-lit book of pictures, concluded that the boy liked books, more vaguely, that he would make a lawyer of him, send him into politics, see him elected to the governorship, the Senate, the presidency. And he unfolded to him time after time all the rude American legendry of the country boys who became great men because they were country boys, poor boys, and hard-working farm boys. But Eliza thought of him as a scholar, a learned man, a professor, and with that convenient after-thought that annoyed Gant so deeply, but by which she firmly convinced herself, she saw in this book-brooder the fruit of her own deliberate design.

"I read every moment I could get the chance the summer before he was born," she said. And then, with a complacent and confidential smile which, Gant knew, always preceded some reference to her family, she said: "I tell you what: it may all come out in the Third Generation."

"The Third Generation be Goddamned!" answered Gant furiously.

"Now, I want to tell you," she went on thoughtfully, speaking with her forefinger, "folks have always said that his grandfather would have made a fine scholar if—"

"Merciful God!" said Gant, getting up suddenly and striding about the room with an ironical laugh. "I might have known that it would come to this! You may be sure," he exclaimed in high excitement, wetting his thumb briefly on his tongue, "that if there's any credit to be given I won't get it. Not from you! You'd rather die than admit it! No, but I'll tell you what you will do! You'll brag about that miserable old freak who never did a hard day's work in his life."

"Now, I wouldn't be so sure of that if I were you," Eliza began, her lips working rapidly.

"Jesus God!" he cried, flinging about the room with his customary indifference to reasoned debate. "Jesus God! What a travesty! A travesty on Nature! Hell hath no fury like a woman scorned!" he exclaimed, indefinitely but violently, and then as he strode about, he gave way to loud, bitter, forced laughter.

Thus, pent in his dark soul, Eugene sat brooding on a fire-lit book, a stranger in a noisy inn. The gates of his life were closing him in from their knowledge, a vast aerial world of phantasy was erecting its fuming and insubstantial fabric. He steeped his soul in streaming imagery, rifling the book-shelves for pictures and finding there such treasures as *With Stanley in Africa*, rich in the mystery of the jungle, alive with combat, black battle, the hurled spear, vast snake-rooted forests, thatched villages, gold and ivory; or Stoddard's *Lectures*, on whose slick heavy pages were stamped the most-visited scenes of Europe and Asia; a Book of Wonder, with enchanting drawings of all the marvels of the age—Santos Dumont in his balloon, liquid

air poured from a kettle, all the navies of the earth lifted two feet
from the water by an ounce of radium (Sir William Crookes), the
building of the Eiffel Tower, the Flatiron Building, the stick-steered
automobile, the submarine. After the earthquake in San Francisco
there was a book describing it, its cheap green cover lurid with
crumbling towers, shaken spires, toppling many-storied houses plung-
ing into the splitting flame-jawed earth. And there was another
called *Palaces of Sin,* or *The Devil in Society,* purporting to be the
work of a pious millionaire, who had drained his vast fortune in
exposing the painted sores that blemish the spotless-seeming hide
of great position, and there were enticing pictures showing the
author walking in a silk hat down a street full of magnificent palaces
of sin.

Out of this strange jumbled gallery of pictures the pieced-out
world was expanding under the brooding power of his imagination:
the lost dark angels of the Doré "Milton" swooped into cavernous
Hell beyond this upper earth of soaring or toppling spires, machine
wonder, maced and mailed romance. And, as he thought of his
future liberation into this epic world, where all the color of life
blazed brightest far away from home, his heart flooded his face with
lakes of blood.

He had heard already the ringing of remote church bells over a
countryside on Sunday night; had listened to the earth steeped in the
brooding symphony of dark, and the million-noted little night things;
and he had heard thus the far retreating wail of a whistle in a
distant valley, and faint thunder on the rails; and he felt the infinite
depth and width of the golden world in the brief seductions of a
thousand multiplex and mixed mysterious odors and sensations, weaving, with a blinding interplay and aural explosions, one into the
other.

He remembered yet the East India Tea House at the Fair, the
sandalwood, the turbans, and the robes, the cool interior and the
smell of India tea; and he had felt now the nostalgic thrill of dew-
wet mornings in Spring, the cherry scent, the cool clarion earth, the
wet loaminess of the garden, the pungent breakfast smells and the
floating snow of blossoms. He knew the inchoate sharp excitement of

hot dandelions in young Spring grass at noon; the smell of cellars, cobwebs, and built-on secret earth; in July, of watermelons bedded in sweet hay, inside a farmer's covered wagon; of cantaloupe and crated peaches; and the scent of orange rind, bitter-sweet, before a fire of coals. He knew the good male smell of his father's sitting-room; of the smooth worn leather sofa, with the gaping horse-hair rent; of the blistered varnished wood upon the hearth; of the heated calf-skin bindings; of the flat moist plug of apple tobacco, stuck with a red flag; of wood-smoke and burnt leaves in October; of the brown tired autumn earth; of honey-suckle at night; of warm nasturtiums; of a clean ruddy farmer who comes weekly with printed butter, eggs and milk; of fat limp underdone bacon and of coffee; of a bakery-oven in the wind; of large deep-hued stringbeans smoking-hot and seasoned well with salt and butter; of a room of old pine boards in which books and carpets have been stored, long closed; of Concord grapes in their long white baskets.

Yes, and the exciting smell of chalk and varnished desks; the smell of heavy bread-sandwiches of cold fried meat and butter; the smell of new leather in a saddler's shop, or of a warm leather chair; of honey and of unground coffee; of barrelled sweet-pickles and cheese and all the fragrant compost of the grocer's; the smell of stored apples in the cellar, and of orchard-apple smells, of pressed-cider pulp; of pears ripening on a sunny shelf, and of ripe cherries stewing with sugar on hot stoves before preserving; the smell of whittled wood, of all young lumber, of sawdust and shavings; of peaches stuck with cloves and pickled in brandy; of pine-sap, and green pine-needles; of a horse's pared hoof; of chestnuts roasting, of bowls of nuts and raisins; of hot cracklin, and of young roast pork; of butter and cinnamon melting on hot candied yams.

Yes, and of the rank slow river, and of tomatoes rotten on the vine; the smell of rain-wet plums and boiling quinces; of rotten lily-pads; and of foul weeds rotting in green marsh scum; and the exquisite smell of the South, clean but funky, like a big woman; of soaking trees and the earth after heavy rain.

Yes, and the smell of hot daisy-fields in the morning; of melted puddling-iron in a foundry; the winter smell of horse-warm stables and smoking dung; of old oak and walnut; and the butcher's smell of meat, of strong slaughtered lamb, plump gouty liver, ground pasty sausages, and red beef; and of brown sugar melted with slivered bitter chocolate; and of crushed mint leaves, and of a wet lilac bush; of magnolia beneath the heavy moon, of dogwood and laurel; of an old caked pipe and Bourbon rye, aged in kegs of charred oak; the sharp smell of tobacco; of carbolic and nitric acids; the coarse true smell of a dog; of old imprisoned books; and the cool fern-smell near springs; of vanilla in cakedough; and of cloven ponderous cheeses.

Yes, and of a hardware store, but mostly the good smell of nails; of the developing chemicals in a photographer's dark-room; and the young-life smell of paint and turpentine; of buckwheat batter and black sorghum; and of a negro and his horse, together; of boiling fudge; the brine smell of pickling vats; and the lush undergrowth smell of southern hills; of a slimy oyster-can, of chilled gutted fish; of a hot kitchen negress; of kerosene and linoleum; of sarsaparilla and guavas; and of ripe autumn persimmons; and the smell of the wind and the rain; and of the acrid thunder; of cold starlight, and the brittle-bladed frozen grass; of fog and the misted winter sun; of seed-time, bloom, and mellow dropping harvest.

And now, whetted intemperately by what he had felt, he began, at school, in that fecund romance, the geography, to breathe the mixed odors of the earth, sensing in every squat keg piled on a pierhead a treasure of golden rum, rich port, fat Burgundy; smelling the jungle growth of the tropics, the heavy odor of plantations, the salt-fish smell of harbors, voyaging in the vast, enchanting, but unperplexing world.

* * *

Three weeks after Eugene's return to the university the war ended. The students cursed and took off their uniforms. But they rang the great bronze bell, and built a bonfire on the campus, leaping around it like dervishes.

Life fell back into civilian patterns. The gray back of winter was broken: the Spring came through.

Eugene was a great man on the campus of the little university. He plunged exultantly into the life of the place. He cried out in his throat with his joy: all over the country, life was returning, reviving, awaking. The young men were coming back to the campus. The leaves were out in a tender green blur: the quilled jonquil spouted from the rich black earth, and peachbloom fell upon the shrill young isles of grass. Everywhere life was returning, awaking, reviving. With victorious joy, Eugene thought of the flowers above Ben's grave.

He was wild with ecstasy because the Spring had beaten death. The grief of Ben sank to a forgotten depth in him. He was charged with the juice of life and motion. He did not walk: he bounded along. He joined everything he had not joined. He made funny speeches in chapel, at smokers, at meetings of all sorts. He edited the paper, he wrote poems and stories—he flung outward without pause or thought.

Sometimes at night he would rush across the country, beside a drunken driver, to Exeter and Sydney, and there seek out the women behind the chained lattices, calling to them in the fresh dawn-dusk of Spring his young goat-cry of desire and hunger.

Lily! Louise! Ruth! Ellen! O mother of love, you cradle of birth and living, whatever your billion names may be, I come, your son, your lover. Stand, Maya, by your opened door, denned in the jungle web of Niggertown.

Sometimes, when he walked softly by, he heard the young men talking in their rooms of Eugene Gant. Eugene Gant was crazy. Eugene Gant was mad. Oh, I (he thought) am Eugene Gant!

* * *

Then a voice said: "He didn't change his underwear for six weeks. One of his fraternity brothers told me so." And another: "He takes a bath once a month, whether he needs it or not." They laughed; one said then that he was "brilliant"; they all agreed.

He caught the claw of his hand into his lean throat. They are talking of me, of me! I am Eugene Gant—the conqueror of nations, lord of the earth, the Siva of a thousand beautiful forms.

In nakedness and loneliness of soul he paced along the streets. Nobody said, I know you. Nobody said, I am here. The vast wheel of life, of which he was the hub, spun round.

Most of us think we're hell, thought Eugene. I do. I think I'm hell. Then, in the dark campus path, he heard the young men talking in their rooms, and he gouged his face bloodily, with a snarl of hate against himself.

I think I am hell, and they say I stink because I have not had a bath. But I could not stink, even if I never had a bath. Only the others stink. My dirtiness is better than their cleanliness. The web of my flesh is finer; my blood is a subtle elixir: the hair of my head, the marrow of my spine, the cunning jointure of my bones, and all the combining jellies, fats, meats, oils, and sinews of my flesh, the spittle of my mouth, the sweat of my skin, is mixed with rarer elements, and is fairer and finer than their gross peasant beef.

There had appeared that year upon the nape of his neck a small tetter of itch, a sign of his kinship with the Pentlands—a token of his kinship with the great malady of life. He tore at the spot with frantic nails; he burned his neck to a peeled blister with carbolic acid—but the spot, as if fed by some ineradicable leprosy in his blood, remained. Sometimes, during cool weather, it almost disappeared; but in warm weather it returned angrily, and he scraped his neck red in an itching torture.

He was afraid to let people walk behind him. He sat, whenever possible, with his back to the wall; he was in agony when he descended a crowded stair, holding his shoulders high so that the collar of his coat might hide the terrible patch. He let his hair grow in a great thick mat, partly to hide his sore, and partly because exposing it to the view of the barber touched him with shame and horror.

He would become at times insanely conscious of spotless youth: he was terrified before the loud good health of America, which is really a sickness, because no man will admit his sores. He shrank back at the memory of his lost heroic fantasies: he thought of Bruce-Eugene, of all his thousand romantic impersonations, and never could he endure himself with an itching tetter upon his flesh. He became morbidly conscious of all his blemishes, real and fancied: for days he would see nothing but people's teeth—he would stare into their mouths when he talked to them, noting the fillings, the extractions, the plates and bridges. He would gaze with envy and fear at the sound ivory grinders of the young men, baring his own, which were regular but somewhat yellowed with smoking, a hundred times a day. He scrubbed at them savagely with a stiff brush until the gums bled; he brooded for hours upon a decaying molar which must one day be extracted, and, wild with despair, he would figure out on paper the age at which he might become toothless.

But if, he thought, I lose only one every two years after I am twenty, I shall still have over fifteen left when I am fifty, since we have thirty-two, including wisdom-teeth. And it will not look so bad, if only I can save the front ones. Then, with his hope in futures, he thought: But by that time perhaps the dentists can give me real ones. He read several dental magazines to see if there was any hope for the transplanting of sound teeth for old ones. Then, with brooding satisfaction, he studied his sensual deeply scalloped mouth with the pouting underlip, noting that even when he smiled he barely revealed his teeth.

He asked the medical students innumerable questions about the treatment or cure of inherited blood maladies, venereal diseases, intestinal and inguinal cancers, and the transference of animal glands to men. He went to the movies only to examine the teeth and muscles of the hero; he pored over the toothpaste and collar advertisements in the magazines; he went to the shower-rooms at the gymnasium and stared at the straight toes of the young men, thinking with desperate sick pain of his own bunched and crooked ones. He stood naked before a mirror, looking at his long gaunt body, smooth and white save for the crooked toes and the terrible spot on his neck—lean, but moulded with delicate and powerful symmetry.

Then, slowly, he began to take a terrible joy in his taint. The thing on his neck that could not be gouged or burnt away he identified with a tragic humor of his blood that plunged him downward at times into melancholia and madness. But there was, he saw, a great health in him as well, that could bring him back victoriously from desolation. In his reading of fiction, in the movies, in the collar advertisements, in all his thousand fantasies of Bruce-Eugene, he had never known a hero with crooked toes, a decaying tooth, and a patch of tetter on his neck. Nor had he ever known a heroine, whether among the society women of Chambers and Phillips, or among the great elegants of Meredith and Ouida, who had borne such a blemish. But, in all his fantasies now, he loved a woman with hair of carrot silk and eyes of a faintly weary violet, webbed delicately at the corners. Her teeth were small, white and irregular, and she had one molar edged with gold which was visible when she smiled. She was subtle, and a little weary: a child and a mother, as old and as deep as Asia, and as young as germinal April who returns forever like a girl, a mistress, a parent, and a nurse.

Thus, through the death of his brother, and the sickness that was rooted in his own flesh, Eugene came to know a deeper and darker wisdom than he had ever known before. He began to see that what was subtle and beautiful in human life was touched with a divine pearl-sickness. Health was to be found in the steady stare of the cats and dogs, or in the smooth vacant chops of the peasant. But he looked on the faces of the lords of the earth—and he saw them wasted and devoured by the beautiful disease of thought and passion. In the pages of a thousand books he saw their portraits: Coleridge at twenty-five, with the loose sensual mouth, gaping idiotically, the vast staring eyes, holding in their opium depths the vision of seas haunted by the albatross, the great white forehead—head mixed of Zeus and the village degenerate; the lean worn head of Cæsar, a little thirsty in the flanks; and the dreaming mummy face of Kublai Khan, lit with eyes that flickered with green fires. And he saw the faces of the great Thothmes, and Aspalta and Mycerinus, and all the heads of subtle Egypt—those smooth unwrinkled faces that held the wisdom of 1,200 gods. And the strange wild faces of the Goth, the Frank, the Vandal, that came storming up below the old tired eyes of Rome. And the weary craftiness on the face of the great Jew, Disraeli; the terrible skull-grin of Voltaire; the mad ranting savagery of Ben Jonson's; the dour wild agony of Carlyle's; and the faces of Heine, and Rousseau, and Dante, and Tiglath-Pileser, and Cervantes—these were all faces on which life had fed. They were faces wasted by the vulture, Thought; they were faces seared and hollowed by the flame of Beauty.

And thus, touched with the terrible destiny of his blood, caught in the trap of himself and the Pentlands, with the little flower of sin and darkness on his neck, Eugene escaped forever from the good and the pretty, into a dark land that is forbidden to the sterilized. The creatures of romantic fiction, the vicious doll-faces of the movie women, the brutal idiot regularity of the faces in the advertisements, and the faces of most of the young college-men and women, were stamped in a mould of enamelled vacancy, and became unclean to him.

The national demand for white shiny plumbing, toothpaste, tiled lunch-rooms, hair-cuts, manicured dentistry, horn spectacles, baths, and the insane fear of disease that sent the voters whispering to the druggist after their brutal fumbling lecheries—all of this seemed nasty. Their outer cleanliness became the token of an inner corruption: it was something that glittered and was dry, foul, and rotten at the core. He felt that, no matter what leper's taint he might carry upon his flesh, there was in him a health that was greater than they could ever know—something fierce and cruelly wounded, but alive, that did not shrink away from the terrible sunken river of life; something desperate and merciless that looked steadily on the hidden and unspeakable passions that unify the tragic family of this earth.

* * *

During these years Eugene would go away from Pulpit Hill, by night and by day, when April was a young green blur, or when the Spring was deep and ripe. But he liked best to go away by night, rushing across a cool Spring countryside full of dew and starlight, under a great beach of the moon ribbed with clouds.

He would go to Exeter or Sydney; sometimes he would go to little towns he had never before visited. He would register at hotels as "Robert Herrick," "John Donne," "George Peele," "William Blake," and "John Milton." No one ever said anything to him about it. The people in those towns had such names. Once he registered at a hotel, in a small Piedmont town, as "Ben Jonson."

The clerk spun the book critically.

"Isn't there an *h* in that name?" he said.

"No," said Eugene. "That's another branch of the family. I have an uncle, Samuel, who spells his name that way."

Sometimes, at hotels of ill-repute, he would register, with dark buried glee, as "Robert Browning," "Alfred Tennyson," and "William Wordsworth."

Once he registered as "Henry W. Longfellow."

"You can't fool me," said the clerk, with a hard grin of disbelief. "That's the name of a writer."

He was devoured by a vast strange hunger for life. At night, he listened to the million-noted ululation of little night things, the great brooding symphony of dark, the ringing of remote churchbells across the country. And his vision widened out in circles over moon-drenched meadows, dreaming woods, mighty rivers going along in darkness, and ten thousand sleeping towns. He believed in the infinite rich variety of all the towns and faces: behind any of a million shabby houses he believed there was strange buried life, subtle and shattered romance, something dark and unknown. At the moment of passing any house, he thought, some one therein might be at the gate of death, lovers might lie twisted in hot embrace, murder might be doing.

He felt a desperate frustration, as if he were being shut out from the rich banquet of life. And against all caution, he determined to break the pattern of custom, and look within. Driven on by this hunger, he would suddenly rush away from Pulpit Hill and, as dusk came on, prowl up and down the quiet streets of towns. Finally, lifted beyond all restraint, he would mount swiftly to a door and ring the bell. Then, to whoever came, reeling against the wall and clutching at his throat, he would say:

"Water! In God's name, water! I am ill!"

Sometimes there were women, seductive and smiling, aware of his trick, but loath to let him go; sometimes women touched with compassion and tenderness. Then, having drunk, he would smile with brave apology into startled and sympathetic faces, murmuring:

"Pardon me. It came on suddenly—one of my attacks. I had no time to go for help. I saw your light."

Then they would ask him where his friends were.

"Friends!" he glanced about wildly and darkly. Then, with a bitter laugh, he said, "Friends! I have none! I am a stranger here."

Then they would ask him what he did.

"I am a Carpenter," he would answer, smiling strangely.

Then they would ask him where he came from.

"Far away. Very far," he would say deeply. "You would not know if I told you."

Then he would rise, looking about him with grandeur and compassion.

"And now I must go!" he would say mysteriously. "I have a long way to go before my journey is done. God bless you all! I was a stranger and you gave me shelter. The Son of Man was treated not so well."

Sometimes, he would ring bells with an air of timid inquiry, saying:

"Is this number 26? My name is Thomas Chatterton. I am looking for a gentleman by the name of Coleridge—Mr. Samuel T. Coleridge. Does he live here? . . . No? I'm sorry. . . . Yes, 26 is the number I have, I'm sure. . . . Thank you . . . I've made a mistake . . . I'll look it up in the telephone directory."

But what, thought Eugene, if one day, in the million streets of life, I should really find him?

These were the golden years.

JAMES BRANCH CABELL

Jurgen

SO it was that Jurgen came into Cocaigne, wherein is the bedchamber of Time. And Time, they report, came in with Jurgen,
since Jurgen was mortal: and Time, they say, rejoiced in this respite
from the slow toil of dilapidating cities stone by stone, and, with
his eyes tired by the finicky work of etching in wrinkles, went happily into his bedchamber, and fell asleep just after sunset on this
fine evening in late June: so that the weather remained fair and
changeless, with no glaring sun rays anywhere, and with one large
star shining alone in clear daylight. This was the star of Venus
Mechanitis, and Jurgen later derived considerable amusement from
noting how this star was trundled about the dome of heaven by a
largish beetle, named Khepre. And the trees everywhere kept their
first fresh foliage, and the birds went about their indolent evening
songs, all during Jurgen's stay in Cocaigne, for Time had gone to
sleep at the pleasantest hour of the year's most pleasant season. So
tells the tale.

And Jurgen's shadow also went in with Jurgen, but in Cocaigne as
in Glathion, nobody save Jurgen seemed to notice this curious
shadow which now followed Jurgen everywhere.

In Cocaigne Queen Anaïtis had a palace, where domes and pin-
nacles beyond numbering glimmered with a soft whiteness above

the top of an old twilit forest, wherein the vegetation was unlike that which is nourished by ordinary earth. There was to be seen in these woods, for instance, a kind of moss which made Jurgen shudder. So Anaïtis and Jurgen came through narrow paths, like murmuring green caverns, into a courtyard walled and paved with yellow marble, wherein was nothing save the dimly colored statue of a god with ten heads and thirty-four arms: he was represented as very much engrossed by a woman, and with his unoccupied hands he was holding yet other women.

"It is Jigsbyed," said Anaïtis.

Said Jurgen: "I do not criticize. Nevertheless, I think this Jigsbyed is carrying matters to extremes."

Then they passed the statue of Tangaro Loloquong, and afterward the statue of Legba. Jurgen stroked his chin, and his color heightened. "Now certainly, Queen Anaïtis," he said, "you have unusual taste in sculpture."

Thence Jurgen came with Anaïtis into a white room, with copper plaques upon the walls, and there four girls were heating water in a brass tripod. They bathed Jurgen, giving him astonishing caresses meanwhile,—with the tongue, the hair, the finger-nails, and the tips of the breasts,—and they anointed him with four oils, then dressed him again in his glittering shirt. Of Caliburn, said Anaïtis, there was no present need: So Jurgen's sword was hung upon the wall.

These girls brought silver bowls containing wine mixed with honey, and they brought pomegranates and eggs and barleycorn, and triangular red-colored loaves, whereon with formal gestures they sprinkled sweet-smelling little seeds. Then Anaïtis and Jurgen broke their fast, eating together while the four girls served them.

"And now," says Jurgen, "and now, my dear, I would suggest that we enter into the pursuit of those curious pleasures about which you were recently telling me."

"I am very willing," responded Anaïtis, "since there is no one of these pleasures but is purchased by some diversion of man's nature. Yet first, as I need hardly inform you, there is a ceremonial to be observed."

"And what, pray, is this ceremonial?"

"Why, we call it the Breaking of the Veil." And Queen Anaïtis explained what they must do.

"Well," says Jurgen, "I am willing to taste any drink once."

So Anaïtis led Jurgen into a sort of chapel, adorned with very unchurchlike paintings. There were four shrines, dedicated severally to St. Cosmo, to St. Damianus, to St. Guignole of Brest, and to St. Foutin de Varailles. In this chapel were a hooded man, clothed in long garments that were striped with white and yellow, and two naked children, both girls. One of the children carried a censer: the other held in one hand a vividly blue pitcher half filled with water, and in her left hand a cellar of salt.

First of all, the hooded man made Jurgen ready. "Behold the lance," said the hooded man, "which must serve you in this adventure."

"I accept the adventure," Jurgen replied, "because I believe the weapon to be trustworthy."

Said the hooded man: "So be it! But as you are, so once was I."

Meanwhile Duke Jurgen held the lance erect, shaking it with his right hand. This lance was large, and the tip of it was red with blood.

"Behold," said Jurgen, "I am a man born of a woman incomprehensibly. Now I, who am miraculous, am found worthy to perform a miracle, and to create that which I may not comprehend."

Anaïtis took salt and water from the taller child, and mingled these. "Let the salt of earth enable the thin fluid to assume the virtue of the teeming sea!"

Then, kneeling, she touched the lance, and began to stroke it lovingly. To Jurgen she said: "Now may you be fervent of soul and body! May the endless Serpent be your crown, and the fertile flame of the sun your strength!"

Said the hooded man, again, "So be it!" His voice was high and bleating, because of that which had been done to him.

"That therefore which we cannot understand we also invoke," said Jurgen. "By the power of the lifted lance,"—and now with his left hand he took the hand of Anaïtis,—"I, being a man born of a woman incomprehensibly, now seize upon that which alone I desire with my whole being. I lead you toward the east. I upraise you above the earth and all the things of earth."

Then Jurgen raised Queen Anaïtis so that she sat upon the altar, and that which was there before tumbled to the ground. Anaïtis placed together the tips of her thumbs and of her fingers, so that her hands made an open triangle; and waited thus. Upon her head was a network of red coral, with branches radiating downward: her gauzy tunic had twenty-two openings, so as to admit all imaginable caresses, and was of two colors, being shot with black and crimson curiously mingled: her dark eyes glittered and her breath came fast.

Now the hooded man and the two naked girls performed their share in the ceremonial, which part it is not essential to record. But Jurgen was rather shocked by it.

None the less, Jurgen said: "O cord that binds the circling of the stars! O cup which holds all time, all color, and all thought! O soul of space! not unto any image of thee do we attain unless thy image show in what we are about to do. Therefore by every plant which scatters its seed and by the moist warm garden which receives and nourishes it, by the commingling of bloodshed with pleasure, by the joy that mimics anguish with sighs and shudderings, and by the contentment which mimics death,—by all these do we invoke thee. O thou, continuous one, whose will these children attend, and whom I now adore in this fair-colored and soft woman's body, it is thou whom I honor, not any woman, in doing what seems good to me: and it is thou who art about to speak, and not she."

Then Anaïtis said: "Yea, for I speak with the tongue of every woman, and I shine in the eyes of every woman, when the lance is lifted. To serve me is better than all else. When you invoke me with a heart wherein is kindled the serpent flame, then you will understand the delights of my garden, and what joy unwordable pulsates therein, and how very potent is the sole desire which uses all of a man. To serve me you will then be eager to surrender whatsoever else is in your life; and other pleasures you will take with your left hand, not thinking of them entirely: for I am the desire which uses all of a man, and so wastes nothing. And I accept you. I yearn toward you, I who am daughter and somewhat more than daughter to the

Sun. I who am all pleasure, all ruin, and a drunkenness of the inmost sense, desire you."

Now Jurgen held his lance erect before Anaïtis. "O secret of all things, hidden in the being of all which lives, now that the lance is exalted I do not dread thee: for thou art in me, and I am thou. I am the flame that burns in every beating heart and in the core of the farthest star. I too am life and the giver of life, and in me too is death. Wherein art thou better than I? I am alone: my will is justice: and there comes no other god where I am."

Said the hooded man behind Jurgen: "So be it! But as you are, so once was I."

The two naked children stood one at each side of Anaïtis, and waited there trembling. These girls, as Jurgen afterward learned, were Alecto and Tisiphonê, two of the Eumenidês. And now Jurgen shifted the red point of the lance, so that it rested in the open triangle made by the fingers of Anaïtis.

"I am life and the giver of life," cried Jurgen. "Thou that art one, that makest use of all! I who am but a man born of a woman, I in my station now honor thee in honoring this desire which uses all of a man. Make open therefore the way of creation, encourage the flaming dust which is in our hearts, and aid us in that flame's perpetuation! For is not that thy law?"

Anaïtis answered, "There is no law in Cocaigne save, Do that which seems good to you."

Then said the naked children: "Perhaps it is the law, but certainly it is not justice. Yet we are little and quite helpless. So presently we must be made as you are: for now you two are no longer two, and your flesh is not shared merely with each other. For your flesh becomes our flesh, and your sins must be accounted our sins now: and we have no choice."

Jurgen lifted Anaïtis from the altar, and they went into the chancel and searched for the adytum. There seemed to be no doors anywhere in the chancel: but presently Jurgen found an opening screened by a pink veil. Jurgen thrust with his lance and broke this veil. He heard the sound of one brief wailing cry: it was followed by soft laughter. So Jurgen came into the adytum.

Black candles were burning in this place, and sulphur too was burning there, before a scarlet cross, of which the top was a circle, and whereon was nailed a living toad. And other curious matters Jurgen likewise noticed.

He laughed, and turned to Anaïtis: now that the candles were behind him, she was standing in his shadow. "Well, well! but you are a little old-fashioned, with all these equivocal mummeries. And I did not know that civilized persons any longer retained sufficient credulity to wring a thrill from god-baiting. Still, women must be humored, bless them! and at last, I take it, we have quite fairly fulfilled the ceremonial requisite to the pursuit of curious pleasures."

Queen Anaïtis was very beautiful, even under his bedimming shadow. Triumphant too was the proud face beneath that curious coral network, and yet this woman's face was sad.

"Dear fool," she said, "it was not wise, when you sang of the Léshy who control the Days, to put an affront upon Monday. But you have forgotten that. And now you laugh because that which we have done you do not understand: and equally that which I am you do not understand."

"No matter what you may be, my dear, I am sure that you will presently tell me all about it. For I assume that you mean to deal fairly with me."

"I shall do that which becomes me, Duke Jurgen—"

"That is it, my dear, precisely! You intend to be true to yourself, whatever happens. The aspiration does you infinite honor, and I shall try to help you. Now I have noticed that every woman is most truly herself," says Jurgen, oracularly, "in the dark."

Then Jurgen looked at her for a moment, with twinkling eyes: then Anaïtis, standing in his shadow, smiled with glowing eyes: then Jurgen blew out those black candles: and then it was quite dark.

A PLAY

EUGENE O'NEILL

The Emperor Jones

CHARACTERS

BRUTUS JONES . . . . *Emperor*
HENRY SMITHERS . . . . *A Cockney Trader*
AN OLD NATIVE WOMAN
LEM . . . . *A Native Chief*
SOLDIERS . . . . *Adherents of Lem*

*The Little Formless Fears; Jeff; The Negro Convicts; The Prison
Guard; The Planters; The Auctioneer; The Slaves; The Congo
Witch-Doctor; The Crocodile God.*

*The action of the play takes place on an island in the West Indies
as yet not self-determined by white Marines. The form of native
government is, for the time being, an empire.*

SCENE ONE

SCENE—*The audience chamber in the palace of the Emperor—a
spacious, high-ceilinged room with bare, white-washed walls.
The floor is of white tiles. In the rear, to the left of center, a*

wide archway giving out on a portico with white pillars. The palace is evidently situated on high ground for beyond the portico nothing can be seen but a vista of distant hills, their summits crowned with thick groves of palm trees. In the right wall, center, a smaller arched doorway leading to the living quarters of the palace. The room is bare of furniture with the exception of one huge chair made of uncut wood which stands at center, its back to rear. This is very apparently the Emperor's throne. It is painted a dazzling, eye-smiting scarlet. There is a brilliant orange cushion on the seat and another smaller one is placed on the floor to serve as a footstool. Strips of matting, dyed scarlet, lead from the foot of the throne to the two entrances.

It is late afternoon but the sunlight still blazes yellowly beyond the portico and there is an oppressive burden of exhausting heat in the air.

As the curtain rises, a native Negro woman sneaks in cautiously from the entrance on the right. She is very old, dressed in cheap calico, bare-footed, a red bandana handkerchief covering all but a few stray wisps of white hair. A bundle bound in colored cloth is carried over her shoulder on the end of a stick. She hesitates beside the doorway, peering back as if in extreme dread of being discovered. Then she begins to glide noiselessly, a step at a time, toward the doorway in the rear. At this moment, SMITHERS *appears beneath the portico.*

SMITHERS *is a tall, stoop-shouldered man about forty. His bald head, perched on a long neck with an enormous Adam's apple, looks like an egg. The tropics have tanned his naturally pasty face with its small, sharp features to a sickly yellow, and native rum has painted his pointed nose to a startling red. His little, washy-blue eyes are red-rimmed and dart about him like a ferret's. His expression is one of unscrupulous meanness, cowardly and dangerous. He is dressed in a worn riding suit of dirty white drill, puttees, spurs, and wears a white cork helmet. A cartridge belt with an automatic revolver is around his waist. He carries a riding whip in his hand. He sees the woman and stops to watch her suspiciously. Then, making up his mind, he steps quickly on tiptoe into the room. The woman, looking back over her shoulder continually, does not see him until it is too late. When she does* SMITHERS *springs forward and grabs her firmly by the shoulder. She struggles to get away, fiercely but silently.*

SMITHERS [*Tightening his grasp—roughly*]: Easy! None o' that, me birdie. You can't wriggle out now. I got me 'ooks on yer.

WOMAN [*Seeing the uselessness of struggling, gives way to frantic terror, and sinks to the ground, embracing his knees supplicatingly*]: No tell him! No tell him, Mister!

SMITHERS [*With great curiosity*]: Tell 'im? [*Then scornfully.*] Oh, you mean 'is bloomin' Majesty. What's the gaime, any 'ow? What are you sneakin' away for? Been stealin' a bit, I s'pose. [*He taps her bundle with his riding whip significantly.*]

WOMAN [*Shaking her head vehemently*]: No, me no steal.

SMITHERS: Bloody liar! But tell me what's up. There's somethin' funny goin' on. I smelled it in the air first thing I got up this mornin'. You blacks are up to some devilment. This palace of 'is is like a bleedin' tomb. Where's all the 'ands? [*The woman keeps sullenly silent.* SMITHERS *raises his whip threateningly.*] Ow, yer won't, won't yer? I'll show yer what's what.

WOMAN [*Coweringly*]: I tell, Mister. You no hit. They go—all go. [*She makes a sweeping gesture toward the hills in the distance.*]

SMITHERS: Run away—to the 'ills?

WOMAN: Yes, Mister. Him Emperor—Great Father. [*She touches her forehead to the floor with a quick mechanical jerk.*] Him sleep after eat. Then they go—all go. Me old woman. Me left only. Now me go too.

SMITHERS [*His astonishment giving way to an immense, mean satisfaction*]: Ow! So that's the ticket! Well, I know bloody well wot's in the air—when they runs orf to the 'ills. The tom-tom 'll be thumping out there bloomin' soon. [*With extreme vindictiveness.*] And I'm bloody glad of it, for one! Serve 'im right! Puttin' on airs, the stinkin' nigger! 'Is Majesty! Gawd blimey I only 'opes I'm there when they takes 'im out to shoot 'im. [*Suddenly.*] 'E's still 'ere all right, ain't 'e?

WOMAN: Yes. Him sleep.

SMITHERS: 'E's bound to find out soon as 'e wakes up. 'E's cunnin' enough to know when 'is time's come. [*He goes to the doorway on right and whistles shrilly with his fingers in his mouth. The old woman springs to her feet and runs out of the doorway, rear. SMITHERS goes after her, reaching for his revolver.*] Stop or I'll shoot! [*Then stopping—indifferently.*] Pop orf then, if yer like, yer black cow. [*He stands in the doorway, looking after her.*]

[JONES *enters from the right. He is a tall, powerfully-built, full-blooded Negro of middle age. His features are typically negroid, yet there is something decidedly distinctive about his face—an underlying strength of will, a hardy, self-reliant confidence in himself that inspires respect. His eyes are alive with a keen, cunning intelligence. In manner he is shrewd, suspicious, evasive. He wears a light blue uniform coat, sprayed with brass buttons, gold braid on the collar, cuffs, etc. His pants are bright red with a light blue stripe down the side. Patent-leather laced boots with brass spurs, and a belt with a long-barreled, pearl-handled revolver in a holster complete his make up. Yet there is something not altogether ridiculous about his grandeur. He has a way of carrying it off.*]

JONES [*Not seeing anyone—greatly irritated and blinking sleepily—shouts*]: Who dare whisper dat way in my palace? Who dare wake up de Emperor? I'll git de hide fravled off some o' you niggers sho'!

SMITHERS [*Showing himself—in a manner half-afraid and half-defiant*]: It was me whistled to yer. [*As JONES frowns angrily.*] I got news for yer.

JONES [*Putting on his suavest manner, which fails to cover up his contempt for the white man*]: Oh, it's you, Mister Smithers. [*He sits down on his throne with easy dignity.*] What news you got to tell me?

SMITHERS [*Coming close to enjoy his discomfiture*]: Don't yer notice nothin' funny today?

JONES [*Coldly*]: Funny? No. I ain't perceived nothin' of de kind!

SMITHERS: Then yer ain't so foxy as I thought yer was. Where's all your court? [*Sarcastically.*] The Generals and the Cabinet Ministers and all?

JONES [*Imperturbably*]: Where dey mostly runs de minute I closes my eyes—drinkin' rum and talkin' big down in de town. [*Sarcastically.*] How come you don't know dat? Ain't you sousin' with 'em most every day?

SMITHERS [*Stung but pretending indifference—with a wink*]: That's part of the day's work. I got ter—ain't I—in my business?

JONES [*Contemptuously*]: Yo' business!

SMITHERS [*Imprudently enraged*]: Gawd blimey, you was glad enough for me ter take yer in on it when you landed here first. You didn' 'ave no 'igh and mighty airs in them days!

JONES [*His hand going to his revolver like a flash—menacingly*]: Talk polite, white man! Talk polite, you heah me! I'm boss heah now, is you fergettin'? [*The Cockney seems about to challenge this last statement with the facts but something in the other's eyes holds and cows him.*]

SMITHERS [*In a cowardly whine*]: No 'arm meant, old top.

JONES [*Condescendingly*]: I accepts yo' apology. [*Lets his hand fall from his revolver.*] No use'n you rakin' up ole times. What I was den is one thing. What I is now 's another. You didn't let me in on yo' crooked work out o' no kind feelin's dat time. I done de dirty work fo' you—and most o' de brain work, too, fo' dat matter— and I was wu'th money to you, dat's de reason.

SMITHERS: Well, blimey, I give yer a start, didn't I—when no one else would. I wasn't afraid to 'ire yer like the rest was—'count of the story about your breakin' jail back in the States.

JONES: No, you didn't have no s'cuse to look down on me fo' dat. You been in jail you'self more'n once.

SMITHERS [*Furiously*]: It's a lie! [*Then trying to pass it off by an attempt at scorn.*] Garn! Who told yer that fairy tale?

JONES: Dey's some tings I ain't got to be tole. I kin see 'em in folk's eyes. [*Then after a pause—meditatively.*] Yes, you sho' give me a start. And it didn't take long from dat time to git dese fool, woods' niggers right where I wanted dem. [*With pride.*] From stow-away to Emperor in two years! Dat's goin' some!

SMITHERS [*With curiosity*]: And I bet you got yer pile o' money 'id safe some place.

JONES [*With satisfaction*]: I sho' has! And it's in a foreign bank where no pusson don't ever git it out but me no matter what come. You didn't s'pose I was holdin' down dis Emperor job for de glory in it, did you? Sho'! De fuss and glory part of it, dat's only to turn de heads o' de low-flung, bush niggers dat's here. Dey wants de big circus show for deir money. I gives it to 'em an' I gits de money. [*With a grin.*] De long green, dat's me every time! [*Then rebuk-ingly.*] But you ain't got no kick agin me, Smithers. I'se paid you back all you done for me many times. Ain't I pertected you and winked at all de crooked tradin' you been doin' right out in de broad day? Sho' I has—and me makin' laws to stop it at de same time! [*He chuckles.*]

SMITHERS [*Grinning*]: But, meanin' no 'arm, you been grabbin' right and left yourself, ain't yer? Look at the taxes you've put on 'em! Blimey! You've squeezed 'em dry!

JONES [*Chuckling*]: No, dey ain't *all* dry yet. I'se still heah, ain't I?

SMITHERS [*Smiling at his secret thought*]: They're dry right now, you'll find out. [*Changing the subject abruptly.*] And as for me breakin' laws, you've broke 'em all yerself just as fast as yer made 'em.

JONES: Ain't I de Emperor? De laws don't go for him. [*Judi-cially.*] You heah what I tells you, Smithers. Dere's little stealin' like you does, and dere's big stealin' like I does. For de little stealin' dey gits you in jail soon or late. For de big stealin' dey makes you Em-peror and puts you in de Hall o' Fame when you croaks. [*Reminis-cently.*] If dey's one thing I learns in ten years on de Pullman ca's listenin' to de white quality talk, it's dat same fact. And when I gits a chance to use it I winds up Emperor in two years.

SMITHERS [*Unable to repress the genuine admiration of the small fry for the large*]: Yes, yer turned the bleedin' trick, all right. Blimey, I never seen a bloke 'as 'ad the bloomin' luck you 'as.

JONES [*Severely*]: Luck? What you mean—luck?

SMITHERS: I suppose you'll say as that swank about the silver bullet ain't luck—and that was what first got the fool blacks on yer side the time of the revolution, wasn't it?

JONES [*With a laugh*]: Oh, dat silver bullet! Sho' was luck! But I makes dat luck, you heah? I loads de dice! Yessuh! When dat murderin' nigger ole Lem hired to kill me takes aim ten feet away and his gun misses fire and I shoots him dead, what you heah me say?

SMITHERS: You said yer'd got a charm so's no lead bullet'd kill yer. You was so strong only a silver bullet could kill yer, you told 'em. Blimey, wasn't that swank for yer—and plain, fat-'eaded luck?

JONES [*Proudly*]: I got brains and I uses 'em quick. Dat ain't luck.

SMITHERS: Yer know they wasn't 'ardly liable to get no silver bullets. And it was luck 'e didn't 'it you that time.

JONES [*Laughing*]: And dere all dem fool, bush niggers was kneelin' down and bumpin' deir heads on de ground like I was a miracle out o' de Bible. Oh Lawd, from dat time on I has dem all eatin' out of my hand. I cracks de whip and dey jumps through.

SMITHERS [*With a sniff*]: Yankee bluff done it.

JONES: Ain't a man's talkin' big what makes him big—long as he makes folks believe it? Sho', I talks large when I ain't got nothin' to back it up, but I ain't talkin' wild just de same. I knows I kin fool 'em—I *knows* it—and dat's backin' enough fo' my game. And ain't I got to learn deir lingo and teach some of dem English befo' I kin talk to 'em? Ain't dat wuk? You ain't never learned ary word er it, Smithers, in de ten years you been heah, dough yo' knows it's money in yo' pocket tradin' wid 'em if you does. But you'se too shiftless to take de trouble.

SMITHERS [*Flushing*]: Never mind about me. What's this I've 'eard about yer really 'avin' a silver bullet moulded for yourself?

JONES: It's playin' out my bluff. I has de silver bullet moulded and I tells 'em when de time comes I kills myself wid it. I tells 'em dat's 'cause I'm de on'y man in de world big enuff to git me. No use'n deir tryin'. And dey falls down and bumps deir heads.

[*He laughs.*] I does dat so's I kin take a walk in peace widout no jealous nigger gunnin' at me from behind de trees.

SMITHERS [*Astonished*]: Then you 'ad it made—'onest?

JONES: Sho' did. Heah she be. [*He takes out his revolver, breaks it, and takes the silver bullet out of one chamber.*] Five lead an' dis silver baby at de last. Don't she shine pretty? [*He holds it in his hand, looking at it admiringly, as if strangely fascinated.*]

SMITHERS: Let me see. [*Reaches out his hand for it.*]

JONES [*Harshly*]: Keep yo' hands whar dey b'long, white man. [*He replaces it in the chamber and puts the revolver back on his hip.*]

SMITHERS [*Snarling*]: Gawd blimey! Think I'm a bleedin' thief, you would.

JONES: No, 'tain't dat. I knows you'se scared to steal from me. On'y I ain't 'lowin' nary body to touch dis baby. She's my rabbit's foot.

SMITHERS [*Sneering*]: A bloomin' charm, wot? [*Venomously.*] Well, you'll need all the bloody charms you 'as before long, s' 'elp me!

JONES [*Judicially*]: Oh, I'se good for six months yit 'fore dey gits sick o' my game. Den, when I sees trouble comin', I makes my getaway.

SMITHERS: Ho! You got it all planned, ain't yer?

JONES: I ain't no fool. I knows dis Emperor's time is sho't. Dat why I make hay when de sun shine. Was you thinkin' I'se aimin' to hold down dis job for life? No, suh! What good is gittin' money if you stays back in dis raggedy country? I wants action when I spends. And when I sees dese niggers gittin' up deir nerve to tu'n me out, and I'se got all de money in sight, I resigns on de spot and beats it quick.

SMITHERS: Where to?

JONES: None o' yo' business.

SMITHERS: Not back to the bloody States, I'll lay my oath.

JONES [*Suspiciously*]: Why don't I? [*Then with an easy laugh.*] You mean 'count of dat story 'bout me breakin' from jail back dere? Dat's all talk.

SMITHERS [*Skeptically*]: Ho, yes!

JONES [*Sharply*]: You ain't 'sinuatin' I'se a liar, is you?

SMITHERS [*Hastily*]: No, Gawd strike me! I was only thinkin' o' the bloody lies you told the blacks 'ere about killin' white men in the States.

JONES [*Angered*]: How come dey're lies?

SMITHERS: You'd 'ave been in jail if you 'ad, wouldn't yer then? [*With venom.*] And from what I've 'eard, it ain't 'ealthy for a black to kill a white man in the States. They burns 'em in oil, don't they?

JONES [*With cool deadliness*]: You mean lynchin' 'd scare me? Well, I tells you, Smithers, maybe I does kill one white man back dere. Maybe I does. And maybe I kills another right heah 'fore long if he don't look out.

SMITHERS [*Trying to force a laugh*]: I was on'y spoofin' yer. Can't yer take a joke? And you was just sayin' you'd never been in jail.

JONES [*In the same tone—slightly boastful*]: Maybe I goes to jail dere for gettin' in an argument wid razors ovah a crap game. Maybe I gits twenty years when dat colored man die. Maybe I gits in 'nother argument wid de prison guard was overseer ovah us when we're wukin' de roads. Maybe he hits me wid a whip and I splits his head wid a shovel and runs away and files de chain off my leg and gits away safe. Maybe I does all dat 'an maybe I don't. It's a story I tells you so's you knows I'se de kind of man dat if you evah repeats one word of it, I ends yo' stealin' on dis yearth mighty damn quick!

SMITHERS [*Terrified*]: Think I'd peach on yer? Not me! Ain't I always been yer friend?

JONES [*Suddenly relaxing*]: Sho' you has—and you better be.

SMITHERS [*Recovering his composure—and with it his malice*]: And just to show yer I'm yer friend, I'll tell yer that bit o' news I was goin' to.

JONES: Go ahead! Shoot de piece. Must be bad news from de happy way you look.

SMITHERS [*Warningly*]: Maybe it's gettin' time for you to resign

—with that bloomin' silver bullet, wot? [*He finishes with a mocking grin.*]

JONES [*Puzzled*]: What's dat you say? Talk plain.

SMITHERS: Ain't noticed any of the guards or servants about the place today, I 'aven't.

JONES [*Carelessly*]: Dey're all out in de garden sleepin' under de trees. When I sleeps, dey sneaks a sleep, too, and I pretends I never suspicions it. All I got to do is to ring de bell and dey come flyin', makin' a bluff dey was wukin' all de time.

SMITHERS [*In the same mocking tone*]: Ring the bell now an' you'll bloody well see what I means.

JONES [*Startled to alertness, but preserving the same careless tone*]: Sho' I rings. [*He reaches below the throne and pulls out a big, common dinner bell which is painted the same vivid scarlet as the throne. He rings this vigorously—then stops to listen. Then he goes to both doors, rings again, and looks out.*]

SMITHERS [*Watching him with malicious satisfaction, after a pause—mockingly*]: The bloody ship is sinkin' an' the bleedin' rats 'as slung their 'ooks.

JONES [*In a sudden fit of anger flings the bell clattering into a corner*]: Low-flung, woods' niggers! [*Then catching Smithers' eye on him, he controls himself and suddenly bursts into a low chuckling laugh.*] Reckon I overplays my hand dis once! A man can't take de pot on a bob-tailed flush all de time. Was I sayin' I'd sit in six months mo'? Well, I'se changed my mind den. I cashes in and resigns de job of Emperor right dis minute.

SMITHERS [*With real admiration*]: Blimey, but you're a cool bird, and no mistake.

JONES: No use'n fussin'. When I knows de game's up I kisses it good-bye widout no long waits. Dey've all run off to de hills, ain't dey?

SMITHERS: Yes—every bleedin' man jack of 'em.

JONES: Den de revolution is at de post. And de Emperor better git his feet smokin' up de trail. [*He starts for the door in rear.*]

SMITHERS: Goin' out to look for your 'orse? Yer won't find any.

They steals the 'orses first thing. Mine was gone when I went for 'im this mornin'. That's wot first give me a suspicion of wot was up.

JONES [*Alarmed for a second, scratches his head, then philosophically*]: Well, den I hoofs it. Feet, do yo' duty! [*He pulls out a gold watch and looks at it.*] Three-thuty. Sundown's at six-thuty or dereabouts. [*Puts his watch back—with cool confidence.*] I got plenty o' time to make it easy.

SMITHERS: Don't be so bloomin' sure of it. They'll be after you 'ot and 'eavy. Ole Lem is at the bottom o' this business an' 'e 'ates you like 'ell. 'E'd rather do for you than eat 'is dinner, 'e would!

JONES [*Scornfully*]: Dat fool no-count nigger! Does you think I'se scared o' him? I stands him on his thick head more'n once befo' dis, and I does it again if he comes in my way . . . [*Fiercely.*] And dis time I leave him a dead nigger fo' sho'!

SMITHERS: You'll 'ave to cut through the big forest—an' these blacks 'ere can sniff and follow a trail in the dark like 'ounds. You'd 'ave to 'ustle to get through that forest in twelve hours even if you knew all the bloomin' trails like a native.

JONES [*With indignant scorn*]: Look-a-heah, white man! Does you think I'se a natural bo'n fool? Give me credit fo' havin' some sense, fo' Lawd's sake! Don't you s'pose I'se looked ahead and made sho' of all de chances? I'se gone out in dat big forest, pretendin' to hunt, so many times dat I knows it high an' low like a book. I could go through on dem trails wid my eyes shut. [*With great contempt.*] Think dese ign'rent bush niggers dat ain't got brains enuff to know deir own names even can catch Brutus Jones? Huh, I s'pects not! Not on yo' life! Why, man, de white men went after me wid bloodhounds where I come from an' I jes' laughs at 'em. It's a shame to fool dese black trash around heah, dey're so easy. You watch me, man! I'll make dem look sick, I will. I'll be 'cross de plain to de edge of de forest by time dark comes. Once in de woods in de night, dey got a swell chance o' findin' dis baby! Dawn tomorrow I'll be out at de oder side and on de coast whar dat French gunboat is stayin'. She picks me up, take me to Martinique when she go dar, and dere I is safe wid a mighty big bankroll in my jeans. It's easy as rollin' off a log.

SMITHERS [*Maliciously*]: But s'posin' somethin' 'appens wrong an' they do nab yer?

JONES [*Decisively*]: Dey don't—dat's de answer.

SMITHERS: But, just for argyment's sake—what'd you do?

JONES [*Frowning*]: I'se got five lead bullets in dis gun good enuff fo' common bush niggers—and after dat I got de silver bullet left to cheat 'em out o' gittin' me.

SMITHERS [*Jeeringly*]: Ho, I was fergettin' that silver bullet. You'll bump yourself orf in style, won't yer? Blimey!

JONES [*Gloomily*]: You kin bet yo whole roll on one thing, white man. Dis baby plays out his string to de end and when he quits, he quits wid a bang de way he ought. Silver bullet ain't none too good for him when he go, dat's a fac'! [*Then shaking off his nervousness—with a confident laugh.*] Sho'! What is I talkin' about? Ain't come to dat yit and I never will—not wid trash niggers like dese yere. [*Boastfully.*] Silver bullet bring me luck anyway. I kin outguess, outrun, outfight, an' outplay de whole lot o' dem all ovah de board any time o' de day er night! You watch me! [*From the distant hills comes the faint, steady thump of a tom-tom, low and vibrating. It starts at a rate exactly corresponding to normal pulse beat—72 to the minute—and continues at a gradually accelerating rate from this point uninterruptedly to the very end of the play.*]

[JONES *starts at the sound. A strange look of apprehension creeps into his face for a moment as he listens. Then he asks, with an attempt to regain his most casual manner.*] What's dat drum beatin' fo'?

SMITHERS [*With a mean grin*]: For you. That means the bleedin' ceremony 'as started. I've 'eard it before and I knows.

JONES: Cer'mony? What cer'mony?

SMITHERS: The blacks is 'oldin' a bloody meetin', 'avin' a war dance, gettin' their courage worked up b'fore they starts after you.

JONES: Let dem! Dey'll sho' need it!

SMITHERS: And they're there 'oldin' their 'eathen religious service—makin' no end of devil spells and charms to 'elp 'em against your silver bullet. [*He guffaws loudly.*] Blimey, but they're balmy as 'ell!

JONES [*A tiny bit awed and shaken in spite of himself*]: Huh! Takes more'n dat to scare dis chicken!

SMITHERS [*Scenting the other's feeling—maliciously*]: Ternight when it's pitch black in the forest, they'll 'ave their pet devils and ghosts 'oundin' after you. You'll find yer bloody 'air 'll be standin' on end before termorrow mornin'. [*Seriously.*] It's a bleedin' queer place, that stinkin' forest, even in daylight. Yer don't know what might 'appen in there, it's that rotten still. Always sends the cold shivers down my back minute I gets in it.

JONES [*With a contemptuous sniff*]: I ain't no chicken-liver like you is. Trees an' me, we'se friends, and dar's a full moon comin' bring me light. And let dem po' niggers make all de fool spells dey'se a min' to. Does yo' s'pect I'se silly enuff to b'lieve in ghosts an' ha'nts an' all dat ole woman's talk? G'long, white man! You ain't talkin' to me. [*With a chuckle.*] Doesn't you know dey's got to do wid a man was member in good standin' o' de Baptist Church? Sho' I was dat when I was porter on de Pullmans, befo' I gits into my little trouble. Let dem try deir heathen tricks. De Baptist Church done pertect me and land dem all in hell. [*Then with more confident satisfaction.*] And I'se got little silver bullet o' my own, don't forgit.

SMITHERS: Ho! You 'aven't give much 'eed to your Baptist Church since you been down 'ere. I've 'eard myself you 'ad turned yer coat an' was takin' up with their blarsted witch-doctors, or whatever the 'ell yer calls the swine.

JONES [*Vehemently*]: I pretends to! Sho' I pretends! Dat's part o' my game from de fust. If I finds out dem niggers believes dat black is white, den I yells it out louder 'n deir loudest. It don't git me nothin' to do missionary work for de Baptist Church. I'se after de coin, an' I lays my Jesus on de shelf for de time bein'. [*Stops abruptly to look at his watch—alertly.*] But I ain't got de time to waste no more fool talk wid you. I'se gwine away from heah dis secon'. [*He reaches in under the throne and pulls out an expensive Panama hat with a bright multi-colored band and sets it jauntily on his head.*] So long, white man! [*With a grin.*] See you in jail some-time, maybe!

SMITHERS: Not me, you won't. Well, I wouldn't be in yer bloody boots for no bloomin' money, but 'ere's wishin' yer luck just the same.

JONES [*Contemptuously*]: You're de frightenedest man evah I see! I tells you I'se safe's 'f I was in New York City. It takes dem niggers from now to dark to git up de nerve to start somethin'. By dat time, I'se got a head start dey never kotch up wid.

SMITHERS [*Maliciously*]: Give my regards to any ghosts yer meets up with.

JONES [*Grinning*]: If dat ghost got money, I'll tell him never ha'nt you less'n he wants to lose it.

SMITHERS [*Flattered*]: Garn! [*Then curiously.*] Ain't yer takin' no luggage with yer?

JONES: I travels light when I wants to move fast. And I got tinned grub buried on de edge o' de forest. [*Boastfully.*] Now say dat I don't look ahead an' use my brains! [*With a wide, liberal gesture.*] I will all dat's left in de palace to you—and you better grab all you kin sneak away wid befo' dey gits here.

SMITHERS [*Gratefully*]: Righto—and thanks ter yer. [*As* JONES *walks toward the door in rear—cautioningly.*] Say, Look 'ere, you ain't goin' out that way, are yer?

JONES: Does you think I'd slink out de back door like a common nigger? I'se Emperor yit, ain't I? And de Emperor Jones leaves de way he comes, and dat black trash don't dare stop him—not yit, leastways. [*He stops for a moment in the doorway, listening to the far-off but insistent beat of the tom-tom.*] Listen to dat roll-call, will you? Must be mighty big drum carry dat far. [*Then with a laugh.*] Well, if dey ain't no whole brass band to see me off, I sho' got de drum part of it. So long, white man. [*He puts his hands in his pockets and with studied carelessness, whistling a tune, he saunters out of the doorway and off to the left.*]

SMITHERS [*Looks after him with a puzzled admiration*]: 'E's got 'is bloomin' nerve with 'im, s'elp me! [*Then angrily.*] Ho—the bleedin' nigger—puttin' on 'is bloody airs! I 'opes they nabs 'im an' gives 'im what's what! [*Then putting business before the pleasure of this thought, looking around him with cupidity.*] A bloke ought to find a 'ole lot in this palace that'd go for a bit of cash. Let's take a look, 'Arry, me lad. [*He starts for the doorway on right as*

[*The Curtain Falls.*]

SCENE TWO

SCENE—*Nightfall. The end of the plain where the Great Forest begins. The foreground is sandy, level ground dotted by a few stones and clumps of stunted bushes cowering close against the earth to escape the buffeting of the trade wind. In the rear the forest is a wall of darkness dividing the world. Only when the eye becomes accustomed to the gloom can the outlines of separate trunks of the nearest trees be made out, enormous pillars of deeper blackness. A somber monotone of wind lost in the leaves moans in the air. Yet this sound serves but to intensify the impression of the forest's relentless immobility, to form a background throwing into relief its brooding, implacable silence.*

[JONES *enters from the left, walking rapidly. He stops as he nears the edge of the forest, looks around him quickly, peering into the dark as if searching for some familiar landmark. Then, apparently satisfied that he is where he ought to be, he throws himself on the ground, dog-tired.*]

Well, heah I is. In de nick o' time, too! Little mo' an' it'd be blacker'n de ace of spades heah-abouts. [*He pulls a bandana handkerchief from his hip pocket and mops off his perspiring face.*] Sho'! Gimme air! I'se tuckered out sho' 'nuff. Dat soft Emperor job ain't no trainin' fo' a long hike ovah dat plain in de brilin' sun. [*Then with a chuckle.*] Cheah up, nigger, de worst is yet to come. [*He lifts his head and stares at the forest. His chuckle peters out abruptly. In a tone of awe.*] My goodness, look at dem woods, will you? Dat nocount Smithers said dey'd be black an' he sho' called de turn. [*Turning away from them quickly and looking down at his feet, he snatches at a chance to change the subject—solicitously.*] Feet, you is holdin' up yo' end fine an' I sutinly hopes you ain't blisterin' none. It's time you git a rest. [*He takes off his shoes, his eyes studiously avoiding the forest. He feels of the soles of his feet gingerly.*] You is still in de pink—on'y a little mite feverish. Cool yo'selfs. Remember you done got a long journey yit befo' you. [*He sits in a weary attitude, listening to the rhythmic beating of the tom-tom. He grumbles in a loud tone to cover up a growing uneasiness.*] Bush niggers! Wonder dey wouldn' git sick o' beatin' dat drum. Sound louder, seem like. I wonder if dey's startin' after me? [*He scrambles to his feet, looking back across the plain.*] Couldn't see dem now, nohow, if dey was hundred feet away. [*Then shaking himself like a wet dog to get rid of these depressing thoughts.*] Sho', dey's miles an' miles behind. What you gittin' fidgety about? [*But he sits down and begins to lace up his shoes in great haste, all the time muttering reassuringly.*] You know what? Yo' belly is empty, dat's what's de matter wid you. Come time to eat! Wid nothin' but wind on yo' stumach, o' course you feels jiggedy. Well, we eats right heah an' now soon's I gits dese pesky shoes laced up! [*He finishes lacing up his shoes.*] Dere! Now le's see. [*Gets on his hands and knees and searches the ground around him with his eyes.*] White stone, white stone, where is you? [*He sees the first white stone and crawls to it—with satisfaction.*] Heah you is! I knowed dis was de right place. Box of grub, come to me. [*He turns over the stone and feels in under it—in a tone of dismay.*] Ain't heah! Gorry, is I in de right place or isn't I? Dere's 'nother stone. Guess dat's it. [*He scrambles to the next stone and turns it over.*] Ain't heah, neither! Grub, whar is you? Ain't heah. Gorry, has I got to go hungry into dem woods—all de night? [*While he is talking he scrambles from one stone to another, turning them over in frantic haste. Finally, he jumps to his feet excitedly.*] Is I lost de place? Must have! But how dat happen when I was followin' de trail across de plain in broad daylight? [*Almost plaintively.*] I'se hungry, I is! I gotta git my feed. Whar's my strength gonna come from if I doesn't? Gorry, I gotta find dat grub high an' low somehow! Why it come dark so quick like dat? Can't see nothin'. [*He scratches a match on his trousers and peers about him. The rate of the beat of the far-off tom-tom increases perceptibly as he does so. He mutters in a bewildered voice.*] How come all dese white stones come heah when I only remembers one? [*Suddenly, with a frightened gasp, he flings the match on the ground and stamps on it.*] Nigger, is you gone crazy mad? Is you lightin' matches to show dem whar you is? Fo' Lawd's sake, use yo' haid. Gorry, I'se got to be careful! [*He stares at the plain behind him apprehensively, his hand on his revolver.*] But how come all dese white stones? And whar's dat tin box o' grub I had all wrapped up in oil cloth?

[*While his back is turned, the* LITTLE FORMLESS FEARS *creep out from the deeper blackness of the forest. They are black, shapeless, only their glittering little eyes can be seen. If they have any describable form at all it is that of a grubworm about the size of a creeping child. They move noiselessly, but with deliberate, painful effort, striving to raise themselves on end, failing and sinking prone again.* JONES *turns about to face the forest. He stares up at the tops of the trees, seeking vainly to discover his whereabouts by their conformation.*]

Can't tell nothin' from dem trees! Gorry, nothin' 'round heah look like I evah seed it befo'. I'se done lost de place sho' 'nuff. [*With mournful foreboding.*] It's mighty queer! It's mighty queer! [*With sudden forced defiance—in an angry tone.*] Woods, is you tryin' to put somethin' ovah on me?

[*From the formless creatures on the ground in front of him comes a tiny gale of low mocking laughter like a rustling of leaves. They squirm upward toward him in twisted attitudes.* JONES *looks down, leaps backward with a yell of terror, yanking out his revolver as he does so—in a quavering voice.*] What's dat? Who's dar? What is. you? Git away from me befo' I shoots you up! You don't? . . .

[*He fires. There is a flash, a loud report, then silence broken only by the far-off, quickened throb of the tom-tom. The formless creatures have scurried back into the forest.* JONES *remains fixed in his position, listening intently. The sound of the shot, the reassuring feel of the revolver in his hand, have somewhat restored his shaken nerve. He addresses himself with renewed confidence.*]

Dey're gone. Dat shot fix 'em. Dey was only little animals—little wild pigs, I reckon. Dey've maybe rooted out yo' grub an' eat it. Sho', you fool nigger, what you think dey is—ha'nts? [*Excitedly.*] Gorry, you give de game away when you fire dat shot. Dem niggers heah dat fo' su'tin! Time you beat it in de woods widout no long waits. [*He starts for the forest—hesitates before the plunge—then urging himself in with manful resolution.*] Git in, nigger! What you skeered at? Ain't nothin' dere but de trees! Git in! [*He plunges boldly into the forest.*]

SCENE THREE

SCENE—*Nine o'clock. In the forest. The moon has just risen. Its beams, drifting through the canopy of leaves, make a barely perceptible, suffused, eerie glow. A dense low wall of underbrush and creepers is in the nearer foreground, fencing in a small triangular clearing. Beyond this is the massed blackness of the forest like an encompassing barrier. A path is dimly discerned leading down to the clearing from left, rear, and winding away from it again toward the right. As the scene opens nothing can be distinctly made out. Except for the beating of the tom-tom, which is a trifle louder and quicker than in the previous scene, there is silence, broken every few seconds by a queer, clicking sound. Then gradually the figure of the negro, JEFF, can be discerned crouching on his haunches at the rear of the triangle. He is middle-aged, thin, brown in color, is dressed in a Pullman porter's uniform, cap, etc. He is throwing a pair of dice on the ground before him, picking them up, shaking them, casting them out with the regular, rigid, mechanical movements of an automaton. The heavy, plodding footsteps of someone approaching along the trail from the left are heard and JONES' voice, pitched in a slightly higher key and strained in a cheering effort to overcome its own tremors.*

De moon's rizen. Does you heah dat, nigger? You gits more light from dis out. No mo' buttin' yo' fool head agin' de trunks an' scratchin' de hide off yo' legs in de bushes. Now you sees whar yo'se gwine. So cheer up! From now on you has a snap. [*He steps just to the rear of the triangular clearing and mops off his face on his sleeve. He has lost his Panama hat. His face is scratched, his brilliant uniform shows several large rents.*] What time's it gittin' to be, I wonder? I dassent light no match to find out. Phoo'. It's wa'm an' dat's a fac'! [*Wearily.*] How long I been makin' tracks in dese woods? Must be hours an' hours. Seems like fo'evah! Yit can't be, when de moon's jes' riz. Dis am a long night fo' yo', yo' Majesty! [*With a mournful chuckle.*] Majesty! Der ain't much majesty 'bout dis baby now. [*With attempted cheerfulness.*] Never min'. It's all part o' de game. Dis night come to an end like everything else. And when you gits dar safe and has dat bankroll in yo' hands you laughs at all dis. [*He starts to whistle but checks himself abruptly.*] What yo' whistlin' for, you po' dope! Want all de worl' to heah you? [*He stops talking to listen.*] Heah dat ole drum! Sho' gits nearer from de sound. Dey're packin' it along wid 'em. Time fo' me to move. [*He takes a step forward, then stops—worriedly.*] What's dat odder queer clickety sound I heah? Dere it is! Sound close! Sound like—sound like —Fo' God sake, sound like some nigger was shootin' crap! [*Frightenedly.*] I better beat it quick when I gits dem notions. [*He walks quickly into the clear space—then stands transfixed as he sees* JEFF —*in a terrified gasp.*] Who dar? Who dat? Is dat you, Jeff? [*Starting toward the other, forgetful for a moment of his surroundings and really believing it is a living man that he sees—in a tone of happy relief.*] Jeff! I'se sho' mighty glad to see you! Dey tol' me you done died from dat razor cut I gives you. [*Stopping suddenly, bewilderedly.*] But how you come to be heah, nigger? [*He stares fascinatedly at the other who continues his mechanical play with the dice.* JONES' *eyes begin to roll wildly. He stutters.*] Ain't you gwine —look up—can't you speak to me? Is you—is you—a ha'nt? [*He jerks out his revolver in a frenzy of terrified rage.*] Nigger, I kills you dead once. Has I got to kill you again? You take it den. [*He fires. When the smoke clears away* JEFF *has disappeared.* JONES *stands trembling—then with a certain reassurance.*] He's gone, anyway. Ha'nt or no ha'nt, dat shot fix him. [*The beat of the far-off tom-tom is perceptibly louder and more rapid.* JONES *becomes conscious of it —with a start, looking back over his shoulder.*] Dey's gittin' near! Dey's comin' fast! And heah I is shootin' shots to let 'em know jes' whar I is. Oh, Gorry, I'se got to run. [*Forgetting the path he plunges wildly into the underbrush in the rear and disappears in the shadow.*]

SCENE FOUR

SCENE—*Eleven o'clock. In the forest. A wide dirt road runs diagonally from right, front, to left, rear. Rising sheer on both sides the forest walls it in. The moon is now up. Under its light the road glimmers ghastly and unreal. It is as if the forest had stood aside momentarily to let the road pass through and accomplish its veiled purpose. This done, the forest will fold in upon itself again and the road will be no more.* JONES *stumbles in from the forest on the right. His uniform is ragged and torn. He looks about him with numbed surprise when he sees the road, his eyes blinking in the bright moonlight. He flops down exhaustedly and pants heavily for a while. Then with sudden anger.*

I'm meltin' wid heat! Runnin' an' runnin' an' runnin'! Damn dis heah coat! Like a strait-jacket! [*He tears off his coat and flings it away from him, revealing himself stripped to the waist.*] Dere! Dat's better! Now I kin breathe! [*Looking down at his feet, the spurs catch his eye.*] And to hell wid dese high-fangled spurs. Dey're what's been a-trippin' me up an' breakin' my neck. [*He unstraps them and flings them away disgustedly.*] Dere! I gits rid o' dem frippety Emperor trappin's an' I travels lighter. Lawd! I'se tired! [*After a pause, listening to the insistent beat of the tom-tom in the distance.*] I must 'a put some distance between myself an' dem— runnin' like dat—and yit—dat damn drum sound jes' de same— nearer, even. Well, I guess I a'most holds my lead anyhow. Dey won't never catch up. [*With a sigh.*] If on'y my fool legs stands up. Oh, I'se sorry I evah went in for dis. Dat Emperor job is sho' hard to shake. [*He looks around him suspiciously.*] How'd dis road evah git heah? Good level road, too. I never remembers seein' it befo'. [*Shaking his head apprehensively.*] Dese woods is sho' full o' de queerest things at night. [*With a sudden terror.*] Lawd God, don't let me see no more o' dem ha'nts! Dey gits my goat! [*Then trying to talk himself into confidence.*] Ha'nts! You fool nigger, dey ain't no such things! Don't de Baptist parson tell you dat many time? Is you civilized, or is you like dese ign'rent black niggers heah? Sho'! Dat was all in yo' own head. Wasn't nothin' dere. Wasn't no Jeff! Know what? You jus' get seein' dem things 'cause yo' belly's empty and you's sick wid hunger inside. Hunger 'fects yo' head and yo' eyes. Any fool know dat. [*Then pleading fervently.*] But bless God, I don't come across no more o' dem, whatever dey is! [*Then cautiously.*] Rest! Don't talk! Rest! You needs it. Den you gits on yo' way again. [*Looking at the moon.*] Night's half gone a'most. You hits de coast in de mawning! Den you'se all safe.

[*From the right forward a small gang of Negroes enter. They are dressed in striped convict suits, their heads are shaven, one leg drags limpingly, shackled to a heavy ball and chain. Some carry picks, the others shovels. They are followed by a white man dressed in the uniform of a prison guard. A Winchester rifle is slung across his shoulders and he carries a heavy whip. At a signal from the* GUARD *they stop on the road opposite where* JONES *is sitting.* JONES, *who has been staring up at the sky, unmindful of their noiseless approach, suddenly looks down and sees them. His eyes pop out, he tries to get to his feet and fly, but sinks back, too numbed by fright to move. His voice catches in a choking prayer.*]

Lawd Jesus!

[*The* PRISON GUARD *cracks his whip—noiselessly—and at that signal all the convicts start to work on the road. They swing their picks, they shovel, but not a sound comes from their labor. Their movements, like those of* JEFF *in the preceding scene, are those of automatons,—rigid, slow, and mechanical. The* PRISON GUARD *points sternly at* JONES *with his whip, motions him to take his place among the other shovelers.* JONES *gets to his feet in a hypnotized stupor. He mumbles subserviently.*]

Yes, suh! Yes, suh! I'se comin'.

[*As he shuffles, dragging one foot, over to his place, he curses under his breath with rage and hatred.*]

God damn yo' soul, I gits even wid you yit, sometime.

[*As if there were a shovel in his hands he goes through weary, mechanical gestures of digging up dirt, and throwing it to the road-side. Suddenly the* GUARD *approaches him angrily, threateningly. He raises his whip and lashes* JONES *viciously across the shoulders with it.* JONES *winces with pain and cowers abjectly. The* GUARD *turns his back on him and walks away contemptuously. Instantly* JONES *straightens up. With arms upraised as if his shovel were a club in his hands he springs murderously at the unsuspecting* GUARD. *In the act of crashing down his shovel on the white man's skull,* JONES *suddenly becomes aware that his hands are empty. He cries despairingly.*]

Whar's my shovel? Gimme my shovel till I splits his damn head! [*Appealing to his fellow convicts.*] Gimme a shovel, one o' you, fo' God's sake!

[*They stand fixed in motionless attitudes, their eyes on the ground. The* GUARD *seems to wait expectantly, his back turned to the attacker.* JONES *bellows with baffled, terrified rage, tugging frantically at his revolver.*]

I kills you, you white debil, if it's de last thing I evah does! Ghost or debil, I kill you again!

[*He frees the revolver and fires point blank at the* GUARD'S *back. Instantly the walls of the forest close in from both sides, the road and the figures of the convict gang are blotted out in an en-shrouding darkness. The only sounds are a crashing in the under-brush as* JONES *leaps away in mad flight and the throbbing of the tom-tom, still far distant, but increased in volume of sound and rapidity of beat.*]

SCENE FIVE

SCENE—*One o'clock. A large circular clearing, enclosed by the serried ranks of gigantic trunks of tall trees whose tops are lost to view. In the center is a big dead stump worn by time into a*

*curious resemblance to an auction block. The moon floods the
clearing with a clear light.* JONES *forces his way in through the
forest on the left. He looks wildly about the clearing with
hunted, fearful glances. His pants are in tatters, his shoes cut
and misshapen, flapping about his feet. He slinks cautiously to
the stump in the center and sits down in a tense position, ready
for instant flight. Then he holds his head in his hands and
rocks back and forth, moaning to himself miserably.*

Oh Lawd! Lawd! Oh Lawd, Lawd! [*Suddenly he throws himself
on his knees and raises his clasped hands to the sky—in a voice of
agonized pleading.*] Lawd Jesus, heah my prayer! I'se a po' sinner,
a po' sinner! I knows I done wrong, I knows it! When I cotches Jeff
cheatin' wid loaded dice my anger overcomes me and I kills him
dead! Lawd, I done wrong! When dat guard hits me wid de whip,
my anger overcomes me, and I kills him dead. Lawd, I done wrong!
And down heah whar dese fool bush niggers raises me up to the
seat o' de mighty, I steals all I could grab. Lawd, I done wrong! I
knows it! I'se sorry! Forgive me, Lawd! Forgive dis po' sinner!
[*Then beseeching terrifiedly.*] And keep dem away, Lawd! Keep dem
away from me! And stop dat drum soundin' in my ears! Dat begin
to sound ha'nted, too. [*He gets to his feet, evidently slightly re-
assured by his prayer—with attempted confidence.*] De Lawd'll
preserve me from dem ha'nts after dis. [*Sits down on the stump
again.*] I ain't skeered o' real men. Let dem come. But dem odders
. . . [*He shudders—then looks down at his feet, working his toes
inside the shoes—with a groan.*] Oh, my po' feet! Dem shoes ain't
no use no more 'ceptin' to hurt. I'se better off widout dem. [*He un-
laces them and pulls them off—holds the wrecks of the shoes in his
hands and regards them mournfully.*] You was real, A-one patin'
leather, too. Look at you now. Emperor, you'se gittin' mighty low!
[*He sits dejectedly and remains with bowed shoulders, staring
down at the shoes in his hands as if reluctant to throw them away.
While his attention is thus occupied, a crowd of figures silently
enters the clearing from all sides. All are dressed in Southern
costumes of the period of the fifties of the last century. There are*

middle-aged men who are evidently well-to-do planters. There is one spruce, authoritative individual—the AUCTIONEER. *There is a crowd of curious spectators, chiefly young belles and dandies who have come to the slave-market for diversion. All exchange courtly greetings in dumb show and chat silently together. There is something stiff, rigid, unreal, marionettish about their movements. They group themselves about the stump. Finally a batch of slaves are led in from the left by an attendant—three men of different ages, two women, one with a baby in her arms, nursing. They are placed to the left of the stump, beside* JONES.

The white planters look them over appraisingly as if they were cattle, and exchange judgments on each. The dandies point with their fingers and make witty remarks. The belles titter bewitchingly. All this in silence save for the ominous throb of the tom-tom. The AUCTIONEER *holds up his hand, taking his place at the stump. The group strain forward attentively. He touches* JONES *on the shoulder peremptorily, motioning for him to stand on the stump—the auction block.*

JONES *looks up, sees the figures on all sides, looks wildly for some opening to escape, sees none, screams and leaps madly to the top of the stump to get as far away from them as possible. He stands there, cowering, paralyzed with horror. The* AUCTIONEER *begins his silent spiel. He points to* JONES, *appeals to the planters to see for themselves. Here is a good field hand, sound in mind and limb as they can see. Very strong still in spite of his being middle-aged. Look at that back. Look at those shoulders. Look at the muscles in his arms and his sturdy legs. Capable of any amount of hard labor. Moreover, of a good disposition, intelligent and tractable. Will any gentleman start the bidding? The* PLANTERS *raise their fingers, make their bids. They are apparently all eager to possess* JONES. *The bidding is lively, the crowd interested. While this has been going on,* JONES *has been seized by the courage of desperation. He dares to look down and around him. Over his face abject terror gives way to mystification, to gradual realization—stutteringly.*]

What you all doin', white folks? What's all dis? What you all lookin' at me fo'? What you doin' wid me, anyhow? [*Suddenly con-*

vulsed with raging hatred and fear.] Is dis a auction? Is you sellin'
me like dey uster befo' de war? [*Jerking out his revolver just as the*
AUCTIONEER *knocks him down to one of the planters—glaring
from him to the purchaser.*] And *you* sells me? And *you* buys me?
I shows you I'se a free nigger, damn yo' souls! [*He fires at the* AUC-
TIONEER *and at the* PLANTER *with such rapidity that the two shots
are almost simultaneous. As if this were a signal the walls of the
forest fold in. Only blackness remains and silence broken by* JONES
*as he rushes off, crying with fear—and by the quickened, ever louder
beat of the tom-tom.*]

SCENE SIX

SCENE—*Three o'clock. A cleared space in the forest. The limbs of
the trees meet over it forming a low ceiling about five feet from
the ground. The interlocked ropes of creepers reaching upward
to entwine the tree trunks give an arched appearance to the
sides. The space thus enclosed is like the dark, noisome hold of
some ancient vessel. The moonlight is almost completely shut
out and only a vague, wan light filters through. There is the
noise of someone approaching from the left, stumbling and
crawling through the undergrowth.* JONES' *voice is heard between chattering moans.*

Oh, Lawd, what I gwine do now? Ain't got no bullet left on'y
de silver one. If mo' o' dem ha'nts come after me, how I gwine
skeer dem away? Oh, Lawd, on'y de silver one left—an' I gotta save
dat fo' luck. If I shoots dat one I'm a goner sho'! Lawd, it's black
heah! Whar's de moon? Oh, Lawd, don't dis night evah come to an
end? [*By the sounds, he is feeling his way cautiously forward.*] Dere!
Dis feels like a clear space. I gotta lie down an' rest. I don't care if
dem niggers does cotch me. I gotta rest.
[*He is well forward now where his figure can be dimly made out.
His pants have been so torn away that what is left of them is no
better than a breech cloth. He flings himself full length, face down-*

ward on the ground, panting with exhaustion. Gradually it seems to grow lighter in the enclosed space and two rows of seated figures can be seen behind JONES. *They are sitting in crumpled, despairing attitudes, hunched, facing one another with their backs touching the forest walls as if they were shackled to them. All are Negroes, naked save for loin cloths. At first they are silent and motionless. Then they begin to sway slowly forward toward each other and back again in unison, as if they were laxly letting themselves follow the long roll of a ship at sea. At the same time, a low, melancholy murmur rises among them, increasing gradually by rhythmic degrees which seemed to be directed and controlled by the throb of the tom-tom in the distance, to a long, tremulous wail of despair that reaches a certain pitch, unbearably acute, then falls by slow gradations of tone into silence and is taken up again.* JONES *starts, looks up, sees the figures, and throws himself down again to shut out the sight. A shudder of terror shakes his whole body as the wail rises up about him again. But the next time, his voice, as if under some uncanny compulsion, starts with the others. As their chorus lifts he rises to a sitting posture similar to the others, swaying back and forth. His voice reaches the highest pitch of sorrow, of desolation. The light fades out, the other voices cease, and only darkness is left.* JONES *can be heard scrambling to his feet and running off, his voice sinking down the scale and receding as he moves farther and farther away in the forest. The tom-tom beats louder, quicker, with a more insistent, triumphant pulsation.*]

SCENE SEVEN

SCENE—*Five o'clock. The foot of a gigantic tree by the edge of a great river. A rough structure of boulders, like an altar, is by the tree. The raised river bank is in the nearer background. Beyond this the surface of the river spreads out, brilliant and unruffled in the moonlight, blotted out and merged into a veil of bluish mist in the distance.* JONES' *voice is heard from the left rising and falling in the long, despairing wail of the chained slaves, to the rhythmic beat of the tom-tom. As his voice sinks into silence, he enters the open space. The expression of his face is fixed and stony, his eyes have an obsessed glare, he moves with a strange deliberation like a sleepwalker or one in a trance. He looks around at the tree, the rough stone altar, the moonlit surface of the river beyond, and passes his hand over his head with a vague gesture of puzzled bewilderment. Then, as if in obedience to some obscure impulse, he sinks into a kneeling, devotional posture before the altar. Then he seems to come to himself partly, to have an uncertain realization of what he is doing, for he straightens up and stares about him horrifiedly— in an incoherent mumble.*

What—what is I doin'? What is—dis place? Seems like—seems like I know dat tree—an' dem stones—an' de river. I remember— seems like I been heah befo'. [*Tremblingly.*] Oh, Gorry, I'se skeered in dis place! I'se skeered! Oh, Lawd, pertect dis sinner!

[*Crawling away from the altar, he cowers close to the ground, his face hidden, his shoulders heaving with sobs of hysterical fright. From behind the trunk of the tree, as if he had sprung out of it, the figure of the* CONGO WITCH-DOCTOR *appears. He is wizened and old, naked except for the fur of some small animal tied about his waist, its bushy tail hanging down in front. His body is stained all over a bright red. Antelope horns are on each side of his head, branching upward. In one hand he carries a bone rattle, in the other a charm stick with a bunch of white cockatoo feathers tied to the end. A great number of glass beads and bone ornaments are about his neck, ears, wrists, and ankles. He struts noiselessly with a queer prancing step to a position in the clear ground between* JONES *and the altar. Then with a preliminary, summoning stamp of his foot on the earth, he begins to dance and to chant. As if in response to his summons the beating of the tom-tom grows to a fierce, exultant boom whose throbs seem to fill the air with vibrating rhythm.* JONES *looks up, starts to spring to his feet, reaches a half-kneeling, half-squatting position and remains rigidly fixed there, paralyzed with awed fascination by this new apparition. The* WITCH-DOCTOR *sways, stamping with his foot, his bone rattle clicking the time. His voice rises and falls in a weird, monotonous croon, without articulate word divisions. Gradually his dance becomes clearly one of a narrative in pantomime, his croon is an incantation, a charm to allay the fierceness of some implacable deity demanding sacrifice. He flees, he is pursued by devils, he hides, he flees again. Ever wilder and wilder becomes his flight, nearer and nearer draws the pursuing evil, more and more the spirit of terror gains possession of him. His croon, rising to intensity, is punctuated by shrill cries. JONES has become completely hypnotized. His voice joins in the incantation, in the cries, he beats time with his hands and sways his body to and fro from the waist. The whole spirit and meaning of the dance has entered into him, has become his spirit. Finally the theme of the pantomime halts on a howl of despair, and is taken up again in a note of savage hope. There is a salvation. The forces of evil demand sacrifice. They must be appeased. The WITCH-DOCTOR points with his wand to the sacred tree, to the river beyond, to the altar, and finally to JONES with a ferocious command. JONES seems to sense the meaning of this. It is he who must offer himself for sacrifice. He beats his forehead abjectly to the ground, moaning hysterically.]*

Mercy, Oh Lawd! Mercy! Mercy on dis po' sinner.

[The WITCH-DOCTOR springs to the river bank. He stretches out his arms and calls to some god within its depths. Then he starts backward slowly, his arms remaining out. A huge head of a crocodile appears over the bank and its eyes, glittering greenly, fasten upon JONES. He stares into them fascinatedly. The WITCH-DOCTOR prances up to him, touches him with his wand, motions with hideous command toward the waiting monster. JONES squirms on his belly nearer and nearer, moaning continually.]

Mercy, Lawd! Mercy!

[The crocodile heaves more of his enormous bulk onto the land. JONES squirms toward him. The WITCH-DOCTOR's voice shrills out in furious exultation, the tom-tom beats madly. JONES cries out in a fierce, exhausted spasm of anguished pleading.]

Lawd, save me! Lawd Jesus, heah my prayer!

[Immediately, in answer to his prayer, comes the thought of the one bullet left him. He snatches at his hip, shouting defiantly.]

De silver bullet! You don't git me yit!

[*He fires at the green eyes in front of him. The head of the crocodile sinks back behind the river bank, the* WITCH-DOCTOR *springs behind the sacred tree and disappears.* JONES *lies with his face to the ground, his arms outstretched, whimpering with fear as the throb of the tom-tom fills the silence about him with a somber pulsation, a baffled but revengeful power.*]

SCENE EIGHT

SCENE—*Dawn. Same as Scene Two, the dividing line of forest and plain. The nearest tree trunks are dimly revealed but the forest behind them is still a mass of glooming shadows. The tom-tom seems on the very spot, so loud and continuously vibrating are its beats.* LEM *enters from the left, followed by a small squad of his soldiers, and by the Cockney trader,* SMITHERS. LEM *is a heavy-set, ape-faced old savage of the extreme African type, dressed only in a loin cloth. A revolver and cartridge belt are about his waist. His soldiers are in different degrees of rag-concealed nakedness. All wear broad palm-leaf hats. Each one carries a rifle.* SMITHERS *is the same as in Scene One. One of the soldiers, evidently a tracker, is peering about keenly on the ground. He grunts and points to the spot where* JONES *entered the forest.* LEM *and* SMITHERS *come to look.*

SMITHERS [*After a glance, turns away in disgust*]: That's where 'e went in right enough. Much good it'll do yer. 'E's miles orf by this an' safe to the Coast, damn 'is 'ide! I tole yer yer'd lose 'im, didn't I?—wastin' the 'ole bloomin' night beatin' yer bloody drum and castin' yer silly spells! Gawd blimey, wot a pack!

LEM [*Gutturally*]: We cotch him. You see. [*He makes a motion to his soldiers who squat down on their haunches in a semicircle.*]

SMITHERS [*Exasperatedly*]: Well, ain't yer goin' in an' 'unt 'im in the woods? What the 'ell's the good of waitin'?

LEM [*Imperturbably—squatting down himself*]: We cotch him.

SMITHERS [*Turning away from him contemptuously*]: Aw! Garn! 'E's a better man than the lot o' you put together. I 'ates the sight o' 'im but I'll say that for 'im. [*A sound of snapping twigs comes from the forest. The soldiers jump to their feet, cocking their rifles alertly.* LEM *remains sitting with an imperturbable expression, but listening intently. The sound from the woods is repeated.* LEM *makes a quick signal with his hand. His followers creep quickly but noiselessly into the forest, scattering so that each enters at a different spot.*]

SMITHERS [*In the silence that follows—in a contemptuous whisper*]: You ain't thinkin' that would be 'im, I 'ope?

LEM [*Calmly*]: We cotch him.

SMITHERS: Blarsted fat 'eads! [*Then after a second's thought— wonderingly.*] Still an' all, it might 'appen. If 'e lost 'is bloody way in these stinkin' woods 'e'd likely turn in a circle without 'is knowin' it. They all does.

LEM [*Peremptorily*]: Sssh! [*The reports of several rifles sound from the forest, followed a second later by savage, exultant yells. The beating of the tom-tom abruptly ceases.* LEM *looks up at the white man with a grin of satisfaction.*] We cotch him. Him dead.

SMITHERS [*With a snarl*]: 'Ow d'yer know it's 'im an' 'ow d'yer know 'e's dead?

LEM: My mens dey got 'um silver bullets. Dey kill him shore.

SMITHERS [*Astonished*]: They got silver bullets?

LEM: Lead bullet no kill him. He got um strong charm. I cook um money, make um silver bullet, make um strong charm, too.

SMITHERS [*Light breaking upon him*]: So that's wot you was up to all night, wot? You was scared to put after 'im till you'd moulded silver bullets, eh?

LEM [*Simply stating a fact*]: Yes. Him got strong charm. Lead no good.

SMITHERS [*Slapping his thigh and guffawing*]: Haw-haw! If yer don't beat all 'ell! [*Then recovering himself—scornfully.*] I'll bet yer it ain't 'im they shot at all, yer bleedin' looney!

LEM [*Calmly*]: Dey come bring him now. [*The soldiers come out of the forest, carrying* JONES' *limp body. There is a little red-*

dish-purple hole under his left breast. He is dead. They carry him *to* LEM, *who examines the body with great satisfaction.* SMITHERS *leans over his shoulder—in a tone of frightened awe.*] Well, they did for yer right enough, Jonsey, me lad! Dead as a 'erring! [*Mockingly.*] Where's yer 'igh an' mighty airs now, yer bloomin' Majesty? [*Then with a grin.*] Silver bullets! Gawd blimey, but yer died in the 'eighth o' style. any'ow! [LEM *makes a motion to the soldiers to carry the body out left.* SMITHERS *speaks to him sneeringly.*]

SMITHERS: And I s'pose you think it's yer bleedin' charms and yer silly beatin' the drum that made 'im run in a circle when 'e'd lost 'imself, don't yer? [*But* LEM *makes no reply, does not seem to hear the question, walks out left after his men.* SMITHERS *looks after him with contemptuous scorn.*] Stupid as 'ogs, the lot of 'em! Blarsted niggers!

[*Curtain Falls.*]

MORE OR LESS LITERARY

VAN WYCK BROOKS

The Writer and
His Audience

DEAN INGE observes, in his *Outspoken Essays,* that those who
are in the habit of disparaging the great Victorians ought to
make a collection of their photographs and compare them with those
of their own little favourites. "Let them set up in a row," he says,
"good portraits of Tennyson, Charles Darwin, Gladstone, Manning,
Newman, Martineau, Lord Lawrence, Burne-Jones, and, if they like,
a dozen lesser luminaries, and ask themselves candidly whether men
of this stature are any longer among us." When this essay first appeared, in the form of a lecture, one of our magazines acted on the
suggestion and drew the deadly parallel: side by side with these
eminent Victorians, who might have been replaced by eminent Americans, it presented the no less familiar features of Messrs. Wells,
Bennett, Chesterton, Shaw, Lloyd George and one or two others.
With the possible exceptions of Shaw and Chesterton, the effect, one
had to admit, was damaging to the moderns: it gave point to Mr.
Orage's remark, apropos of the Victorian character, that his own generation (and ours) has "provided the soul of the world with nothing
so fine." What was it they lacked, these heads of our contemporaries?
In juxtaposition with the heads of their predecessors, they were at
as great a disadvantage as the politicians at Washington who sit
surrounded by the marble busts of Houdon and his disciples.

Taken from *Sketches in Criticism,* by Van Wyck Brooks, published and copyright 1932 by E. P. Dutton & Co., Inc., New York.

The difference can hardly be ascribed to the fortuities of dress and fashion. Capes and beards, to be sure, impart to the human aspect a wondrous venerability: no one, for instance, to judge from photographs, ever looked more the authentic *vates* than the forgotten author of *Festus*. The personages of two generations ago imposed themselves upon the outer eye; but it is not merely this that gives to so many of the Victorians, both English and American, their air of authority. It was partly the religious depth of their convictions, and partly something else. In its proper definition, authority is not only power but delegated power. Some secret principle in society determines the preeminence at a given moment of this type or that; and literature, which has ceased to speak, from its own point of view, as it used to speak (with whatever derelictions in the matter of form), the words of "the immensities and the eternities," has also ceased to speak for the human race. If the faces of our modern writers are so often marked either by impudence or an excessive shyness, it is largely because, lacking the intrinsic power, they lack also the delegated power of public spokesmen.

For, say what we will, literature depends upon some deep law of supply and demand. Whether we can ever apprehend that law is one of the main problems of criticism; it was a problem that occupied Taine, and nothing more clearly proves the frivolity of our own criticism than the fact that we pay so little attention to it at a time when literature has been driven to the very periphery of the human consciousness. In this country our minds are so busy with beginnings, with first works and opening careers, that we are impatient of any attempt to take a long view of our situation: we assume that discussions of literary form are all that are necessary to produce a race of artists. We do not observe that when writers are not adjusted to society, discussions of form can merely lead to the point where, having an adequate command of their medium, writers have nothing to say. A literature of this kind is only a substitute for chess; it is a game for a few hundred people, a very different thing from the literature that Goethe had in mind when he said that the writer who lacks the sense that he is writing for a million readers has mistaken his vocation. And we can surely make no greater mistake than to be satisfied with the expectation of a mere private or group-literature.

The great writer always expresses what Renan called "the silent spirit of collective masses." For the great writer to exist, there must also exist a secret, unspoken understanding in the society from which he emerges. He responds to this understanding, he voices it, he feels that he is needed; and who can doubt that this fact accounts for the self-confidence of the Victorian writers, for their astonishing tenacity of life, the volume, the depth, the sustained power of their utterance? We, too, before the great dispersal, had in this country, in a less degree, a literature that expressed the general mind; and how admirably our writers throve on the sense that they were fulfilling a genuine popular need! There is a passage in Howells' *Years of My Youth* that partially explains the calm pertinacity of so many of our old men of letters. Howells, who had been living in Cambridge, had returned to Ohio and was sitting one evening with the Garfield family on the verandah that overlooked their lawn. "I was beginning to speak," he says, "of the famous poets I knew when Garfield stopped me with 'Just a minute!' He ran down into the grassy space first to one fence and then to the other at the sides, and waved a wild arm of invitation to the neighbours who were also sitting on their back porches. 'Come over here!' he shouted. 'He's telling about Holmes, and Longfellow, and Lowell, and Whittier!' And at his bidding, dim forms began to mount the fences and follow him up to his verandah. 'Now go on!' he called to me, when we were all seated, and I went on, while the whippoorwills whirred and whistled round, and the hours drew toward midnight." Nation for nation, and writer for writer, we have there the sort of correspondence between the mind of the individual and the mind of the "collective mass" that is always to be found in the great literary epochs.

One doubts if there exists in America a writer who has reached the age of fifty without believing that he could have written ten times more and better if only someone—some one, some thing, he never knows what or who—had wished him to do so. It is easy to ridicule this feeling, still easier to explain it in various false and discreditable ways; but one hears it on the lips and sees it in the faces of too many sincere men not to know that it cannot be dismissed in any such fashion. It is essential for the artist to feel that he is needed; it is natural for him to wish to be needed and to wither when that support is withdrawn. And it is this assurance, this birthright, as every artist feels it to be, that our writers of the passing generation have been obliged to forgo: hence their vague but deep and general sense that they have been somehow cheated. Too many of the seats of authority in this country are occupied by hardy vulgarians, while the aging men who have contributed most to the real thought of the time creep about in corners with scarcely more of the will-to-live than Jack London possessed at the end, with scarcely more of the will-to-complete their thought than William James possessed. The rising generation, to be sure, inherits the small cooperating public for which Henry Adams seemed always to be looking in vain; but even this, as yet, is a very different public from the public which the great Victorians knew.

THOMAS BEER

The Titaness

THEY laid Jesse James in his grave and Dante Gabriel Rossetti
died immediately. Then Charles Darwin was deplored and then,
on April 27, 1882, Louisa May Alcott hurried to write in her journal:
"Mr. Emerson died at 9 P. M. suddenly. Our best and greatest American gone. The nearest and dearest friend Father has ever had and
the man who helped me most by his life, his books and his society.
Illustrious and beloved friend, good-bye!" So she made a lyre of yellow jonquils for Ralph Waldo Emerson's preposterous funeral and
somehow steered Bronson Alcott through the dreary business until
he stood beside the coffin in the damp cemetery and mechanically
drawled out the lines of a dire poem. Under the shock the tall old
idler was a mere automaton with a bloodless face that startled watch-
ers as he stepped back from the grave into which his one importance
sank. Emerson was going from him! He was losing his apologist, his
topic. His fingers fell on the shoulder of a little boy who had pressed
forward to see and the grip became so cruel that Louisa saw and her
hoarse voice rose in the hush, commanding: "Pa! Let go! You're hurt-
ing Georgie's arm!" But her father could hear nothing. She stooped
and wrenched the child's arm free.

All summer long, Bronson Alcott paced through Concord's placid

Reprinted from *Hanna, Crane and the Mauve Decade* by Thomas Beer, by permission of Alfred A. Knopf, Inc. Copyright 1926, 1941 by Alfred A. Knopf, Inc.

loveliness, being Bronson Alcott still, still ready to let flow the wonderous volume of his stored inanity on any victim. But ghosts may have stalked with him beneath the royal elms, for when his school of limp philosophers gathered in July, he said to Frances Hedges: "I am the last. They are all gone but me." And they were gone—Hawthorne, Thoreau, the obsessed Sumner and the bloody Theodore Parker; and now Emerson had left him. True, Holmes survived, and so did Lowell. But they had never been too friendly, and neither was young Howells a great admirer, nor that dapper, handsome poet, much too suave—his name was Aldrich—who once so upset a session of the Radical Club by reciting some satirical verses about an improper woman in a harem. * * *

No, Bronson Alcott was wasted on this new society of fribbles and light poets in which men applauded the ribaldries of Mark Twain, whose flippancy Louisa had reproved in her "Eight Cousins," in which the Radical Club was forgotten. His occupation and his audience ceased beside Emerson's flowery casket. Emerson had approved him in all his stages—Platonist schoolmaster, vegetarian, communist, transcendentalist, abolitionist. Bronson Alcott had repaid the devotion with devotion. A new phrase of his Emerson roused in the shallow pond of his intelligence the noisy splash of a log rolled down some slope into a tepid flood. As he lounged from hotel to hotel in summers, he spoke of Emerson as warmly as he spoke of Duty or Domestic Loyalty or Purity or Unselfishness. For Alcott was not an ungrateful man, although an idealist by profession and practice. Idealism is best supported on an income and, after the death of his proud wife's father, Alcott had no banker.

He somehow married the daughter of Samuel May, a rather leonine lady, kin to the Sewalls and Frothinghams. She refused food when her husband's idiotic communist farm at Harvard failed, perhaps from sheer exhaustion, as she had toiled in the fields with her impubic children while Alcott, clad in white linen, talked to callers and explained his high purposes to Margaret Fuller under shady trees. Emerson rescued the family. Emerson brooded affectionately over the growing girls while Mrs. Alcott had an employment office in Boston, on behalf of Alcott's inexhaustible idealism. The older daughters wore frocks bestowed by cousins and an aunt. Louisa went out as a maid once, and once contemplated marriage with a wealthy unloved suitor and once considered suicide. She taught school; she wrote trash for newspapers; she ran errands. Alcott addressed her as "duty's faithful child" in one of his insufferable poems and rhetorically clasped her to his bosom in recognition of her merits, which, he wrote to a friend, gave him every satisfaction. It seems fair. Her first, forgotten novel "Moods" had just made a stir, even causing Henry James, Junior—"a very literary youth," says Louisa's journal —to commit an act of enthusiasm in print. But "Moods" did not sell and Emerson's benevolence continued. It appears that he found for Alcott a paying post in the hospital service at Washington when war broke out, but he was obliged to tell the offering powers that Mr. Alcott had "other projects," which consisted, as far as there is record, in a hearty admiration of the Bostonian excitement over a situation highly profitable to Boston, together with some occasional speeches for the holy cause.

Louisa went to nursing in the hospitals and Alcott quite closely approached the rim of slaughter when he had to bring her home in icy trains, delirious with typhoid and pneumonia, all the way from Washington to Concord. What Louisa thought of his notions about tending a sick daughter we shall never know, as she destroyed much of her journal in the autumn of 1887 when she was so wrecked that she took refuge with Dr. Rhoda Lawrence and sat making penwipers of flannel in the shape of carnations, waiting for death at the age of fifty-three.* But the experience gave her material for "Hospital and Campfire Sketches." She became popular, and money oozed on the arid contours of Alcott's massive debts. Then her publisher wanted a book for girls. She didn't much like girls. Girls, it is possible, had always been rather shy of the Alcott sisters with their bad gowns and their curious papa. But she could write of herself and her family, so she wrote that first part of "Little Women"—and there it is, simple and as effortless as though she had spilled bright rags of silk from her lap on sunlit grass beneath a blowing lilactree.

Louisa May Alcott was famous. Her bones ached; her voice had

* Louisa May Alcott died at fifty-five, in 1888.——Ed. note.

become hoarse and coarse; doctors gave her opiates and treatments that would scare a modern physician badly; she had no use for popularity and no taste for the world that now blandished before her. Pleasure? A trip to Europe with her youngest sister, May. She must nurse her mother and pay Pa's debts and make sure of the family's future. Alcott went beaming and rosy in the very best broadcloth and linen to lecture on Duty, Idealism and Emerson before larger audiences, which now looked eagerly at the grandfather of "Little Women." Duty's child was hard at work, writing "moral pap for the young," in her own phrase, and paralysing a thumb by making three copies of a serial at once. Once she walked across the lawns of Vassar among the thronging girls who tore bits of lace from her dull gown, shook hands with Maria Mitchell, the astronomer, who privately held that Miss Alcott's books were namby-pamby nonsense, but thought the tall spinster a fine woman. And once at Syracuse she faced a congress of her sex and heard its applause as women wrung her fingers. She worked, and Alcott prattled to and fro. Her mother slowly died after looking up at Alcott with the singular remark, "You have laid a very soft pillow for me to go to sleep on." And in the summer of 1882 she worked still, arranging monstrous lunches and teas for the students of the Alcottian school of philosophy, scolding her adored, handsome nephews, permitting Miss Frances Hedges to help her with preserves and ginger cakes, and pausing between jobs to mend a coat or stitch a baseball for any lad who swung over the fence and came prowling around to the kitchen in search of Miss Lou. Men had no interest for Louisa, but a court of adolescents hummed about her to be lectured for sneaking off to Boston to see that awful French troupe in *La Grande Duchesse* and *La Belle Hélène,* and to be fed ginger cakes. Little Miss Hedges had come to be irradiated by the wisdom of Bronson Alcott, but she fell into subjection before Alcott's daughters and wrote to her father in crude Illinois: "I just cannot see anything remarkable or interesting in Mr. Alcott at all, but it is a *privilege* to know Miss Alcott and Mrs. Pratt [the "Meg" of "Little Women"]. They had the awfullest time when they were girls. Sometimes they did not have enough to eat and I have met some ladies here who think that Mr. Alcott has always treated his family shamefully . . ." Alcott would probably have been much astonished to know that anybody had such thoughts about him. There is an indurating quality in the practice of idealism. It is true that Louisa's journal contains notes of restlessness under the spell of duty. In April of 1877 she wrote: "I'm selfish. I want to go away and rest in Europe. Never shall," and in August of 1882 she sent word after Miss Hedges that she was going to take her favourite nephew, Johnny Pratt, out to California and have "a good, long, selfish rest." Never did. In September her father collapsed and thereafter lay a prisoner in a pretty room lined with books, chattering more and more feebly, but chattering still.

All this while the fat volumes of Louisa May Alcott had gone swarming in ugly covers across America from the press of Roberts Brothers, spreading the voice not of Bronson Alcott but of Abba May, his wife, a Puritan lady born in 1799. Her biographer admits that Louisa was unfitted by nature to comprehend Bronson Alcott. In the journal he is "my handsome old philosopher" but it isn't evident that his child cared for transcendentalism. In "Little Women," "Little Men" and "Jo's Boys," Pa is the merest shadow, and the heroic males of the long series are either handsome lads or brisk, successful bearded doctors, men who would hardly lug a delirious lady four hundred miles in railway coaches and who always have cash in pocket. Such philosophy as the books hold is just what Abba May had taught her children, and when the young folk of the tales have flared into a moment of wilful hedonism, it is a firm, kind lady, middle-aged, who steps forward and puts them right. Louisa was writing "moral pap." She couldn't conceive an unmoral book for children, and her own morality hadn't shifted since it was pressed into her by Ma, who had Louisa analyse her small self in a diary for inspection. Pa's lessons, such as "Appollo eats no meat and has no beard . . ." seem to have faded from her completely. God's ministrant is always female, sometimes abetted in virtue by one of the bearded doctors, and always a success. The children wriggle for a breath and then are towed meekly in the cool tide of rectitude. One learns a deal of Abba May Alcott in the progress. She was charmed with "Eight Cousins," in which her representative rebukes current books for boys, the nonsense of Horatio Alger and Oliver Optic, with a fleet slap for "Innocents Abroad," and comments "It gives them such wrong ideas of life and business; shows them so much evil and vulgarity that they need not know about . . . It does seem to me that someone should write stories that should be lively, natural and helpful—tales in which the English should be good, the morals pure and the characters such as we can love in spite of the faults that all may have . . ." She must have been delighted with "Rose in Bloom," in which Rose Campbell gives talks on conduct to other girls in the dressing-rooms of balls, throws over her lover when he comes in a state of champagne to wish her a happy New Year, and waltzes only with her male cousins. She did not live to read "Jo's Boys," which decided that men who have been, no matter how forgivably, in prison may not woo pure young girls. Righteous diversion? A jolly picnic on the river or a set of patriotic tableaux; a romp on the sands at Nonquit; red apples and a plate of gingerbread after sledding in winter; tennis and rootbeer under the elms in summer.

It is a voice of that fading generation which crowned William Dean Howells and shuddered with pleasure as it dabbled its hands in strong Russian waters, for Miss Alcott found "Anna Karenina" most exciting and liked "Kings in Exile" with its pictures of a dissolute Europe. She would even recommend *Le Père Goriot* as suitable reading for a girl of eighteen, but as for "Huckleberry Finn," why, "if Mr. Clemens cannot think of something better to tell our pure-minded lads and lasses, he had best stop writing for them" . . . But she went on writing moral pap for the young and it sold prodigiously. The critics paid no particular attention. Miss Alcott wrote admirably for our little folk. It seems to have struck nobody that Miss Alcott's first audience, the girls who had wept over "Little Women" in the latter '60's were now rearing their daughters in an expanded world on the same diet. In 1882 Joseph Choate turned on a witness in one of his cross-examinations with the cry, "Good God, madame! Did you think that your husband was one of Miss Alcott's boys?" but the lawyer was a profane fellow, given to whist and long dinners. There was no discussion of Miss Alcott's morality, and certainly nobody talked of her art: she wrote for the young.

As spring of 1888 drew near, certain improvident small Bostonians in the region of Louisburg Square's marshalled prettiness were aware of a benevolent goddess whose dark carriage came daily to a rented house. If you ran quickly to open the door, you were sure of a hoarse joke and some pennies and, if you were a small male, a kiss and the loan of a laced handkerchief should your nose need wiping. The goddess, known by the rather Syriac title of "Msalkot," was in the form of a tall lady whose handsome body shivered constantly under furred wraps and whose brown hair showed no grey. Sometimes she came out of the house with a plate of some quivering dessert or a bunch of black foreign grapes untouched by the dotard upstairs in his hired shrine. Sometimes she came out weeping quietly on the arm of a grave nephew if Pa had not known her that day. Once she picked up little Patrick Keogh and held him against her very barrenness all the way to Dunreath Place and gave him a bath in Rhoda Lawrence's tub. She had nothing left for herself. Her sister's sons were grown. Her will was made, asking that she be buried across the feet of her family, as she had always cared for them in life and would rest better so. On March 3rd some acute infant may have noted that the lady wore no furs. Chill wind pursued the carriage as she drove away. In the morning came the daze and agony of a new pain. She asked: "Is it not meningitis?" But at noon she could not know that Bronson Alcott had stopped talking, and before a second sunset Duty's child went hurrying after him.

The journals observed that she had been an admirable writer for the young. Mayo Hazeltine stated casually that "Miss Alcott has found imitators among writers who aspired to something more than the entertainment of nurseries." The gentle, forgotten Constance Woolson exclaimed on paper: "How she has been imitated!" and resumed the imitation of Henry James, a habit in which she so far progressed that "A Transplanted Boy" might have been written and destroyed by James himself. It was plain, to be sure, that a cooing legion was now busy in devising tales on the Alcottian formula, and one follower, Margaret Sydney, was simply a vulgar duplicate of Miss Alcott. But the reviewers generally had little to say of an influence, loosed and active for a quarter of a century, embedded in grown women from the nursery, familiar as a corset. Louisa May Alcott passed without judgment or summary. The critics faced thrilling importations just then and space must be kept for the discussion of "Robert Elsmere," an announcement by a Mrs. Humphry Ward that she had receded from strict belief in the divine origin of Jesus Christ, a fact somehow more exhilarating than the similar recession of her kinsman Matthew Arnold. And then there was "As in a Looking-Glass" with delicious illustrations by George Du Maurier, in whose pages one learned of a raffish woman who married a virtuous landholder and then poisoned herself when her past rose to be a nuisance. Its morality had to be discussed in long columns, just as the morality of its stepchild, "The Second Mrs. Tanqueray," would be discussed sixty months later. These foreign wares had natural precedence of the case of an American spinster, born of a dis-moded philosopher, and full justice had been done when six notices mentioned that Louisa May Alcott was a type of the nation's pure and enlightened womanhood.

Even before the Civil War, orators had flung to the female margin of their audiences some variation of a phrase that always concluded with the trisyllabic word, "womanhood." Theodore Parker used "our pure and enlightened womanhood" four times in two years. Daniel Sickles produced "our world conquering and enlightened womanhood" a few days before he shot his wife's paramour in the streets of Washington. Roscoe Conkling sprinkled his speeches with references to "a pure, enlightened and progressive womanhood" and had more than six hundred babies named after him, to say nothing of one proved "Roscina Conkling" in Ohio. Chester Arthur begot "our cultured and enlightened womanhood" shortly after he startled a dinner in his honour at Saratoga by remarking that he might be President of the United States but his private life was nobody's damned business. Ulysses Grant was also President, but he said nothing much about women and was defended by his doctors and family in his last days from committees of ladies and ancillary clergymen demanding that he sign warnings against the use of alcohol and tobacco. Robert Ingersoll spoke touchingly of the nobility of womanhood quite often, and his version of the tribute is identical with that used by Susan Brownell Anthony and Lucy Stone. There was some convention of the editorial desk and platform in favour of a noble womanhood currently to be viewed in America, and the phrase echoed broadly in 1889 when a yearning for suffrage crystallized under the leadership of Elizabeth Cady Stanton. Miss Grace Ralston caught the words from air about her and made use of "the nobility of womanhood" to a courtly, charming gentleman in a Bostonian drawing-room. "Just what," he asked the girl, "is the nobility of womanhood?" Miss Ralston was annoyed. She had in her possession a dried rose once the property of Elizabeth Stanton and some letters from Lucy Stone. The nobility of womanhood was . . . why, it was the nobility of womanhood! The pleasant gentleman seemed amazingly dull. What precisely was the nobility of womanhood? Miss Ralston had to lecture him stringently. The nobility of womanhood meant the nobility of womanhood! Anybody knew that! "Yes," said William James, "but just what is it, my dear?"

The year 1889 is stippled with unrecorded criticisim of American womanhood, besides the printed observation of Rudyard Kipling who found it wasted time to call on the grand pirates of San Francisco in their homes as wives and daughters adopted the dark young man from India. The house belonged to the womenfolk and it was vain to hint that he had come to see its owner. In March Mlle. Suzanne Beret was appalled by the strangeness of Cleveland as she taught French in a wealthy family and wrote to a cousin in New York: "The ladies talk of nothing but adultery to each other, although they never tell amusing stories of love-affairs . . . I do not accustom myself to the rudeness with which young girls treat men older than themselves. M. Eltinoit * made Miss X a compliment on her costume at a dinner last week by saying she resembled Sarah Bernhardt. She responded: 'Shut up! How dare you compare me to such a woman!' . . . They treat their sons and husbands as rudely before people as though they were bad servants . . . They are much more loyal to each other than Frenchwomen would be . . ." She could make nothing of such a situation. Home-sickness overcame her and she went back to Nantes and to matrimony. In June a Mrs. Edward Wharton of Boston gave

* Elton Hoyt

offence to a matron from Chicago by remarking on the rudeness of American ladies to their sons, but was something forgiven on account of a lovely white parasol. In October the curious Grant Allen gave some advice to an English friend starting for New York and concluded: "Be careful about involving yourself in arguments with ladies. American women take offence easily. With them argument is not intellectual but always emotional and if you attack any little belief or vanity you will find that they can be very rude indeed." Allen knew countless Americans and was himself a Canadian. He later chose to refer rather coldly to "American girls indulged by 'poppa' and spoiled beyond endurance by 'mamma' who make life intolerable and ordinary conversation inaudible for a considerable distance around them," although, among his many avocations, he was a feminist and raised a storm with a feminist novel, "The Woman Who Did," in 1895. His whole literary course was unsteady and a perplexity to critics. He applauded good popular art as good popular art and found the low comedian, Dan Leno, more amusing than Sir Henry Irving. He wrote readable bits of botany, translated from Catullus, composed guide-books, and invented, in a story, a prelude to the psychological entertainments of Sigmund Freud. One comes to-day on his name in volumes of reminiscence or in dusty copies of the *Strand* with some surprise ... But, for all these dubious undertones, 1889 was a year of triumph for American womanhood. Without parade or notice, outside Chicago, a settlement for the poor was opened by Jane Addams and Ellen Starr in September with the name, "Hull House," and at Lake Forest, on Christmas Day, Helen Kimball, a child of ten, was asked to define the word "author" and with the speed of true intelligence answered: "An author is a dreadful person who likes to write books." The last decade of the nineteenth century could now begin.

It began with a handsome exhortation from Phillips Brooks, who urged it to be a good decade. Susan Anthony wished it well, but symptoms of frivolity appeared too soon. In the West some young Indians imagined that they saw a Son of the Great Spirit walking the waters and their aboriginal fancy led them to represent this messenger as having nail-pierced hands and feet. The absurdity didn't prevent tribes from believing that a promise of a happier land teeming with buffalo had been made. So land agents and commanders of outlying forts were alarmed by the Ghost Dance. Naked altogether or striped with paint and floating wolfskins, lads spun and trotted in monotonous rhythms. Some whisper ran down deserts into Mexico and there they danced with green feathers laced to ankles above feet that padded in the noise of drums. Old Sitting Bull now had callers at his shack. His attitude toward the paleface had always been tinged by a dour conservatism, and after Major Kossuth Elder translated to him Longfellow's awful poem on the death of Custer at the Little Big Horn he was heard to state a preference for Negroes. It is said that he was spider in a vast conspiracy, red and black, to drive the white man altogether from America but unhappily he was killed before his plans had time to mature . . . In the East, too, dancing held the eye. Dandies packed Koster and Bial's profane hall nightly to applaud the stamp and flutter of Carmencita as the tall Spaniard whirled and swayed in smoky light. Ladies came veiled to inspect the prodigy and she outdid in gossip the fame of Richard Harding Davis or of Richard Mansfield, who returned to female favour in the "Beau Brummell" of a young playwright, Clyde Fitch. Carmencita's red and yellow gowns covered her legs entirely and her shoulders were hidden in sleeves. It is plain that she wore corsets and nothing lewd is recorded of her performances, in public, while in private she seems to have been an estimable, stupid creature, like most artists, but in October the peace of the *Sun's* office was invaded by five matrons from Chicago, headed by a Mrs. Walker, who demanded that Charles Dana suppress Carmencita forthwith. The editor was habitually deferential to women and notably patient in conversation with fools, but his cynical humour roused behind the kindly mask. He asked if the committee had seen the Spaniard dance. No, but she was an immoral person and the *Sun* must wither this ribald bloom straightway. Chicago then contained a dive of ferocious note among men, mentioned discreetly in journals when it vanished and since recalled in the documents of psychiatrists. Did the ladies not think that they should suppress "the Slide" before they began to rearrange New York? They had never heard of such a place. "Well," said Dana, "you go back to Chicago and have them shut the Slide, and then I'll have Carmencita run out of town for you." The committee bustled forth . . . Carmencita danced and danced. In 1893 male tourists went secretly and timidly to behold the old assemblies at the Slide when the World's Fair packed Chicago. But on April 7, 1891, Dana wrote to an old friend in Illinois: "I do not see why you cannot keep your lady reformers at home. They come in here so thick and fast that I am thinking of attaching a portcullis to my office just to keep them out. If I do not let them waste my time proposing some foolish amendment to the laws they insult me by mail, and if I do see them they insult me anyhow. If you hear of any more nuisances starting for the *Sun,* tell them to try Godkin at the *Post.*"

VERNON L. PARRINGTON

The Gilded Age

I

FREE AMERICA

THE pot was boiling briskly in America in the tumultuous post-war years. The country had definitely entered upon its freedom and was settling its disordered household to suit its democratic taste. Everywhere new ways were feverishly at work transforming the countryside. In the South another order was rising uncertainly on the ruins of the plantation system; in the East an expanding factory economy was weaving a different pattern of industrial life; in the Middle Border a recrudescent agriculture was arising from the application of the machine to the rich prairie soil. All over the land a spider web of iron rails was being spun that was to draw the remotest outposts into the common whole and bind the nation together with steel bands. Nevertheless two diverse worlds lay on the map of continental America. Facing in opposite directions and holding different faiths, they would not travel together easily or take comfort from the yoke that joined them. Agricultural America, behind which lay two and a half centuries of experience, was a decentralized world, democratic, individualistic, suspicious; industrial America, behind which lay only half a dozen decades of bustling experiment, was a

From *Main Currents in American Thought*, Volume 3, by Vernon L. Parrington, copyright, 1930, by Harcourt, Brace and Company, Inc.

centralizing world, capitalistic, feudal, ambitious. The one was a decaying order, the other a rising, and between them would be friction till one or the other had become master.

Continental America was still half frontier and half settled country. A thin line of homesteads had been thrust westward till the outposts reached well into the Middle Border—an uncertain thread running through eastern Minnesota, Nebraska, Kansas, overleaping the Indian Territory and then running west into Texas—approximately halfway between the Atlantic and the Pacific. Behind these outposts was still much unoccupied land, and beyond stretched the unfenced prairies till they merged in the sagebrush plains, gray and waste, that stretched to the foothills of the Rocky Mountains. Beyond the mountains were other stretches of plains and deserts, vast and forbidding in their alkali blight, to the wooded coast ranges and the Pacific Ocean. In all this immense territory were only scattered settlements—at Denver, Salt Lake City, Sacramento, San Francisco, Portland, Seattle, and elsewhere—tiny outposts in the wilderness, with scattered hamlets, mining camps, and isolated homesteads lost in the great expanse. On the prairies from Mexico to Canada—across which rumbled great herds of buffalo—roved powerful tribes of hostile Indians who fretted against the forward thrust of settlement and disputed the right of possession. The urgent business of the times was the subduing of this wild region, wresting it from Indians and buffalo and wilderness; and the forty years that lay between the California gold rush of '49 and the Oklahoma Land Rush of '89 saw the greatest wave of pioneer expansion—the swiftest and most reckless—in all our pioneer experience. Expansion on so vast a scale necessitated building, and the seventies became the railway age, bonding the future to break down present barriers of isolation, and opening new territories for later exploitation. The reflux of the great movement swept back upon the Atlantic coast and gave to life there a fresh note of spontaneous vigor, of which the Gilded Age was the inevitable expression.

It was this energetic East, with its accumulations of liquid capital awaiting investment and its factories turning out the materials needed to push the settlements westward, that profited most from the conquest of the far West. The impulsion from the frontier did much to drive forward the industrial revolution. The war that brought devastation to the South had been more friendly to northern interests. In gathering the scattered rills of capital into central reservoirs at Philadelphia and New York, and in expanding the factory system to supply the needs of the armies, it had opened to capitalism its first clear view of the Promised Land. The bankers had come into control of the liquid wealth of the nation, and the industrialists had learned to use the machine for production; the time was ripe for exploitation on a scale undreamed-of a generation before. Up till then the potential resources of the continent had not even been surveyed. Earlier pioneers had only scratched the surface—felling trees, making crops, building pygmy watermills, smelting a little iron. Mineral wealth had been scarcely touched. Tools had been lacking to develop it, capital had been lacking, transportation lacking, technical methods lacking, markets lacking.

In the years following the war, exploitation for the first time was provided with adequate resources and a competent technique, and busy prospectors were daily uncovering new sources of wealth. The coal and oil of Pennsylvania and Ohio, the copper and iron ore of upper Michigan, the gold and silver, lumber and fisheries, of the Pacific Coast, provided limitless raw materials for the rising industrialism. The Bessemer process quickly turned an age of iron into an age of steel and created the great rolling mills of Pittsburgh from which issued the rails for expanding railways. The reaper and binder, the sulky plow and the threshing machine, created a large-scale agriculture on the fertile prairies. Wild grass-lands provided grazing for immense herds of cattle and sheep; the development of the corn-belt enormously increased the supply of hogs; and with railways at hand the Middle Border poured into Omaha and Kansas City and Chicago an endless stream of produce. As the line of the frontier pushed westward new towns were built, thousands of homesteads were filed on, and the speculator and promoter hovered over the prairies like buzzards seeking their carrion. With rising land-values money was to be made out of unearned increment, and the creation of booms was a profitable industry. The times were stirring and it was a shiftless fellow who did not make his pile. If he had been too late to file on desirable acres he had only to find a careless homesteader who had failed in some legal technicality and "jump his claim." Good bottom land could be had even by late-comers if they were sharp at the game.

This bustling America of 1870 accounted itself a democratic world. A free people had put away all aristocratic priviliges and conscious of its power went forth to possess the last frontier. Its social philosophy, which it found adequate to its needs, was summed up in three words—preëmption, exploitation, progress. Its immediate and pressing business was to dispossess the government of its rich holdings. Lands in the possession of the government were so much idle waste, untaxed and profitless; in private hands they would be developed. They would provide work, pay taxes, support schools, enrich the community. Preëmption meant exploitation and exploitation meant progress. It was a simple philosophy and it suited the simple individualism of the times. The Gilded Age knew nothing of the Enlightenment; it recognized only the acquisitive instinct. That much at least the frontier had taught the great American democracy; and in applying to the resources of a continent the lesson it had been so well taught the Gilded Age wrote a profoundly characteristic chapter of American history.

II

FIGURES OF EARTH

In a moment of special irritation Edwin Lawrence Godkin called the civilization of the seventies a chromo civilization. Mark Twain, with his slack western standards, was equally severe. As he contemplated the slovenly reality beneath the gaudy exterior he dubbed it the Gilded Age. Other critics with a gift for pungent phrase have flung their gibes at the ways of a picturesque and uncouth generation. There is reason in plenty for such caustic comment. Heedless, irreverent, unlovely, cultivating huge beards, shod in polished top-boots— the last refinement of the farmer's cowhides—wearing linen dickeys over hickory shirts, moving through pools of tobacco juice, erupting

in shoddy and grotesque architecture, cluttering its homes with un-
gainly walnut chairs and marble-topped tables and heavy lambre-
quins, the decade of the seventies was only too plainly mired and
floundering in a bog of bad taste. A world of triumphant and un-
abashed vulgarity without its like in our history, it was not aware
of its plight, but accounted its manners genteel and boasted of ways
that were a parody on sober good sense.

Yet just as such comments are, they do not reach quite to the
heart of the age. They emphasize rather the excrescences, the casual
lapses, of a generation that underneath its crudities and vulgarities
was boldly adventurous and creative—a generation in which the
democratic freedoms of America, as those freedoms had taken shape
during a drab frontier experience, came at last to spontaneous and
vivid expression. If its cultural wealth was less than it thought, if
in its exuberance it was engaged somewhat too boisterously in stamping its own plebeian image on the work of its hands, it was only
natural to a society that for the first time found its opportunities
equal to its desires, a youthful society that accounted the world its
oyster and wanted no restrictions laid on its will. It was the ripe
fruit of Jacksonian leveling, and if it ran to a grotesque individualism—if in its self-confidence it was heedless of the smiles of older
societies—it was nevertheless by reason of its uncouthness the most
picturesque generation in our history; and for those who love to
watch human nature disporting itself with naïve abandon, running
amuck through all the conventions, no other age provides so fascinating a spectacle.

When the cannon at last had ceased their destruction it was a
strange new America that looked out confidently on the scene. Something had been released by the upheavals of half a century, something
strong and assertive that was prepared to take possession of the continent. It did not issue from the loins of war. Its origins must be
sought elsewhere, further back in time. It had been cradled in the
vast changes that since 1815 had been reshaping America: in the
break-up of the old domestic economy that kept life mean and drab,
in the noisy enthusiasms of the new coonskin democracy, in the ro-
manticisms of the California gold rush, in the boisterous freedoms

discovered by the forties and fifties. It had come to manhood in the battles of a tremendous war, and as it now surveyed the continent, discovering potential wealth before unknown, it demanded only freedom and opportunity—a fair race and no favors. Everywhere was a welling-up of primitive pagan desires after long repressions— to grow rich, to grasp power, to be strong and masterful and lay the world at its feet. It was a violent reaction from the narrow poverty of frontier life and the narrow inhibitions of backwoods religion. It had had enough of skimpy, meager ways, of scrubbing along hoping for something to turn up. It would go out and turn it up. It was consumed with a great hunger for abundance, for the good things of life, for wealth. It was frankly materialistic and if material goods could be wrested from society it would lay its hands heartily to the work. Freedom and opportunity, to acquire, to possess, to enjoy—for that it would sell its soul.

Society of a sudden was become fluid. With the sweeping-away of the last aristocratic restraints the potentialities of the common man found release for self-assertion. Strange figures, sprung from obscure origins, thrust themselves everywhere upon the scene. In the reaction from the mean and skimpy, a passionate will to power was issuing from unexpected sources, undisciplined, confused in ethical values, but endowed with immense vitality. Individualism was being simplified to the acquisitive instinct. These new Americans were primitive souls, ruthless, predatory, capable; single-minded men; rogues and rascals often, but never feeble, never hindered by petty scruple, never given to puling or whining—the raw materials of a race of capitalistic buccaneers. Out of the drab mass of common plebeian life had come this vital energy that erupted in amazing abundance and in strange forms. The new freedoms meant diverse things to different men and each like Jurgen followed after his own wishes and his own desires. Pirate and priest issued from the common source and played their parts with the same picturesqueness. The romantic age of Captain Kidd was come again, and the black flag and the gospel banner were both in lockers to be flown as the needs of the cruise determined. With all coercive restrictions put away the democratic genius of America was setting out on the road of manifest destiny.

Analyze the most talked-of men of the age and one is likely to find a splendid audacity coupled with an immense wastefulness. A note of tough-mindedness marks them. They had stout nippers. They fought their way encased in rhinoceros hides. There was the Wall Street crowd—Daniel Drew, Commodore Vanderbilt, Jim Fisk, Jay Gould, Russell Sage—blackguards for the most part, railway wreckers, cheaters and swindlers, but picturesque in their rascality. There was the numerous tribe of politicians—Boss Tweed, Fernando Wood, G. Oakey Hall, Senator Pomeroy, Senator Cameron, Roscoe Conkling, James G. Blaine—blackguards also for the most part, looting city treasuries, buying and selling legislative votes like railway stock, but picturesque in their audacity. There were the professional keepers of the public morals—Anthony Comstock, John B. Gough, Dwight L. Moody, Henry Ward Beecher, T. De Witt Talmage—ardent proselytizers, unintellectual, men of one idea, but fiery in zeal and eloquent in description of the particular heaven each wanted to people with his fellow Americans. And springing up like mushrooms after a rain was the goodly company of cranks—Victoria Woodhull and Tennessee Claflin, "Citizen" George Francis Train, Henry Bergh, Ben Butler, Ignatius Donnelly, Bob Ingersoll, Henry George—picturesque figures with a flair for publicity who tilled their special fields with splendid gestures. And finally there was Barnum the Showman, growing rich on the profession of humbuggery, a vulgar greasy genius, pure brass without any gilding, yet in picturesque and capable effrontery the very embodiment of the age. A marvelous company, vital with the untamed energy of a new land. In the presence of such men one begins to understand what Walt Whitman meant by his talk of the elemental.

Created by a primitive world that knew not the machine, they were marked by the rough homeliness of their origins. Whether wizened or fat they were never insignificant or commonplace. On the whole one prefers them fat, and for solid bulk what generation has outdone them? There was Revivalist Moody, bearded and neckless, with his two hundred and eighty pounds of Adam's flesh, every ounce of which "belonged to God." There was the lyric Sankey, afflicted with two hundred and twenty-five pounds of human frailty, yet looking as smug as a banker and singing "There were ninety and nine" divinely through mutton-chop whiskers. There was Boss Tweed, phlegmatic and mighty, overawing rebellious gangsters at the City Hall with his two hundred and forty pounds of pugnacious rascality. There was John Fiske, a philosophic hippopotamus, warming the chill waters of Spencerian science with his prodigious bulk. There was Ben Butler, oily and puffy and wheezy, like Falstaff larding the lean earth as he walked along, who yearly added more flesh to the scant ninety-seven pounds he carried away from Waterville College. And there was Jim Fisk, dressed like a bartender, huge in nerve as in bulk, driving with the dashing Josie Mansfield down Broadway—prince of vulgarians, who jovially proclaimed, "I worship in the Synagogue of the Libertines," and who on the failure of the Erie coup announced cheerfully, "Nothing is lost save honor!"

Impressive as are the fat kine of Egypt, the lean kine scarcely suffer by contrast. There were giants of puny physique in those days. There was Uncle Dan'l Drew, thin as a dried herring, yet a builder of churches and founder of Drew Theological Seminary, who pilfered and cheated his way to wealth with tobacco juice drooling from his mouth. There was Jay Gould, a lone-hand gambler, a dynamo in a tubercular body, who openly invested in the devil's tenements as likely to pay better dividends, and went home to potter lovingly amongst his exotic flowers. And there was Oakey Hall, clubman and playwright, small, elegant, and unscrupulous; and Victoria Woodhull who stirred up the Beecher case, a wisp of a woman who enraged all the frumpy blue-stockings by the smartness of her toilet and the perfection of her manners; and little Libby Tilton with her tiny wistful face and great eyes that looked out wonderingly at the world—eyes that were to go blind with weeping before the candle of her life went out. It was such men and women, individual and colorful, that Whitman and Mark Twain mingled with, and that Herman Melville—colossal and dynamic beyond them all—looked out upon sardonically from his tomb in the Custom House where he was consuming his own heart.

They were thrown up as it were casually out of the huge caldron of energy that was America. All over the land were thousands like them, self-made men quick to lay hands on opportunity if it knocked at the door, ready to seek it out if it were slow in knocking, recognizing no limitations to their powers, discouraged by no shortcomings in their training. When Moody set out to bring the world to his Protestant God he was an illiterate shoe salesman who stumbled over the hard words of his King James Bible. Anthony Comstock, the roundsman of the Lord, was a salesman in a dry-goods shop, and as careless of his spelling as he was careful of his neighbors' morals. Commodore Vanderbilt, who built up the greatest fortune of the time, was a Brooklyn ferryman, hard-fisted and tough as a burr-oak, who in a lifetime of over eighty years read only one book, *Pilgrim's Progress,* and that after he was seventy. Daniel Drew was a shyster cattle-drover, whose arid emotions found outlet in periodic conversions and backslidings, and who got on in this vale of tears by salting his cattle and increasing his—and the Lord's wealth— with every pound of water in their bellies—from which cleverness is said to have come the Wall Street phrase, "stock-watering." Jim Fisk was the son of a Yankee peddler, who, disdaining the unambitious ways of his father, set up for himself in a cart gilded like a circus-wagon and drove about the countryside with jingling bells. After he had made his pile in Wall Street he set up his own opera house and proposed to rival the Medici as a patron of the arts—and especially of the artists if they were of the right sex. A surprising number of them—Moody, Beecher, Barnum, Fisk, Comstock, Ben Butler—came from New England; Jay Gould was of Connecticut ancestry; but Oakey Hall was a southern gentleman; Fernando Wood, with the face of an Apollo and the wit of an Irishman, was the son of a Philadelphia cigar-maker and much of his early income was drawn from sailors' groggeries along the waterfront; Tweed was a stolid New Yorker, and Drew was a York State country boy.

What was happening in New York was symptomatic of the nation. If the temple of Plutus was building in Wall Street, his devotees were everywhere. In Chicago, rising higgledy-piggledy from the ashes of the great fire, Phil Armour and Nelson Morris were laying out stockyards and drawing the cattle and sheep and hogs from remote prairie farms to their slaughter-houses. In Cleveland, Mark Hanna was erecting his smelters and turning the iron ore of Michigan into dollars, while John D. Rockefeller was squeezing the small fry out of the petroleum business and creating the Standard Oil monopoly. In Pittsburgh, Andrew Carnegie was applying the Bessemer process to steel-making and laying the foundations of the later steel trust. In Minneapolis, C. C. Washburn and Charles A. Pillsbury were applying new methods to milling and turning the northern wheat into flour to ship to the ends of the earth. In San Francisco, Leland Stanford and Collis P. Huntington were amassing huge fortunes out of the Southern Pacific Railway and bringing the commonwealth of California to their feet. Everywhere were boomtown and real-estate promoters, the lust of speculation, the hankering after quick and easy wealth.

In the great spaces from Kansas City to Sacramento the frontier spirit was in the gaudiest bloom. The experiences of three centuries of expansion were being crowded into as many decades. In the fifties the highway of the frontier had run up and down the Mississippi River and the golden age of steamboating had brought a motley life to Saint Louis; in the seventies the frontier had passed far beyond and was pushing through the Rocky Mountains, repeating as it went the old frontier story of swagger and slovenliness, of boundless hope and heroic endurance—a story deeply marked with violence and crime and heart-breaking failure. Thousands of veterans from the disbanded armies, northern and southern alike, flocked to the West to seek their fortunes, and daily life there soon took on a drab note from the alkali of the plains; yet through the drabness ran a boisterous humor that exalted lying to a fine art—a humor that goes back to Davy Crockett and the Ohio flatboatmen. Mark Twain's *Roughing It* is the epic of the Pony Express, as *Life on the Mississippi* is the epic of the preceding generation.

The huge wastefulness of the frontier was everywhere, East and West. The Gilded Age heeded somewhat too literally the Biblical injunction to take no thought for the morrow, but was busily intent on squandering the resources of the continent. All things were held

cheap, and human life cheapest of all. Wild Bill Hickok with forty
notches on his gun and a row of graves to his credit in Boot Hill
Cemetery, and Jesse James, most picturesque of desperadoes, levying
toll with his six-shooter on the bankers who were desecrating the free
spirit of the plains with their two per cent a month, are familiar
heroes in Wild West tales; but the real plainsman of the Gilded
Age, the picturesque embodiment of the last frontier, was Captain
Carver, the faultless horesman and faultless shot, engaged in his
celebrated buffalo hunt for the championship of the prairies. Wag-
ering that he could kill more buffalo in a day than any rival hero
of the chase, he rode forth with his Indian marker and dropping
the miles behind him he left an endless trail of dead beasts properly
tagged, winning handsomely when his rival's horse fell dead from
exhaustion. It was magnificent. Davy Crockett's hundred and five
bears in a season was but 'prentice work compared with Captain
Carver's professional skill. It is small wonder that he became a hero
of the day and his rifle, turned now to the circus business of breaking glass balls thrown from his running horse, achieved a fame far
greater than Davy's Betsy. With his bold mustaches, his long black
hair flying in the wind, his sombrero and chaps and top-boots, he
was a figure matched only by Buffalo Bill, the last of the great
plainsmen.

Captain Carver was picturesque, but what shall be said of the
thousands of lesser Carvers engaged in the same slaughter, market-
hunters who discovered a new industry in buffalo-killing? At the
close of the Civil War the number on the western plains was estimated at fifteen millions. With the building of the Union Pacific
Railroad they were cut asunder into two vast herds, and upon these
herds fell the hunters with the new breech-loading rifles, shooting
for the hide market that paid sixty-five cents for a bull's hide and
a dollar and fifteen cents for a cow's. During the four years from
1871 to 1874 nearly a million head a year were slain from the
southern herd alone, their skins ripped off and the carcasses left
for the coyotes and buzzards. By the end of the hunting season of
1875 the vast southern herd had been wiped out, and with the
building of the Northern Pacific in 1880 the smaller northern herd

soon suffered the same fate. The buffalo was gone with the hostile Indians—Sioux and Blackfeet and Cheyennes and a dozen other tribes. It was the last dramatic episode of the American frontier, and it wrote a fitting climax to three centuries of wasteful conquest. But the prairies were tamed, and Wild Bill Hickok and Captain Carver and Buffalo Bill Cody had become romantic figures to enthrall the imagination of later generations.

It was the abundant harvest of those freedoms that America had long been struggling to achieve, and it was making ready the ground for later harvests that would be less to its liking. Freedom had become individualism, and individualism had become the inalienable right to preëmpt, to exploit, to squander. Gone were the old ideals along with the old restraints. The idealism of the forties, the romanticism of the fifties—all the heritage of Jeffersonianism and the French Enlightenment—were put thoughtlessly away, and with no social conscience, no concern for civilization, no heed for the future of the democracy it talked so much about, the Gilded Age threw itself into the business of money-getting. From the sober restraints of aristocracy, the old inhibitions of Puritanism, the niggardliness of an exacting domestic economy, it swung far back in reaction, and with the discovery of limitless opportunities for exploitation it allowed itself to get drunk. Figures of earth, they followed after their own dreams. Some were builders with grandiose plans in their pockets; others were wreckers with no plans at all. It was an anarchistic world of strong, capable men, selfish, unenlightened, amoral—an excellent example of what human nature will do with undisciplined freedom. In the Gilded Age freedom was the freedom of buccaneers preying on the argosies of Spain.

BURTON RASCOE

Two Writers

FIRST MEETING WITH WILLA CATHER

I MET Miss Willa Cather for the first time to-day at lunch with
Thomas Beer. She impressed me at once as a remarkable woman,
in a way I had so far from expected that I was some time in orientating
myself to her personality and so getting my ease. She is full-blooded,
vigorous, substantial, sure of herself, matter-of-fact, businesslike, and
somehow I had expected her to be reticent, uncommunicative, rather
sweet and softish. She looks as though she might conduct a great law
practice or a successful dairy farm, superintend a telephone exchange
or run a magazine with equal efficiency, ideas and energy.

The first thing I heard her say concerned matters of a practical
nature. She said that she refused to autograph books sent to her for
the quite legitimate reason that lately her publisher is bringing out
limited autographed editions of her work, and for her to autograph
books sent to her would cut in on his business. One bookseller had
had the nerve, she said, to send her twenty-five books to autograph
for sale, but she sent them back with promptitude and gave him a
bit of her mind. She is fond of the table and she discourses with
gusto on food; she knows where the best meals are to be had in
Paris, London and New York; she taxies uptown frequently from

Bank Street to eat at a restaurant where the food is so good that she told Beer, who had never been there: "Young man, the next time I see you I want you to have been at Voisin's"; she sent back her chicken pie, reminding the waiter curtly that it was insufficient in sauce and that it is not to be eaten dry. She is free from the usual inhibitions to comfortable and easy discourse; she uses good, colloquial and pungent words. I could have embraced her with joy and admiration when she exclaimed, the moment a certain academic critic's name was mentioned, "Oh, that mutton-head!" That is, in my opinion, precisely what he is, and no one had ever said it before. She is brief, decisive and sharp in her criticism of writers and of people. When Beer said he had been called to task for not mentioning Octave Thanet in his book and said he had not read her, Miss Cather replied, "There's no reason why you should; she was a carpenter. Her stories are well-nailed, uninteresting goods boxes." *(From "A Bookman's Daybook," New York Tribune, February 18, 1924.)*

First Visit to Dreiser

This afternoon I went to see Theodore Dreiser, who has come on from Hollywood for the winter and is living in St. Luke's Place, next door to Sherwood Anderson. Although we had exchanged brief notes from time to time for several years, I had never met Dreiser until to-day. He is more youthful looking than I expected him to be, remembering that he published "Sister Carrie" more than twenty years ago. He is tall, without superfluous flesh and only slightly stooped. His hair is gray, his eyes deep-set, his cheeks so full as to seem puffy, his lips thick. He has no gestures and is the most immobile writer I ever saw, apparently capable of sitting at ease for an hour without moving a muscle. His voice is well modulated, soft and without any nasal quality. He speaks slowly, with the average stammer, and there is a certain air of humility and gentleness in his bearing. I got from him the same sort of impression of dogged persistency, honesty, sincerity, frankness and hungry curiosity about life that I get from his writings. He greeted me with a friendly casualness one has toward friends of long standing. He had a sheaf of manuscript in his hand and after he had got a match for my cigarette (he doesn't smoke) he sat down and explained, in a timid and bashful manner, that he had been writing poems and that he was anxious to know what I thought of them. He said he would like to send me the batch of poems he has written over a long period of years and have me make frank notes of comment on each one.

"They are free verse sort of things," he said. "Just moods and impressions and attempts to get into a few words something I feel about the color and beauty and strangeness of life. I have been writing them off and on for years. I don't know whether they are any good or not, but they are things I had to write just the way they are written."

I asked him to read some of them to me, knowing that I had been much more sympathetic toward Sherwood Anderson's "Mid-American Chants" after hearing Sherwood recite them than I had upon reading them in *The Little Review;* but Dreiser picked out five and handed them to me. I had almost wanted to laugh when he told me he was writing poetry, so redundant, cacophanous and deficient in word values is he in his prose; but these strange pieces had life and heart in them, like his plodding, cumbrous novels, and moreover, they have the impress of authentic poetic emotion. Here was ineluctable sadness with a poignancy in no way rhetorical, glimpses of beauty caught in images from life in a city street— astonishing things, really, yet somehow the sort of fumbling grasps of poetic essentials one would expect of him did one ever think of him expressing himself in verse, free or otherwise.

He works daily, he told me, from 10 until 3 or 4, uninterruptedly without lunching. He is still writing "The Bulwark," the third volume of the trilogy which includes "The Financier" and "The Titan," and he has also written eight of a series of fifteen portraits of women, which is to be a companion volume to "Twelve Men." That book, "Twelve Men," he said, is apparently the best liked of all his books. More copies of it have been sent to him for his signature than of all the others combined.

He recited to me without bitterness, indeed with an amused resignation, the rebuffs he had had, the difficulties he still encounters in finding a market for his writings, the hostility of the reviewers, the trenchant personal abuse that has been heaped upon him gratuitously by critics, the hard time he has had in making a living. Of the series of fine and original portraits in "Twelve Men" he was able to dispose of only one to a magazine, although, he said, "I hawked them all in every editorial office. Everybody said they were no good until after they came out in book form and critics here and there began to praise them. Then the editors wanted me to write more like them."

Dreiser's tenacity of purpose in the face of all possible odds against him has been not the least noble aspect of his writing career. Against a storm of critical derision, mere indignation, the hounding of the vice society, rejection slips, insufficient financial returns, discouragements and abuse, he has made no compromise whatever; he has expressed himself unequivocably, sincerely as he felt. He is at once a proud and humble man, without arrogance or a sense of martyrdom, driven by a desire to write of life as he sees it, as well and as truthfully as he can. He moved, a pathmaker, with heavy crunching, powerful steps, through the brambles and thickets of American literary prejudice, making way for a host of more graceful but less powerful writers to follow him, and who in the blithe heedlessness of youth will never be properly grateful for the work he has done until it turns out, as it reasonably may, that he has done not the most artistic but the most significant work of his period in America's age of democratic industrialism, that it was his genius which most accurately reflected the peculiar aspects of that age. *(From "A Bookman's Daybook," New York Tribune, December 18, 1922.)*

FRANCES NEWMAN

"This Side of Paradise"

IT is not, of course, necessary that all American reviewers—critic is rather a lofty word—should have read "Sinister Street" once a month or so during the six years that one has been privileged to do so, and perhaps one official skimming might have been dimmed by the intervention of a fairly prolonged war. But an equally casual skimming of the reviews of "This Side of Paradise" has revealed in only the New Republic a glance at Mr. Fitzgerald's "acquisitive eye on 'Sinister Street.' " And as the next line continued "without its obesity," one gathers that this R.V.A.S. has no very tender regard for Michael Fane. But if "Sinister Street" was until very lately the apple of one's eye and if even the discovery of a new apple has not caused one to love it less, the perusal of "This Side of Paradise" becomes nothing less than agony. * * *

Now, naturally, one knows no more of Mr. Fitzgerald's literary affections than he has seen fit to reveal in print, but it rather seems that his memory is much more highly developed than his imagination and that he has no idea how good a memory he really has. As some forgotten writer said when "Queed" was first delighting the world, Mr. Harrison might have imitated Robert Chambers, but he had instead risen to the altitude of imitating the author of "Septimus,"

Reprinted by permission from *The Atlanta Constitution* of February 13, 1921.

and so one might take it kindly that young Mr. Fitzgerald has hitched his wagon to Mr. Mackenzie rather than to Ralph Barbour, and so, if it were only Mr. Walpole or Mr. Cannan or even Aldous Huxley, one could. But the vulgarizing of one's perfect book is more than can be endured in silence.

Mr. Fitzgerald certainly did not sit down with the desire to write a story of youth and after casting about for a model, say to himself that he would write an American parody of "Sinister Street." No one in his senses would do that. So it must follow that he has been betrayed by his too retentive memory. The suffering of witnessing the desecration of an idol has made the reading of every one of his words impossible, so it is quite possible that one has missed the most distressing of the affinities between the career of Amory Blaine and Michael Fane—one had not, until the moment of writing them, realized that the names rhyme—and one may also have missed some of Mr. Fitzgerald's felicities, even all of them. This sincere flattery begins at the very beginning, by a caricature of Mrs. Fane, that vague and charming woman, which after being united with some of the less pleasing frailties of Michael's nurse, is called the sophisticated mother of Amory. Mr. Fitzgerald has even provided a dignitary of the Catholic church for Amory to discuss his divergences from other boys with—quite as Michael had his Mr. Viner for the same high use. And just, also, as Michael had his Wilmot to introduce him to Oscar Wilde and Walter Pater and Mademoiselle de Maupin, even to the decadents of another age—Petronius and Apuleius and Suetonius, Amory had his D'Inviliers to discover to him the glories of "Dorian Gray" and Swinburne and Pater, of Gautier, and Huysmans, of "the racier sections of Rabelais, Bocaccio, Petronius and Suetonius." And Michael was called Narcissus by this Wilmot; Mr. Fitzgerald has provided a section entitled "Narcissus on Duty." The first book of "Sinister Street" is called "Dreaming Spires," and most properly, since Matthew Arnold gave the phrase to Oxford; the entry of Amory into Princeton is heralded by the title "Spires and Gargoyles." Michael was teased by his governess because his sympathies were the sympathies of the late G. A. Henty, even to the point of sympathizing with the American colonists against his own British forebears;

Amory had all the "Henty biasses," even to the point of sympathizing with the southern confederacy. Michael was rigid about dividing Oxford into "good eggs and bad men"; Amory's world was divided into "slickers and big-men." And there are endless phrases and incidents that have risen from poor Mr. Fitzgerald's subconscious mind rather than from his observation.

Such a comparison is undoubtedly vain and frivolous, but this young man, in the phrase of his period, has positively "asked for it." To one who cherishes "Sinister Street" and one who cherishes some hope for the American novel, it is impossible to read "This Side of Paradise" without having one's blood-pressure about mount to a dangerous degree and without one's temperature becoming unendurable. And it would not be so very annoying if any number of critics for whom one had a high regard had not taken it so very seriously. Such panegyrics as might have greeted the plays of Euripides or the Divine Comedy—but which certainly did not—have flowed from the most respectable sources; the book has had both the success of esteem and the success of popularity.

As for the ways in which "This Side of Paradise" differs from "Sinister Street," except for a few essentially trivial ones, a comparison would be rather like one between "Irene" and "Tristran and Isolde." There is, however, the fundamental one that Michael Fane, in spite of some eccentricities of ancestry, was a gentleman. And there is also the difference that Mr. Fitzgerald's youths serve Athena and Aphrodite quite interchangeably. . . . But both of these books end with a crisis of youth and a cry in the dark—rather significantly, the darkness of Rome and the darkness of New Jersey.

Of course, Mr. Fitzgerald is young—so young that he thinks eight years passed between the eighteenth amendment and the day when the Fifth Avenue traffic lights were still a subject of conversation—and Dr. Johnson might charitably decide that one should be surprised to find it done at all. But if one must have youth, let us have Daisy Ashford's youth and let us not be confronted with a choice between Mr. Fitzgerald's youthful patchwork and Miss Opal Whiteley's childish labor.

But the crowning glory of "This Side of Paradise" may be regarded as the fact that about his twenty-third year this Amory Blaine "was where Goethe was when he began 'Faust'; he was where Conrad was. when he wrote 'Almayer's Folly.' " Now, quite apart from the difficulty of conceiving that Goethe and Conrad were at the same place, one grieves for the loss it is to American letters that this gifted Amory should be only the creation of Mr. Fitzgerald's brain. *(From "Carnegie Library Notes," Atlanta Constitution, February 13, 1921.)*

An Exchange of Letters

38 West 59 Street, New York
February 26, 1921

My dear Miss Newman:

While it astonished me that so few critics mentioned the influence of Sinister Street on This Side of Paradise, I feel sure that was much more in intention than in literal fact. It occurred to me to write an American version of the history of that sort of young man—in which, no doubt, I was hindered by lack of perspective as well as by congenital short-comings.

But I was also hindered by a series of resemblances between my life and that of Michael Fane which, had I been a more conscientious man, might have precluded my ever attempting an autobiographical novel. I have five copies of Youth's Encounter at present in my library, sent me by people who stumbled on the book and thought that it was an amazing parallel to my own life. When I was twenty-one and began This Side of Paradise my literary taste was so unformed that Youth's Encounter was still my "perfect book." My book quite naturally shows the influence to a marked degree. However, I resent your details. Both Shane Leslie in the Dublin Review and Maurice Francis Egan in the Catholic World took me to task for painting "Monsignor Darcy" from the life. He was, of course, my best friend, the Monsignor Sigorney Fay, to whom the book was

dedicated. He was known to many Catholics as the most brilliant
priest in America. The letters in the book are almost transcriptions
of his own letters to me.

Amory Blaine's mother was also an actual character, the mother of
a friend of mine, whose name I cannot mention. There is such an
obvious connection between her early career and that of the cook in
Youth's Encounter that I appreciate your pointing it out to me. You
see I object to being twice blamed—once for transcribing a character from life and once for stealing him from another author. I have
had numerous comments from Princeton about putting J—— into
the book as "Thomas P. D'Invilliers," and now I am told that I
borrowed the dilettante aesthete Wilmot from MacKenzie. "Spires
and Gargoyles" was possibly suggested by "Dreaming Spires" but
the terms "slicker" and "big men" were in use at Princeton when
I first went there—before Youth's Encounter was written.

It seems to me that you have marred a justified criticism by such
pettinesses as comparing the names "Blaine" and "Fane," and by remarking on the single occurrence of the word "Narcissus" in Sinister
Street. You seem to be unconscious that even MacKenzie had his
sources such as Dorian Grey and None Other Gods and that occasionally we may have drunk at the same springs. Incidentally
Michael's governess did *not* tease him about G. A. Henty.

This is the first letter of any kind I have ever written to a critic
of my book and I shall probably regret this one before the day is
over. I sent the novel to Mencken with the confession that it derived
itself from MacKenzie, Wells and Tarkington, with half a dozen
additional overtones, but there are comparisons you brought up that
make me as angry as my book evidently made you. It is as if I accused Floyd Dell of being a plagiarist because both our mooncalfs
wrote poetry and both walked toward a dark town at the last, whispering of their lost loves—or said that Cabell's Jurgen is an imitation of The Revolt of the Angels, or even, to use another Tristan
and Irene comparison, compared your article with P. 138 of
Mencken's Prejudices, 1st Series.

Yours very truly,

F. Scott Fitzgerald

Atlanta, March 4, 1921

My dear Mr. Fitzgerald

Please do not regret that you wrote to me—I enjoyed your letter greatly, particularly the deadly thrust about the unformed state of your literary taste at twenty-one. And I am truly sorry that I should have annoyed you, for my quarrel was much more with American criticism than with you. But if you find that as Irene is to Tristan and Isolde, so am I to Mencken, I do not see why you do not just put me down as an oafish inhabitant of the Sahara of the Bozart.

There are only two points in your letter that I think it necessary for me to answer. I do not think, and I did not say, that D'Invilliers is like Wilmot or that your priest is like Father Viner. I have no very clear conception of either one. As to the affair of the Henty books, I remember the incident perfectly, but I did not verify it, and it is quite possible that it is in some other English story. I bow to your superior memory for Mackenzie and apologize unreservedly. And as for Mrs. Fane, of course elegant idiots are all too common on both sides of the Atlantic, but the kind of thing I meant is typified in her reply to Michael's remark that he is thinking of being a priest —"Oh, Michael, and you look so particularly nice in tweeds." The quotation may not be exact.

I was not quoting Mencken on Mr. Harrison. It was something decidedly less violent, for in my opinion there is not so much space below Mencken as there is between the two aforementioned operas.

I think the remarks you quoted are probably not really those that made you most angry. But if you had seen the posters with which Mr. Hearst has Atlanta placarded just now concerning your "wonderful story of the adolescent he-vamp," you might have agreed that I could hardly do as much to injure your reputation.

Very truly yours,

FRANCES NEWMAN

45 West Eleventh Street

(F.N. had sent to Mr. Cabell her correspondence with Mr. Fitzgerald, across the top of whose letter to her she had written: "I feel as if I had pulled a spoiled baby's curls and made him cry. Please send it back—first blood, you know.")

March 7, 1921

Dear Miss Newman:

Herewith (to begin) is Fitzgerald's letter, and I honestly confess I think you dealt overharshly with him. What may be in him there is no saying: but I rather fancy the notion there is a great deal. You see, we all have to begin with something: and I, who began with The Eagle's Shadow, am the last person in the world to be hypercritical. Well! . . .

Yours faithfully,

JAMES BRANCH CABELL

ERNEST BOYD

Aesthete: Model 1924

H E is a child of this Twentieth Century, for the Yellow Nineties
had flickered out in the delirium of the Spanish-American War
when his first gurgles rejoiced the ears of his expectant parents. . . .
His thirtieth birthday is still on the horizon, his literary baggage is
small, or non-existent—but he is already famous; at least, so it seems
to him when he gazes upon his own reflection in the eyes of his
friends, and fingers aggressively the luxurious pages of the magazine of which he is Editor-in-Chief, Editor, Managing Editor, Associate Editor, Contributing Editor, Bibliographical Editor, or Source
Material Editor. His relationship to the press must always be editorial, and to meet the changed conditions of the cosmos, a changed
conception of the functions of an editor provides him with a vast
selection of titles from which to choose. The essential fact is that
he has an accredited mouthpiece, a letter-head conferring authority,
a secure place from which to bestride the narrow world in which
he is already a colossus. Thus he is saved from those sordid encounters with the harsh facts of literary commerce which his predecessors
accepted as part of the discipline of life: Meredith reading manuscripts for Chapman & Hall, Gissing toiling in New Grub Street,
Anatole France writing prefaces for Lemerre's classics, Dreiser polishing dime novels for Street & Smith. * * *

Reprinted by permission from *The American Mercury*, January 1924. Copyright
1924 and 1952, The American Mercury.

When he went to Harvard—or was it Princeton or Yale?—in the
early years of the Woodrovian epoch, he was just one of so many
mute and inglorious Babbitts preparing to qualify as regular fellows.
If some brachycephalic shadow lay across the Nordic blondness of his
social pretensions, then, of course, the pilgrimage assumed something
of the character of a great adventure into the Promised Land, the
penetration to an Anglo-Saxon Lhasa. His immediate concern, in any
case, was to resemble as closely as possible every man about him, to
acquire at once the marks of what is known as the education of a
gentleman, to wit, complete and absolute conformity to conventions,
the suppression of even the faintest stirrings of eccentric personality.
To this day he feels a little embarrassed when he calls on his father
in Wall Street, carrying a walking-stick and wearing a light tweed
suit, but he trusts that even the door-opener's scorn will be softened
by the knowledge that here is an artist, whose personality must be
untrammeled.

Those who knew the Aesthete during the period of his initiation
will recall how he walked along the banks of his Yankee Isis, or
lolled behind the bushes, discussing Life; how he stood at the Leif
Ericson monument and became aware of the passage of time; —
Eheu fugaces, labuntur anni, he now would say, especially if he were
writing a notice of the Music Box Review; how he went to the
cemetery to contemplate the graves of William and Henry James,
and noted in himself the incipient thrill of Harvard pride and acquired New Englandism. But these gentle pursuits did not mean so
much to him at first as the more red-blooded diversions of week-ends
in Boston, and such other fleshy sins as that decayed city might with
impunity offer. More refined were the evening parties on the northern
side of town where, in a background of red plush curtains and chairs
but recently robbed of their prudish antimacassars, whispers of romantic love might be heard from well-behaved young women, whose
highest destiny, before lapsing legally into the arms of a professor,
was to be remembered when, at a later stage, a sonnet evolved from
a brain beginning to teem creatively. For the rest, football games
and lectures, the former seriously, the latter intermittently, main-

tained in him the consciousness of the true purpose of a university education.

From the excellent Professors Copeland and Kittredge he distractedly and reluctantly acquired a knowledge of the elements of English composition and of the more virtuous facts of English literature. He read, that is to say, fragments of the classical authors and dutifully absorbed the opinions of academic commentators upon them. American literature was revealed to him as a pale and obedient provincial cousin, whose past contained occasional indiscretions, such as Poe and Whitman, about whom the less said the better. Latin and French were filtered through the same kind of sieve, but without so many precautions, for in neither case was it possible for the aspirant after knowledge to decipher easily the kind of author to whom the urge of adolescence would naturally drive him. The Loeb classics left the un-Christian passages in the original, while the estimable Bohn unkindly took refuge in Italian, the language of a "lust-ridden country," as Anthony Comstock points out in that charming book of his, *Traps for the Young*. However, he still possesses enough Latin to be able to introduce into his written discourse appropriate tags from the Dictionary of Classical Quotations, though his quantities, I regret to say, are very weak. I have heard him stress the wrong syllable when speaking of Ouspensky's *Tertium Organum*, although he will emend a corrupt passage in Petronius, and professes to have read all the obscurer authors in Gourmont's *Latin Mystique*.

There came finally a subtle change in his outlook, from which one must date the actual birth of the Aesthete as such—*der Aesthetiker an sich,* so to speak. I suspect it was after one of those parties in the red plush drawing-rooms, when he returned to his rooms with what seemed like the authentic beginnings of a sonnet in his ears. From that moment he had a decided list in the direction of what he called "creative work." While the stadium shook with the hoarse shouts of the rabble at football games he might be observed going off with a companion to indulge in the subtle delights of intellectual conversation. His new friends were those whom he had at first dismissed as negligible owing to their avowed intention of not being he-men. The pulsation of new life within him prompted him to turn a more sympathetic eye upon this hitherto despised set, and they, in their turn, welcomed a new recruit, for the herd instinct is powerful even amongst the intellectual. Under this new guidance he came into contact with ideas undreamt of in the simple philosophy of the classroom.

Strange names were bandied about, curious magazines, unwelcomed by the college library, were read, and he was only too glad to discover that all the literary past of which he was ignorant or strangely misinformed counted as nothing in the eyes of his newly emancipated friends. From the pages of the *Masses* he gathered that the Social Revolution was imminent, that Brieux was a dramatist of ideas; in the *Little Review* he was first to learn the enchantment of distance as he sat bemused by its specimens of French and pseudo-French literature. Thus the ballast of which he had to get rid in order to float in the rarefied atmosphere of Advanced Thought was quite negligible. He had merely to exchange one set of inaccurate ideas for another.

II

It was at this precise moment in his career that the Wilsonian storming of Valhalla began. With the call to arms tingling in his blood, the Aesthete laid aside the adornments of life for the stern realities of a military training camp. Ancestral voices murmured in his ears, transmitted by instruments of dubious dolichocephalism, it is true, but perhaps all the more effective on that account, for Deep calls unto Deep. I will not dwell upon the raptures of that martial period, for he himself has left us his retrospective and disillusioned record of it, which makes it impossible to recapture the original emotion. * * * By luck or cunning, however, he succeeded in getting out of the actual trenches, and there, in the hectic backwash of war, he cultivated the tender seeds just beginning to germinate. He edited his first paper, the *Doughboy's Dreadnought,* or under the auspices of the propaganda and vaudeville department made his first contribution to literature, "Young America and Yugo-Slavia." Simultaneously with this plunge into arms and letters, he made his first venture into the refinements of sex, thereby extending his French vocabulary and gaining that deep insight into the intimate life of France which is still his proudest possession.

When militarism was finally overthrown, democracy made safe, and a permanent peace established by the victorious and united Allies, he was ready to stay on a little longer in Paris, and to participate in the joys of La Rotonde and Les Deux Magots. There for a brief spell he breathed the same air as the Dadaists, met Picasso and Philippe Soupault, and allowed Ezra Pound to convince him that the French nation was aware of the existence of Jean Cocteau, Paul Morand, Jean Giraudoux and Louis Aragon. From those who had nothing to say on the subject when Marcel Proust published *Du Côté de Chez Swann* in 1914 he now learned what a great author the man was, and formed those friendships which caused him eventually to join in a tribute to Proust by a group of English admirers who would have stoned Oscar Wilde had they been old enough to do so when it was the right thing to do.

The time was now ripe for his repatriation, and so, with the same critical equipment in French as in English, but with a still imperfect control of the language as a complication, the now complete Aesthete returned to New York, and descended upon Greenwich Village. His poems of disenchantment were in the press, his war novel was nearly finished, and it was not long before he appeared as Editor-in-Chief, Editor, Managing Editor, Associate Editor, Contributing Editor, Assistant Editor, Bibliographical Editor or Source Material Editor of one of the little reviews making no compromise with the public (or any other) taste. Both his prose and verse were remarkable chiefly for typographical and syntactical eccentricities, and a high pressure of unidiomatic, misprinted French to the square inch. His further contributions (if any) to the art of prose narrative have consisted of a breathless phallic symbolism—a sex obsession which sees the curves of a woman's body in every object not actually flat, including, I need hardly say, the Earth, our great Mother.

But it is essentially as an appraiser of the arts, as editor and critic, that the young Aesthete demands attention. He writes a competent book review and awakes to find himself famous. The next number of the magazine contains a study of his aesthetic, preferably by the author whose work he has favorably reviewed. By the end of the year a publisher announces a biographical and critical study of our young friend and his fame is secured. He can now discourse with impunity about anything, and he avails himself of the opportunity. He has evolved an ingenious style, florid, pedantic, technical, full of phrases so incomprehensible or so rhetorical that they almost persuade the reader that they must have a meaning. But the skeptical soon discover that this is an adjustable and protean vocabulary, that by a process of reshuffling the same phrases will serve for an artistic appreciation of Charlie Chaplin, an essay on Marcel Proust, or an article on Erik Satie. His other expedient is an arid and inconceivable learning, picked up at second hand. Let him discuss *The Waste Land* and his erudition will rival the ponderous fatuity of T. S. Eliot himself. * * *

Nevertheless, information is the one thing the Aesthete dreads. To be in the possession of solid knowledge and well-digested facts, to have definite standards, background and experience, is to place oneself outside the pale of true aestheticism. While foreign literature is his constant preoccupation, the Aesthete has no desire to make it known. What he wants to do is to lead a cult, to communicate a mystic faith in his idols, rather than to make them available for general appreciation. Articles on the subject are an important feature of his magazines, but they consist, as a rule, of esoteric witticisms and allusive gossip about fourth-rate people whom the writer happens to have met in a café. He will sweep aside the finest writers in French as lumber, launch into ecstasies over some Dadaist, and head the article with a French phrase which is grammatically incorrect, and entirely superfluous, since it expresses no idea that could not be correctly rendered in English. If one protest that the very title of a book which is a masterpiece of style has been mistranslated, that the first page has several gross errors, the Aesthete will blandly point out that in paragraph two there are four abstract nouns each with a different termination. It is useless to show him that there are no equivalent nouns in the text. Finally, one gives up arguing, for one remembers that Rimbaud once wrote a poem about the color of the vowels. Literary history must repeat itself. * * *

"Two souls," in the words of the German bard, "dwell in the breast" of the Aesthete, and his allegiance is torn between the sales-manager's desk, where, it appears, the Renaissance artist of to-day is to be found, and the esoteric editorial chair where experiments are made with stories which "discard the old binding of plot and narra-tive," the substitute being "the structural framework which appeals to us over and above the message of the line."

Thus it becomes possible simultaneously to compare Gertrude Stein with Milton and to chant the glories of the machine age in America. This dualism, obviously, foreshadows the ultimate disintegration of the type, although for the moment the process is ingeniously dis-guised by such devices as the printing of prose bearing all the out-ward marks of super-modern eccentricity but made up cunningly of a pattern woven from phrases culled from billboards and the advertis-ing pages of the magazines; by reproducing the weirdest pictures together with business-like photographs of cash-registers and tele-phones.

Here the Aesthete departs from the traditions of the species at his peril. Hitherto his technique has been perfect, for it has been his practice to confine his enthusiasm to works of art that are either as obscure or as inessential, or both, as his own critical comment. Now his incantations lose their potency when applied to matters within the experience and comprehension of the plain people, and not one cubit is added to the stature of William S. Hart, so far as his de-votees are concerned, by the knowledge that his name is pronounced with aesthetic reverence on the Left Bank of the Seine.

The process of change is at work, for the transitional youth is al-ready in at least one editorial chair, frowning upon the frivolities of the Jazz Age, calling for brighter and better books, his dreams haunted by fears of Sodom and Gomorrah. The Aesthete, meanwhile, is retiring with an intellectual *Katzenjammer*, which produces in some cases a violent and unnatural nausea, a revulsion against the wild delights of his former debauches. In others the result is a return to the cosy hearth of the American family; his head aches a little but his hand is steady. He is refreshed by a journalistic Bromo-Seltzer. There is pep in the swing of his fist upon the typewriter as he sits down to a regular and well-paid job, convincing others, as his employer has convinced him, that he really knows what the public wants.

BURTON RASCOE

"Aesthete: Model 1924"— Timeless and Universal

H E [Edmund Wilson] told me that Malcolm Cowley and Matthew Josephson were much cut up about Boyd's skit in the
American Mercury called "Aesthete: Model 1924." Especially was
Cowley vexed, it seems, and believes that the literary cause (whatever it is) that he is interested in has been very seriously damaged
by what he considers an ill-natured attack.

This is very curious, for, although I recognized the features of any
number of other people in Boyd's composite picture, I didn't recognize Cowley, and I asked Wilson what Cowley had written besides
some book reviews in *Broom*.

Wilson said he had written some poetry, some of it very good; but
that Boyd had not given any indication of including Cowley in his
portrait.

This piece of Boyd's seems to have caused a great stir, out of all
proportion to its manifest intention, which is merely a deft bit of
kidding. That it is ill-natured or even damning to the young men I
cannot see; by a change of years and a few appurtenances it might
have been a composite picture of Mencken, Nathan, Boyd and Stuart
P. Sherman in their youth; for it will be remembered that as a young
man in college Professor Sherman was an aesthete of the model of

From *A Bookman's Daybook*. By permission of Liveright Publishing Corp.
Copyright 1929 by Horace Liveright, Inc.

the Yellow Nineties, and that he wore a yellow cornflower in his buttonhole, recited "Cynara" soulfully, and spouted Baudelaire; and that Mencken wrote an introduction to a volume of plays translated from the French of Eugène Brieux and saluted them as nothing less than epoch-making in ideas and dramaturgy; and that Boyd hasn't yet shaved the beard he grew as a young man in Paris when all the geniuses of the Left Bank wore beards.

There is nothing disgraceful that I can see about the fact that a number of young men have the courage to interest themselves in cultural matters rather than grow into Babbitts, and if some aspects of their cultural enthusiasms are ludicrous they are no less admirable on that account. If Cowley or any one else who fancies himself ridiculed in Boyd's skit can't take a kidding, he is hopeless. A similar piece might have been written about the Irish Renaissance, during which Yeats, Synge, Stephens and Joyce emerged; in fact, George Moore rather did it; and one might be written about every cultural center in Europe. *(From "A Bookman's Daybook," New York Tribune, December 24, 1923.)*

GEORGE JEAN NATHAN

The Code of a Critic

NO less than once a week I am asked by some otherwise amiable person why I, after all these years, persist still in consecrating my time and what measure of talent I may possess to a critical consideration of the theater. "You have said your say," they tell me. "The Theater is too trivial for your later years. Why continue? Why not devote your effort to books on other and more important subjects?" I have been told this so often of late that it has begun to disturb me a bit. It is time, I conclude, to seek counsel with myself. Why, then, let me ask of myself, *do* I persist?

Performing, in the first volume of his *Prejudices*, a critical phlebotomy upon me, H. L. Mencken made the following observation: "At the brink of forty years, he remains faithful to the theater; of his books, only one does not deal with it, and that one is a very small one. In four or five years he has scarcely written of aught else. I doubt that anything properly describable as enthusiasm is at the bottom of this assiduity; perhaps the right word is curiosity . . . I sometimes wonder what keeps such a man in the theater, breathing bad air nightly, gaping at prancing imbeciles, sitting cheek by jowl with cads. Perhaps there is, at bottom, a secret romanticism—a lingering residuum of a boyish delight in pasteboard and spangles, gaudy colors and soothing sounds, preposterous heroes and appetizing wenches. . . ."

It is true that enthusiasm does not figure in my effort. I am, constitutionally, given to enthusiasm about nothing. But it is not true that curiosity is at the bottom of my effort. While curiosity is an habitual impulse with me, it has no part—or at best a very small part—in my devotion to the theater. To the final indictment, however, I offer a plea of guilty, though with reservations. The theater is, to me, a great toy; and upon the toys of the world what Mr. Mencken alludes to as my lingering residuum of boyish delight concentrates itself. What interests me in life—and my years have since he wrote marched across the frontier of forty—is the surface of life: life's music and color, its charm and ease, its humor and loveliness. The great problems of the world—social, political, economic and theological—do not concern me in the slightest. I care not who writes the laws of a country so long as I may listen to its songs. I can live every bit as happily under a King, or even a Kaiser, as under a President. One church is as good as another to me; I never enter one anyway, save only to delight in some particularly beautiful stained-glass window, or in some fine specimen of architecture, or in the whiskers of the Twelve Apostles. If all the Armenians were to to be killed tomorrow and if half of Russia were to starve to death the day after, it would not matter to me in the least. What concerns me alone is myself, and the interests of a few close friends. For all I care the rest of the world may go to hell at today's sunset. I was born in America, and America is to me, at the time of writing, the most comfortable country to live in—and also, at the time of writing, the very pleasantest—in the world. This is why, at the time of writing, I am here, and not in France, or in England, or elsewhere. But if England became more comfortable and more pleasant than America tomorrow, I'd live in England. And if I lived in England I should be no more interested in the important problems of England than I am now interested in the important problems of America. My sole interest lies in writing, and I can write as well in one place as in another, whether it be Barcelona, Spain or Coon Rapids, Iowa. Give me a quiet room, a pad of paper, eight or nine sharp lead

pencils, a handful of thin, mild cigars, and enough to eat and drink
—all of which, by the grace of God, are happily within my means—
and I do not care a tinker's dam whether Germany invades Belgium
or Belgium Germany, whether Ireland is free or not free, whether
the Stock Exchange is bombed or not bombed, or whether the nations of the earth arm, disarm, or conclude to fight their wars by
limiting their armies to biting each other . . . On that day during
the world war when the most critical battle was being fought, I sat
in my still, sunlit, cozy library composing a chapter on esthetics
for a new book on the drama. And at five o'clock, my day's work
done, I shook and drank a half dozen excellent apéritifs.

Such, I appreciate, are not the confessions that men usually make,
for they are evil and unpopular confessions. My only apology for
them is that they are true. That is the kind of dog I happen to be,
and, I take it, a curse upon me for it! But if some tremendous event
were breaking upon the world and men and women were shaking
their heads in terrified foreboding, I know myself well enough to
know that if I had an agreeable engagement for the same evening
I should keep it, were the streets flowing with lava and the heavens
thundering forth their "Feuersnot." I speak, of course, figuratively,
for if it so much as rains I do not challenge my comfort to the point
of going out and getting my hat wet. What I mean to say, in plain
English, is that if it rested with me to decide upon the fate of
the West Virginia coal miners or to hear Fritz Kreisler play the
fiddle, the West Virginia coal miners would have to wait until the
next day. The Soviet theory of government doesn't interest me one-
tenth so much as Gordon Craig's theory of the theater. Whether the
Methodists will go to heaven or to hell when they die doesn't interest me one-twentieth so much as Adele Astaire's dancing. And
whether the Japs will conquer Los Angeles or Los Angeles the Japs
doesn't interest me one-hundredth as much as whether Anatole
France's next novel will be as fine as his memorable *Revolt of the
Angels*. I am not glibly posing myself here as an "artist," an aloof,
exotic and elegant fellow with a maroon bud in his lapel and his
nose in the air. I am merely a man gifted, as I see it, with an admirable practicability: one who believes that the highest happiness

in life comes from doing one's job in the world as thoroughly well as one knows how, from viewing the world as a charming, serio-comic, childish circus, from having a few good, moderately witty friends, from avoiding indignation, irritation and homely women, and from letting the rest—the uplift, the downlift, the whole kit and caboodle—go hang. Selfish? To be sure. What of it?

PERCY HAMMOND

Those Very First Nighters

NOTHING, it has been said, is so characteristic of New York as its friendliness to visitors from out of town. Let a guest approach and we open the gates, roll out the red carpet, spread the canopies, and send a band to the depot to meet him. Flags fly; the air is filled with confetti and the loud "halloos" of welcome.

"Place," we say to him, "your little hand in ours, and we shall take you to see the sights. You are not interested in fish? Then we shall omit the Aquarium. But in our zoölogical gardens pleasing elephants swing their lithe proboscides, and the wary wart-hog is at hand, eager to divert you. In case you are a bookworm, repair with us to the libraries; or if you are fond of art and archaeology, many museums are available for your edification."

You may, in the event that you are both literary and athletic, take a brisk walk around the Reservoir in Central Park to watch the heroes and heroines of New York fiction pursuing their romantic exercises. If patriotic, Grant's mausoleum is available and the effigies of General Sherman, and Franz Sigel.

If you like, you may look at the Hudson River, that mighty, mystic stream—as ancient as the Nile and much more sophisticated. Fifth Avenue is hard by, and sinister Broadway, of which it has been sung that there is a broken heart for every light upon it. If fond of fisticuffs, the pugilists at Madison Square Garden will engage in gentle gladiations. Commodious omnibuses wait on many street corners to transport you to Chinatown and Coney Island, to the residence of Charles M. Schwab and the birthplace of Theodore Roosevelt.

If you need the relaxing influence of dancing and other insobrieties, we have provided supper clubs wherein, despite the vigilance of a Puritan constabulary, vinous eye may look into vinous eye across the hootch and chicken sandwiches. It may interest you to scrutinize the Pittsburgh banker's son in one of these ruddy rendezvous as he tells the shrewd milliner from Altoona that she is the only woman he ever loved. And to watch her as she yearns for her room at the Ritz, replying, "Be yourself, Big Boy, be yourself."

These are the commonplaces of our hospitality, the habitual deeds of good-fellowship, the fresh log in the fireplace. It is our desire, if not our passion, to be open-armed. If, as our guest, you are robbed, bilked, or assassinated, as you may be in your home town, we provide you with policemen and competent district attorneys to avenge you. Our bootleggers are alert and well-bestowed; our magistrates humane and sagacious; our morgues and penitentiaries adequate. As Ed Howe of the Atchison *Globe* said to a traffic policeman who permitted his daughter, Miss Effie, to motor illegally through a one-way street:

> Oh! call it by some other name,
> For friendship sounds too cold.

It is no more than right, then, that so wide-armed an institution should reserve one little pleasure to itself—one chamber in its vast open house whence it may retire occasionally and be alone. This New York retreat to which guests are not bidden and which the keys of the city will not unlock is the First Night at the theatres. There, and there only, are the real New Yorkers unsociable, asking for privacy. Sequestered among themselves in restful seclusion, they find comfort. Now and then, of course a pushing outsider intrudes in the sanctum, but he meets with small cordiality. The First Night is New York's and New York's alone. As the signboards say in the rural districts, "No Trespassing Allowed on These Premises." The charters and franchises that admit you to the Stock Exchange or Van Cortlandt Park are useless as credentials to one of Mr. Belasco's or Miss Jane Cowl's "openings." To pass these sacred frontiers one must be native or at least naturalized.

It is the belief of New York dramatists, producers, and actors that nobody knows much about a play unless he is a New York first nighter. The "New York verdict" is to them the ultimate decree in dramatic judgments. They may be aware that human beings exist in Harrisburg and Stamford, and that the inhabitants of Chicago, Philadelphia, and Brooklyn are no more ignorant of life and the theatre than are the residents of Manhattan. The people of Denver, and other points West, read H. G. Wells and Miss Edna Ferber; they go to Yale and other universities, and they are as well versed in the sins and the atonements as the New York first night crowd. But to the New York man of the theatre their disapproval of an entertainment is as insignificant as their applause.

I asked an American manager why he was so contemptuous of an opening performance in Brooklyn or Newark and so obsequious about one across the river in New York. "Have not," I inquired, "the Brooklyn first nighters got organs, dimensions, senses, affections, passions? Are they not fed with the same food, interested in the same plots, and cheered by the same songs and dances? A soap-maker regards a soap-user in Fort Wayne with as much respect as he does one in New York. The breakfast foods are contrived to nourish the suburbanite as well as the metropolitan. Velasquez was overjoyed when peasants liked his pictures, and Molière read all his plays to his cook. Successful magazines and periodicals are edited and written as carefully for the Lincoln Avenues as they are for Forty-second Street. The manufacturers of chewing gums will tell you that if the flavour does not last in Zanesville, it will be impermanent also in Times Square. Why, then, should the Drama be so exclusively of New York?"

"Well," this impresario answered, "everybody connected with the theatre lives in New York, from stars to scene painters. If they think of anything else than New York it is in terms of New York.

And they think of it in the way they believe the New York first nighters will think of it. They write, produce, and act to please that first night audience, and they are blind to all others. If an author composes a rural play, it is certain that he will want to have a traffic cop standing beside the town pump. By the way," this manager added, "perhaps you can tell me why the New York dramatic critics ignore a play when it is produced in Brooklyn, Atlantic City, or New Rochelle, and get all excited about it when it comes a week later to Broadway?"

Since these New York premieres are so important, let us try to attend one, carefully passported and viséd by a regular New Yorker. The entertainment may be one of the several *Follies* or a more serious effort supervised by Winthrop Ames, Arthur Hopkins, or George Tyler. We shall arrive punctually so that we may stand upon the curbstone and observe the celebrities as they approach. What a spectacle it is! The Mardi Gras, the Field of the Cloth of Gold, Carnival Time in Venice, Old Home Week in Hollywood, all in a night!

Bud Fisher draws up in a limousine, followed a moment later by Bugs Baer and James Montgomery Flagg. Then a Vanderbilt, a couple of Astors, and a Gould or two arrive in taxicabs. Avery Hopwood and William Anthony McGuire saunter along and engage in deep conversation with Dr. Frank Crane and Rube Goldberg. Bernard M. Baruch, Theodore Dreiser, Claire Briggs, Odd McIntyre, Ring Lardner, Harold Ross of *The New Yorker*, Harry Sinclair, Babe Ruth, and Frank Crowninshield. Who, you will ask, is that dejected boy on whose musical visage pale melancholy sits enthroned in gloom? Is he the composer of "Abide With Me"? Whereupon you will be informed that he is Irving Berlin, author of "Alexander's Ragtime Band." With him are the Selwyns, Edgar and Archibald, Martin Hermann, who directs the destinies of the A. H. Wood enterprises, and Gene Buck, the musical revue librettist. The ticket brokers come in swarms to estimate the values of the play.

Ssh! The critics are approaching. Upon their fronts deliberation sits and princely counsel. The carriage man takes Alan Dale's hat and stick amid a reverential silence. A cry "Make way!" is heard, and Alexander Woollcott appears, immersed in meditation. Burns Mantle and Walter Winchell are now seen, arm in arm, discussing, as they walk along, the *Oedipus* and *Abie's Irish Rose*. They frown a little at such cheers as may be raised, and the demonstration is quickly suppressed. The sidewalk teems with distinguished characters— dramatists, *entrepreneurs*, reviewers, executive editors, column con- ductors, film stars, actors, actresses, some minor poets, and, no doubt, an adventuress or two. There they are—a brilliant entourage for the impending accouchement—bright and voluble courtiers in an ante- room awaiting the birth of another Broadway drama.

The curtain goes up, and there is loud applause for the scenery. An obscure debutante comes in, representing a maidservant, and there is another demonstration. Ovations follow for all the players as they enter, and also as they exeunt. Between the acts there are visiting and exchange of opinion concerning the play. Like professional critics, these laymen have their pet phrases. The auditorium fairly sings with a chorus of "Awfully worth while," and "Isn't it adorable?" In other, less cultured communities, the audience usually describes the acting and the drama as "cute" or "cunning."

At the intermissions we are confronted with an embarrassment of pleasures. Shall we remain inside and watch the "aisle actors" as they perform their modest histrionics; or shall we venture to the sidewalk and listen to the line-pullers as they pull their witty lines? Well, after observing for a moment a distinguished reviewer as he illustrates with gestures how Mansfield would have played the lead- ing rôle in Broadway, let us hasten to the foyers and be regaled by the merry entr'acte banter and repartee of the first night humorists. You may see Professor Brander Matthews whispering to Clayton Ham- ilton, and you can imagine that he is saying, "I'm afraid it's a suc- cess." Or Robert Benchley remarking to Professor Wm. Lyon Phelps that he likes Peggy Hopkins Joyce because she has never got a nickel out of him. "Are you with this show?" you may hear Miss Edna Ferber inquire of Franklin P. Adams, as Mr. Adams emerges from the stage alley between the acts. "No," Mr. Adams will respond, "I'm against it."

But we must seek out Mr. Kelcey Allen, the critic of *Women's Wear*, for the jauntiest expressions of opinion. It was Mr. Allen who, on the opening night of Lionel Barrymore's débâcle in *Macbeth,* gave sententious advice to Mr. McBride, the ticket broker. Mr. McBride, sitting next to Mr. Allen, was wondering whether or not he should buy a lot of seats for *Macbeth,* when the line was spoken, "Lay on, MacDuff!"

"Lay off, McBride," whispered Mr. Allen, and Mr. McBride did so, greatly to his profit.

"This is Mr. Allen," I say, introducing you and hoping for the best. Whereupon Mr. Allen will remark: "If the guy who wrote this show has a lot of enemies, he's even with them all."

The New York first night audience is the Ku Klux of the drama. Its judgments are not final; but its shallow precepts are the frightened creed of all the playwrights from Sidney Howard to Samuel Shipman. When, if ever, an American dramatist endeavours a serious play, he finds this siren congregation looking over his shoulder and telling him what and what not to write. The Drama Leagues and the Culture Clubs should strive to abolish this nefarious institution, and succour the stage from the influences of a selfish insularity.

ALEXANDER WOOLLCOTT

"East Lynne"

AT the Greenwich Village Theatre last evening, the actors and some of the audience had lots and lots of fun making sport of poor, old "East Lynne." It was a revival made in the same mood and for the same purpose that animated the facetious resuscitation of "Fashion" by this very crowd a couple of years or so back.

But this time, for some obscure reason, I felt a curious impulse to fly to the defense. When the players were flinging themselves around the stage in the monstrous poses of a bygone day and when, at each soliloquy and each aside, the audience tittered scrupulously, I had to suppress an unworthy yearning to rise, lift one superb hand to still the tumult and cry out: "Stop, she's somebody's mother."

The point of such a production—roughly akin as it is to one of Master Held's bogus woodcuts—is, I suppose, that grandpa and grandma were not quite bright. In the '70's, the '80's and even the '90's veritable freshets of tears attended each performance of this silly, old play made out of Mrs. Henry Wood's lugubrious novel. For the piece was a favorite with the stock company audiences and was nightly clasped to the same bosoms which, back home under the evening lamps, also heaved convulsively in response to "St. Elmo."

And I suppose, too, that in 1960, the little experimental group down at that funny old theatre on Morningside Heights will revive "Abie's Irish Rose" and the archaeologists in the audience will fairly shake with condescending amusement at the kind of theatrical fare which used to so entrance poor old Mr. Woollcott and poor old Mr. Benchley when they were lads. If any such revival does take place in 1960, I intend to come back from Avignon to guard our memories. And if the insufferable upstarts of the press of that day venture to say that "Abie" was much overrated in my day, I shall beg leave to inquire: "By whom?"

Also, I kept wondering last evening whether, if "East Lynne" were played honestly with some such actress as Margaret Anglin as *Lady Isabel,* we would find that there was a tear left in it after all.

At the Greenwich Village, of course, it was played with the tongue in the cheek—the caricaturing capitally managed by Mary Blair, Charles Fleming and as that "bold, bad man," *Sir Francis Levison* (whom the audience hissed with gusto), Stanley Howlett. It was played with a rheumatic curtain, fearful op'ry house scenery and a great, antiquarian relish—plus entr'acte ballads, such as "Take Back Your Gold," and, of course, the famous incidental strains of "Then You'll Remember Me."

It should be added that, instead of costuming it in the styles affected when the play was new, the management elected to use the mode of the early '90's when, to be sure, "East Lynne" was still going strong in more rural areas.

It was all idly and pleasantly amusing enough as a stunt, but I must confess to a certain embarrassment when the era of Marion Talley, Lady Cathcart and "Abie's Irish Rose" has the effrontery to titter at the naiveté of any bygone day. *(New York World, March 11, 1926.)*

"An American Tragedy"

THEY tell me that Horace Liveright, our doughty fellow towns-man who not only published "An American Tragedy" as a novel but also engineered its present success upon the stage, has decided to attend no more performances of the play. His reason for this stupefying renunciation, it seems, is that the play as performed nightly at the Longacre (matinees Wednesday and Saturday) moves him too profoundly. Each time he has attended a performance the Liveright depths have been so shaken that next day he was just a wreck.

Now, if all has gone as planned, the mighty Dreiser himself, but recently returned from foreign parts, has at last seen this puppet show contrived from his overwhelming novel. And it would not surprise me a bit to hear that he too would refrain from a return visit to the Longacre. Indeed, I would even learn without amazement that he had sworn off after the second act. I do not know how perceptive a playgoer Theodore Dreiser is, but I should think the mess the theatre has made of "An American Tragedy" would permanently impair his health.

It seems to me a gauche, spasmodic, almost childishly concocted melodrama, preposterously miscast. It is, I might add, a great success. Nor can its conspicuous rush of trade be dismissed as the mere temporary stampede of the ardent Dreiserites to see their cherished book done into a play. After all, the sales of "An American Tragedy" to date come to something less than 52,000 copies, and besides in the audience in which I was embedded on Thursday night I doubt if one in fifty had ever heard of Theodore Dreiser. Indeed, after listening to the entr'acte chatter and looking at the faces agape and breathing hard in my vicinity, I was moved to wonder whether my neighbors had recently read anything more taxing than the memoirs of the reticent Mrs. Browning.* From this audience the capitally written and well acted seduction scene in *Roberta Alden's* mean little bedroom elicited a hubbub that was neither laughter nor tears nor protest. It was just a chorus of squeals and in a dim light the Longacre rather suggested a large, emotion-swept sty.

To get as many of the bare facts of the book into a play as possible Patrick Kearney had to pack tight, and then sit on the lid. The resultant telescoping of the story has the odd effect of transforming Dreiser's puzzled, storm-tossed, inert bit of American driftwood into an intensive Lothario. Indeed, as the play, with the nimbleness of a mountain goat, leaped from *Roberta's* dingy bed to *Sondra's* pillowy sofa on Thursday night, I could hear the dilettante bookworms around me murmuring: "Gee, that kid is cert'n'y a fast worker. That's what he is, a fast worker. Yes, sir, a fast worker."

It seems to me too that Morgan Farley was the worst imaginable choice for the central rôle. That, of course, is a faint exaggeration. One would prefer him, let us say, to Louis Mann in the rôle. Or Gail Kane. But he does come near to being the exact opposite of the quality which Dreiser's work called for. It is a trifle too much like casting Clifton Webb as *Huckleberry Finn*.

As everyone knows, "An American Tragedy" had its origins in the arrest, trial and execution of an ornery young nobody named Chester Gillette. What led Dreiser into the field of that murder and bade him fence it in as his own was its great normality, its suggestion of disaster happening to the folks across the street. This was no Thaw case, lunatic spawn of the white lights, no Leopold and Loeb case, monstrously peopled as with creatures from some nether world. When, twenty years ago, the hapless Chester Gillette pushed poor

Grace Brown beneath those whispering Adirondack waters, we were all sick with the sense that it was one of us who had done this thing. And Dreiser, brooding on what unperceived, casual wrong turning must have sent this drifting youth to the death house instead of to the brotherhood of Rotary, wrought at last the plotting epic called "An American Tragedy." It is a great book, great in proportion as it earns the tacit subtitle "Even as You and I." The play called for an actor who would suggest implicitly the average humdrum American youngster. Mr. Farley is a museum piece.

In addition to this natural handicap, his performance seemed to me quite distressing. He is a great one to dart about, being wistful with his elbows. And dramatic schools should be led in droves to watch one scene of his as an admonishing example. That is the scene in which the play tries to reproduce from the book the slow, sick, floundering indecision by which the plan to do away with *Roberta* rises like a shape of mist in *Clyde's* miasmic torment.

First *Clyde* is discovered alone in his lodgings. Enter landlady, equipped with newspaper to read aloud to him an account of a drowning in Big Bittern Lake, a canoe upsetting, a girl's death. As soon as he is left alone, *Clyde* must seize the paper and read it to himself and, since Mr. Farley is the kind of actor who expresses even mild surprise by wrenching his face out of drawing, you can imagine the playground for the emotions which that mobile face becomes during this reading. A playground? Nay, a Coney Island for the emotions, with merry-go-rounds, loop-the-loops and everything. Then, in case the audience should not be any too bright, *Clyde* next hurls the paper to the floor, trembles violently, then picks the paper up again with the agility of a slow motion picture, points to the article in the manner of a show window demonstrator and even says out loud: "Roberta cannot swim." He then shudders six times. If an intelligence test of subsequent audiences should indicate that even this is insufficient, I would suggest that Mr. Farley then lie face down on the floor and do an Australian crawl stroke as just another helpful hint. (*New York World, October 25, 1926.*)

GILBERT SELDES

"I Am Here To-day": Charlie Chaplin

FOR most of us the grotesque effigy dangling from the electric sign or propped against the side of the ticket-booth must remain our first memory of Charlie Chaplin. The splay feet, the moustache, the derby hat, the rattan walking-stick, composed at once the image which was ten years later to become the universal symbol of laughter. *"I am here to-day"* was his legend, and like everything else associated with his name it is faintly ironic and exactly right. The man who, of all the men of our time, seems most assured of immortality, chose that particularly transient announcement of his presence, "I am here to-day," with its emotional overtone of "gone to-morrow," and there is always something in Charlie that slips away. "He does things," said John S. Sargent once, "and you're lucky if you see them." Incredibly lucky to live when we have the chance to see them.

It is a miracle that there should arise in our time a figure wholly in the tradition of the great clowns—a tradition requiring creative energy, freshness, inventiveness, change—for neither the time nor the country in which Charlie works is exceptionally favourable to such a phenomenon. Stranger still is the course he has run. It is simple to take *The Kid* as the dividing line, but it is more to the point to consider just the phases of Charlie's popularity, for each phase corresponds to one of the attacks now being made upon his integrity. He is on the top of the world, an exposed position, and we are all sniping at him; even his adherents are inclined to say that "after all" he is "still" this or the other thing. One goes to his pictures as one went to hear Caruso, with a ghoulish speculation as to the quantity of alloy in the "golden voice." It is because Charlie has had all there ever was of acclaim that he is now surrounded by deserters.

That he exists at all is due to the camera and to the selective genius of Mack Sennett. It is impossible to dissociate him entirely from the Keystone comedy where he began and worked wonders and learned much. The injustice of forgetting Sennett and the Keystone when thinking of Chaplin has undermined most of the intellectual appreciation of his work, for although he was the greatest of the Keystone comedians and passed far beyond them, the first *and decisive* phase of his popularity came while he was with them, and the Keystone touch remains in all his later work, often as its most precious element. It was the time of Charlie's actual contact with the American people, the movie-going populace before the days of the great moving pictures. He was the second man to be known widely by name—John Bunny was the first—and he achieved a fame which passed entirely by word of mouth into the category of the common myths and legends of America, as the name of Buffalo Bill had passed before. By the time the newspapers recognized the movie as a source of circulation, Charlie was already a known quantity in the composition of the American mind and, what is equally significant, he had created the first *Charlot*. The French name which is and is not Charlie will serve for that figure on the screen, the created image which is, and at the same time is more than, Charlie Chaplin, and is less. Like every great artist in whatever medium, Charlie has created the mask of himself—many masks, in fact—and the first of these, the wanderer, came in the Keystone comedies. It was there that he first detached himself from life and began to live in another world, with a specific rhythm of his own, as if the pulse-beat in him changed and was twice or half as fast as that of those who surrounded him. He created then that trajectory across the screen which is absolutely his own line of movement. No matter what the actual facts are, the curve he plots is always the same. It is of one who seems to enter from a corner of the screen, becomes entangled or involved in a force greater than himself as he advances upward and to the center; there he spins like a marionette in a whirlpool, is flung from side to side, always in a parabola which seems centripetal until the madness of the action hurls him to refuge or compels him to flight at the opposite end of the screen. He wanders in, a stranger, an impostor, an anarchist; and passes again, buffeted, but unchanged.

* * *

His successes in this period were confined to those films in which the world intruded with all its natural crassness upon his detached existence. There was a film in which Charlie dreamed himself back into the Stone Age and played the God of the Waters—wholly without success because he contrasted his fantasy with another fantasy in the same tempo, and could neither sink into nor stand apart from it. But in *His Night Out* the effect is perfect, and is intensified by the alternating coincidence and syncopation of rhythm in which Ben Turpin worked with him. Charlie's drunken line of march down a stairway was first followed in parallel and then in not-quite-parallel by Turpin; the degree of drunkenness was the same, then varied, then returned to identity; and the two, together, were always entirely apart from the actuality of bars and hotels and fountains and policemen which were properties in their existence. In this early day Charlie had already mastered his principles. He knew that the broad lines are funny and that the fragments—which are delicious—must "point" the main line of laughter. I recall, for example, an exquisite moment at the end of this film. Turpin is staggering down the street, dragging Charlie by the collar. Essentially the funny thing is that one drunkard should so gravely, so soberly, so obstinately take care of another and should convert himself into a policeman to do it; it is funny that they should be going nowhere, and go so doggedly. The lurching-forward body of Turpin, the singular angle formed with it by Charlie's body almost flat on the ground, added to the spectacle. And once as they went along Charlie's right hand fell to one side, and as idly as a girl plucks a water-lily from over the side of a canoe he plucked a daisy from the grass border of the path, and smelled it. The function of that gesture was to make everything that went before, and everything that came after, seem funnier; and it succeeded by creating another, incongruous image out of the picture before our eyes. The entire world, a moment earlier, had been aslant and distorted and wholly male; it righted itself suddenly and created a soft idyll of tenderness. Nearly everything of Charlie is in that moment, and I know no better way to express its elusive quality than to say that as I sat watching the film a second time, about two hours later, the repetition of the gesture came with all the effect of surprise, although I had been wondering whether he could do it so perfectly again.

*　*　*

It was foreordained that the improvised kind of comedy should give way to something more calculated, and in Charlie's case it is particularly futile to cry over spilled milk because for a long time he continued to give the *effect* of impromptu; his sudden movements and his finds in the way of unsuspected sources of fun are exceptional to this day. In *The Pawnshop* Charlie begins to sweep and catches in his broom the end of a long rope, which, instead of being swept away, keeps getting longer, actively fighting the broom. I have no way to prove it, but I am sure from the context that this is all he had originally had in mind to do with the scene. Suddenly the tape on the floor creates something in his mind, and Charlie transforms the backroom of the pawnshop into a circus, with himself walking the tightrope—a graceful, nimble balancing along the thin line of tape on the floor, the quick turn and coming forward, the conventional bow, arms flung out, smiling, to receive applause at the end. Again, as ever, he has created an imaginary scene out of the materials of the actual.

The plotting of these comedies did not destroy Charlie's inventiveness and made it possible for him to develop certain other of his characteristics. The moment the vagrant came to rest, the natural man appeared, the paradoxical creature who has the wisdom of simple souls and the incalculable strength of the weak. Charlie all through the middle period is at least half Tyl Eulenspiegel. It is another way for him to live apart from the world by assuming that the world actually means what it says, by taking every one of its conventional formulas, its polite phrases and idioms, with dreadful seriousness. He has created in Charlot a radical with an extraordinary logical mind. Witness Charlot arriving late at the theatre and stepping on the toes of a whole row of people to his seat at the far end; the gravity of his expressions of regret is only matched by his humiliation when he discovers that he is, after all, in the wrong row and makes his way back again and all through the next row to his proper place. It is a careful exaggeration of the social fiction that when you apologise you can do anything to anyone. The same feeling underlies the characteristic moment when Charlot is fighting and suddenly stops, takes off his hat and coat, gives them to his opponent to hold, and then promptly knocks his obliging adversary down. Revisiting once an old Charlie, I saw him do this, and a few minutes later saw the same thing in a new Harold Lloyd; all there is to know of the difference between the two men was to be learned there; for Lloyd, who is a clever fellow, made it seem a smart trick so to catch his enemy off guard, while Chaplin made the moment equal to the conventional crossing of swords or the handshake before a prize fight.

* * *

The Kid was undoubtedly a beginning in "literature" for Charlie. I realize that in admitting this I am giving the whole case away, for in the opinion of certain critics the beginning of literature is the end of creative art. This attitude is not so familiar in America, but in France you hear the Charlot of *The Kid* spoken of as "theatre," as one who has ceased to be of the film entirely. I doubt if this is just. Like the one other great artist in America (George Herriman,* with whom he is eminently in sympathy), Charlie has always had the Dickens touch, a thing which in its purity we do not otherwise discover in our art. Dickens himself is mixed; only a part of him is

---

* George Herriman, 1881-1944. American cartoonist, creator of "Krazy Kat" and "Ignatz Mouse."——Ed. note.

literature, and that not the best, nor is that part essentially the one which Charlie has imported to the screen. *The Kid* had some bad things in it: the story, the halo round the head of the unmarried mother, the quarrel with the authorities; it had an unnecessary amount of realism and its tempo was uncertain, for it was neither serious film nor Keystone. Yet it possessed moments of unbelievable intensity and touches of high imagination. The scenes in and out-side the doss-house were excellent and were old Charlie; the glazier's assistant was inventive and the training of Coogan to look like his foster-father was beautiful. Far above them stood the beginning of the film: Charlot, in his usual polite rags, strolling down to his club after his breakfast (it would have been a grilled bone) and, avoiding slops as Villon did, twirling his cane, taking off his finger-less gloves to reach for his cigarette case (a sardine box), and select-ing from the butts one of quality, *tamping* it to shake down the excess tobacco at the tip—all of this, as Mr. Herriman pointed out to me, was the creation of the society gentleman, the courageous refusal to be undermined by slums and poverty and rags. At the end of the film there was the vision of heaven: apotheosis of the long suffering of Charlot at the hands of the police, not only in *The Kid* —in a hundred films where he stood always against the authorities, always for his small independent freedom. The world in which even policemen have wings shatters, too; but something remains. The in-vincible Charlot, dazed by his dream, looking for wings on the actual policeman who is apparently taking him to jail, will not down. For as they start, a post comes between them, and Charlot, without the slightest effort to break away, too submissive to fight, still dodges back to walk round the post and so avoid bad luck. A moment later comes one of the highest points in Charlie's career. He is ushered into a limousine instead of a patrol wagon—it is the beginning of the happy ending. And as the motor starts he flashes at the spectators of his felicity a look of indescribable poignancy. It is frightened, it is hopeful, bewildered; it lasts a fraction of a second and is blurred by the plate glass of the car. I cannot hope to set down the quality of it, how it becomes a moment of unbearable intensity and how one is breathless with suspense—and with adoration.

For, make no mistake, it is adoration, not less, that he deserves and has from us. He corresponds to our secret desires because he alone has passed beyond our categories, at one bound placing himself outside space and time. His escape from the world is complete and extraordinarily rapid, and what makes him more than a figure of romance is his immediate creation of another world. He has the vital energy, the composing and the functioning brain. This is what makes him aesthetically interesting, what will make him for ever a school not only of acting, but of the whole creative process.

* * *

The slowing-up of Charlie's physical energies and the deepening of his understanding may well restore to him his appreciation of those early monuments to laughter which are his greatest achievement. He stood then shod in absurdity, but with his feet on the earth. And he danced on the earth, an eternal figure of lightness and of the wisdom which knows that the earth was made to dance on. It was a green earth, excited with its own abundance and fruitfulness, and he possessed it entirely. For me he remains established in possession. As it spins under his feet he dances silently and with infinite grace upon it. It is as if in his whole life he had spoken only one word: "I am here *to-day*"— the beginning before time and the end without end of his wisdom and of his loveliness.

LIGHT VERSE

DOROTHY PARKER

One Perfect Rose

A single flow'r he sent me, since we met.
   All tenderly his messenger he chose;
Deep-hearted, pure, with scented dew still wet—
   One perfect rose.

I knew the language of the floweret;
   "My fragile leaves," it said, "his heart enclose."
Love long has taken for his amulet
   One perfect rose.

Why is it no one ever sent me yet
   One perfect limousine, do you suppose?
Ah no, it's always just my luck to get
   One perfect rose.

From *The Portable Dorothy Parker.* Copyright 1926, 1944 by Dorothy Parker. Reprinted by permission of The Viking Press, Inc., New York.

Unfortunate Coincidence

By the time you swear you're his,
    Shivering and sighing,
And he vows his passion is
    Infinite, undying—
Lady, make a note of this:
    One of you is lying.

Fighting Words

Say my love is easy had,
    Say I'm bitten raw with pride,
Say I am too often sad,—
    Still behold me at your side.

Say I'm neither brave nor young,
    Say I woo and coddle care,
Say the devil touched my tongue,—
    Still you have my heart to wear.

But say my verses do not scan,
    And I get me another man!

CHRISTOPHER MORLEY

The Old Mandarin
on His Travels

When I visited America
I saw two things that struck me as extraordinary:
People packed in the subway
Rocking uneasily on their hams
Endlessly studying the newspapers;
And people packed in the movies
Endlessly staring at the films.
I said to myself
If the American people ever develop Minds
There are two great industries
That will crash.

An American Mystic

But you do not understand the subway,
Said an American mystic
Sitting next me at the Rotary Club.
It is a travelling hermitage,

From *Translations From the Chinese*, Copyright, 1922, 1949, by Christopher Morley. Published by J. B. Lippincott Company.

A flying monastery,
A nunnery that moves at fifty miles an hour.
Into its roaring wagons
Thoughtful men and women descend with joy:
They know that there,
The only place in the whole city,
They can meditate undisturbed.

He Likes to Give Both Sides
of the Matter

And as for the newspapers
(Said another)
You forget that they are the last friend
Many a poor devil has.
Go down to Battery Park
And see the chaps lying on the grass.
Newspapers are their blankets,
Their pillows, their sunshades;
Newspapers their Bibles.
After everything else has gone
A poor bum will cling to his newspaper
As his last link with life.

DON MARQUIS

The Song of Mehitabel

this is the song of mehitabel
of mehitabel the alley cat
as i wrote you before boss
mehitabel is a believer
in the pythagorean
theory of the transmigration
of the soul and she claims
that formerly her spirit
was incarnated in the body
of cleopatra
that was a long time ago
and one must not be
surprised if mehitabel
has forgotten some of her
more regal manners

i have had my ups and downs
but wotthehell wotthehell
yesterday sceptres and crowns
fried oysters and velvet gowns
but today i herd with bums

but wotthehell wotthehell
i wake the world from sleep
as i caper and sing and leap
when i sing my wild free tune
wotthehell wotthell
under the blear eyed moon
i am pelted with cast off shoon
but whotthehell wotthehell

do you think that i would change
my present freedom to range
for a castle or moated grange
wotthehell wotthehell
cage me and i d go frantic
my life is so romantic
capricious and corybantic
and i m toujours gai toujours gai

i know that i am bound
for a journey down the sound
in the midst of a refuse mound
but wotthehell wotthehell
oh i should worry and fret
death and i will coquette
there s a dance in the old dame yet
toujours gai toujours gai

i once was an innocent kit
wotthehell wotthehell
with a ribbon my neck to fit
and bells tied onto it
o wotthehell wotthehell
but a maltese cat came by
with a come hither look in his eye
and a song that soared to the sky
and wotthehell wotthehell
and i followed down the street

the pad of his rhythmical feet
o permit me again to repeat
wotthehell wotthehell
my youth i shall never forget
but there s nothing i really regret
wotthehell wotthehell
there s a dance in the old dame yet
toujours gai toujours gai

the things that i had not ought to
i do because i ve gotto
wotthehell wotthehell
and i end with my favorite motto
toujours gai toujours gai

boss sometimes i think
that our friend mehitabel
is a trifle too gay

FRANKLIN P. ADAMS

A Wish

I do not yearn for prairies wide;
   I crave to tramp no tangled wood;
I hunger for no hills. I tried. . . .
   It did no good.

And yet I wish I wished to roam;
   I wish I craved the open sea
Or loved the meadow for my home,
   The life that's free.

I wish I craved to see the corn,
   Or ached to glimpse some native spot;
And yet to be where I was born
   I hanker not.

I wish I yearned to see the hut
   Of boyhood, if for but a minute.
Not that I like this wishing, but
   There's money in it.

From: *So Much Velvet* by Franklin P. Adams. Copyright 1924 by Doubleday & Company, Inc.

At the Circus

I watched the clowns at the circus,
  And I noted their comic art,
And I mused the while how the daily smile
  Might cover a breaking heart.

Perhaps, I thought (I was conscious
  The thing had been thought before)
They are mournful folk who do not joke
  When the nightly task is o'er.

And I thought (I'm a pensive person;
  And this thought was somewhat new)
They have no fun when their work is done—
  And they're sad when they're working, too.

SAMUEL HOFFENSTEIN

You Have a Most
Attractive Pan

You have a most attractive pan,
And I'm a very foolish man,
And, what between the two, I fell
As deep as Dante into hell;
But do you, in your triumph, think
I'll stay forever on the blink,
And pine and pale and waste away
And grow cadaverous and gray—
A wreck, a rum, a shard? Well, maybe
You are right about it, baby!

Lovely Lady

Lovely lady, who does so
All my waking haunt,
Tell me, tell me, do you know
What the hell you want?

Lady, to whose feet I'd bring
The world, if I could win it,
Are you sure of anything
For a single minute?

You whose eyes can kindle flame
Only Death could smother,
Tell me, please, does any dame
Differ from another?

Was the apple applesauce
Eve ate in the garden?
Aren't you all a total loss?
No? I beg your pardon!

You Buy—

You buy some flowers for your table;
You tend them tenderly as you're able;
You fetch them water from hither and thither—
What thanks do you get for it all? They wither.

LIVES AND TIMES

FRANKLIN P. ADAMS

The Diary of Our Own
Samuel Pepys

Monday, November 1, 1920

LAY late, and to the office by subway, and finished S. Lewis's "Main Street," the best book I have read in as long as I can recall; and at my scrivening till evening.

Wednesday, May 17, 1922

To call A. Woollcott the critick this morning to say goodby to him, as he sails this afternoon for Europe, but I would not go to the ship, forasmuch as I hate lengthy farewells as much as I do funerals. So to the office, and all day there, and W. Lippmann to my office, and said, How about a soda, so we to have some, and I home, and did two hours' hard labour before dinner, at copying paragraphs from my scrapbook, and an hour after dinner, and so with my wife to a cinema theatre, and on the way there I saw V. Herbert * come from the subway, walking alone and nobody recognizing him at all. Yet if there be a greater composer living in America, I know not who he may be. And most of his work hath been done to lyrics that were between bad and mediocre, except the early

---

* Victor Herbert, the composer; died in 1924.

ones of Harry B. Smith, most of Henry Blossom's, and all of David Stevens's. At the cinema theatre I marvelled how long they kept a title exposed for the spectators to read, for it seemed to me a six-year-old child could read it five times over before they turned it off. A picture of Mayor Hylan was hissed, which, methought, was as low as sportsmanship could go. Compared to such a hisser, one who calls a stranger by telephone to call him a bad name is almost a hero.

Thursday, December 24, 1925

Up, and my malady vanished, by some miracle or other, and so to the office, and there all day, save to a shoppe to buy my wife a cork-screw for a Yuletide gift, and so to A. Woollcott's, and found a fine present for me, some finer cigarres than I am wont to buy, and a fair bound volume of Housman's Poems, with "A Shropshire Lad" and "Last Poems" made into one book, a book I had liefer own than any. So home, for Christmas Eve with my wife, and we had some presents under a fine tree, and had a pretty time of it. And my wife, out of her great heart, gave me a pair of andirons and some metal-polish, and I told her they were just what I wanted, and we played some Christmas musique upon the player-piano, and four Benéts came in, and Nell gives me a great buss, and F. Root and Olive and Charles come in, and we brewed some hot punch, and Will said "This is Punch Week," but I said, "Nay, this is weak punch," which God knoweth it was.

October 27, 1926

Queen Marie is traveling about in a great luxury in this country and in Canada, I read, and a vast amount of money is being expended by somebody, and there are tayles of the Queen's great candor and frankness, and I think it would be a good idea to say to her, "All right. How much does your country want?" and say either Yes or No. For it seems to me the money spent on silk hats by members of reception committees here and there would keep Rumania in funds for years.

November 17, 1926

To the office, and so home and at my scrivening, and then Dorothy
Parker come to see me, and I overjoyed to see her, and she told me
about her peregrinations abroad, and I asked her about Ernest Hemingway, and how old he was, and she said, "Well, I don't know.
You know, all writers are either twenty-nine or Thomas Hardy."
And we talked of this and that, and I told her that unless somebody
should be John Milton in a few days I should have to award her a
watch for the best piece wrote in my column this year. So Miss R.
West to dinner, and stopped all evening, and we talked of murder
and letters and marriage and this and that. So to bed, and read in
Frances Newman's "The Hard Boiled Virgin," a deeply interesting
book, with the longest sentences ever I read, and the most carefully
written, and thus far no word of conversation or dialogue.

November 29, 1926

Early up, and S. Adams there for breakfast with me, and talked
of letters and life and this and that, and so to the office, where all
day at my tasks, and in the evening to the theatre with Miss Maurine
Watkins, a handsome blue-eyed girl, and we saw S. Howard's "Ned
McCobb's Daughter," which I deemed easily the best play he ever
wrote, and as well acted as might be imagined. Forasmuch as nowhere have I ever seen anything better than Mr. Alfred Lunt's acting
as Babe Callahan, he assuming the role of a bootlegger, and his
bearing and his accent, with its inflections, and his dress, all so
perfect as to give me the greatest delight I have had in the theatre.
And Miss Eames very good, too methought, and Miss Margalo Gill-
more the best ever I saw her, acting with heart-breaking beauty. So
took Miss Watkins home in a metred cab, but then sent it away and
went home in the subway, a great wave of economy coming over me,
and so home and read "The Whispering Gallery," an almost incredibly dull recounting of trivial observations, made with no wit nor
acumen.

Wednesday, February 2, 1927

Today I saw a copy of a book called "Ask Me Another!" which

is a compilation of fifty questionnaires, all the questions being answered in a word or two and all facts and not opinions. Now I do not believe that a person who could answer every question correctly in the book would for that reason be a better or more useful or interesting person than he who could not answer half. But I have observed that it is usually the vague, dull, sloppy-minded persons who say, "These tests are no absolute index of knowledge or wisdom," as though anybody said that they were. But I know this: that a hundred persons who can answer three out of four questions on general information are more successful, more interesting, and happier, too, than a hundred persons who can answer one or two. For the race is oftenest to the swift.

Monday, February 28, 1927

Till late at the office, and heard a tayle how Dorothy Parker's publishers were about to advertise her as "another A. A. Milne," or some such phrase, and now Rob Benchley is going about calling her "Dotty-the-Pooh." Read this day how the Rev. Dr. John Haynes Holmes had made a sermon about Mr. Mencken, and I think he might have said it all in a quatrain, such as—

> *I like Mr. Mencken,*
> *His voice is so loud:*
> *He hates all the boobs,*
> *And he rails at the crowd.*

So home for dinner, and stopped in all evening, reading "Black April," by Julia Peterkin, a tale of Negro life in South Carolina, wrote with great beauty and skill, and a vastly interesting story, too.

Wednesday, March 2, 1927

This morning Mr. George Ruth come to town, and told the pressmen that he would not accept less than $100,000 a year, and I hope he gets it or more, as I think he attracts more money than that to the parks where he plays. But Lord! how weary it maketh me when petty persons compare this salary to the President's, or to their own, saying "How hard I work, and how little I earn!" But this man chooseth to be a writer or a truckman, and that one a ballplayer, and if so be he is fortunate enough to have the qualities that a great public will pay to see displayed, who is anybody to complain of that? For all I would have to do, I tell myself, to get a larger salary than Babe Ruth's would be to be a greater ballplayer, and if I am not, I have no right to complain, nor do I, but say, "Huzzah for Mr. Ruth!" Heard this afternoon that he hath accepted $70,000 a year, and that will make many persons happy, forasmuch as they will justify their own incompetence by saying he is losing $30,000 a year, which is more than most of us have to lose. So in the evening to see J. Lawson's play, "Loud Speaker," which I deemed a pretentious and humorless piece, but Mr. Romney Brent did better, methought, than the play merited. Nor was the play rebellious enough against convention to begin at the announced time, but did not start until 9 o'clock instead of half an hour earlier.

Monday, June 13, 1927

Up by 8 o'clock, and to the office by a devious way, to get through the crowds that were waiting to see Lindbergh, it being a day when few save journalists were required to work, and some of those who did work were presented with a day off, and others were forced not to work, and were paid nothing for their holiday. But I never saw the city in such a gay and happy mood in all my life, and what with the noise of bands in the park and visitors in the office, it was hard to finish my stint, which I was too excited by the electricity in the air to do with my accustomed serenity. Come Dorothy Parker to the office, too, and I glad of seeing her. So home, and on the way I tried to think of a poem about Columbus and Lindbergh, but I could get no forwarder with it than—

> *Not since Columbus discovered America in an effort*
> *to find a passage to the West Indies*
> *Has there been such an achievement as the trans-*
> *Atlantic non-stop of Lindy's.*

So home, and told my wife about the poem I had in mind, but she said it needed polishing, which discouraged me greatly, so I discarded the idea utterly, in great dejection.

Friday, March 30, 1928

Early up of a rainy, misling morning, and to office, and read a piece of Heywood Broun's in *The Nation,* and I award him the prize for the year's most potent piece of satirical criticism, for he is speaking of Louis Bromfield's "A Critique of Criticism," and he says: "Mr. Bromfield says that most American critics are merely exhibitionists. His essay was written shortly after he had completed a lecture tour of the women's clubs in the Middle West." And as for Mr. Bromfield's talking about the Columbus complex that critics have, Lord, why should not a critic be proud to be the first to acclaim this or that writer? For either a critic wants to be a Columbus or a sheep. And even if he is a Columbus he gets scant credit for his discovery, for in a million who know about Mr. Bromfield I doubt that there is one who knows who was the first critic to say, "Here is a first class writer, who will improve with time." I do not know myself, and I doubt whether even Mr. Bromfield knows.

Monday, October 28, 1929

Lay long, till near 9 o'clock, and so up and at my work, and so to the office, where I found great turmoil over the descending prices of stocks, the turmoil being so great that one journalist did ask for my opinion, which made me laugh albeit my heart was breaking. So Alison Smith comes to my office, and hearing somebody say something about the stock of A. T. & T., said that she thought she could make a fortune in American Kiss & Tell, which I thought to nominate for the Wheeze-of-the-Month. So home, and for a walk with my boy to the Square, and came upon Rob Rudd and Will Hill, and had a talk with them, and so home to dinner, and in the evening did some reading in E. Hemingway's "A Farewell to Arms," abandoning myself to it, as A. Woollcott implored me to do, and I did like it far better than when I read it in the magazine, yet do have a hard time forgetting the style of it. But I can forget Dreiser's style, which I dislike far more than I do Hemingway's.

H. L. MENCKEN

The Hills of Zion

IT was hot weather when they tried the infidel Scopes at Dayton, Tenn., but I went down there very willingly, for I was eager to see something of evangelical Christianity as a going concern. In the big cities of the Republic, despite the endless efforts of consecrated men, it is laid up with a wasting disease. The very Sunday-school superintendents, taking jazz from the stealthy radio, shake their fire-proof legs; their pupils, moving into adolescence, no longer respond to the proliferating hormones by enlisting for missionary service in Africa, but resort to necking instead. Even in Dayton, I found, though the mob was up to do execution upon Scopes, there was a strong smell of antinomianism. The nine churches of the village were all half empty on Sunday, and weeds choked their yards. Only two or three of the resident pastors managed to sustain themselves by their ghostly science; the rest had to take orders for mail-order pantaloons or work in the adjacent strawberry fields; one, I heard, was a barber. On the courthouse green a score of sweating theologians debated the darker passages of Holy Writ day and night, but I soon found that they were all volunteers, and that the local faithful, while interested in their exegesis as an intellectual exercise, did not permit it to impede the indigenous debaucheries. Exactly

twelve minutes after I reached the village I was taken in tow by a
Christian man and introduced to the favorite tipple of the Cumber-
land Range: half corn liquor and half Coca-Cola. It seemed a dreadful dose to me, but I found that the Dayton illuminati got it down
with gusto, rubbing their tummies and rolling their eyes. I include
among them chief local proponents of the Mosaic cosmogony. They
were all hot for Genesis, but their faces were far too florid to belong
to teetotalers, and when a pretty girl came tripping down the main
street, which was very often, they reached for the places where their
neckties should have been with all the amorous enterprise of movie
actors. It seemed somehow strange.

An amiable newspaper woman of Chattanooga, familiar with
those uplands, presently enlightened me. Dayton, she explained,
was simply a great capital like any other. That is to say, it was to
Rhea county what Atlanta was to Georgia or Paris to France. That
is to say, it was predominantly epicurean and sinful. A country girl
from some remote valley of the county, coming into town for her
semi-annual bottle of Lydia Pinkham's Vegetable Compound, shivered on approaching Robinson's drug-store quite as a country girl
from up-state New York might shiver on approaching the Metropolitan Opera House. In every village lout she saw a possible white-
slaver. The hard sidewalks hurt her feet. Temptations of the flesh
bristled to all sides of her, luring her to Hell. This newspaper
woman told me of a session with just such a visitor, holden a few
days before. The latter waited outside one of the town hot-dog and
Coca-Cola shops while her husband negotiated with a hardware
merchant across the street. The newspaper woman, idling along and
observing that the stranger was badly used by the heat, invited her
to step into the shop for a glass of Coca-Cola. The invitation
brought forth only a gurgle of terror. Coca-Cola, it quickly appeared, was prohibited by the country lady's pastor, as a levantine
and Hell-sent narcotic. He also prohibited coffee and tea—and pies!
He had his doubts about white bread and boughten meat. The newspaper woman, interested, inquired about ice-cream. It was, she found,
not specifically prohibited, but going into a Coca-Cola shop to get
it would be clearly sinful. So she offered to get a saucer of it, and

bring it out to the sidewalk. The visitor vacillated—and came near being lost. But God saved her in the nick of time. When the newspaper woman emerged from the place she was in full flight up the street. Later on her husband, mounted on a mule, overtook her four miles out the mountain pike.

This newspaper woman, whose kindness covered city officials as well as Alpine Christians, offered to take me back in the hills to a place where the old-time religion was genuinely on tap. The Scopes jury, she explained, was composed mainly of its customers, with a few Dayton sophisticates added to leaven the mass. It would thus be instructive to climb the heights and observe the former at their ceremonies. The trip, fortunately, might be made by automobile. There was a road running out of Dayton to Morgantown, in the mountains to the westward, and thence beyond. But foreigners, it appeared, would have to approach the sacred grove cautiously, for the upland worshipers were very shy, and at the first sight of a strange face they would adjourn their orgy and slink into the forest. They were not to be feared, for God had long since forbidden them to practise assassination, or even assault, but if they were alarmed a rough trip would go for naught. So, after dreadful bumpings up a long and narrow road, we parked our car in a little woodpath a mile or two beyond the tiny village of Morgantown, and made the rest of the approach on foot, deployed like skirmishers. Far off in a dark, romantic glade a flickering light was visible, and out of the silence came the rumble of exhortation. We could distinguish the figure of the preacher only as a moving mote in the light: it was like looking down the tube of a dark-field microscope. Slowly and cautiously we crossed what seemed to be a pasture, and then we stealthily edged further and further. The light now grew larger and we could begin to make out what was going on. We went ahead on all fours, like snakes in the grass.

From the great limb of a mighty oak hung a couple of crude torches of the sort that car inspectors thrust under Pullman cars when a train pulls in at night. In the guttering glare was the preacher, and for a while we could see no one else. He was an immensely tall and thin mountaineer in blue jeans, his collarless shirt open at the

neck and his hair a tousled mop. As he preached he paced up and
down under the smoking flambeaux, and at each turn he thrust his
arms into the air and yelled "Glory to God!" We crept nearer in
the shadow of the cornfield, and began to hear more of his discourse.
He was preaching on the Day of Judgment. The high kings of the
earth, he roared, would all fall down and die; only the sanctified
would stand up to receive the Lord God of Hosts. One of these he
mentioned by name, the king of what he called Greece-y.[1] The king
of Greece-y, he said, was doomed to Hell. We crawled forward a
few more yards and began to see the audience. It was seated on
benches ranged round the preacher in a circle. Behind him sat a row
of elders, men and women. In front were the younger folk. We
crept on cautiously, and individuals rose out of the ghostly gloom.
A young mother sat suckling her baby, rocking as the preacher paced
up and down. Two scared little girls hugged each other, their pig-
tails down their backs. An immensely huge mountain woman, in a
gingham dress, cut in one piece, rolled on her heels at every "Glory
to God!" To one side, and but half visible, was what appeared to be
a bed. We found afterward that half a dozen babies were asleep
upon it.

The preacher stopped at last, and there arose out of the darkness
a woman with her hair pulled back into a little tight knot. She began
so quietly that we couldn't hear what she said, but soon her voice
rose resonantly and we could follow her. She was denouncing the
reading of books. Some wandering book agent, it appeared, had come
to her cabin and tried to sell her a specimen of his wares. She refused to touch it. Why, indeed, read a book? If what was in it was
true, then everything in it was already in the Bible. If it was false,
then reading it would imperil the soul. This syllogism from the Cal-
iph Omar complete, she sat down. There followed a hymn, led by
a somewhat fat brother wearing silver-rimmed country spectacles.
It droned on for half a dozen stanzas, and then the first speaker
resumed the floor. He argued that the gift of tongues was real and
that education was a snare. Once his children could read the Bible,
he said, they had enough. Beyond lay only infidelity and damnation.

[1] Grecia? Cf. Daniel viii, 21.

Sin stalked the cities. Dayton itself was a Sodom. Even Morgantown had begun to forget God. He sat down, and a female aurochs in gingham got up. She began quietly, but was soon leaping and roaring, and it was hard to follow her. Under cover of the turmoil we sneaked a bit closer.

A couple of other discourses followed, and there were two or three hymns. Suddenly a change of mood began to make itself felt. The last hymn ran longer than the others, and dropped gradually into a monotonous, unintelligible chant. The leader beat time with his book. The faithful broke out with exultations. When the singing ended there was a brief palaver that we could not hear, and two of the men moved a bench into the circle of light directly under the flambeaux. Then a half-grown girl emerged from the darkness and threw herself upon it. We noticed with astonishment that she had bobbed hair. "This sister," said the leader, "has asked for prayers." We moved a bit closer. We could now see faces plainly, and hear every word. At a signal all the faithful crowded up to the bench and began to pray—not in unison, but each for himself. At another they all fell on their knees, their arms over the penitent. The leader kneeled facing us, his head alternately thrown back dramatically or buried in his hands. Words spouted from his lips like bullets from a machine-gun—appeals to God to pull the penitent back out of Hell, defiances of the demons of the air, a vast impassioned jargon of apocalyptic texts. Suddenly he rose to his feet, threw back his head and began to speak in the tongues [2]—blub-blub-blub, gurgle-gurgle-gurgle. His voice rose to a higher register. The climax was a shrill, inarticulate squawk, like that of a man throttled. He fell headlong across the pyramid of supplicants.

From the squirming and jabbering mass a young woman gradually detached herself—a woman not uncomely, with a pathetic homemade cap on her head. Her head jerked back, the veins of her neck swelled, and her fists went to her throat as if she were fighting for breath. She bent backward until she was like half a hoop. Then she suddenly snapped forward. We caught a flash of the whites of her eyes. Presently her whole body began to be convulsed—great throes that began

[2] Mark xvi, 17.

at the shoulders and ended at the hips. She would leap to her feet, thrust her arms in air, and then hurl herself upon the heap. Her praying flattened out into a mere delirious caterwauling. I describe the thing discreetly, and as a strict behaviorist. The lady's subjective sensations I leave to infidel pathologists, privy to the works of Ellis, Freud and Moll. Whatever they were, they were obviously not painful, for they were accompanied by vast heavings and gurglings of a joyful and even ecstatic nature. And they seemed to be contagious, too, for soon a second penitent, also female, joined the first, and then came a third, and a fourth, and a fifth. The last one had an extraordinary violent attack. She began with mild enough jerks of the head, but in a moment she was bounding all over the place, like a chicken with its head cut off. Every time her head came up a stream of hosannas would issue out of it. Once she collided with a dark, undersized brother, hitherto silent and stolid. Contact with her set him off as if he had been kicked by a mule. He leaped into the air, threw back his head, and began to gargle as if with a mouthful of BB shot. Then he loosed one tremendous, stentorian sentence in the tongues, and collapsed.

By this time the performers were quite oblivious to the profane universe and so it was safe to go still closer. We left our hiding and came up to the little circle of light. We slipped into the vacant seats on one of the rickety benches. The heap of mourners was directly before us. They bounced into us as they cavorted. The smell that they radiated, sweating there in that obscene heap, half suffocated us. Not all of them, of course, did the thing in the grand manner. Some merely groaned and rolled their eyes. The female ox in gingham flung her great bulk on the ground and jabbered an unintelligible prayer. One of the men, in the intervals between fits, put on his spectacles and read his Bible. Beside me on the bench sat the young mother and her baby. She suckled it through the whole orgy, obviously fascinated by what was going on, but never venturing to take any hand in it. On the bed just outside the light the half a dozen other babies slept peacefully. In the shadows, suddenly appearing and as suddenly going away, were vague figures, whether of believers or of scoffers I do not know. They seemed to come and go in couples. Now and then a couple at the ringside would step out and vanish

into the black night. After a while some came back, the males looking somewhat sheepish. There was whispering outside the circle of
vision. A couple of Model T Fords lurched up the road, cutting holes
in the darkness with their lights. Once someone out of sight loosed
a bray of laughter.

All this went on for an hour or so. The original penitent, by this
time, was buried three deep beneath the heap. One caught a glimpse,
now and then, of her yellow bobbed hair, but then she would vanish
again. How she breathed down there I don't know; it was hard
enough six feet away, with a strong five-cent cigar to help. When the
praying brothers would rise up for a bout with the tongues their
faces were streaming with perspiration. The fat harridan in gingham
sweated like a longshoreman. Her hair got loose and fell down over
her face. She fanned herself with her skirt. A powerful old gal she
was, plainly equal in her day to a bout with obstetrics and a week's
washing on the same morning, but this was worse than a week's
washing. Finally, she fell into a heap, breathing in great, convulsive
gasps.

Finally, we got tired of the show and returned to Dayton. It was
nearly eleven o'clock—an immensely late hour for those latitudes—
but the whole town was still gathered in the courthouse yard, listening to the disputes of theologians. The Scopes trial had brought them
in from all directions. There was a friar wearing a sandwich sign
announcing that he was the Bible champion of the world. There was
a Seventh Day Adventist arguing that Clarence Darrow was the beast
with seven heads and ten horns described in Revelation XIII, and
that the end of the world was at hand. There was an evangelist made
up like Andy Gump, with the news that atheists in Cincinnati were
preparing to descend upon Dayton, hang the eminent Judge Raulston,
and burn the town. There was an ancient who maintained that no
Catholic could be a Christian. There was the eloquent Dr. T. T.
Martin, of Blue Mountain, Miss., come to town with a truck-load
of torches and hymn-books to put Darwin in his place. There was a
singing brother bellowing apocalyptic hymns. There was William
Jennings Bryan, followed everywhere by a gaping crowd. Dayton
was having a roaring time. It was better than the circus. But the note

of devotion was simply not there; the Daytonians, after listening a while, would slip away to Robinson's drug-store to regale themselves with Coca-Cola, or to the lobby of the Aqua Hotel, where the learned Raulston sat in state, judicially picking his teeth. The real religion was not present. It began at the bridge over the town creek, where the road makes off for the hills.

CHRISTOPHER MORLEY

Conrad and the Reporters

THE gist of the adventure, I can see now, is in the relation between Conrad and the reporters. It is pleasant to contemplate
the paradox: a quite genuine meeting of spirit between the long-
thoughtful Ulysses who crushes his grapes of thought secretly, lei-
surely, and these inquisitive young men who (whether they like it
or not) are compelled to catch their thoughts young. It would be
hard to say, let me add, which is the more painful task—Mr. Conrad's, or the Reporter's. For if you allow a thought to grow and
mature in your mind, it gradually clothes itself and walks out decently raimented. If you have to chase it in its infancy, the task is as
perplexing as catching, scrubbing, and decking a lively child for a
party.

Among the reporters who went down the bay to meet Joseph Conrad on the *Tuscania* there were some of those gayly intrepid souls
to whom one assignment is much the same as another, and who would
question a Pope, an ectoplast, a Coué, or an Einstein with the same
cheery irrelevance. There were others, knowing something of Mr.
Conrad's ways of thinking and feeling, who were anxious. They
were troubled, first, on Mr. Conrad's behalf, knowing with what

From "The Bowling Green" by Christopher Morley, *New York Evening Post*,
May 3, 4, 1923. Reprinted in *Conrad and the Reporters* by Christopher Morley,
Doubleday, Page and Company 1923. Used by permission of the author.

horror he would encounter the insensate rush of questioners. They were troubled also on behalf of their own country, hating that a visitor so truly loved and honored should have his first impression marred and irritated by this fantastic absurdity. It is odd that though New York's one most charmingly youthful passion is to know what her callers think of her seaward loveliness, she makes it—by bombarding them with trivialities as they come up the harbor—impossible for them to think at all.

Now how far, one wonders, is trespass upon the privacy of others permissible? Just so far, I think, as the sum of human virtue is likely to be increased thereby. And because most of the literary commentators on Mr. Conrad have tended to give too grim a portrait, I feel that he would forgive a sympathetic attempt to show him as he appeared in what must have been a difficult experience.

I had always imagined a much burlier man: a man much more dour, austere, and remote. The first and most important thing to convey is that, to this little group of attentive students, the instant feeling towards Mr. Conrad was not quite one of awe, but the most honest, tender affection. A spare, almost fragile figure, garbed with clerical sobriety in a black overcoat, white muffler, and a round bowler hat, his left arm bandaged (he suffers painfully from gout), there was something beautifully gentle and kindly in his manner. As one of the reporters said afterwards, racking his wits to express the occasion, "he looked like a perplexed physician." Perplexed was the right word; it might almost have been put down as timid, for Mr. Conrad was evidently in horror of the ordeal of being catechized by a number of strangers. And in that backward-slanted head, with its strong angle of jaw and beard, the deeply carved face, the dark brown heavy-lidded eyes, there was also a faint spark of grimness. One knew that he had resolved to do everything possible to meet these strange demands; and yet that there was a "shadow-line" beyond which trespass was inadvisable.

But it is the gentle, friendly simplicity that the reporters felt most strongly. The photographers—who are barbarians, relentless and persistent—swarmed upon him first, uttering sharp cries of instruction. "Take your hat off, Mr. Conrad!"—"Stand behind that rail!"

The reporters, more delicate-minded souls, were indignant; Mr. Conrad turned despairing eyes toward them as he tried, patiently, to follow instructions. "Take your hat off, Mr. Conrad!" one ruffian kept shouting. But of the conduct of the photographers one does not like to speak.

Capt. Bone, anxious to spare his guest, spirited him away to the captain's cabin, and here the reporters were able to sit down quietly with him. And here it was plain that our fears—both for him and for ourselves—had been exaggerated. How charming he was! Sitting on the sofa, with shy but most humane cordiality he told us what a happiness it had been to be at sea once more. One of the reporters was inspired to call him Captain, and this pleased him. He spoke of the ships that had been dear to him long ago, gravely mentioning their lovely names—the *Otago* (his first command)—the *Skimmer of the Seas* (a Lowestoft coaster)—the *Tremolino*, the *Duke of Sutherland*, the *Loch Etive*, the *Adowa* (a steamship), in which he wrote Chapter Ten of *Almayer's Folly* while he was expecting her to sail for America. But she never did. "This is my furthest West," he said. "Of course I've often been out to Australia, running the easting down, but this is my first time across the Western Ocean." He had been delighted by his first view of the Clyde, which he had never seen before, "being a London skipper." Capt. Bone had read him John Burroughs's essay on the Clyde. We explained to him that this is the Glasgow shipmaster's favorite piece of literature, and that every voyage he looks about for a kinsprit passenger to whom he may introduce it. Conrad chuckled. Yes, Capt. Bone had read him other favorites, too. *The Old Soak*, for instance, which had amused him greatly. He couldn't understand why English publishers hadn't brought it out. "It deals with a universal theme!"

From ships and the sea ("You must remember, my sea life is very long," he said. "It all merges, now, into one solid impression. I have had three different lives.") we got on to American literature. He spoke of Poe—whom he read in French, as a boy; and Emerson, and Walt Whitman. But, asked further about Whitman (whose influence in France, he said, had been enormous) he said, "My mind

is not critical. I have not the general culture to be a literary critic.
You must remember that the conditions of sea life do not permit it."
He spoke with great affection of Henry James. It was James who
first mentioned John Burroughs to him. Conrad chuckled at the
thought of Burroughs. "The man who chased a nightingale," he
said.

How lovely he was! The frankness of his smile was underlaid by
an uneasy terror, which grew less, however, as he realized that these
young men honestly meant to be friendly. Interviewing is a dangerously ticklish art. Several of the little group were terrified for fear
some one would ask some fool question which would disturb the
happy rapprochement, so unexpectedly attained. There was one perilous person who was pining to say "What are your methods of
work?" We could see the question teetering on the edge of his lips.
Every time he opened his mouth the whole equilibrium was in danger. What a gross infliction, also, is the whole business! To hold a
man up for his money is a peccadillo compared to it. To hold him up
and demand those most preciously guarded possessions—his memories, his opinions, his sentiments—this is truculence indeed. *(From
"The Bowling Green," New York Evening Post, May 3, 1923.)*

Happiness * * * consists in finding the right words. How is one
to find those that will express the feeling of being on the *Tuscania*'s
bridge, that May Day morning, with Joseph Conrad? I suppose my
tone of voice now lays me open to the charge of idolatry (there are
worse charges, incidentally. And the chief argument against idolatry
is not that it is unbecoming to the worshiper, but that it may be embarrassing or repugnant to the idol). The feeling of the reporters,
as they stood decently apart while Mr. Conrad got a tranquil view
of New York rising from the hyaline dimness of the spring sky, was
not the mere admiration of an individual, however brave, sensitive,
or potent. It was a sense of doing honor, through this man, to a certain phase of the human spirit: a sense of homage to one who *had*
found the right words; who had, through long and patient years,
tried to utter the unsayable tremors of the mind. At a time when
we are repeatedly and wearisomely assured that the Cyrus Curtis

kind of thing (admirable enough in its own innocent way) is the ultimate benison of human success, there was something purging in contemplating achievement of a different sort.

The harbor, from the high passage of *Tuscania*'s bridge, lay as smoothly shining as a ballroom floor; and, oddly enough, as though to pay respect to their spokesman, an unusual number of sailing vessels were moving. Muirhead Bone, with a face of happy excitement, was busy at a drawing board where he had already sketched and colored the massive forecastle of the ship and the great cairn of brown tin trunks which are the familiar sign of British emigrants. Now, on the horizon of his drawing, M. B. was swiftly filling in the profile of the city. There was a delicious amusement in noting that most of the interviewers were quite unaware of the identity of Mr. Muirhead Bone, a man quite as eminent in his own field as Mr. Conrad in his. The photographers presently made another ugly rush, and cornered Mr. Conrad in the wing of the bridge; somehow or other Muirhead Bone found himself included in this picture; but, as he humorously remarked when these ruffians afterwards asked him to account for himself, "they were frightfully disgusted when they found I wasn't another author." Meanwhile the reporters, with ecstatic pleasure, were comparing notes on the deck below. Those who had taken shorthand memoranda (which, as shorthand memoranda usually are, were badly garbled) were verifying the facts from those who had merely listened. They had done so much better than they had expected. "Did you hear him say that writing is a fearful grind?" they cheerfully ejaculated. "That's the lead, all right." "What did he say exactly when he was asked which is his favorite book?" "He said 'It depends on the day.'" And so it went down in at least one avid notebook, and eventually appeared (in the New York *Times,* to my delight) that Mr. Conrad's best-loved work is *It Depends on the Day.* "There's hardly a man here," one of the group had ejaculated, "who hasn't read your books!" Alas, one fears that was not quite accurate. For, in spite of the affectionate clearness with which the master had spoken of some of the vessels of his past, another paper —the *Mail,* wasn't it?—had him down as having commanded a schooner, *The Skimmer of the Seas,* for twelve years. High spirited skimmers of the seas of interview are the ship-news reporters. They dip their wings in facts and skim away.

Meanwhile, as Capt. Bone explained to Conrad, the *Tuscania* was "sailing up Broadway." Her great stem was pointed straight at that terrific chine that opens up between the Equitable and the Singer (names that seemed to strike Mr. Conrad with some allegorical value), that deeply notched axe-cut into the stone fabric of Manhattan that stands for the mariner as a line of direction for the deep-water channel. The grizzled old quartermaster (we shall never forget having seen him play the haggis in at one or two Scottish parties aboard the old *Columbia*) stood gravely at the wheel, somewhat troubled (I couldn't help thinking) at the unusual incursion of outsiders into this holy precinct. Conrad, at one of the wheelhouse windows, watched the rising bristle of New York. I do not think that much escaped him. It was evident that, long ago, he had formed a clear idea of the geography of our region. Cooper, it seems, had put the East River into his mind; and (if I caught him rightly) he had gathered some impression of the Jersey side from Max Adeler. (I did not feel it quite courteous to admit that I have never read Max Adeler.) Brooklyn, the Brooklyn Bridge, Jersey City, the Battery, all these he seemed to greet and relish in his mind as things mentally familiar for a lifetime. The little plumes of steam that float like feathers from the tips of the high buildings, softly dissipating into that exquisite cool blue air, pleased him greatly. Muirhead Bone, with a face of growing ecstasy, was pondering the criss-cross skeleton of that great building that is going up near Bowling Green.

Of course what the infatuated ship-news reporter is always dumbly hoping for is that the Great Visitor—whoever it may be—will some day say something about this Skyline of ours that will effectually and eventually label it. The ship-news reporter, humble fellow, has that same obscure hankering for the right word that troubles the greatest of his fellows. But at any rate Mr. Conrad was wise enough not to attempt it. One had a feeling that, by the time the *Tuscania* passed the Battery he had seen as much as he could hold together in one clutch of the mind. He was tired, and Capt. Bone had a chair put for him in the sunny corner of the bridge. Here, presently, more sedative topics were discussed. He was greatly interested in watching the pilot; and remarked that in the old days pilots did not smoke on duty. This, naturally, led towards Capt. Bone's famous invention, the Dog's Wool tobacco; and then (after a parenthesis on the *Tusitala,* whose picture he had admired) Mr. Conrad admitted one of the problems that was troubling him. "I can only smoke one thing," he said, and mentioned a well-known brand of French cigarette. "I have only three left," he said. "Three packets?" we inquired in alarm, "or three single cigarettes?" "Three poor little cigarettes," he said (with that note of tremulous tenderness that seems characteristic; and with a sort of beseeching appeal in his brown eyes). He pulled out a small cigarette case and showed them. Only three. "Do you suppose," he said, *"Do* you suppose there is somewhere we can get some?"

So one of the first envoys across the gangplank after *Tuscania* docked, carried the message to Conrad's waiting host that the first and most urgent thing to do was to stop the car on the way uptown and lay in a bale of *Marylands. (From "The Bowling Green," New York Evening Post, May 4, 1923.)*

BURTON RASCOE

Morley, Conrad and the
Interviewers

CHRISTOPHER MORLEY is still beefing because we ship news reporters had the appalling irreverence to ask Joseph Conrad questions and because the photographers were so disrespectful of Morley's god as to ask him to pose for his picture. As one of the ship news reporters—if only for one day, through the kindly offices of Mr. Petrie, *The Tribune's* ship news reporter—I would add my mite of resentment to Morley's aspersions. * * *

Contrary to Morley's ill-tempered report, my own observation on this now historic occasion was that we reporters and photographers not only treated Conrad with the utmost respect but we showed Morley a courtesy which, it would now appear, he hardly deserved.

Morley knew Captain Bone and he had corresponded with Conrad; Conrad, who is shy and modest, was visibly frightened by the interviews; Mr. Cunningham of *The Evening World* suggested that we keep quiet and let Morley put the questions. While the great man was getting his bearings and entering into a calm and affable relationship with us, every reporter stood back, hat in hand, humble and respectful, while Morley asked questions whose answers could not possibly have the slightest news value.

During that half hour of questioning so respectful and sympathetic toward Conrad were the reporters that not one of us had the impertinence to ask a pertinent question. If we reporters had been bad mannered we might have got some stuff which would have made a good story. Instead we were, one and all, hard put to get a "lead" for our copy.

As for the photographers, they were working under difficulties. They are employed to take photographs, which demand sunlight; they were given only a few minutes and they had to work in haste; they were excited and anxious and therefore, perhaps, a little gruff. But it was not Conrad, it was Morley who was offended when one of them asked Conrad to take off his hat. Had the photographers been really bad mannered they would have told Morley that only by courtesy was he managing the show; and they would have shown him where he got off when he said to them while they were taking their snaps of Conrad, "I'll give you just thirty seconds more!" It would hardly have excused them if they had reported back to their employers that they hadn't been able to take any picture of Conrad because Christopher Morley wouldn't let them. "Whothehell is Christopher Morley?" they would have been asked, and, quite properly, they would have got the gate when they answered: "He's a newspaper man." *(From "A Bookman's Daybook," New York Tribune, May 7, 1923.)*

CHRISTOPHER MORLEY

Conrad and the Reporters

WE ARE a little aghast at the comments made by some of our fellow reporters on our stumbling attempt to record the arrival of Conrad. It proves to us, as we have always maintained, that journalism is (in general) not a subdivision of literature, but something utterly and totally different, pointed in a different way. For the general run of cheerful contradictions that we have received from professional colleagues is this: that to the reporter all individuals are much on a par; that he must grab off a few bright and startling details as rapidly as possible; that he must quote verbatim the random utterances of the victim; and that it makes no difference who on earth he or she may be, provided there emerges some quaint, surprising or pathetic outline of human interest. * * * If our sharpshooting method of reporting is so nobly representative, why is it that whenever (by the oddity of circumstance) a newspaper man himself chances to be interviewed he exhibits such uncontrollable agitation? *(From "The Bowling Green," New York Evening Post, May 10, 1923.)*

From "The Bowling Green" by Christopher Morley, *New York Evening Post,* May 10, 1923. Reprinted in *Conrad and the Reporters* by Christopher Morley, Doubleday, Page and Company 1923. Used by permission of the author.

THEODORE DREISER

My Brother Paul

I LIKE best to think of him as he was at the height of his all-too-brief reputation and success, when, as the author and composer of various American popular successes ("On the Banks of the Wabash," "Just Tell Them That You Saw Me," and various others), as a third owner of one of the most successful popular music publishing houses in the city and as an actor and playwright of some small repute, he was wont to spin like a moth in the white light of Broadway. By reason of a little luck and some talent he had come so far, done so much for himself. In his day he had been by turn a novitiate in a Western seminary which trained aspirants for the Catholic priesthood; a singer and entertainer with a perambulating cure-all oil troupe or wagon ("Hamlin's Wizard Oil") traveling throughout Ohio, Indiana and Illinois; both end- and middle-man with one, two or three different minstrel companies of repute; the editor or originator and author of a "funny column" in a Western small city paper; the author of the songs mentioned and a hundred others; a black-face monologue artist; a white-face ditto, at Tony Pastor's, Miner's and Niblo's of the old days; a comic lead; co-star and star in such melodramas and farces as "The Danger Signal," "The Two Johns," "A

Tin Soldier," "The Midnight Bell," "A Green Goods Man" (a farce which he himself wrote, by the way), and others. The man had a genius for the kind of gaiety, poetry and romance which may, and no doubt must be, looked upon as exceedingly middle-class but which nonetheless had as much charm as anything in this world can well have. He had at this time absolutely no cares or financial worries of any kind, and this plus his health, self-amusing disposition and talent for entertaining, made him a most fascinating figure to contemplate.

* * *

As I look back now on my life, I realize quite clearly that of all the members of my family, subsequent to my mother's death, the only one who truly understood me, or, better yet, sympathized with my intellectual and artistic point of view, was, strange as it may seem, this same Paul, my dearest brother. Not that he was in any way fitted intellectually or otherwise to enjoy high forms of art and learning and so guide me, or that he understood, even in later years (long after I had written "Sister Carrie," for instance) what it was that I was attempting to do; he never did. His world was that of the popular song, the middle-class actor or comedian, the middle-class comedy, and such humorous aesthetes of the writing world as Bill Nye, Petroleum V. Nasby, the authors of the Spoopendyke Papers, and "Samantha at Saratoga." As far as I could make out—and I say this in no lofty, condescending spirit, by any means—he was entirely full of simple, middle-class romance, middle-class humor, middle-class tenderness and middle-class grossness, all of which I am very free to say early disarmed and won me completely and kept me so much his debtor that I should hesitate to try to acknowledge or explain all that he did for or meant to me.

Imagine, if you can, a man weighing all of three hundred pounds, not more than five feet ten-and-one-half inches in height and yet of so lithesome a build that he gave not the least sense of either undue weight or lethargy. His temperament, always ebullient and radiant, presented him as a clever, eager, cheerful, emotional and always highly illusioned person with so collie-like a warmth that one found him compelling interest and even admiration. Easily cast down at times by the most trivial matters, at others, and for the most part, he was so spirited and bubbly and emotional and sentimental that your fiercest or most gloomy intellectual rages or moods could scarcely withstand his smile. This tenderness or sympathy of his, a very human appreciation of the weaknesses and errors as well as the toils and tribulations of most of us, was by far his outstanding and most engaging quality, and gave him a very definite force and charm. * * *

Of all characters in fiction he perhaps most suggests Jack Falstaff, with his love of women, his bravado and bluster and his innate good nature and sympathy. Sympathy was really his outstanding characteristic, even more than humor, although the latter was always present. One might recite a thousand incidents of his generosity and out-of-hand charity, which contained no least thought of return or reward. I recall that once there was a boy who had been reared in one of the towns in which we had once lived who had never had a chance in his youth, educationally or in any other way, and, having turned out "bad" and sunk to the level of a bank robber, had been detected in connection with three other men in the act of robbing a bank, the watchman of which was subsequently killed in the mêlée and escape. Of all four criminals only this one had been caught. Somewhere in prison he had heard sung one of my brother's sentimental ballads, "The Convict and the Bird," and recollecting that he had known Paul wrote him, setting forth his life history and that now he had no money or friends.

At once my good brother was alive to the pathos of it. He showed the letter to me and wanted to know what could be done. I suggested a lawyer, of course, one of those brilliant legal friends of his—always he had enthusiastic admirers in all walks—who might take the case for little or nothing. There was the leader of Tammany Hall, Richard Croker, who could be reached, he being a friend of Paul's. There was the Governor himself to whom a plain recitation of the boy's unfortunate life might be addressed, and with some hope of profit.

All of these things he did, and more. He went to the prison (Sing Sing), saw the warden and told him the story of the boy's life, then went to the boy, or man, himself and gave him some money. He was introduced to the Governor through influential friends and permitted to tell the tale. There was much delay, a reprieve, a commutation of the death penalty to life imprisonment—the best that could be done. But he was so grateful for that, so pleased. You would have thought at the time that it was his own life that had been spared.

"Good heavens!" I jested. "You'd think you'd done the man an inestimable service, getting him in the penitentiary for life!"

"That's right," he grinned—an unbelievably provoking smile. "He'd better be dead, wouldn't he? Well, I'll write and ask him which he'd rather have."

*   *   *

As I have said, I always prefer to think of him at this, the very apex or tower window of his life. For most of this period he was gay and carefree. The music company of which he was a third owner was at the very top of its success. Its songs, as well as his, were everywhere. He had in turn at this time a suite at the Gilsey House, the Marlborough, the Normandie—always on Broadway, you see. The limelight district was his home. He rose in the morning to the clang of the cars and the honk of the automobiles outside; he retired at night as a gang of repair men under flaring torches might be repairing a track, or the milk trucks were rumbling to and from the ferries. He was in his way a public restaurant and hotel favorite, a shining light in the theater managers' offices, hotel bars and lobbies and wherever those flies of the Tenderloin, those passing lords and celebrities of the sporting, theatrical, newspaper and other worlds, are wont to gather. One of his intimates, as I now recall, was "Bat" Masterson, the Western and now retired (to Broadway!) bad man; Muldoon, the famous wrestler; Tod Sloane, the jockey; "Battling" Nelson; James J. Corbett; Kid McCoy; Terry McGovern—prize-fighters all. Such Tammany district leaders as James Murphy, "The" McManus, Chrystie and Timothy Sullivan, Richard Carroll, and even Richard Croker, the then reigning Tammany boss, were all on his visiting list. He went to their meetings, rallies and district doings generally to sing and play, and they came to his "office" occasionally.

Various high and mighties of the Roman Church, "fathers" with fine parishes and good wine cellars, and judges of various municipal courts, were also of his peculiar world. He was always running to one or the other "to get somebody out," or they to him to get him to contribute something to something, or to sing and play or act, and betimes they were meeting each other in hotel grills or elsewhere and having a drink and telling "funny stories." * * *

It was wonderful, the loud clothes, the bright straw hats, the canes, the diamonds, the "hot" socks, the air of security and well-being, so easily assumed by those who gain an all too brief hour in this pretty, petty world of make-believe and pleasure and pseudo-fame. Among them my dearest brother was at his best. It was "Paul" here and "Paul" there— "Why, hello, Dresser, you're just in time! Come on in. What'll you have? Let me tell you something, Paul, a good one—" More drinks, cigars, tales—magnificent tales of successes made, "great shows" given, fights, deaths, marvelous winnings at cards, trickeries in racing, prize-fighting; the "dogs" that some people were, the magnificent, magnanimous "God's own salt" that others were. The oaths, stories of women, what low, vice-besmeared, crime-soaked ghoulas certain reigning beauties of the town or stage were—and so on and so on ad infinitum. * * *

Ah, me! Ah, me! That one could be so great, and that it should not last for ever and for ever!

Another of his outstanding characteristics was his love of women, a really amusing and at times ridiculous quality. He was always sighing over the beauty, innocence, sweetness, this and that, of young maidenhood in his songs, but in real life he seemed to desire and attract quite a different type—the young and beautiful, it is true, but also the old, the homely and the somewhat savage—a catholicity of taste I could never quite stomach. It was "Paul dearest" here and "Paul dearest" there, especially in his work in connection with the music-house and the stage. In the former, popular ballad singers of both sexes, some of the women most attractive and willful, were most numerous, coming in daily from all parts of the world apparently to find songs which they could sing on the American or even the English stage * * *

And how he fascinated them, the women! Their quite shameless daring where he was concerned! Positively, in the face of it I used to wonder what had become of all the vaunted and so-called "stabilizing morality" of the world. None of it seemed to be in the possession of these women, especially the young and beautiful. They were distant and freezing enough to all who did not interest them, but let a personality such as his come into view and they were all wiles, bending and alluring graces. It was so obvious, this fascination he had for them and they for him, that at times it took on a comic look.

"Get onto the hit he's making," one would nudge another and remark.

"Say, some tenderness, that!" This in reference to a smile or a melting glance on the part of a female.

"Nothing like a way with the ladies. Some baby, eh, boys?"— this following the flick of a skirt and a backward-tossed glance perhaps, as some noticeable beauty passed out.

"No wonder he's cheerful," a sour and yet philosophic vaudevillian, who was mostly out of a job and hung about the place for what free meals he could obtain, once remarked to me in a heavy and morose undertone. "If I had that many women crazy about me I'd be too!"

And the results of these encounters with beauty! Always he had something most important to attend to, morning, noon or night, and whenever I encountered him after some such statement "the important thing" was, of course, a woman. As time went on and he began to look upon me as something more than a thin, spindling, dyspeptic and disgruntled youth, he began to wish to introduce me to some of his marvelous followers, and then I could see how completely dependent upon beauty in the flesh he was, how it made his life and world * * *

But his great forte was of course his song-writing, and of this, before I speak of anything else, I wish to have my say. It was a gift, quite a compelling one, out of which, before he died, he had made thousands, all spent in the manner described. Never having the least power to interpret anything in a fine musical way, still he was always full of music of a tender, sometimes sad, sometimes gay, kind—that of the ballad-maker of a nation. He was constantly attempting to work them out of himself, not quickly but slowly, brooding as it were over the piano wherever he might find one and could have a little solitude, at times on the organ (his favorite instrument), improvising various sad or wistful strains, some of which he jotted down, others of which, having mastered, he strove to fit words to * * *

And what pale little things they were really, mere bits and scraps of sentiment and melodrama in story form, most asinine sighings over home and mother and lost sweethearts and dead heroes such as never were in real life, and yet with something about them, in the music at least, which always appealed to me intensely and must have appealed to others, since they attained so wide a circulation. They bespoke, as I always felt, a wistful, seeking, uncertain temperament, tender and illusioned, with no practical knowledge of any side of life, but full of a true poetic feeling for the mystery and pathos of life and death, the wonder of the waters, the stars, the flowers, accidents of life, success, failure. Beginning with a song called "Wide Wings" (published by a small retail music-house in Evansville, Indiana), and followed by such national successes as "The Letter That Never Came," "I Believe It, For My Mother Told Me So" (!), "The Convict and the Bird," "The Pardon Came Too Late," "Just Tell Them That You Saw Me," "The Blue and the Grey," "On the Bowery," "On the Banks of the Wabash," and a number of others, he was never content to rest and never really happy, I think, save when composing. During this time, however, he was at different periods all the things I have described—a black-face monologue artist, and end- and at times a middle-up man, a publisher, and so on.

I recall being with him at the time he composed two of his most famous successes: "Just Tell Them That You Saw Me," and "On the Banks of the Wabash," and noting his peculiar mood, almost amounting to a deep depression which ended a little later in marked elation or satisfaction, once he had succeeded in evoking something which really pleased him.

The first of these songs must have followed an actual encounter with some woman or girl whose life had seemingly if not actually gone to wreck on the shore of love or passion. At any rate he came into the office of his publishing house one gray November Sunday afternoon—it was our custom to go there occasionally, a dozen or more congenial souls, about as one might go to a club—and going into a small room which was fitted up with a piano as a "try-out" room (professionals desiring a song were frequently taught it in the office), he began improvising, or rather repeating over and over, a certain strain which was evidently in his mind. A little while later he came out and said, "Listen to this, will you, Thee?"

He played and sang the first verse and chorus. In the middle of the latter, so moved was he by the sentiment of it, his voice broke and he had to stop. Tears stood in his eyes and he wiped them away. A moment or two later he was able to go through it without wavering and I thought it charming for the type of thing it was intended to be. Later on (the following spring) I was literally astonished to see how, after those various efforts usually made by popular music publishers to make a song "go"—advertising it in the *Clipper* and *Mirror,* getting various vaudeville singers to sing it, and so forth—it suddenly began to sell, thousands upon thousands of copies being wrapped in great bundles under my very eyes and shipped express or freight to various parts of the country. Letters and telegrams, even, from all parts of the nation began to pour in—"Forward express today—copies of Dresser's 'Tell Them That You Saw Me.' " The firm was at once as busy as a bee-hive, on "easy street" again, as the expression went, "in clover." Just before this there had been a slight slump in its business and in my brother's finances, but now once more he was his most engaging self. Every one in that layer of life which understands or takes an interest in popular songs and their creators knew of him and his song, his latest success. He was, as it were, a revivified figure on Broadway. His barbers, barkeepers, hotel clerks, theatrical box-office clerks, hotel managers and the stars and singers of the street knew of it and him. Some enterprising button firm got out a button on which the phrase was printed. Comedians on the stage, newspaper paragraphers, his bank teller or his tailor, even staid business men wishing to appear "up-to-date," used it as a parting salute * * *

It was the same with "On the Banks of the Wabash," possibly an even greater success, for it came eventually to be adopted by his native State as its State song, and in that region streets and a town were named after him. In an almost unintentional and unthinking way I had a hand in that, and it has always cheered me to think that I had, although I have never had the least talent for musical composition or song versification. It was one of those delightful summer Sunday mornings (1896, I believe), when I was still connected with his firm as editor of the little monthly they were issuing, and he and myself, living with my sister E—— that we had gone over to this office to do a little work. I had a number of current magazines I wished to examine; he was always wishing to compose something, to express that ebullient and emotional soul of his in some way.

"What do you suppose would make a good song these days?" he asked in an idle, meditative mood, sitting at the piano and thrumming while I at a nearby table was looking over my papers. "Why don't you give me an idea for one once in a while, sport? You ought to be able to suggest something."

"Me?" I queried, almost contemptuously, I suppose. I could be very lofty at times in regard to his work, much as I admired him— vain and yet more or less dependent snip that I was. "I can't write those things. Why don't you write something about a State or a river? Look at 'My Old Kentucky Home,' 'Dixie,' 'Old Black Joe'— why don't you do something like that, something that suggests a part of America? People like that. Take Indiana—what's the matter with it—the Wabash River? It's as good as any other river, and you were 'raised' beside it."

I have to smile even now as I recall the apparent zest or feeling with which all at once he seized on this. It seemed to appeal to him immensely. "That's not a bad idea," he agreed, "but how would you go about it? Why don't you write the words and let me put the music to them? We'll do it together!"

"But I can't," I replied. "I don't know how to do those things. You write it. I'll help—maybe."

After a little urging—I think the fineness of the morning had as much to do with it as anything—I took a piece of paper and after meditating a while scribbled in the most tentative manner imaginable the first verse and chorus of that song almost as it was published. I think one or two lines were too long or didn't rhyme, but eventually either he or I hammered them into shape, but before that I rather shamefacedly turned them over to him, for somehow I was convinced that this work was not for me and that I was rather loftily and cynically attempting what my good brother would do in all faith and feeling.

He read it, insisted that it was fine and that I should do a second verse, something with a story in it, a girl perhaps—a task which I solemnly rejected.

"No, you put it in. It's yours. I'm through."

Some time later, disagreeing with the firm as to the conduct of the magazine, I left—really was forced out—which raised a little feeling on my part; not on his, I am sure, for I was very difficult to deal with.

Time passed and I heard nothing. I had been able to succeed in a somewhat different realm, that of the magazine contributor, and although I thought a great deal of my brother I paid very little attention to him or his affairs, being much more concerned with my own. One spring night, however, the following year, as I was lying in my bed trying to sleep, I heard a quartette of boys in the distance approaching along the street in which I had my room. I could not make out the words at first but the melody at once attracted my attention. It was plaintive and compelling. I listened, attracted, satisfied that it was some new popular success that had "caught on." As they drew near my window I heard the words "On the Banks of the Wabash" most mellifluously harmonized.

I jumped up. They were my words! It was Paul's song! He had another "hit" then—"On the Banks of the Wabash," and they were singing it in the streets already! * * *

The final phase of course related to his untimely end. He was not quite fifty-five when he died, and with a slightly more rugged quality of mind he might have lasted to seventy. It was due really to the failure of his firm (internal dissensions and rivalries, in no way due to him, however, as I have been told) and what he foolishly deemed to be the end of his financial and social glory. His was one of those simple, confiding, non-hardy dispositions, warm and colorful but intensely sensitive, easily and even fatally chilled by the icy blasts of human difficulty, however slight. You have no doubt seen some animals, cats, dogs, birds, of an especially affectionate nature, which when translated to a strange or unfriendly climate soon droop and die. They have no spiritual resources wherewith to contemplate what they do not understand or know. Now his *friends* would leave him. Now that bright world of which he had been a part would know him no more. It was pathetic, really. He emanated a kind of fear. Depression and even despair seemed to hang about him like a cloak. He could not shake it off. And yet, literally, in his case there was nothing to fear, if he had only known.

And yet two years before he died, I knew he would. Fantastic as it may seem, to be shut out from that bright world of which he deemed himself an essential figure was all but unendurable. He had no ready money now, not the same amount anyhow. He could not greet his old-time friends so gayly, entertain so freely. Meeting him on Broadway shortly after the failure and asking after his affairs, he talked of going into business for himself as a publisher, but I realized that he could not. He had neither the ability nor the talent for that, nor the heart. He was not a business man but a song-writer and actor, had never been anything but that. He tried in this new situation to write songs, but he could not. They were too morbid. What he needed was some one to buoy him up, a manager, a strong confidant of some kind, some one who would have taken his affairs in hand and shown him what to do. As it was he had no one. His friends, like winter-frightened birds, had already departed. Personally, I was in no position to do anything at the time, being more or less depressed myself and but slowly emerging from difficulties which had held me for a number of years.

About a year or so after he failed my sister E—— announced that Paul had been there and that he was coming to live with her * * * A few months later he was ostensibly connected with another publishing house, but by then he was feeling so poorly physically and was finding consolation in some drinking and the caresses

of those feminine friends who have, alas, only caresses to offer. A
little later I met a doctor who said, "Paul cannot live. He has per-
nicious anaemia. He is breaking down inside and doesn't know it.
He can't last long. He's too depressed." I knew it was so and what
the remedy was—money and success once more, the petty pettings
and flattery of that little world of which he had been a part but
which now was no more for him. Of all those who had been so lav-
ish in their greetings and companionship earlier in his life, scarcely
one, so far as I could make out, found him in that retired world to
which he was forced. One or two pegged-out actors sought him and
borrowed a little of the little that he had; a few others came when
he had nothing at all. His partners, quarreling among themselves
and feeling that they had done him an injustice, remained religiously
away. He found, as he often told my sister, broken horse-shoes (a
"bad sign"), met cross-eyed women, another "bad sign," was pursued apparently by the inimical number thirteen—and all these little
straws depressed him horribly. Finally, being no longer strong
enough to be about, he took to his bed and remained there days at
a time, feeling well while in bed but weak when up. For a little
while he would go "downtown" to see this, that and the other person, but would soon return. One day on coming back home he found
one of his hats lying on his bed, accidentally put there by one of
the children, and according to my sister, who was present at the
time, he was all but petrified by the sight of it. To him it was the
death-sign. Some one had told him so not long before!!!

Then, not incuriously, seeing the affectional tie that had always
held us, he wanted to see me every day. He had a desire to talk to
me about his early life, the romance of it—maybe I could write a
story some time, tell something about him! (Best of brothers, here
it is, a thin little flower to lay at your feet!) To please him I made
notes, although I knew most of it. On these occasions he was always
his old self, full of ridiculous stories, quips and slight *mots,* all in
his old and best vein. He would soon be himself, he now insisted.

Then one evening in late November, before I had time to call
upon him (I lived about a mile away), a hurry-call came from E——.
He had suddenly died at five in the afternoon; a blood-vessel had

burst in the head. When I arrived he was already cold in death, his
soft hands folded over his chest, his face turned to one side on the
pillow, that indescribable sweetness of expression about the eyes
and mouth—the empty shell of the beetle. There were tears, a band
of reporters from the papers, the next day obituary news articles,
and after that a host of friends and flowers, flowers, flowers. It is
amazing what satisfaction the average mind takes in standardized
floral forms—broken columns and gates ajar!

Being ostensibly a Catholic, a Catholic sister-in-law and other
relatives insistently arranged for a solemn high requiem mass at the
church of one of his favorite rectors. All Broadway was there, more
flowers, his latest song read from the altar. Then there was a carriage procession to a distant Catholic graveyard somewhere, his
friend, the rector of the church, officiating at the grave. It was so
cold and dreary there, horrible. Later on he was removed to Chicago.

But still I think of him as not there or anywhere in the realm of
space, but on Broadway between Twenty-ninth and Forty-second
Streets, the spring and summer time at hand, the doors of the grills
and bars of the hotels open, the rout of actors and actresses ambling
to and fro, his own delicious presence dressed in his best, his
"funny" stories, his songs being ground out by the hand organs, his
friends extending their hands, clapping him on the shoulder, cackling
over the latest idle yarn.

Ah, Broadway! Broadway! And you, my good brother! Here is the
story that you wanted me to write, this little testimony to your memory, a pale, pale symbol of all I think and feel. Where are the thousand yarns I have laughed over, the music, the lights, the song?

Peace, peace. So shall it soon be with all of us. It was a dream.
It is. I am. You are. And shall we grieve over or hark back to
dreams?

KIN HUBBARD

Sayings of Abe Martin

It's no disgrace to be poor, but it might as well be.

Th' word "slob" sounds jest exactly like one looks.

Never leave any alcohol around where there's a feller who says, "We're better off without it."

How'd you like t' be marooned in Napoleon, Indianny, an' dependin' on th' Congress t' git you out?

Marriages are made in Heaven, an' very few o' em ever git back t' th' factory.

Some o' these days somebuddy's goin' t' git in such a mess he won't be able t' find a criminal lawyer famous enough t' git him out.

Never offer a bandit a check.

H. L. MENCKEN

The Husbandman

LET the farmer, so far as I am concerned, be damned forever-more. To Hell with him, and bad luck to him. He is a tedious fraud and ignoramus, a cheap rogue and hypocrite, the eternal Jack of the human pack. He deserves all that he ever suffers under our economic system, and more. Any city man, not insane, who sheds tears for him is shedding tears of the crocodile.

No more grasping, selfish and dishonest mammal, indeed is known to students of the *Anthropoidea*. When the going is good for him he robs the rest of us up to the extreme limit of our endurance; when the going is bad he comes bawling for help out of the public till. Has anyone ever heard of a farmer making any sacrifice of his own inter-ests, however slight, to the common good? Has anyone ever heard of a farmer practising or advocating any political idea that was not absolutely self-seeking—that was not, in fact, deliberately designed to loot the rest us to his gain? Greenbackism, free silver, the govern-ment guarantee of prices, bonuses, all the complex fiscal imbecilities of the cow State John Baptists—these are the contributions of the virtuous husbandmen to American political theory. There has never been a time, in good seasons or bad, when his hands were not itch-ing for more; there has never been a time when he was not ready to

Reprinted from *A Mencken Chrestomathy* by H. L. Mencken, by permission of Alfred A. Knopf, Inc. Copyright 1924, 1949 by Alfred A. Knopf, Inc.

support any charlatan, however grotesque, who promised to get it for him. Only one issue ever fetches him, and that is the issue of his own profit. He must be promised something definite and valuable, to be paid to him alone, or he is off after some other mountebank. He simply cannot imagine himself as a citizen of a commonwealth, in duty bound to give as well as take; he can imagine himself only as getting all and giving nothing.

Yet we are asked to venerate this prehensile moron as the *Ur-burgher,* the citizen *par excellence,* the foundation-stone of the state! And why? Because he produces something that all of us must have— that we must get somehow on penalty of death. And how do we get it from him? By submitting helplessly to his unconscionable black-mailing—by paying him, not under any rule of reason, but in propor-tion to his roguery and incompetence, and hence to the direness of our need. I doubt that the human race, as a whole, would submit to that sort of high-jacking, year in and year out, from any other neces-sary class of men. But the farmers carry it on incessantly, without challenge or reprisal, and the only thing that keeps them from reduc-ing us, at intervals, to actual famine is their own imbecile knavery. They are all willing and eager to pillage us by starving us, but they can't do it because they can't resist attempts to swindle each other. Recall, for example, the case of the cottongrowers in the South * * * they agreed among themselves to cut down the cotton acreage in order to inflate the price—and instantly every party to the agreement began planting *more* cotton in order to profit by the abstinence of his neighbors. That abstinence being wholly imaginary, the price of cotton fell instead of going up—and then the entire pack of scoun-drels began demanding assistance from the national treasury—in brief, began demanding that the rest of us indemnify them for the failure of their plot to blackmail us.

The same demand is made sempiternally by the wheat farmers of the Middle West. It is the theory of the zanies who perform at Washington that a grower of wheat devotes himself to that banal art in a philanthropic and patriotic spirit—that he plants and harvests his crop in order that the folks of the cities may not go without bread. It is a plain fact that he raises wheat because it takes less labor than any other crop—because it enables him, after working no more than sixty days a year, to loaf the rest of the twelve months. If wheat-raising could be taken out of the hands of such lazy *fellahin* and organized as the production of iron or cement is organized, the price might be reduced by two-thirds, and still leave a large profit for *entrepreneurs*. But what would become of the farmers? Well, what rational man gives a hoot? If wheat went to $10 a bushel tomorrow, and all the workmen of the cities became slaves in name as well as in fact, no farmer in this grand land of freedom would consent voluntarily to a reduction of as much as ⅛ of a cent a bushel. "The greatest wolves," said E. W. Howe, a graduate of the farm, "are the farmers who bring produce to town to sell." Wolves? Let us not insult *Canis lupus*. I move the substitution of *Hyaena hyaena*.

Meanwhile, how much truth is in the common theory that the husbandman is harassed and looted by our economic system, that the men of the cities prey upon him—specifically, that he is the chronic victim of such devices as the tariff, railroad regulation, and the banking system? So far as I can make out, there is none whatever. The net effect of our present banking system is that the money accumulated by the cities is used to finance the farmers, and that they employ it to blackmail the cities. As for the tariff, is it a fact that it damages the farmer, or benefits him? Let us turn for light to the worst tariff act ever heard of in human history: that of 1922. It put a duty of 30 cents a bushel on wheat, and so barred out Canadian wheat, and gave the American farmer a vast and unfair advantage. For months running the difference in the price of wheat on the two sides of the American-Canadian border—wheat raised on farms not a mile apart —ran from 25 to 30 cents a bushel. Danish butter was barred out by a duty of 8 cents a pound—and the American farmer pocketed the 8 cents. Potatoes carried a duty of 50 cents a hundredweight—and the potato-growers of Maine, eager to mop up, raised such an enormous crop that the market was glutted, and they went bankrupt, and began bawling for government aid. High duties were put, too, upon meats, upon cheese, upon wool—in brief, upon practically everything that the farmer produced. But his profits were taken from him by even higher duties upon manufactured goods, and by high freight rates? Were they, indeed? There was, in fact, no duty at all upon many of the things he consumed. There was no duty, for example, upon shoes. The duty upon woolen goods gave a smaller advantage to the manufacturer than the duty on wool gave to the farmer. So with the duty on cotton goods. Automobiles were cheaper in the United States than anywhere else on earth. So were all agricultural implements. So were groceries. So were fertilizers.

But here I come to the brink of an abyss of statistics, and had better haul up. The enlightened reader is invited to investigate them for himself; they will bring him, I believe, some surprises. They by no means exhaust the case against the consecrated husbandman. I have said that the only political idea he can grasp is one which promises him a direct profit. It is, alas, not quite true: he can also grasp one which has the sole effect of annoying and damaging his enemy, the city man. The same mountebanks who get to Washington by promising to augment his gains and make good his losses devote whatever time is left over from that enterprise to saddling the rest of us with oppressive and idiotic laws, all hatched on the farm. There, where the cows low through the still night, and the jug of Peruna stands behind the stove, and bathing begins, as at Biarritz, with the vernal equinox—there is the reservoir of all the nonsensical legislation which makes the United States a buffoon among the great nations. It was among the country Methodists, practitioners of a theology degraded almost to the level of voodooism, that Prohibition was invented, and it was by country Methodists, nine-tenths of them actual followers of the plow, that it was fastened upon the rest of us, to the damage of our bank accounts, our dignity and our viscera. What lay under it, and under all the other crazy enactments of its category, was no more and no less than the yokel's congenital and incurable hatred of the city man—his simian rage against everyone who, as he sees it, is having a better time than he is.

The same animus is visible in innumerable other moral statutes, all ardently supported by the peasantry. For example, the Mann Act. The aim of this amazing law, of course, is not to put down adultery; it is simply to put down that variety of adultery which is most agreeable. What got it upon the books was the constant gabble in the rural

newspapers about the byzantine debaucheries of urban antinomians—
rich stockbrokers who frequented Atlantic City from Friday to Monday, movie actors who traveled about the country with beautiful
wenches, and so on. Such aphrodisiacal tales, read beside the kitchen-
stove by hinds condemned to monogamous misery with stupid,
unclean and ill-natured wives, naturally aroused in them a vast detestation of errant cockneys, and this detestation eventually rolled up
enough force to attract the attention of the quacks who make laws
at Washington. The result was the Mann Act. Since then a number
of the cow States have passed Mann Acts of their own, usually forbidding the use of automobiles "for immoral purposes." But there is
nowhere a law forbidding the use of cow-stables, hay-ricks and other
such familiar rustic ateliers of sin. That is to say, there is nowhere a
law forbidding yokels to drag virgins into infamy by the crude
technic practised since Tertiary times on the farms; there are only
laws forbidding city youths to do it according to the refined technic
of the great Babylons.

Such are the sweet-smelling and altruistic agronomists whose sorrows are the *Leitmotiv* of our politics, whose welfare is alleged to
be the chief end of democratic statecraft, whose patriotism is the so-
called bulwark of this so-called Republic.

ROBERT BENCHLEY

Bringing Back the Morris Dance

I DON'T know why I never thought to speak of it before, but we don't do nearly enough Morris-dancing in this country. These fine early summer days (or early winter days, or whenever you read this) it seems a shame to be devoting ourselves to golf and tennis and drinking when we might be out of doors prancing around a pole and falling down every few feet.

In Merrie Englandie they used to have quite a good time doing this, and there is no reason why we shouldn't today, except that good poles are hard to get. Poles with ribands on them are practically unknown. The thing to do is get a pole and put the ribands on yourself, and then you are sure that they are fresh.

Of course, it is not necessary to have a pole for your Morris dance, but it is better because then you have something to lean against when you get tired. (I am tired before I start, just thinking about it.) The chief thing for Morris-dancing is a smock and lots of ribands. I am sorry to keep harping on this riband business, but you are just nobody in Morris-dancing circles unless you have a lot of ribands hanging off you. These serve to float in the wind and to trip you up. I am going right ahead in this thesis on the assumption that "ribands" are the same as our "ribbons," although I haven't

looked it up. If they are something entirely different, then I am
getting myself into a terrible mix-up and might better stop right
here.

Bells are also worn strapped to the dancers' legs to give warning
to the other dancers and to show where each individual is at any
given time. These dances used to run on 'way into the night sometimes, and without the bells there would be nasty collisions and perhaps serious injury. It is essential that the bells be strapped tightly
to the legs, otherwise the dancer will have to keep stooping and
hitching them up every few steps, thereby spoiling the symmetry of
the dance figure. If the bells *are* loose and there is no way of tightening them, the next best thing is to have a very small child run
along beside the dancer and hold them up. It would have to be a
very small child, though, so small as to be almost repulsive.

I had always thought (when I thought of it at all) that the name
"Morris dance" came from William Morris who designed the old
Morris chairs. By the way, did you ever see a Morris chair that
wasn't old? They must have been new *sometime,* when they were
bought, but by the time anyone ever got to looking at them the
seats were all sunken in and the arms covered with cigarette burns.
Perhaps that was the way William Morris designed them. I frankly
don't know. As I look back on them now, it also seems that they
were always awfully low, so low as to be almost a part of the floor.
It was always very difficult to get up out of one, once you got in,
and I wouldn't be surprised if a great many people are still sitting
in them, which would account for a great many people that have
been missing for a long time. Expeditions might be started to go and
get missing people out of Morris chairs—or maybe you don't care.

Well, anyway, it *wasn't* that William Morris who worked up the
Morris dance, because he came a great deal later and was too busy
with chairs, anyway. I understand that the Moors of Spain did the
first Morris dances, and called it the "Morisco," probably a trade
name like "Nabisco" and "Delco." It is barely possible that one
of the Marx Brothers' ancestors, named Mawruss, invented it and
began that pleasing trick of nomenclature which has resulted in
"Groucho," "Harpo," "Chico," and "Zeppo" among his descend-

ants. At any rate, the dance that the Moors used to do was the "Morisco" and "Morris" was as near as the English could get the name. You would think that a great big nation like England could get the little name "Morisco" right. But no.

We are told that, in Merrie Englandie, one of the dancers was always decked out as Robin Hood "with a magpye's plume to his capp and a russat bearde," which is as lousy spelling as you will see grouped together in any one sentence anywhere. At first, the only music was that of the bells, but that got pretty tiresome after a while and they brought out a flute, or "tabor," which probably added nothing. I can, offhand, think of nothing more dismal.

Of course, I hope that you don't think that I am under the impression that the Morris dance was the *first* outdoor dancing done by people. I am not quite *that* much of a ninny. The first records that we have of such things are those of the Egyptians about 5000 B.C. (And what a long time ago *that* was!) Nobody knows what they had to dance about in 5000 B.C., but they were hard at it, for we find pictures of them dancing on their sarcophagi. That is, they didn't dance on their sarcophagi, but they drew pictures on their sarcophagi of dancing, which must have been almost as painful. In this dance, eight maidens from the local maidenry danced around and around with no particular idea in mind, finally falling down when they got tired, which was in anywhere from ten to fifteen minutes. This left them with the rest of the afternoon free, but they probably weren't good for much.

Most of all folk dancing that followed this has been based on the same idea—round, and round, and round, and then stop. In the Chinese dances they did a great deal of banging as they danced, striking swords on shields and scowling, but there is no record of anyone ever getting hurt. They got awfully tired, though. That seems to be the story of all group dancing through the ages, people getting awfully tired. It is a wonder that no one ever thought of just not dancing at all.

Sometimes, of course, the dances did mean something, usually an appeal to the Rain God to do something about the crops. The Egyptians had a dance like this, but one year they did it *too* well and got nothing *but* rain; so they had to work in a figure which was an appeal to the Sun God to come and drive away the Rain God. This resulted in a lot of hard feeling between the Sun God and the Rain God and the entire dance had to be discontinued, with the result that, for about fifty years, no crops came up at all.

But we are getting away from our Morris dance, which is perhaps just as well. By the sixteenth century you would have thought that people would be working up something new in the line of dancing, but the only difference between the Morris dance and that one of the Egyptians was the bells on the legs. The Egyptians also danced sideways a lot, which made it difficult for them to get anywhere much. The English rustics did know enough to dance forward and back, but that isn't much of a development for over six thousand years, is it?

A lot of people try to read a sex meaning into dancing, but that seems to me to be pretty far-fetched. By the time you have been panting and blowing around in a circle for five or ten minutes, keeping your mind steadily on maintaining your balance and not tripping, sex is about the *last* thing that would enter your head. Havelock Ellis even goes so far as to say that all life is essentially a dance, that we live in a rhythm which is nothing but a more cosmic form of dancing. This may be true of some people, but there are others, among whom I am proud to count myself, to whom life is static, even lethargic, and who are disciples of the Morris who designed the Morris chair rather than the Morris of the dance.

Havelock Ellis can dance through life if he wants to, but I think I'll sit this one out, if you don't mind.

JOSEPH HERGESHEIMER

San Cristóbal de la Habana

THERE are certain cities, strange to the first view, nearer the
heart than home. But it might be better to acknowledge that, perhaps, the word home has a wider and deeper significance than any
mere geographical and family setting. Many men are alien in houses
built from the traditions of their blood; the most inaccessible and
obdurate parts of the earth have always been restlessly sought by individuals driven not so much by exterior pressure as by a strange
necessity to inhabit a barren copper mountain, a fever coast, or follow
to the end of a life a river lost in a savage remoteness, hiding
the secret of their unquenchable longing.

Not this, precisely, happened to me, approaching Havana in the
early morning, nothing so tyrannical and absolute; yet, watching the
silver greenness of Cuba rising from the blue sea, I had a premoni-
tion that what I saw was of peculiar importance to me. I grew at once
impatient and sharply intent on the resolving of a nebulous and ver-
dant mass into the details of dense slopes, slopes that showed, from
the sea to their crowns, no break in a dark foliage. The sombreness
of the leaves immediately marked the land from an accustomed region of bright maples—they were at once dark, glossy, and heavy,
an effect I had often tried to describe, and their presence in such

---

utter expanses filled me with pleasure. It was exactly as though the smooth lustrous hills before me had been created out of an old mysterious desire to realize them in words.

Undoubtedly their effect belonged to the sea, the sky, and the hour in which they were set. The plane of the sea, ruffled by a wind like a willful and contrarily exerted force, was so blue that its color was lost in the dark intensity of tone; while the veils of space were dissolved in arcs of expanding light. The island seemed unusually solid and isolated, as complete within itself as a flower in air, and saturated with romance. That was my immediate feeling about Cuba, taking on depth across water profounder than indigo . . . it was latent with the emotional distinction which so signally stirred me to write * * *

What I tried to discover, rushed through broad avenues and streets hardly more than passageways, was the special characteristic of a city which had already possessed me. And, ignorant of the instantaneous process that formed the words, I told myself that it was a mid-Victorian Pompeii. This was a modification of my first impression, a truer approximation, for it expressed the totality of marble façades inadmissible architecturally, yet together holding a surprising and pleasant unity. No one, I thought excitedly, had ever rightly appreciated Havana; it required a very involved understanding, a feeling not entirely admirable. No, it wasn't Hellenic, not what might be called in the first manner; it hadn't the simplicity of great spirit, a true epoch; Havana was artificial, exotic: Spain touched everywhere by the tropics, the tropics—without a tradition—built into a semblance of the baroque.

It was rococo, and I liked it; an admission, I believe, laying me open to certain charges; for the rococo was universally damned; the Victorian period had been equally condemned . . . and I liked it. Why, God knew! Ornament without use, without reference to its surface and purpose, invited contempt. A woman in a hoop skirt was an absurdity; black walnut furniture carved and gilded beyond recognition, nonsense. Yet they had my warm attachment. Havana claimed me for its own—a city where I could sit at tables in the open and gaze at parterres of flowers and palms and statues and fountains,

where, in the evening, a band played the light arias of La Belle
Hélène.

*   *   *

Havana was identified as an authentic part of my inheritance. I
was—in a purely inner manner—to understand it, to have for it the
affectionate recognition, the sense of familiarity, of which I have already spoken. The city was wholly expressed by the fanlight sparkling with the shifting radiance of the blazing day. It was possible,
without leaving the room, to grasp the essential spirit of a place so
largely unseen. Then it occurred to me that, indeed, I had seen
Havana, and that the wisest thing to do was to leave at once, to
go back with my strong feeling uncontaminated by trivial facts; but
a more commonplace impulse, a limiting materialism, pointed out
that, since I had come away for a change of scene, I had best realize
a semblance of my intention. Still those colors, like a bouquet of
translucent tulips, easily outweighed in importance all that I subsequently gained; they gave the emotional pitch, the intellectual note,
of whatever followed—a mood, an entire existence, into which I
walked with the turning of a sapphire-blue knob.

*   *   *

The sun, that I had seen rising on the undiscovered hills of Cuba,
was sinking behind the apprehended city; it touched the caryatids of
the Gallego Club and enveloped, in a diminished gold like a fine
suffusion of precious dust, the circular avenue, the royal palms, the
flambeau trees and Indian laurels, of the plaza. The whiteness of the
buildings, practically unbroken, everywhere took on the tone of every
moment: now they were faintly aureate, as though they had been
lightly touched by a gilder's brush; the diffused shadows were violet.
The shadows slowly thickened and merged; they seemed to swell
upward from the streets, the Parque; and the buildings, in turn, became lavender, and then, again, a glimmering white. Only the lifted
green of the palms was changeless, positive, until it was lost in
darkness.

A great many people appeared below, moving with an air of deter-
mination on definite ways. The faces of the men were darkened by

the contrast of their linen; I couldn't see their features; but what struck me at once was the fact that there were, practically, no women along the streets. It was a tide of men. This, at first, gave me an impression of monotony, of stupidity—women were an absolute essential to the variety of any spectacle; and here, except for an occasional family group hurrying to a café, a rare stolid shape, they were utterly lacking.

The reason, however, quickly followed the observed truth; this was, in spirit, Spain, and Spain was saturated with Morocco, a land where women, even the poorest, were never publicly exhibited. Havana was a city of balconies, of barred windows, of houses impenetrable, blank, to the streets, but open on the garden rooms of patios. And suddenly—while the moment before I had been impatient at the bareness resulting from their absence—I was overwhelmingly conscious of the pervading influence of charming women. Here they were infinitely more appealing than in places where they were set out in the rows of a market, sometimes like flowers, but more often resembling turnips and squashes. Here, with extreme flattery, women were regarded as dangerous, as always desirable, and capable of folly.

It was a society where a camellia caught in the hair, a brilliant glance across a powdered cheek, lace drawn over a vivid mouth, were not for nothing. In the world from which I had come these gestures, beauties, existed; but they were general, and meaningless, rather than special—the expression of a conventional vanity without warmth. There was an agreement that any one might look, the intensest gaze was invited, with the understanding that almost none should desire; and a cloak of hypocrisy had been the result; either that or the beauty was mechanical, the gesture furtive and hard.

For Havana a woman was, in principle, a flower with delicate petals easily scattered, a perfume not to be rudely, indiscriminately spent; a rose, it was the implication, had its moment, its perfection of eager flushed loveliness, during which what man would not reach out his hand: After that . . . but the seed pods were carefully, jealously, tended. And here, in addition to so much else, was another shared attitude drawing me toward Havana—an enormous preference for women who had the courage of their emotions over those com- pletely circumspect except in situations morally and financially solid. * * *

I debated comfortably the security of a dinner coat, slightly varied, perhaps, by white flannels; but in the end decided in favor of a more informal jacket of Chinese silk with the flannels. A shirt, the socks and scarf, were objects of separate importance; but when they were combined there was a prevailing shade of green . . . I had no in- clination to apologize for lingering over these details, but it might be necessary to warn the seekers after noble truisms that I had no part in their righteous purpose. Even noble truths, in their popular defi- nitions, had never been a part of my concern: at the beginning I was hopelessly removed from them, and what was an instinct had become, in an experience of life not without supporting evidence, the firmest possible attitude. A tone of candor, if my reflections were to have the slightest interest or value, was my first necessity; and candor com- pelled me to admit that I thought seriously about the jacket which finally slipped smoothly over my shoulders.

It was an undeniable fact that I was newly in a land of enormous interest, which, just then, held the most significant and valuable crop growing on earth. But that didn't detain my imagination for a mo- ment. The Havana that delighted me, into which I found myself so happily projected, was a city of promenading and posted theatre programmes, of dinners and drinks and fragrant cigars. I was aware that from such things I might, in the end, profit; but I'd get nothing, nothing in the world from stereotyped sentiments and places and solemn gabbled information. * * *

The day wheeled from south to west. I was perfectly contented to linger doing nothing, scarcely thinking, in the subdued and dark- ened heat. There was a heavy passage of trunks through the echoing hall without, the melancholy calling of the evening papers rose on the air; I was enveloped in the isolation of a strange tongue. To sit as still as possible, as receptive as possible, to stroll aimlessly, watch indiscriminately, was the secret of conduct in my situation. Nothing could be planned or provided for. The thing was to get enjoyment from what I did and saw; what benefit I should receive, I knew from long experience, would be largely subconscious. I had been in Havana scarcely more than a day, and already I had collected a hundred impressions and measureless pleasure. How wise I had been to come . . . extravagantly, with—as it were—a flower in my coat, a gesture of protest, of indifference, to all that the world now emphasized.

DAMON RUNYON

The Eternal Blonde

Long Island City, New York, April 19, 1927.

A CHILLY looking blonde with frosty eyes and one of those marble, you-bet-you-will chins, and an inert, scare-drunk fellow that you couldn't miss among any hundred men as a dead set-up for a blonde, or the shell game, or maybe a gold brick.

Mrs. Ruth Snyder and Henry Judd Gray are on trial in the huge weatherbeaten old court house of Queens County in Long Island City, just across the river from the roar of New York, for what might be called for want of a better name, The Dumbbell Murder. It was so dumb.

They are charged with the slaughter four weeks ago of Albert Snyder, art editor of the magazine, *Motor Boating,* the blonde's husband and father of her nine-year-old daughter, under circumstances that for sheer stupidity and brutality have seldom been equalled in the history of crime.

It was stupid beyond imagination, and so brutal that the thought of it probably makes many a peaceful, home-loving Long Islander of the Albert Snyder type shiver in his pajamas as he prepares for bed.

They killed Snyder as he slumbered, so they both admitted in confessions—Mrs. Snyder has since repudiated hers—first whacking him on the head with a sash weight, then giving him a few whiffs of chloroform, and finally tightened a strand of picture wire around his throat so he wouldn't revive.

This matter disposed of, they went into an adjoining room and had a few drinks of whiskey used by some Long Islanders, which is very bad, and talked things over. They thought they had committed "the perfect crime," whatever that may be. It was probably the most imperfect crime on record. It was cruel, atrocious and unspeakably dumb.

They were red-hot lovers then, these two, but they are strangers now. They never exchanged a glance yesterday as they sat in the cavernous old court room while the citizenry of Long Island tramped in and out of the jury box, and the attorneys tried to get a jury of twelve men together without success.

Plumbers, clerks, electricians, merchants, bakers, butchers, barbers, painters, salesmen, machinists, delicatessen dealers, garage employes, realtors and gardeners from the cities and the hamlets of the County of Queens were in the procession that marched through the jury box answering questions as to their views on the death penalty, and their sympathies toward women, and other things.

Out of fifty men, old and young, married and single, bald and hairy, not one was found acceptable to both sides. Forty-three were excused, the State challenged one peremptorily, the attorneys for Mrs. Snyder five, and the attorneys for Gray one. Each defendant is allowed thirty peremptory challenges, the State thirty against each defendant.

At this rate they may be able to get a jury before the Long Island corn is ripe. The State is asking that Mrs. Snyder and her meek looking Lothario be given the well-known "hot seat" in Sing Sing, more generally known as the electric chair, and a lot of the talesmen interrogated today seemed to have a prejudice against that form of punishment.

Others had opinions as to the guilt or innocence that they said they couldn't possibly change. A few citizens seemed kindly disposed toward jury service, possibly because they haven't anything at hand for the next few weeks, but they got short shrift from the lawyers. The jury box was quite empty at the close of the day's work.

Mrs. Snyder, the woman who has been called a Jezebel, a lineal descendant of the Borgia outfit, and a lot of other names, came in for the morning session of court stepping along briskly in her patent-leather pumps with little short steps.

She is not bad-looking. I have seen much worse. She is thirty-three and looks just about that, though you cannot tell much about blondes. She has a good figure, slim and trim, with narrow shoulders. She is of medium height and I thought she carried her clothes off rather smartly. She wore a black dress and a black silk coat with a collar of black fur. Some of the girl reporters said it was dyed ermine; others pronounced it rabbit.

They made derogatory remarks about her hat. It was a tight-fitting thing called, a, I believe, a beret. Wisps of her straw-colored hair straggled out from under it. Mrs. Snyder wears her hair bobbed, the back of the bobbing rather ragged. She is of the Scandinavian type. Her parents are Norwegian and Swedish.

Her eyes are blue-green, and as chilly looking as an ice cream cone. If all that Henry Judd Gray says of her actions the night of the murder is true, her veins carry ice water. Gray says he dropped the sash weight after slugging the sleeping Snyder with it once and that Mrs. Gray picked it up and finished the job.

Gray's mother and sister, Mrs. Margaret Gray, and Mrs. Harold Logan, took seats in the court room just behind Mrs. Snyder. At the afternoon session, Mrs. Gray, a small determined-looking woman of middle age, hitched her chair over so she was looking right into Mrs. Snyder's face.

There was a rather grim expression in Mrs. Gray's eyes. She wore a black hat and a black coat with a fur collar, a spray of artificial flowers were pinned to the collar. Her eyelids were red as if she had been weeping.

The sister, Mrs. Logan, is plump and pleasant looking. Gray's wife has left him flat, in the midst of his troubles and gone to Norwalk, Conn., with their nine-year-old daughter. She never knew her husband was playing that Don Juan business when she thought he was out peddling corsets. That is she never knew it until the murder.

Gray, a spindly fellow in physical build, entered the court room with quick, jerky little steps behind an officer, and sat down between his attorneys, Samuel L. Miller and William L. Millard. His back was to Mrs. Snyder who sat about ten feet distant. Her eyes were on a level with the back of his narrow head.

Gray was neatly dressed in a dark suit, with a white starched collar and a subdued tie. He has always been a bit on the dressy side, it is said. He wears big, horn-rimmed spectacles and his eyes have a startled expression. You couldn't find a meeker, milder looking fellow in seven states, this man who is charged with one of the most horrible crimes in history.

He occasionally conferred with his attorneys as the examination of the talesmen was going forward, but not often. He sat in one position almost the entire day, slumped down in his chair, a melancholy figure for a fellow who once thought of "the perfect crime."

Mrs. Snyder and Gray have been "hollering copper" on each other lately, as the boys say. That is, they have been telling. Gray's defense goes back to old Mr. Adam, that the woman beguiled him, while Mrs. Snyder says he is a "jackal," and a lot of other things besides that, and claims that he is hiding behind her skirts.

She will claim, it is said, that while she at first entered into the conspiracy to kill her husband, she later tried to dissuade Gray from going through with it, and tried to prevent the crime. The attorneys will undoubtedly try to picture their respective clients as victims of each other.

Mrs. Snyder didn't want to be tried with Gray, but Gray was very anxious to be tried with Mrs. Snyder. It is said that no Queens County jury ever sent a woman to death, which is what the State will ask of this jury, if it ever gets one. The relations among the attorneys for the two defendants are evidently not on the theory of "one for all and all for one." Probably the attorneys for Gray do not care what happens to Mrs. Snyder, and probably the attorneys for Mrs. Snyder feel the same way about Gray.

Edgar Hazelton, a close-trimmed dapper looking man, with a

jutting chin and with a pince-nez balanced on a hawk beak, who
represents Mrs. Snyder, did most of the questioning of the talesmen
for the defense. His associate, Dana Wallace, is a former district
attorney of Queens County, and the pair are said to be among the
ablest lawyers on Long Island. It is related that they have defended
eleven murder cases without a conviction going against them.

Supreme Court Justice Townsend Scudder is presiding over the
court room, which has a towering ceiling with a stained glass sky-
light, and heavy dark oak furniture with high-backed pews for the
spectators. Only no spectators were admitted today because the room
was needed for the talesmen.

The court room is so huge it was difficult to hear what was going
on at any distance from the bench. I believe it is the largest court
room in the country. It was here that the trial scene in the picture
Manslaughter was filmed.

In the court room on the floor below was held the trial of Mrs.
Nack in the famous Guldensuppe murder thirty years ago, when
the reporters used carrier pigeons to take their copy across the river
to Park Row.

Microphones have been posted on the tables, and amplifiers have
been rigged up on the walls, probably the first time this was ever
done in a murder trial, but the apparatus wasn't working any too
well today, and one hundred and twenty newspaper writers scattered
around the tables listened with their hands cupped behind their ears.

Here is another record, the number of writers covering the trial.
We have novelists, preachers, playwrights, fiction writers, sports
writers and journalists at the press benches. Also we have nobility in
the persons of the Marquis of Queensbury and Mrs. Marquis. The
Marquis is a grandson of the gent whose name is attached to the
rules governing the manly art of scrambling ears, but the young man
wore a pair of fancy-topped shoes yesterday that surprised me. It
isn't done you know, really!

The Reverend John Roach Straton was present wearing a Buster
Brown necktie that was almost unclerical. A Catholic priest was on
hand, but he carried no pad or pencil to deceive us. Some of the
writers came attended by their secretaries, which shows you how far

we have gone since the days of the carrier pigeons at the Gulden-suppe trial.

There were quite a number of philosophers. I have been requested by my Broadway constituency to ascertain if possible what, if any-thing, philosophy suggests when a hotsy-totsy blonde with whom a guy is enamoured tells him to do thus and so. But then a philoso-pher probably never gets tangled up with blondes, or he wouldn't be a philosopher.

Mrs. Snyder showed signs that might have been either nervous-ness or just sheer impatience during the day. Her fingers constantly toyed with a string of black beads at her throat. Her entire set-up suggested mourning. She has nice white hands, but they are not so small as Gray's. His hands are quite effeminate.

In fact, the alienists who examined Gray and pronounced him quite sane say he is effeminate in many ways. Gray showed no signs of nervousness or any particular animation whatever. He just sat there. It must be a strain on a man to sit for hours knowing the eyes of a woman who is trying to get him all burned up are beating against the back of his neck and not turn around and give her at least one good hot glare.

HEYWOOD BROUN

Sacco and Vanzetti

WHEN at last Judge Thayer in a tiny voice passed sentence upon Sacco and Vanzetti, a woman in the courtroom said with terror: "It is death condemning life!"

The men in Charlestown Prison are shining spirits, and Vanzetti has spoken with an eloquence not known elsewhere within our time. They are too bright, we shield our eyes and kill them. We are the dead, and in us there is not feeling nor imagination nor the terrible torment of lust for justice. And in the city where we sleep smug gardeners walk to keep the grass above our little houses sleek and cut whatever blade thrusts up a head above its fellows.

"The decision is unbelievably brutal," said the Chairman of the Defense Committee, and he was wrong. The thing is worthy to be believed. It has happened. It will happen again, and the shame is wider than that which must rest upon Massachusetts. I have never believed that the trial of Sacco and Vanzetti was one set apart from many by reason of the passion and prejudice which encrusted all the benches. Scratch through the varnish of any judgment seat and what will you strike but hate thick-clotted from centuries of angry verdicts? Did any man ever find power within his hand except to use it as a whip?

From *Collected Edition of Heywood Broun,* copyright, 1941, by Heywood Hale Broun. Reprinted by permission of Harcourt, Brace and Company, Inc.

Gov. Alvan T. Fuller never had any intention in all his investigation but to put a new and higher polish upon the proceedings. The justice of the business was not his concern. He hoped to make it respectable. He called old men from high places to stand behind his chair so that he might seem to speak with all the authority of a high priest or a Pilate.

What more can these immigrants from Italy expect? It is not every prisoner who has a President of Harvard University throw on the switch for him. And Robert Grant is not only a former Judge but one of the most popular dinner guests in Boston. If this is a lynching, at least the fish peddler and his friend the factory hand may take unction to their souls that they will die at the hands of men in dinner coats or academic gowns, according to the conventionalities required by the hour of execution.

Already too much has been made of the personality of Webster Thayer. To sympathizers of Sacco and Vanzetti he has seemed a man with a cloven hoof. But in no usual sense of the term is this man a villain. Although probably not a great jurist, he is without doubt as capable and conscientious as the average Massachusetts Judge, and if that's enough to warm him in wet weather by all means let him stick the compliment against his ribs.

Webster Thayer has a thousand friends. He has courage, sincerity and convictions. Judge Thayer is a good man, and when he says that he made every effort to give a fair trial to the Anarchists brought before him, undoubtedly he thinks it and he means it. Quite often I've heard the remark: "I wonder how that man sleeps at night?" On this point I have no first hand information, but I venture to guess that he is no more beset with uneasy dreams than most of us. He saw his duty and he thinks he did it.

And Gov. Fuller, also, is not in any accepted sense of the word a miscreant. Before becoming Governor he manufactured bicycles. Nobody was cheated by his company. He loves his family and he pays his debts. Very much he desires to be Governor again, and there is an excellent chance that this ambition will be gratified. Other Governors of Massachusetts have gone far, and it is not fantastic to assume that some day he might be President. His is not a master mind, but he is a solid and substantial American, chiming in heartily with all our national ideals and aspirations.

To me the tragedy of the conviction of Sacco and Vanzetti lies in the fact that this was not a deed done by crooks and knaves. In that case we could have a campaign with the slogan "Turn the rascals out," and set up for a year or two a reform Administration. Nor have I had much patience with any who would like to punish Thayer by impeachment or any other process. Unfrock him and his judicial robes would fall upon a pair of shoulders not different by the thickness of a fingernail. Men like Holmes and Brandeis do not grow on bushes. Popular government, as far as the eye can see, is always going to be administered by the Thayers and Fullers.

It has been said that the question at issue was not the guilt or innocence of Sacco and Vanzetti, but whether or not they received a fair trial. I will admit that this commands my interest to some extent, but still I think it is a minor phase in the whole matter. From a Utopian point of view the trial was far from fair, but it was not more biased than a thousand which take place in this country every year. It has been pointed out that the Public Prosecutor neglected to call certain witnesses because their testimony would not have been favorable to his case. Are there five District Attorneys, is there one, in the whole country who would do otherwise?

Again Prof. Frankfurter has most clearly shown that the prosecution asked a trick question in regard to the pistol, and made the expert seem to testify far more concretely than he was willing to commit himself. That was very wrong, but not unique. Our judicial processes are so arranged that it is to the interest of District Attorneys to secure convictions rather than to ascertain justice, and if it would profit his case, there is not one who would not stoop to confuse the issue in the minds of the jurymen.

Eleven of the twelve who convicted Sacco and Vanzetti are still alive, and Gov. Fuller talked to them. He reports somewhat naively that they all told him that they considered the trial fair. Did he expect them to report, "Why, no, Governor, we brought in a verdict of guilty just out of general depravity"?

By now there has been a long and careful sifting of the evidence in the case. It is ridiculous to say that Sacco and Vanzetti are being railroaded to the chair. The situation is much worse than that. This is a thing done cold-bloodedly and with deliberation. But care and deliberation do not guarantee justice. Even if every venerable college president in the country tottered forward to say "guilty" they could not alter facts. The tragedy of it all lies in the fact that though a Southern mountain man may move more quickly to a dirty deed of violence, his feet are set no more firmly in the path of prejudice than a Lowell ambling sedately to a hanging.

I said of Calvin Coolidge that I admired his use of "I do not choose," but he was dealing with a problem wholly personal and had every right to withhold his reasons. For Gov. Fuller I can't say the same. These are the lives of others with which he is dealing. In his fairly long statement he answers not a single point which has been made against the justice of the conviction. The deliberations of himself and his associates were secret, and seemingly it is his intention that they shall remain secret. A gentleman does not investigate and tell.

I've said these men have slept, but from now on it is our business to make them toss and turn a little, for a cry should go up from many million voices before the day set for Sacco and Vanzetti to die. We have a right to beat against tight minds with our fists and shout a word into the ears of the old men. We want to know, we will know —"Why?" *(New York World, August 5, 1927.)*

MORRIS MARKEY

Fear, Inc.

WE call them gangsters and gunmen and racketeers, what time an outburst of their peevish temper flips a new murder into the front pages, reminding us of their existence—and from the security of our righteous lives we reprove and envy them a little for their failure to abide by our rules. From the movies and the Sunday supplements and the Inside Dope of Mr. Hearst's crime reporters we fashion our transient images of them—images that fade and disappear, of course, when the latest murder at their hands has faded into the record of Mr. Whalen's * unsolved mysteries. Vaguely we fancy them as marauding brigands, sitting with loaded pistols and baleful eyes waiting for another chance to kill somebody. They (according to the gaudy pictures given us) are the scum and the outcasts of the world, parasites upon the citizens—debonair and romantic sometimes with their swift lives and their strange vendettas—but on the whole violent and irrational fellows awaiting their grim retribution, which is Sing Sing. Their crimes? Well, something to do with prohibition and high-jacking and racketeering. . . .

We are encouraged to think of them after this fashion because we

* Grover Whalen, 1886—. Police Commissioner of New York City, 1928-30; perennial Chairman of the Mayor's Committee on Reception to Distinguished Guests.——Ed. note.

only hear of them through their occasional bloody crimes or the melodramas written about those crimes. As a matter of fact, the life of the gangsters and the gunmen and the racketeers is very little concerned with bloody crime, or with any very stirring felony at all. It is, by and large, a quite monotonous life, relieved from the humdrum only by the remarkable sums of money that it produces.

I think of the most powerful and respected racketeer among us: An Irish-American in his forties, neither tall nor short, dressed somewhat flashily but not conspicuously so, with a very long and toughened face (toughened, you might guess, from years on a steamboat deck, or a baseball diamond, or a circus lot). He occupies a very large and considerably over-decorated office in a Columbus Circle building. In the office, sitting at the genuine mahogany desks, are young stenographers who peck at commonplace typewriters and hurry with their spike heels over extremely thick green carpets. They spend a part of their time arranging papers in commonplace steel filing cabinets and answering buzzers and getting numbers over the telephone. On the walls are autographed portraits of celebrities and an original newspaper cartoon or two.

In short, this workshop of our racketeer varies in no respect whatever, as far as its outward aspects are concerned, from that of an up-to-date advertising agency or theatrical producer or a Wall Street broker. The racketeer himself lives ordinarily the sort of existence that is followed by advertising agents and producers and brokers. He arrives at his office in the late forenoon. He has many conferences during and after the luncheon hour. He dines in a public place, generally, and spends his evening at a speakeasy or night club.

His business, which he orders and manages with extreme efficiency, may be explained simply. He has organized the principal dairymen and the principal poultrymen of the metropolitan district into leagues for their own protection against uncouth competition. In return for his forethought in thus safeguarding their interests, the poultrymen and the dairymen naturally pay him a handsome fee. Suggestions that he did not really earn this money, emanating from the District Attorney, were met by the dairymen and poultrymen themselves with indignant denials. They were, they told the District

Attorney, deeply indebted to our racketeer. He was aid and counsel in their struggle for business. They would not think of testifying against him under any circumstances.

They refused to testify against him, as a matter of fact, because they were mortally afraid of the consequences. Indeed, it was upon this not uncommon emotion of fear that our gentleman built his profitable enterprise. Certain poultrymen and certain dairymen, invited at the outset to join the association, declined. A few days later their establishments were set upon and their property destroyed—by tablets to sour their milk or heavily loaded lorries to crash into their delivery trucks in the case of the dairymen, and in the case of the poultrymen by the death of some thousands of terrified hens. It would be cheaper, the others decided, to pay the membership fee and be discreet, even if the amount seemed altogether exhorbitant.

As almost everybody knows, the profession of racketeer was imported from Chicago, where cruder men, in a cruder setting, have practiced it with high profit for years. Only two things are necessary for the hanging out of a shingle; an extraordinarily cool business head on the shoulders of the leader, and a close-knit gang of worthies handy with club or pistol.

Racketeering impinged itself upon New York life with that grace and lack of excitement which give us so much pride, for two reasons: first, because the potential victims had already heard of the futility of resistance to the system as practiced in Chicago—and second, because the man destined to control New York's racketeering was an uncommonly able fellow, already dominating with terrible ease the organized criminal operations of Manhattan.

This gentleman, when he was quite ready, adapted racketeering to the New York scene, and with the acquisition of a trade that was, for all practical purposes, beyond the law, he gave over the more hazardous enterprises that he once pursued. Of course, he kept his finger in the pie of prohibition. It is such easy money for a man with organization.

The fact remains, beyond dispute, that our racketeer still dwells in the atmosphere of the underworld. That is partly because of his inherent temperament and partly because he is, after all, engaged in a contemptuous war upon the rules laid down by legislatures and police. Also, his shoulders are lifted above the mob of his fellows, and any man whose head goes up above the multitude is likely to have a cobblestone heaved at him any moment. So instead of a private detective for his bodyguard (after the manner of our more hated bankers) he carried with him two dapper fellows who know the interior architecture of Dannemora and who are without peers at close-range pistol work or the swinging of a full bottle against threatening heads. Instead of a squad of policemen on motorcycles acting as equerries for his car (after the manner of the city governors) he drives an automobile which is, within itself, impregnable to attack.

A certain romantic history hangs about this car. The King of the Belgians, it seems, has a hobby of building magnificent armored automobiles with his own hands—as Peter the Great built clocks. He turns out of his elegant shop about one car every two years. The first went to the King of Spain, the second to the Prince of Wales, and the third, through the devious channels of an American millionaire and a brokerage house, to our celebrated gentleman of Broadway. Its one-inch steel plate looks no more forbidding than the enameled sheetmetal that covers our Detroit models, but it turns back high-penetration bullets. Its cowling hides a sub-machine gun. Its speed and pick-up are almost incalculable because the throttle has never been wide open.

Thus lives our racketeer: surrounded by a certain hint of danger, to be sure, but devoted chiefly to the prosy collection of fees from the members of his two prosy associations—fees which they pay him to protect them from himself. He is competent and highly successful in a nebulous business made more difficult by the fact that all the law is against him. He makes the struggling efforts of coal and steel and lumber merchants, with tariffs and lobbies, seem like apprentice labors.

Of course, his work has been imitated by lesser men. One group of greedy fellows, for example, set out to establish themselves in the building-trades racket. They presented themselves to the contractor for a new apartment house and offered, for a not too modest sum, to protect him from the fury of a gang that was out to get him and his new job. Unless the sum was paid over, the racketeers themselves provided the opposition gang and burned the new building when it was half completed.

But that is a little crude. Too violent by far, and destined for a quick end, for insurance companies were the victims and insurance companies are no policemen when it comes to wrecking their natural enemies.

Beneath the racketeering of both the suave sort and the rude there goes on the pretty little trade of bootlegging, and it is from this, as a matter of fact, that most of our gang quarrels arise. Such quarrels, for example, as that which left the bodies of the Cassidy brothers dead upon the floor of the Hotsy-Totsy Club not many weeks ago.

Our gentleman of the beginning of this story carries on a sideline, as it were, of providing kegged beer for a large group of midtown speakeasies. Perhaps this is his avocation, pursued in the moments of release from his more pressing duties in the office.

The beer trade is organized in a rather interesting way. The factor receives a shipment of a thousand kegs. He does not wish to store them. So he calls on the speakeasy proprietors and offers them the right to purchase for immediate delivery.

"Take a hundred kegs," is the suggestion.

"But I can't use that much," says the proprietor.

"A hundred kegs will be delivered tonight," says the factor. He nods, and terminates the conversation after receiving cash payment.

The proprietor can stomach this, because he has to. But when, the next day, a rival wholesaler offers him a hundred kegs more, he is in something of a quandary. He manages to remain meek, but informs his first salesman of the circumstances.

"Forget it," says the first salesman. "Our crowd will take care of you on that." The competing salesman is warned that any effort to force delivery will mean a sudden spray of bullets. Occasionally there is a death.

In the Hotsy-Totsy Club episode, however, the action was a little too fast for the routine to be followed.

Mr. Jack Diamond, proprietor of the place, had plenty of beer. The Messrs. Cassidy insisted that he must buy another lot from them, on the spot. There was no opportunity to call in the usual aid from the wholesalers, and so Mr. Diamond fell back upon his own excellent pistol. His bartender, one Entratta alias Green, appears to have followed suit. Then bullets were shot into the bodies of the Cassidy boys. Diamond put on his hat, beckoned to Green, and walked quietly down the stairs to the street. He has not been seen since, although Green was miraculously arrested in Chicago. As it falls out, there will be nobody to testify against Green, and nothing very serious will happen to him.

But such violent occurrences—even such incidents as the killing of a Rothstein (who was important because he was both rich and a dramatic, celebrated figure who had never been jailed) are merely episodic. They disturb the routine of business for a little while, and they serve to recall to our pious selves that gangs exist among us, but they are not the vital elements of gang life itself. The vital elements, on the other hand, are the huge and easy profits, taken by a shrewd application to business—a business that has as much technique as the selling of vacuum cleaners and, on the whole, as much excitement.

A recent communication from our boss racketeer even bore the small imprint of a rubber stamp: "Dictated but not read." *(From "A Reporter at Large," The New Yorker, September 28, 1928.)*

THE NEW YORKER

Notes and Comment

THE Waldorf is going to pieces. The traffic towers have been dug up by the roots from Fifth Avenue. The green line in the subway has been replaced by lights. Peggy Joyce is renouncing her citizenship. The hippopotamus in the Bronx Zoo is dead. The lately acquired battleships have departed from the North River. Life is slipping away, crumbling all around us. Still, nothing seems to make a dent in the town. It occurred to us that if forty-two battleships could slink away with so little fuss, there's no telling what could be removed from New York and not be missed. We will wager (wagers like this being pretty safe) that if the Chanin Building were removed over night and nothing said about it in the papers, less than six per cent of the population would miss it the next day, and more than ten per cent would live the rest of their urban lives and never know it had come and gone.—(*May 18, 1929*)

It's a duty and a pleasure to note that the carriage trade is favoring the old Rialto Theatre in Hoboken. The players are enjoying, in the murk of the Jersey shore, a popularity not equalled anywhere on well-lighted Broadway. Not only is that old thriller, "After Dark," which Harry Wagstaff Gribble discovered in the Public Library, a perfect vehicle in which to display lightheartedness and hide amateurishness, but 1929 has turned out to a favorable year for a new growth in the theatre—or rather a return to traditions that have been lost. We've been to Hoboken several times lately, and its warmth and easy-going spirit are a vast relief after the chilling monotony of the Manhattan theatrical district. To pay a dollar or two for a seat instead of four dollars is something; to go somewhere far from the fierce arena of Times Square is much; and to approach darkly along a waterfront instead of edging along painfully in a taxi phalanx is a boon which is proving sweet to thousands.

Mr. Morley so dimly hoped for the success of his theatre that at first, we are told, he thought of calling it The Crown and Elephant, as being the crown of his ambitions and the elephant on his hands. A sudden turn of events changed the picture completely and success sprang from a lucky combination of things. By restoring the audience to their rightful estate and giving them an opportunity to boo the villain and stamp their feet in time to the sad songs, the Hoboken Theatrical Company achieves its simple triumph and the playgoers achieve their simple happiness—since the human animal derives a faint superior glow from sharing in the ridicule of anything at all. This stamping of the feet became at one time so alarmingly metrical that the patrons had some doubts as to whether the theatre would hang together under the vibration; so the manager had it inspected, and it was found durable.

That Hoboken life agrees with the townsfolk of Manhattan has been an alarming and wholesome discovery to producers on this side of the river, vindicating the contention of that vigorous contender, St. John Ervine, who has been shouting for the dispersal of the theatres from Broadway. The Rialto's boom has extended to the restaurants near River Street; and the proprietor of the Hofbrau, we heard the other night, is now so overcome with gratitude for his sudden increase in business that he has volunteered to redecorate the theatre at his own expense. He has also opened an annex to his establishment to care for the overflow. Further, the Company has leased another theatre in Hudson Street, the Lyric, and is talking about putting on "The Black Crook," a spectacle in which ladies once appeared in tights, to the demoralization of our fathers and grandfathers.

All this is mightily pleasing, and after a couple of merry evenings in the friendly smoke of German cooking, one is likely to declare impulsively that one doesn't particularly care whether one ever again ventures into the whitelight heart of Broadway, whose ever mounting and paramounting millions have a curious debilitating effect on the soul, and whose taxis must be feed a block in advance. Anyone who wishes to establish theatres in Yorkville, Spuyten Duyvil, Battery Park, Chelsea, or Montauk Point has our permission and a promise of our patronage. (*January 26, 1929*)

Mr. Coolidge, the little Vermonter, has appeared against many strange backgrounds. Surely the most incongruous of all was the langorous Georgia island, where the double-breasted business suit bobbed up against the bearded oaks, the Spanish ruins, and the warm mystery of the Southland. Reading the account of his doings, we were thinking how times had fallen off. From that island, pirates once put to sea. Later, Spanish friars lived there in a mission. From a timber of one of the island's trees was hewn the keel of the frigate Constitution. How pale by contrast must have been the scene this past week—a strange little twentieth-century sprite, who, surrounded by photographers, guarded by secret-service men, and tagged by reporters, phoned Washington every day from his bedroom, and dedicated, in a high nasal voice, an ancient and uncomplaining tree. —(*January 5, 1929*)

The odds ought to be eight hundred to one on Mr. Walker, not eight to one. It may be true that in the time he devotes to civic affairs he personally does little, beyond changing a police commissioner and handling such matters of broad policy, but his attitude toward accomplishment does not seem to be antagonistic and somebody, we know not who—the borough presidents, or the bosses of Tammany, or the civil-service engineers in the Department of Plant and Structures, possibly—gets some things done, subways built, tunnels dug, streets cleaned, asphalt laid—not enough, Allah knows, but some. The city struggles on. Meantime Walker does things of infinitely greater importance. He lives. He is gay, carefree, obviously happy. He makes whoopee, stays up late, rises late. He dresses snappy and talks snappy. He dines with the Biddles and is photographed with Colleen Moore. Thus he has become the symbol of some odd million glamour-starved souls numbly seeking escape from reality. In importance he ranks ahead of Roxy's, Babe Ruth's home-run score, Ziegfeld's chorus, the tabloids, the Edison test, the Snooks case, or Lindbergh's or Rockefeller's private lives. He's five hundred years ahead of his time. Or maybe only one hundred, at the rate we're going.—(*August 17, 1929*)

CONTRIBUTORS

Contributors

Franklin P. Adams, 1881—. Best-known works: *Half a Loaf, The Diary of Our Own Samuel Pepys, Toboganning on Parnassus, The Melancholy Lute.*

Conrad Aiken, 1889—. Best-known works: *The Jig of Forslin, The House of Dust, Priapus and the Pool, Blue Voyage, Bring! Bring! and Other Stories, Selected Poems.*

Sherwood Anderson, 1876-1941. Best-known works: *Winesburg, Ohio; The Triumph of the Egg, Horses and Men, Death in the Woods, A Story Teller's Story, Dark Laughter.*

Thomas Beer, 1889-1940. Best-known works: *The Mauve Decade, Mrs. Egg and Other Americans* (collected short stories), *Stephen Crane, Hanna, Sandoval.*

Robert Benchley, 1889-1945. Best-known works: *Love Conquers All, 20,000 Leagues Under the Sea: or David Copperfield, The Treasurer's Report, My Ten Years in a Quandry, Inside Benchley.*

Stephen Vincent Benét, 1898-1943. Best-known works: *John Brown's Body, Thirteen O'Clock, Johnny Pye and the Fool-Killer.*

Ernest Boyd, 1887-1946. Best-known works: *Ireland's Literary Renaissance, Portraits: Real and Imaginary, Literary Blasphemies.*

Van Wyck Brooks, 1886—. Best-known works: *America's Coming-of-Age, The Ordeal of Mark Twain, The Flowering of New England, New England: Indian Summer, The World of Washington Irving, The Times of Melville and Whitman, The Confident Years.*

Heywood Broun, 1889-1939. Best-known works: *Anthony Comstock* (with Margaret Leech), *Seeing Things At Night, The Boy Grew Older, Collected Edition of Heywood Broun* (compiled by Heywood Hale Broun).

James Branch Cabell, 1879—. Best-known works: *The Rivet in Grandfather's Neck, Beyond Life, Jurgen, The High Place, The Cream of the Jest, The Silver Stallion.*

Hart Crane, 1899-1932. Best-known works: *White Buildings, The Bridge, Collected Poems.*

E. E. Cummings, 1894—. Best-known works: *The Enormous Room, Tulips and Chimneys, XLI Poems, Collected Poems.*

John Dos Passos, 1896—. Best-known works: *Three Soldiers, Manhattan Transfer, U.S.A.* (comprising *The 42nd Parallel, Nineteen Nineteen, The Big Money*), *District of Columbia* (comprising *The Adventures of a Young Man, Number One, Grand Design*).

Theodore Dreiser, 1871-1945. Best-known works: *Sister Carrie, Jennie Gerhardt, The Financier, The Titan, The "Genius," An American Tragedy, Twelve Men.*

T. S. Eliot, 1888—. Best-known works: *Prufrock and Other Observations, The Waste Land, Poems, 1909-1925, Ash Wednesday, Murder in the Cathedral, Collected Poems* (1936), *Four Quartets, The Cocktail Party, Selected Essays.*

F. Scott Fitzgerald, 1896-1940. Best-known works: *This Side of Paradise, The Beautiful and Damned, The Great Gatsby, Tender Is the Night, Tales of the Jazz Age, All the Sad Young Men, Taps at Reveille, The Last Tycoon.*

Robert Frost, 1875—. Best-known works: *A Boy's Will, North of Boston, New Hampshire, West-Running Brook, Collected Poems.*

Ellen Glasgow, 1874-1945. Best-known works: *Virginia, Life and Gabriella, Barren Ground, The Romantic Comedians, They Stooped to Folly, The Sheltered Life, Vein of Iron.*

Percy Hammond, 1873-1936. Best-known works: *But—Is It Art?, This Atom in the Audience.*

H. D. (Hilda Doolittle), 1886—. Best-known works: *Sea Garden, Hymen, Palimpsest.*

Ernest Hemingway, 1898—. Best-known works: *In Our Time, Men Without Women, The Sun Also Rises, A Farewell to Arms, Death in the Afternoon, For Whom the Bell Tolls, The Fifth Column and the First Forty-nine.*

Joseph Hergesheimer, 1880—. Best-known works: *The Three Black Pennys, Java Head, Linda Condon, The Bright Shawl, San Cristóbal de la Habana, Balisand.*

Samuel Hoffenstein, 1890-1947. Best-known works: *Poems in Praise of Practically Nothing, Year In, You're Out.*

Frank McKinney Hubbard ("Kin" Hubbard), 1868-1930. Best-known works: *Abe Martin, Hoss Sense and Nonsense; Abe Martin's Almanack, Abe Martin on Things in General.*

Ring Lardner, 1885-1933. Best-known works: *You Know Me, Al; The Big Town, How to Write Short Stories, The Love Nest, Round Up* (collected stories).

Sinclair Lewis, 1885-1951. Best-known works: *Main Street, Babbitt,*

Arrowsmith, Dodsworth, Elmer Gantry, The Man Who Knew Coolidge, It Can't Happen Here.

Amy Lowell, 1874-1925. Best-known works: *A Dome of Many-Coloured Glass, Sword Blades and Poppy Seeds, What's O'Clock?, John Keats.*

Morris Markey, 1899-1950. Best-known works: *That's New York, This Country of Yours, Well Done!*

Don Marquis, 1878-1937. Best-known works: *Hermione, The Old Soak, Sonnets to a Red Haired Lady, archy and mehitabel.*

H. L. Mencken, 1880—. Best-known works: *In Defense of Women, A Book of Prefaces, Prejudices* (six series), *The American Language, Treatise on the Gods, A Mencken Chrestomathy* (selected excerpts).

Edna St. Vincent Millay, 1882-1950. Best-known works: *Renascence and Other Poems, A Few Figs from Thistles, Second April, The Harp-Weaver and Other Poems, Fatal Interview, Conversation at Midnight.*

Marianne Moore, 1887—. Best-known works: *Observations, The Pangolin and Other Verse, Collected Poems* (1951).

Christopher Morley, 1890—. Best-known works: *Where the Blue Begins, Thunder on the Left, Kitty Foyle, John Mistletoe* (autobiography).

George Jean Nathan, 1882—. Best-known works: *The World in Falseface, The Popular Theatre, The Autobiography of an Attitude, Art of the Night, The Bachelor Life, The World of George Jean Nathan* (selected writings, edited by Charles Angoff).

Frances Newman, 1888-1928. Best-known works: *The Hard-Boiled Virgin, Dead Lovers Are Faithful Lovers, The Short Story's Mutations* (a critical anthology).

Eugene O'Neill, 1888—. Best-known works: *The Long Voyage Home, Beyond the Horizon, The Emperor Jones, The Hairy Ape, Anna Christie, Desire Under the Elms, Strange Interlude, Mourning Becomes Electra.*

Dorothy Parker, 1893—. Best-known works: *Enough Rope, Sunset Gun, Death and Taxes, After Such Pleasures, Not So Deep As a Well* (collected verse), *Laments for the Living, Here Lies* (collected stories).

Vernon Louis Parrington, 1871-1929. Best-known work: *Main Currents in American Thought.*

Burton Rascoe, 1892—. Best-known works: *A Bookman's Daybook, Before I Forget* and *We Were Interrupted* (autobiography), *Titans of Literature.*

Damon Runyon, 1884-1946. Best-known works: *Guys and Dolls, Blue Plate Special, The Best of Runyon, A Slight Case of Murder* (play, with Howard Lindsay).

Carl Sandburg, 1878—. Best-known works: *Chicago Poems, Smoke and Steel, Slabs of the Sunburnt West, The American Songbag, The People, Yes; Abraham Lincoln* (six volumes), *Complete Poems.*

Gilbert Seldes, 1893—. Best-known works: *The Seven Lively Arts, The Years of the Locust.*

Wallace Stevens, 1879—. Best-known works: *Harmonium, Ideas of Order, The Man With the Blue Guitar, The Auroras of Autumn.*

Ruth Suckow, 1892—. Best-known works: *Country People, Iowa Interiors, The Folks, The Kramer Girls.*

James Thurber, 1894—. Best-known works: *The Owl in the Attic, My Life and Hard Times, My World—and Welcome to It!, The Thurber Carnival, The Thurber Album.*

Thomas Wolfe, 1900-1938. Best-known works: *Look Homeward, Angel; Of Time and the River, The Web and the Rock, You Can't Go Home Again.*

Alexander Woollcott, 1887-1943. Best-known works: *Shouts and Murmurs, Enchanted Aisles, Going to Pieces, While Rome Burns, Long, Long Ago, The Woollcott Readers* (Ed.).

Elinor Wylie, 1885-1928. Best-known works: *Nets to Catch the Wind, Black Armour, Angels and Earthly Creatures, The Venetian Glass Nephew, The Orphan Angel.*